JUL   2022

AGENT
JOSEPHINE

AGENT JOSEPHINE

AMERICAN BEAUTY, FRENCH HERO, BRITISH SPY

DAMIEN LEWIS

PublicAffairs

NEW YORK

For my father, and for Lesley,
for first taking me to the heart
of the Josephine Baker story.

And for Peter Watson –
gone but not forgotten.

PublicAffairs
Hachette Book Group
1290 Avenue of the Americas, New York, NY 10104
www.publicaffairsbooks.com
@Public_Affairs

Printed in the United States of America

Originally published in hardcover in Great Britain in 2022 by Quercus Editions Ltd

First US Edition: July 2022

Published by PublicAffairs, an imprint of Perseus Books, LLC, a subsidiary of Hachette Book Group, Inc. The PublicAffairs name and logo is a trademark of the Hachette Book Group.

The Hachette Speakers Bureau provides a wide range of authors for speaking events. To find out more, go to www.hachettespeakersbureau.com or call (866) 376-6591.

The publisher is not responsible for websites (or their content) that are not owned by the publisher.

Typeset by CC Book Production Ltd.

Picture credits in order of appearance:
1 – Studio Harcourt; 2, 18, 27, 28, 29 – Le Service Historique de la Défense; 3 – Paillole family;
4 – Bertrand-Hugues and Bernadette Abtey; 5, 26 – Brian Hammond; 6, 13, – Unknown, courtesy of J.P. Reggiori; 7 – Paris Match; 8 – Bundesarchiv; 9, 14, 22, 23, 24 – Public domain; 10 – Imperial War Museum; 11, 12 – Paul Biddle; 15 – Hulton Archive/Getty Images; 16 – Roger-Viollet; 17, 20, 36, 38 – Author's collection; 19 – Philippe Verrier; 21 – Tango Images / Alamy Stock Photo; 25 – Renault Family Estate; 30 – Yorkshire Air Museum; 31 – Ullstein/Getty; 32 – Robert A. Schmuhl/United States Holocaust Memorial Museum; 33 – J.P. Reggiori; 34 – Prosthetic Head; 35 – Tim Spicer; 37 - Science History Images/Alamy Stock Photo

Library of Congress Control Number: 2022934998

ISBNs: 9781541700666 (hardcover), 9781541700680 (e-book)

LSC-C

Printing 1, 2022

'What is the use of living, if it be not to strive for noble causes and to make this muddled world a better place for those who live it after we are gone?'

Winston Churchill

'More is achieved by love than hate.
Hate is the downfall of any race or nation.'

Josephine Baker

Contents

Author's Note

The writing of this book has presented an unusual set of challenges, and mostly due to the secrecy that surrounded, and still surrounds, operations of the security services. In 1949, the main protagonist of this book, Josephine Baker, who was a special agent serving on espionage duties for the Allies during the Second World War, told her biographer, Marcel Sauvage, precious little about her wartime activities on behalf of the Allies, and very deliberately so. She rarely if ever spoke or wrote in detail about any of her wartime work, and went to her grave in 1975 taking many of those secrets with her.[1]

In 1975, the year of Josephine Baker's death, Colonel Paul Paillole, her immediate chief at the Deuxième Bureau – basically, the French equivalent of the British Secret Intelligence Service (SIS) or the American CIA – published his own account of his war years, entitled *Services Spéciaux 1935–1945*. In The Author's Introduction, Paillole explained why he came to take the decision to break the rigid code of secrecy, by which he still felt bound some three decades after the end of the Second World War, and which is defined by the saying that 'What is secret should remain secret.' He had chosen to do so to counter falsehoods that had arisen in the interim, while still acknowledging that much could not be written, and that the code of silence was one in which he still ardently believed and by which he was bound. As Paillole made clear, even after the thirty-year-rule had elapsed, any such public release of material still needed to be processed through the relevant French authorities.[2]

A few years earlier, the acclaimed French Resistance hero, Colonel Rémy – real name Gilbert Renault – who became a prominent author after the war, wrote his own account of Josephine Baker's war and that of her Deuxième Bureau partner, Captain Jacques Abtey. It is entitled *J.A.: Épisodes de la vie d'un agent du S.R. et du contre-espionnage français*. In the introduction to that book, which is based upon extensive interviews with the key protagonists, Rémy explained how the aim of writing it was chiefly to honour Josephine Baker and her colleagues' war effort. It was a homage chiefly to her – and Captain Abtey's – wartime service. That a man of Colonel Rémy's stature felt compelled to tell their wartime story reflects the importance and status it held, at least in Colonel Rémy's eyes.[3]

However, Rémy also outlined how the constraints of secrecy binding French security service agents were far more stringent than what was expected of those who served in the French Resistance. In short, those waging the espionage war were privy to secrets of far greater sensitivity and longevity than those who had waged a guerrilla war to drive out the enemy. As Rémy explained, the war of the shadows – the espionage war – never ended, whereas the role of the Resistance was over once peace was declared. The sensitivities and the need for secrecy regarding the former endures. As a result, even in Rémy's account some names, places, dates, and even the events portrayed had been suitably disguised. Much had been left out, due to issues of ongoing sensitivity and secrecy.[4]

In 1949, and again in 1967, Captain Abtey wrote accounts of his wartime service, the first book entitled *La Guerre Secrète de Joséphine Baker*, and the second, *2ème Bureau Contre Abwehr* (which is co-authored with an Abwehr – German military intelligence – veteran of the Second World War). In the latter volume, Abtey writes of how the rules concerning French intelligence work require that any files concerning those operations are closed to the public for several decades at the very least. Indeed, some of the most important Second World War-era files concerning Captain Abtey and Josephine Baker's wartime service were only released to the public in 2020, more than seventy-five years after the events they pertain to. As a point of note, the French government and the French security services should be applauded in deciding that files concerning the activities of their intelligence agencies can be released after appropriate time has elapsed. As far as I am aware, there are no such laws or practices concerning the equivalent British agencies, and few if any files, no matter their vintage, are ever released to the public.[5]

I also believe that the concept of 'plausible deniability' has been applied to some, if not all of the above accounts, as any number of the activities described therein – or indeed deliberately left out of some of the accounts – were on the very cusp of what was legal and sanctioned and acceptable, at least outside times of war. Needless to say, the war and the long and savage occupation of France pitted French men and French women against each other, and loyalties were often conflicted and opaque. The history of much of this remains sensitive, and often accounts were written with a view to not upsetting the status quo, or to avoid attracting opprobrium to the protagonists. Stories concerning French collaboration with the Nazis during the Occupation remain particularly sensitive. The rights and wrongs are still hotly debated and for many this remains a sensitive subject.

Then there are the intricacies and layers of secrecy which attach to the wartime operations of special agents themselves. Rarely in reports submitted to military and political leaders are the sources of the intelligence made clear, only the reliability of those sources (I elaborate upon this further in the main body of this book). Moreover, during the Second World War agents of different Allied nations had a vested interest in claiming ownership of key war-winning intelligence as delivered to their taskmasters, regardless of its true genesis. As just one example, the 12 Apostles – the American Vice Consuls who were dispatched to French North Africa to spy on behalf of US President Roosevelt – hoovered up intelligence from a vast array of largely non-American sources, and took the lion's share of the credit for having secured it. Josephine Baker was by then a French national, as were many of her special agent colleagues; the Polish spymaster codenamed Rygor was another key source for the Apostles.

As one final layer of intrigue, there is also a supposedly fictional account that deals in some depth with Josephine Baker and Jacques Abtey's wartime service, but which is, by the author's own admission, actually a true story in which he has had to disguise some names, dates and minor details. That extraordinary tale, written by Austrian author Johannes Mario Simmel, and called in English *It Can't Always Be Caviar*, tells the wartime story of Hans Müssig, a German national, although Simmel uses the pseudonym 'Thomas Lieven' for Müssig in the book. Müssig, a fervent anti-Nazi, was a most unusual character. He was also something of a French intelligence agent and he proved a very useful and dynamic colleague for Jacques Abtey and Josephine Baker, one who refused to be hamstrung by tradition or convention.

Unpicking and sifting the fact from the fiction and identifying the deliberate obfuscations in the above accounts, and cross-referencing that with the wartime and post-war files and the plethora of other documents that have survived, has been a challenge. Very likely, I have not always reached the right conclusion, although I have endeavoured strenuously to do so. Nevertheless, I believe that the story as told in the following pages is as close to the truth as can ever be reached from the vast amount of often-contradictory material that is available. It remains the most credible, plausible and convincing account, one backed up by the most numerous and reliable sources.

There are sadly few survivors from the Second World War activities described in these pages. Throughout the decade spent researching and writing this book I have sought to be in contact with as many as possible, plus surviving family members of those who have passed away. If there are further witnesses to the stories told who are inclined to come forward, please do get in touch, as I will endeavour to include further recollections, where relevant, in future editions.

The time spent by Allied special agents operating far from friendly territory tended to be stressful and traumatic and wreathed in layers of secrecy, and many chose to take their stories to their graves. Memories tend to differ and apparently none more so than those concerning such work. The written accounts that do exist tend to differ, and locations and chronologies are sometimes contradictory. Nevertheless, I have endeavoured to provide an accurate sense of place and time. Where various accounts of a mission or an event appear to be particularly confused, the methodology I have used to determine where, when and how events took place is the 'most likely' scenario. If two or more testimonies or sources point to a particular time or place or sequence of events, I have opted to use that account. The dialogue used in the pages that follow is in all cases taken from either contemporaneous accounts, or from accounts written after the war by the individuals portrayed.

The above notwithstanding, any mistakes herein are entirely of my own making, and I would be happy to correct any in future editions. Likewise, while I have attempted to locate the copyright holders of the photos, sketches and other images, and of the written material quoted in this book, that has not always been straightforward or easy. Again, I would be happy to correct any errors or omissions in future editions.

Note: 'Black girl.' 'Coloured.' 'Negro.' 'Wench.' These and other terms in *Agent Josephine* may be found by readers today to be offensive, but they were the language used at the time. As this was the language used then, I have included such phraseology when quoting from the actual words used by the characters portrayed, or their writing, in an effort to relate this story as authentically as possible, remaining true to the time in which it took place. In doing so, I seek to reflect the realities of the age depicted and so as to avoid censoring history. We need to learn the vital lessons from the past. That being said, I have rendered the N-word as 'n*****', as readers may find it particularly troubling.

Preface

I like to think every book begins with a journey; a first step. This one has involved an exceptionally long and tortuous and at times challenging road. There are several reasons for this, and I go on to enumerate them in the section that follows, but much of it has to do with the fact that Josephine Baker and her fellow special agents operated wholly in the shadows during the Second World War, and in many ways they wished their wartime exploits to remain obfuscated thereafter. But for now, to start with, I'd like to tell the story of what first opened my eyes to Josephine Baker's secret war – what set my feet firmly on the path.

My father and my stepmother, Lesley, live in France, in a beautiful medieval-era château that they purchased as a near-ruin with cattle still living in some of the buildings. Over the next several decades they renovated and restored it painstakingly – stone by stone, tile-by-tile and ornate carving by ornate carving. A labour of love. So ancient are the roots of the place, that some of the building-blocks have been reused from castles of an even greater vintage, from which medieval knights set forth to prosecute the Crusades. In some places, the huge stones boasting carvings of crucifixes or coats of arms or other heraldry have been reused in a somewhat haphazard fashion, for the building of this new – fifteenth-century! – château, such that they appear upside-down or skew-whiff, the writing or iconography seeming at first glance to be scrambled. A few of the carved building blocks even originate from the ruins of a Roman villa, and a bronze statue discovered in the grounds is now housed in the Louvre museum, in Paris.

Unsurprisingly, a love of châteaux – and of ancient history and of buildings of all types – runs deep in their blood. So it was that several years back they took a trip to the Dordogne and, among a number of visits to other historic sites, they decided to take a look around the Château des Milandes. Milandes – both the amazing, turreted château itself and the splendid gardens – is open to the public, and they went there expecting to enjoy a day immersed in the centuries-old history of the place, as expressed in the magic and majesty of limestone, slate, iron, oak and stained glass. They did indeed experience a day of magic and wonder, but not quite as they had anticipated.

Château des Milandes happened to be the wartime and post-war home of one of the most famous and highly paid female entertainers of the 1920s and '30s, Josephine Baker. As a black American singer and dancer she had emigrated to France in the early 1920s, when still only nineteen years old, seeking fame and fortune. She would find it chiefly in Paris, from where she would become a global star of stage, screen and song. At first, in the early 1920s, she set Paris alight with her sexually charged, 'exotic', semi-naked dance routines, which both scandalised, provoked and captivated her audiences. But as the years progressed and her fame mushroomed – she was reputedly the most photographed woman in the world by the late 1920s – she matured into a singer, dancer and movie star with real gravitas. She gained superstar status and fabulous riches, and she was admired and courted by the wealthy, the famous and royalty alike. Just prior to the war she had made Château des Milandes her home, after Paris, and it has been preserved to this day as a fabulous memorial to her life and works.

But what most surprised both my father and Lesley during their visit was that Josephine Baker had also played a little-known, clandestine role during the war, as a sometime Resistance fighter and very possibly also a special agent or spy. Indeed, one entire wing of the château – the French Resistance Room, to them the most striking – is dedicated to displaying and showcasing the story of Josephine Baker's war years. Of course, they had known of the star's existence, but they had not known that she had carried out a series of daring wartime exploits that had earned for her no less than the Médaille de la Résistance avec Palme, the Croix de Guerre, and the Légion d'Honneur, France's highest decoration for civil or military service.

It would be an understatement to say that their interest was piqued, and shortly they reached out to me, for obvious reasons. In due course I took my family to visit, with my father and Lesley there to help guide us. To say we were captivated is an understatement. The château itself is enchanting, but its owner, Angélique de Saint-Exupéry, has done an incredible job in renovating the place and transforming it into a living memorial to Josephine Baker's life and work. The day flew by, and as we spent the last hour exploring the château grounds – which are breathtaking – we were tailed everywhere by a black and white cat. My youngest daughter, who is a total sucker for animals, whether dogs, cats, rabbits, squirrels or whatever, promptly named the moggie 'Patch', and by the end of our visit she was carrying Patch everywhere.

At the exit, one of the charming young ladies who worked at the château asked us if the cat was ours. Surprised, we told her no, we presumed it lived at Milandes. No, she told us, it was a stray that had only just turned up. She was worried that the cat would get reported to the local vet, who would very likely have her destroyed. My daughter was distraught. We should adopt Patch, she insisted. Fathers cannot say no to daughters. It is an established fact. I told the young assistant that I would telephone her the following morning, and that if no one had come to claim Patch we would drive right over and fetch her. Of course, as fathers tend to, I had an ulterior motive: it would be an excuse for me to return to the château and spend a little longer in the French Resistance Room, studying more closely all the fantastic history it reveals.

As luck would have it, by the next morning Patch had been claimed. The interest of the Lewis family moved on: Patch would not after all be spirited to England, and there were other sites to see and adventures to be had. The Dordogne, it has to be said, is full of both. But my mind did not move on. It remained captivated by the story embodied in Château des Milandes. As I pondered it I found myself wrestling with a conundrum. How was it that a woman of such global renown could have ended up performing some sort of 'grey' role, serving as a spy in the Second World War? Surely, her very notoriety and fame militated against any such clandestine role. And surely, a woman of such unique and distinctive celebrity would have been the least likely candidate ever to spy for France, or for any of the Allies.

And so, as one tends to, I began to dig.

The story that emerged was simultaneously mysterious, tantalising and sensational. Josephine Baker had been born into poverty in St Louis, Missouri, in the American Midwest, a city that hugs the banks of the sluggish, meandering Mississippi River. She had left as soon as she was able, making her way to New York, seeking the limelight of the Broadway stage. But by her own account, prejudice – America was still prone to racial segregation and the so-called Jim Crow laws – held her back. In 1925 she had sailed for France, seeking to escape all of that, and very quickly she had captured the hearts of Parisians. She found France to be largely free of prejudice, as was wider Europe, at least in comparison to what she had experienced in the USA. Paris was the city that embraced her, that she fell in love with and made her home.

But then had come the rise of Nazi Germany. Josephine, who told many versions of her rags-to-riches life story, seemed to have little fixed, immutable past, or wider history, but by the late 1930s she had become transfixed by a burning hunger to fight and to defeat the threat emanating from Berlin. To her, the rise of Hitler, Goering and Eichmann, plus the Führer's other henchmen, threatened all that she had come to believe in and all that she held dear. If the forces of Nazi Germany invaded, she would once again be forced to flee from prejudice and hatred. But where could she go, if the entire world was to be engulfed in the struggle for freedom, as seemed inevitable? Where would she run to next? Or should she choose instead to stay and to fight?

In truth, there was little debate in Josephine's mind. She had always been a fighter, ever since she had packed her bags and left St Louis, with little or no idea of how she would make it in the world. She resolved that whatever the cost, whatever it might entail, she would stay and embrace the struggle. Of course, she had little idea what form the fight might take, and even less sense of how a black woman of such global renown could possibly play a role. That was until she was approached by a French intelligence agent called Captain Jacques Abtey, though he was not using his real name at the time. Abtey and his bosses at the Deuxième Bureau – an arm of what would be the equivalent of Britain's Secret Intelligence Service (SIS), or the CIA – had a very clear sense of how Josephine might help fight the war of the shadows. It was exactly because she was so famous, instantly recognisable and universally loved – at least outside of Nazi circles – that she could serve such a potent role.

So it was that Josephine was recruited as an 'Honourable Correspondent' – what amounts to a voluntary, unpaid, freelance intelligence agent, or spy. So far, so good. But it was now that things began to get a little challenging, the road ahead less well-travelled or clearly defined. The story of Josephine Baker's wartime exploits, and that of her closest fellows, her band of brothers – for almost exclusively she was surrounded by male spies and assorted male adventurers during the war – remained enigmatic and shrouded in mystery. I wondered why this was so? Why, when her life of stardom was so incredibly well publicised – there have been dozens of books written about Josephine Baker the superstar; thousands of media articles – did her wartime exploits remain so veiled in obscurity? It did not make a great deal of sense.

The deeper I dug, the more I began to detect answers; reasons. First, there was the wholesale destruction of wartime files that took place as France's secret agencies, in a helter-skelter retreat from the advancing forces of the enemy, put to the torch tonnes of archives. When Paris was evacuated, prior to the June 1940 arrival of the enemy, hundreds of funeral pyres smouldered across the city, as the last of those sensitive papers were consumed by the flames. Then, those files that did remain were very often seized by the invading forces, and in many cases carted back to Germany, so they could be studied in detail, in an effort to ensure that Berlin won the intelligence war. And when the tide of war finally turned, and Germany itself was invaded by the Allies, much of what survived of those archives was seized by the Allies, often never to be returned. In the case of the Russians, the French were still trying to secure the return of the wartime papers of the Deuxième Bureau – that is, if they even still existed – many decades after the end of the war.[1]

Sadly, yet more wanton destruction took place immediately post-war, and very often because the secret agencies that proliferated in wartime weren't seen as being needed – or indeed very much in favour – in a time of peace. As just one example, with the Special Operations Executive (SOE) – Churchill's Ministry for Ungentlemanly Warfare, which was charged with waging clandestine war behind enemy lines – some 85 per cent of all their files were destroyed. With the British Special Air Service (SAS), which, like the SOE, was disbanded at war's end, it is only due to a small miracle that any records survive today. There are numerous similar examples from wartime agencies across the Allied nations. And in the case of Britain's Secret Intelligence Service, even if that agency's wartime files have been preserved, the SIS has a blanket policy of absolute secrecy: nothing is ever released to the public, and it appears likely that nothing ever will be.

All of that being said, it is remarkable what actually has survived and is available to study. My search – my job of detective work, for that is exactly what it felt like – took me deep into the London National Archives, at Kew, where thankfully key wartime files have endured, including those concerning a smuggling fleet operated by His Majesty's Government to run weapons, explosives, radios and secret agents to and from enemy-occupied lands, while at the same time smuggling illegal goods, and which quickly became a highly profitable, self-financing, blockade-busting intelligence-gathering operation. Extraordinary. If it featured in a James Bond novel it would be criticised as fanciful, but it is entirely true. It took me to one of the French equivalents of Kew,

Le Service Historique de la Défense, which is housed in the vast and severe-seeming Château des Vincennes, where wartime files are secreted of such a sensitive nature that they would only be released in the final stages of my research, after more than seventy-five years had passed since they were sealed. Without having access to those archives, this story would have been exceedingly difficult to tell.

It took me to several Paris archives, and from there to municipal museums across France that memorialise the history of the French Resistance; to the Churchill Archives Centre, in Cambridge; to the Beinecke Rare Book & Manuscript Library archives at Yale; and to the archives of the Federal Bureau of Investigation (FBI), an agency which itself collaborated with Josephine Baker and her fellows during the war, only to turn against her post-war. It took me to archives spread across Germany, and to an esteemed British professor of German and military history, and to an RSHA (Reich Security Main Office) internal telephone directory from the war years, which he insisted I should read. Plus it took me into the heart of the New York Mafia, who at the outbreak of the war had cut an ultra-secret deal with the American Government, codenamed Operation Underworld, to use the Mafia's extensive criminal networks to aid the Allies' cause. Again, quite extraordinary.

It took me to veterans of the conflict who had also fought and served in the war of the shadows; it took me to interview those who performed on stage with Josephine Baker and grew to know and love her, and to understand what made her so suited to a clandestine role. It took me to the sons and daughters of the key characters who made up Josephine Baker's shadow army – French, American and British – to hear from them the stories of those who had served in a knife-edge battle waged in the depths of fear, wherein betrayal, capture, torture and death were only ever one step away. Finally, it took me to the private family archives of one of the war's foremost SIS agents, who was also one of the chief models for Ian Fleming's James Bond, a man whose wartime exploits would once again be considered as fantastical fiction, if they weren't 100 per cent true, and whose role in Josephine Baker's wartime story is utterly captivating.

It took me to requesting that files be opened that were never going to be opened, or not for a good while anyway: some of these secrets remain just that – secrets which are not yet ripe for the telling, or at least not as far as those in power are concerned. It took me through a series of seemingly wild goose chases, where I knew the files I wanted existed and were supposedly open to the public, but where no official actually seemed able to place their hands upon them. It compelled me to open and keep rigorous records of several dozen files of my own research – shelves groaning under the load – as I tried to piece together, to fathom, to cross-reference and to elucidate the story of Josephine Baker's war. Repeatedly, I had to sift fact from fiction and to flush out the deliberate obfuscations that have taken place concerning much of the war in France – including Josephine's story – which of course pitted French men and women against each other, turning Resistance fighter against collaborator against special agent against soldier against spy. Much of this history remains raw and controversial and disputed to this day. Much remains inconvenient and unsaid.

Some of this journey – of necessity – was 'digital'. Researched partly during a time of Covid, it meant that some overseas journeys simply were not possible. Regardless, I do not believe my inability to go to certain locations or physically sit in certain archives has lessened the reach of my research. And for all the twists and turns and the rabbit holes and the blind alleyways, I kept being pulled back into the story, like a twitch on the thread. Never for one moment did Josephine's wartime tale disappoint. Indeed, it is more incredible than I had ever imagined possible, and defined by raw courage, maverick daring, double- and triple-bluff and fabulous chutzpah. It is full to the brim with the intrigue, the cut and thrust and the unique tradecraft of the world of espionage, plus the dagger-in-the-back that so often comes with it. Of course, it also delves deeply into the world of the Resistance fighter, the guerrilla operator and the regular soldier. It involves bribery, corruption, torture, assassinations, fake passports, currency trafficking, high-society partying, exotic locations to die for, stunning desert adventures, lovers' trysts and much, much more.

It also involves unimaginable selflessness, bravery, courage and sheer guts and generosity of spirit on a scale to take the very breath away.

Josephine's adversaries more often than not proved merciless, murderous, cut-throat and immensely cunning, turning deception, manipulation and the power of raw fear and prejudice to their ends. Mostly, when facing them, her only defence was her extraordinary self-possession, her courage and her nerve. On many levels she had been an actor all of her life: from her earliest years, her career and her life had played out on the public stage. And on many levels, that ability to act – to be all things to all people, when necessary – was her greatest asset as a spy.

But there was something else, something perhaps of even more significance: Josephine had never once had it easy. At every stage she had had to fight, to graft and to work unbelievably hard to get ahead. Josephine was blessed with a core of steely fortitude – an unbreakable spirit that was hard wired into her soul. Always and everywhere her ability to survive, to suffer but to keep going no matter what, to remain undaunted and to believe that good would triumph over evil, shines through. Even at the Allies' darkest hour, even when serving alongside long-lived, seasoned agents, it was Josephine who proved the chief inspiration; a powerhouse; unbreakable. From the very earliest days she was their muse, and in time it would become clear that the student – the rookie agent – was fast becoming the master.

Of course, Josephine was a flawed human being; a vulnerable individual, who tended to wear her foibles and her insecurities on her sleeve. But as with so many tragic heroes, she is all the more laudable for it. Arguably, bereft of her human flaws she would never have made such a fine special agent. Her own failings made her better able to empathise with and to understand the failings, foibles and the weaknesses of others, including her enemies, and to turn those to her advantage. Moreover, the finest special agents need to have been schooled in life, and ideally in the school of hard knocks. They need to have been rejected, to have failed, to have had to fight and fight again, and they need to have learned to deal with all the repeated setbacks.

During the war, this was one of Josephine's stand-out attributes: no matter how dark the fates seemed and how impossible the odds, she never once contemplated giving up or giving in.

On that level, Josephine had much in common with those wartime leaders whom she most admired: General Charles de Gaulle, Franklin D. Roosevelt and Winston Churchill. Disregarding any controversy that may surround such figures today, during the war – and during their lives – Josephine was drawn to their unbreakable, unshakeable spirit of resistance. She was equally at home rubbing shoulders with world leaders and senior generals as she was with tribal chiefs, Moroccan street beggars, Spanish gypsy dancers or the poorest of the poor in a Paris tenement block. Hailing from the background that she did, with the tough upbringing she had had, and having endured the prejudices and setbacks of her early years, and ultimately having enjoyed the runaway, stratospheric successes that she had in Paris and worldwide, she could relate.

She was also a groundbreaker and a pioneer. The deployment of women on front-line operations – whether espionage or warfare – is still the subject of fierce debate. Yet almost eighty years ago Josephine was leading men on missions to the front lines of war and beyond, often operating deep within lands menaced by the enemy, and sometimes, inevitably, she would be forced to operate alone. Of course, she was not the only one doing so. There were numerous women who served in the Resistance and on clandestine operations against the Germans, but it was certainly not the norm. In that sense she broke the mould. She became a role model for women the world over, and would do so increasingly during her life and work post-war.

During seven years of wartime operations – she was recruited as a special agent prior to the war – she risked her life again and again, the cumulative effect of which was to lead her repeatedly to the very brink of death. By her own admission, and by the accounts of those who served alongside her, she was stalked by the Grim Reaper repeatedly. But while there was such a vital cause to fight for – vanquishing Nazism – she remained unwilling to shuffle off this mortal coil. She believed we die only when we decide we are ready to die. She was certainly not willing to do so during the Occupation, when sweet freedom needed to be fought for and won. And incredibly, during the process of doing all of that, she would never once accept a penny of pay from the Allies, and indeed she would exhaust much of her pre-war fortune, selling off her precious gems and gold – the fruit of the superstar years – to finance her activities and the Allied cause.

The war was Josephine's coming of age. It was a watershed moment; a pivot in her life and career. Before it she had been a glittering and beguiling superstar, blessed with beauty, talent and an ability to charm and to connect with her audience that few performers have rivalled. Prior to the war, she had been an inspiration to many of the world's foremost performers. Shirley Bassey would say of her that she was the 'grande diva magnifique' – a performer without equal, and a singer and dancer who would very likely never be rivalled. After the war, Josephine would again become a celebrated superstar, but she would also take up the cudgels for the battle for freedom and civil liberties in all its forms. She would never forget the lesson of the war years: freedom must be fought for, every day. She would herself remark that all of her accolades from the long years of fame and fortune were as nothing compared to her wartime work.

That being said, this is not a book telling Josephine Baker's life story: there are many of those. Rather it recounts the story of her wartime exploits as a special agent for the Allies and as a spirited and brave supporter of the Allied troops. The wider canvas of the war provides a vital backdrop, while Josephine's earlier life serves to flesh out her character, elucidating how and why she was such a unique and extraordinary figure. It shows how she, along with her band of fellow agents and assorted adventurers, helped turn the tide of the war and made a very real contribution to Allied victory. Even prior to the war, Josephine had been identified as an enemy of the Nazi state – top figures in Hitler's circle despised all that she stood for. She was targeted, but of course she was not alone in facing a gruesome fate if unmasked by the enemy. All those who worked with her, and helped her, and inspired her, and guided her – and at times taught her how to be a world-beating special agent – faced the same terrible consequences if captured.

They were an unconventional band. They were brazenly, astoundingly brave. But they were also mavericks, law-breakers, and at times they tore apart convention. They opted to cut deals with whoever they had to – gangsters, forgers, fugitives, assassins – to wage war in freedom's cause. The ends justified the means. They spoke truth to power. They told the unvarnished truth and said what needed to be said, even when it was not what Allied leaders might want to hear, and damn the consequences. Unsurprisingly, in doing so they were not always looked upon with great kindness or sympathy from those on high. Even so, they did what had to be done, no matter what the risks or the cost, until the war was won.

Damien Lewis
Dorset, UK
2022

CHAPTER ONE

A Traitor Unmasked

As his chauffeur nosed the sleek black Rolls-Royce through the dawn streets of Paris, Wilfred 'Biffy' Dunderdale had little inkling that his actions over the coming months would have such immense historic significance, or that he would end up serving as a role model for the world's most famous (fictional) secret agent, '007' – James Bond.[1]

As the chief of Britain's Secret Intelligence Service – SIS; also known as MI6 – in France, it was almost inevitable that Dunderdale, and Bond's creator, Ian Fleming, would serve together in the espionage capitals of the world. Indeed, they would first do so in Paris just as the city was poised to fall to Nazi Germany's onslaught.[2] The two men had a great deal in common: both were scions of wealthy Scottish dynasties; both would join Boodle's, the centuries-old London club steeped in diplomacy and espionage, where they would rub shoulders with the likes of Winston Churchill; both were Royal Naval commanders by profession, which served as their entry-point into the world of espionage. Clichéd though it might sound, both were also drawn to fast cars and fine wine, and they were destined to become firm friends.[3]

With swept-back dark hair, eyes creased with laughter-lines and a deep dimple in his chin, Dunderdale was blessed with boyish – almost mischievous – good looks. Charming, suave, impeccably-dressed – his father was a shipping magnate, and Dunderdale was of independent means – he was often to be seen wearing gold Cartier cufflinks, a long ebony cigarette holder clamped between his teeth, the same as favoured by the fictional Bond, and with a bottle of vintage champagne never far from hand.[4]

Yet beneath the chummy, clubbable, debonair look, this Paris spymaster was no soft touch, as the level expression behind his gaze hinted at. Belying his diminutive stature – Dunderdale stood five-feet-six-inches tall – he was a tough and resolute foe, not to mention loyal to a fault. He'd earned the singular nickname 'Biffy' due to his prowess at boxing, and he was known to have something of a cutthroat, piratical streak. Beneath its immaculate and sumptuous exterior, his Rolls-Royce was no pushover either: it was fitted with concealed bullet-proof steel plates and glass.

A hugely likeable, if eccentric and unconventional character, Dunderdale was determined to do whatever it took to get the job done, and no matter who he might rub up the wrong way. His actions that spring 1938 morning would epitomise that spirit. In the Irish capital, Dublin, British intelligence agents had stumbled upon what increasingly looked to be the work of France's greatest pre-war traitor. That man's identity was yet to be unmasked, but right now Dunderdale had on his person evidence of treachery and perfidy most foul, and at such a level that all of France was threatened, not to mention her foremost ally, Great Britain.[5]

As Dunderdale appreciated, such disloyalty could not go unchallenged; the betrayer needed to be hunted down before any further harm might be wrought. The world teetered on the brink of war. Much that the politicians might deny it, those fighting the war in the shadows – the war of the secret services – knew what was coming. Adolf Hitler was hell-bent on avenging what he saw as the injustices heaped upon Germany following the First World War, and of winning global domination under the credo of Nazism; of forging his dark kingdom – his Third Reich. And if he succeeded, as Dunderdale and his colleagues well knew, freedom would die in darkness.

At first glance Dunderdale and his chauffeur – Paul Kilesso, a gnarled giant of an Ukrainian – were the most unlikely of pairings. But ever since Dunderdale's youthful recruitment into the SIS, the two had been inseparable – firm friends; loyal unto death. Kilesso, a former cavalry officer, had fought at Verdun, in the Great War, in defence of France, and Dunderdale had convinced him not to return home at war's end. Instead, he had persuaded Kilesso that he would be far better off running the Hotel du Havre, at 37 Boulevard Montparnasse, in Paris, which was operated as a SIS safe house, being used to harbour agents, cash and espionage equipment. Kilesso doubled as Dunderdale's driver, just as he was doing today.[6]

Quietly, smoothly, he nosed the gleaming Rolls into a vacant parking spot in Paris' 7th arrondissement and killed the engine. To their front, cloaked in the shadows of that early spring morning, lay the Avenue de Tourville headquarters of the Deuxième Bureau, France's counter-espionage service. Though woefully understaffed, the handful of men beavering away beneath this ancient domed edifice were some of the best spy-hunters in the business; past-masters at turning the enemy's strategies, resources and agents back against them. If only they had a smidgen more money and agents and clout, they would be unbeatable. But backing from the political hierarchy was woefully lacking, as Paris fervently – blindly – gambled that France wouldn't be catapulted into another war with the old enemy.

In short, too many heads were buried too firmly in the sand.

Inside the Avenue de Tourville headquarters, Dunderdale's Deuxième Bureau colleagues were on tenterhooks. Little could or ever would be said over open phone lines. Paris, indeed, all of France, was awash with German agents, as the Abwehr, Nazi Germany's much expanded intelligence service, sought to overwhelm and subvert her enemies. Berlin had watchers and listeners everywhere. Germany's omnipresent *Forschungsamt* – the ultra-secret telephone, mail and radio intercept and code-breaking service – had spread its tentacles across the length and breadth of Germany, as the Nazi elite turned that nation into a terrifying police state, one in which all dissent was crushed. With a staff numbering several thousand, the *Forschungsamt* had extended its reach into France and Britain, for the sea was no impediment to radio-interception.[7]

As for the Abwehr, so brazen had their agents become, they were openly taking telephone calls at the German embassy in Paris, from sources across France, knowing that the Deuxième Bureau was bound to be listening. It was almost as if Germany's intelligence service was challenging Paris – the French authorities – to challenge them. *To do something.* To indulge in an act of 'provocation', one that could be used as 'justification' for ever greater belligerence, provoking an ever-more vitriolic tide of propaganda from Joseph Goebbels – *Reichsminister* of Public Enlightenment and Propaganda – plus an ever-more vigorous beating of the drums of war.

Dunderdale's colleagues at the Deuxième Bureau manned the German Desk, though they were but a paltry few. Their chief, Commander Paul Paillole, was exactly what Dunderdale would expect from such a man in such a position. A champion fencer, Paillole had been schooled at Saint-Cyr, the foremost French military academy – the equivalent of Britain's Sandhurst or America's West Point. After service in the North African colonies, chiefly Algeria, he had fully intended to follow a traditional soldier's career. His posting to the Deuxième Bureau had come completely from out of the blue, but true to form – a rigorous man of duty – he had made the cat-and-mouse game of counter-espionage very much his own.[8]

Tall, slender, dark-haired, with angular, almost emaciated features, Paillole had proved a demanding boss, one keen to forge ever closer links with the Deuxième Bureau's foremost ally, the Secret Intelligence Service. In him, Dunderdale had found a committed opponent to the rise of Nazi Germany, an enthusiastic anglophile and an archetypal patriotic Frenchman. By contrast, Paillole's deputy, and Dunderdale's other key partner in this war of the shadows, wasn't exactly cut from the same cloth, or so first appearances might suggest.

Captain Maurice Léonard Abtey – known to all as 'Jacques' – was blond, with pale-blue eyes and classic Nordic good looks, and he was as much at home speaking German as French. Born and brought up in the Alsace region, on France's eastern border with Germany, in lands which historically were claimed as much by Berlin as by Paris, Abtey readily admitted that their family name was very likely of German origin.[9] His family was steeped in German culture as much as it was that of France. Prior to being recruited into the Deuxième Bureau, he had graduated from the French Centre for Advanced Germanic Studies, in Strasbourg, becoming ever more immersed in the German nation's language and values.[10]

But in fact it was his very 'German-ness' that made him such an asset. Abtey could talk like the enemy, think like the enemy and he looked like the archetypal Nazi foe. Perhaps in an effort to undercut his ordered, disciplined, Germanic side, there was something of the rebel – the spirited maverick – in Abtey, just as there was in Dunderdale.[11] As the latter liked to cruise the streets of Paris in his bullet-proof Rolls-Royce, so the former was in the habit of commuting to work not on the Paris metro, nor even by bicycle, but paddling a kayak on the grey-green waters of the Seine, which weaves its way through the heart of Paris with a meandering, looping ease.

From early spring to the darkest days of winter, kayak-time proved decompression-time – a precious hour away from the desk and the mind-bending intrigues of work.[12] Living in the Vanves suburb of Paris, the six-kilometre paddle took Abtey beneath the Billancourt and Alma bridges, whereupon he would tie up his canoe and make the remainder of the commute on foot. 'Once on the water, I forgot about spies, suspects, reports, intelligence, anonymous letters,' Abtey would write. Or most usually he would.[13] In the coming weeks his thoughts would keep drifting to the very betrayal that Dunderdale was in the process of uncovering.

Late the previous evening Dunderdale had telephoned unexpectedly, keeping communication to the absolute minimum. Might he call around at the Deuxième Bureau's office first thing the following morning, he'd asked? Before agreeing to a meeting, the staff on the German Desk had asked the obvious question: was the matter as serious as it seemed it might be?

'It's serious,' Dunderdale had confirmed, simply.[14]

Nothing further needed to be said: Dunderdale's reputation went before him. Brought up and schooled in Odessa, Ukraine, from where his father ran the family shipping business, his entry into the world of espionage had begun spectacularly, if somewhat prematurely. At age eighteen he'd joined the Royal Navy, being mentioned in dispatches twice for individual acts of bravery towards the end of the First World War. He'd then volunteered for an unusually hazardous mission, one aimed at discovering if the communists – who were even then seizing power in Russia – had got their hands on some particularly sophisticated weaponry.

At the height of the war the American armaments firm, the Electric Boat Company (today part of General Dynamics Corp.), had sold Russia a dozen partially assembled mini-submarines, Russia then being an ally.[15] As far as anyone knew, the mini-subs were still in Odessa, the Black Sea port city to where they had been shipped. Dunderdale spoke fluent Russian and had only recently graduated from school in Odessa, plus for some reason he still had his school uniform with him, packed in a trunk and stowed aboard the Royal Navy vessel on which he served. Put ashore dressed as an Odessa schoolboy, he made for his former housemaster's home, seeking to discover what exactly had happened to those diminutive submarines.[16]

'What on earth are you doing here, Dunderdale?' his former housemaster greeted him, with undisguised incredulity.

Having explained his unlikely mission, the housemaster banished the schoolboy spy to the attic, for his discovery would spell trouble. He happened to have a relative who worked in the Odessa docks, he explained, from whom he was sure to discover the fate of those mini-subs. Dunderdale, meanwhile, was to remain hidden at all times.

'Your Latin was always behind,' the housemaster scolded, as he banished his former pupil to the room beneath the eaves. 'You can work up there to improve it!'[17]

The very next day the housemaster had the answer to Dunderdale's quest, and the teenage agent left his hideout and made his pre-arranged pick-up with the Royal Navy – mission accomplished, or almost ... It was decided that those mini-subs could not be left in communist hands. They were subsequently sabotaged, in a dramatic mission of underwater derring-do, in which Dunderdale again played a key role. For such extraordinary bouts of heroism, in June 1921 Dunderdale would earn an MBE – The Most Excellent Order of the British Empire, a chivalric honour. He was just twenty-one years old.[18] Recruited into the SIS – what else was anyone to do with him? – a string of similarly colourful adventures followed, before Dunderdale earned his Paris posting. A born secret agent, a good decade later he was resolutely stalking that city's streets, intent on defeating those enemies who plot and scheme in the shadows.[19]

Exiting his Rolls-Royce, Dunderdale stepped into an ancient clanking lift with a sliding wire door, which spirited him into the bowels of the Avenue de Tourville headquarters, set directly beneath the giant Dome of the Church of the Invalides. Prior to the Eiffel Tower being built, this was the highest building in all Paris, and it houses Napoleon Bonaparte's tomb. There, deep in the catacombs, a small, dark iron door barred the way. To be admitted, Dunderdale had first to ring a bell set into the centuries-old stonework, before announcing his name and purpose into a wire mesh-covered peephole. Only when the doorkeeper was fully satisfied as to his identity was he permitted entry.[20]

The closely guarded domain of French counter-espionage exuded spycraft, plus a certain respect and esteem for one's adversary – in this case, chiefly the Abwehr. On one wall was displayed the motto of the German intelligence service from the First World War: *Der Nachrichtendienst ist ein Herrendienst* – the Intelligence Service is a service of gentlemen. In other words, theirs was a higher calling, and only those with courage and an unbreakable moral fortitude need apply.[21]

According to Paillole, honour was critical in such a seemingly amoral profession: 'We had to be all the more rigorous, for we were dealing with terribly ambiguous, frightening and sometimes sordid situations.'[22] Serving as an intelligence officer required very different qualities from that of a regular soldier. As Paillole had learned, you had to throw off the military straitjacket; flexibility and lateral thinking were key. You had to learn the rules, in order to break the rules, before *rewriting* the rules. Somewhat unexpectedly, Paillole had found this suited him down to the ground, and it was something that likewise seemed to come naturally to his colleague, Jacques Abtey.[23]

Once admitted into Paillole's lair, Dunderdale took from a locked leather briefcase a thick envelope addressed in French to a Dublin mailbox. Tipped off by the FBI, MI5, Britain's domestic intelligence service – Ireland was seen as domestic, or home, territory – had learned that the Dublin post office box served as a 'dead letter drop' for the Abwehr, an anonymous and supposedly untraceable address in a neutral country to which could be sent sensitive information. MI5 had set up surveillance and intercepted this and a previous missive before they reached German hands.[24]

What had led the FBI to the innocent-looking PO box was in itself one hell of a tale, concerning a concerted effort by Berlin to establish a spy ring deep inside the USA. But that was firmly FBI business. The first envelope had been steamed open, and found to contain a single, brief page – an alert as to when the next substantive cache of documents would arrive from France. It had been resealed and returned to the PO box, so as not to arouse suspicion. But the present parcel now being delivered by Dunderdale was an entirely different matter: it was stuffed thick with papers.

With great care, Paillole and Abtey proceeded to steam open the envelope and photograph the contents, which concerned certain details of the French naval fleet stationed in the Mediterranean. The pages looked as if they had been torn from a school exercise book, and the intelligence they contained was handwritten, with only an 'A' for a signature. It provided precious little to go on as to the identity of the traitor. Frustratingly, the postmark was from a post office in Paris, not so far distant from the Deuxième Bureau's Avenue de Tourville headquarters.[25]

Paillole ordered the envelope resealed, after which it was to be dispatched to its intended destination post haste. Admittedly, they would be delivering valuable intelligence into the hands of the enemy – the Abwehr. At that time the modern French fleet was the fourth most powerful in the world, after Great Britain, the USA and Japan. If war was coming, those French warships were bound to play a key role in the defence of Western Europe. But that was a price Paillole deemed worth paying, to keep the traitor active and to buy time to hunt, trace and trap him.

Paillole's team rushed into action. At the headquarters of the French Admiralty, the naval intelligence staff were 'flabbergasted' at the details the handwritten notes revealed. The first line read: 'The Mediterranean fleet can set sail in twenty-four hours.' The nation's warships had indeed been placed on an extremely high state of readiness, but only a few score French naval officers were aware of this. That narrowed the field of suspects a little. A foremost expert was asked to analyse the informant's handwriting. He concluded that the mystery author 'A' was a young man aged around thirty, thickset and powerfully built, but who lacked both a high degree of education and a strong personality.

Paillole and Abtey crunched the numbers, looking for a naval officer who fitted the description and whose surname began with 'A'. That narrowed the field a little more. But for now at least, all they could do was await the traitor's next move.

Bar an enlightened few, all of Paris was in denial. Less than two decades had passed since the First World War had come to a close, and France was still trying to shake off the war's long shadow: just short of two million French soldiers and civilians had perished, so many more wounded. This was a city – a people – that was war-weary, that hungered for entertainment, for laughter and for light. To that end, a short drive from the Deuxième Bureau's Paris headquarters, one of the city's most-celebrated entertainers was giving Parisians and foreign visitors alike exactly what they hungered for, and as almost no other female performer seemed able to.

At her own nightclub, Chez Josephine, the distinctive figure of Josephine Baker, superstar, stepped into the limelight . . . or rather the muted, intimate lighting that conjured up just the kind of cosy, magical feel that such a venue required. American by birth, in part a descendant of slaves, Josephine had been brought up in grinding poverty, and it was in France – and chiefly Paris – that she had first found fame and fortune. As a result, she loved the city and its people with all her heart and soul. Her nightly performances at Chez Josephine embodied all of that. She gave to her guests all that she had, somehow making each and every one of them feel special, as if she were dancing and singing and glittering and captivating especially for him or for her.

That ability to reach out and embrace and touch her audiences was one of her most unique and potent assets. One of the other things that distinguished her, and indeed her club, was her runaway love of animals. One of the signatures of her acts was the exotic four-legged cast who joined her on stage, Josephine herself appearing like the 'most beautiful panther', as the famous French novelist Sidonie-Gabrielle Colette would describe her. Several of Josephine's menagerie had taken up residence in her club, which gave it a distinctive Doctor-Dolittle-esque air, as Toutoute the goat and Albert the pig cavorted with the guests . . . for of course, if a goat and pig could take to the floor, what excuse did the human clientele have not to let their hair down and dance?

The moment that Josephine breezed into Chez Josephine, more often than not at one o'clock in the morning, having already performed an evening show at one of Paris' top theatres, the atmosphere was transformed. She would step between the tables, pulling beards and patting bald heads and everywhere making light and laughter, before dousing Albert with a few squirts of Je Reviens perfume, by Worth. As she did so, it became obvious that her greatest talent wasn't her voice, though it was captivating, or her svelte, lissome form, though she could dance like almost no one else seemed able; it was her sheer strength of personality and her ability to relate; to forge connections. Her very presence made a world menaced by war seem a better, brighter, more joyful place, and in the intimate environ of her club she could truly sparkle.

Stepping onto the dance floor she would begin to twirl and gyrate to the beat of the jazz, improvising her steps seemingly without thinking, almost subconsciously, as the rhythm found its pace and its place in her soul. She could do so endlessly, for hours, hypnotically, never seeming to tire. But eventually, realising she was dancing mostly alone, she would drag the remainder of her guests out into the limelight. Soon, the entire establishment would be rocking with the beat as the good times rolled.

'I want people to shake off their worries the way a dog shakes off his fleas,' declared Josephine of her club.[26] 'I never amused myself more. I made jokes ... Everyone did the Charleston, the boys, the maîtres d'hotel, the cook, the cashier, the errand boys, the goat and the pig ... all in the midst of streamers, balls and all night the lights keep changing.'[27]

A reviewer for the French language newspaper, *Le Soir*, would paint an enchanting picture of Chez Josephine: 'Midnight. Naked shoulders ... Blue chandeliers throw a soft light ... to the slow dying of the jazz ... A world exhausted ... Suddenly a shiver goes through the sold-out room ... Josephine Baker has just made her entrance. Simple, quick, amiable, she slides between the tables ... Joy, absent until now, has returned ... She dances, then suddenly remembering she is the owner ... she forces a customer to dance with her ... until everybody is on the dance floor.'[28]

By anyone's reckoning, Josephine had succeeded in her aim: she had taught Paris to enjoy itself again and to rediscover its heart. The people loved her for it. Or at least, mostly they did. By her own account, she had left the land of her birth, America, due to the segregation and the Jim Crow laws that had meant she really could not make it as a performer there. By contrast, Paris – all of Europe – had embraced her. She had found it remarkably free of prejudice; a promised land in which she could be all she had dreamed she might be and more. But from time to time the unwelcome sentiments of her youth and her teenage years had come back to haunt her, even here.

A few years back she'd been invited to announce that a

twenty-seven-year-old American called Charles Lindbergh had made the first solo transatlantic flight, landing his aircraft, *The Spirit of St Louis*, at the nearby Paris Le Bourget airfield. Of course, Josephine was overjoyed and she felt hugely honoured. Not only was she American by birth, but she hailed from the city of St Louis, after which Lindbergh had named his aircraft. As she knew full well, people both sides of the Atlantic were transfixed by Lindbergh's incredible exploits, which had monopolised headlines.

She was performing that evening at the Folies-Bergère, a Paris music hall which then was the most famous and lavish in the world. 'Good news, ladies and gentlemen,' she announced, pausing theatrically to make the announcement. 'Charles Lindbergh has arrived.' The news caused such an outpouring of joy and wonder that it almost, but not quite, stopped the show. Later, she and fellow revellers retired to a chic Paris restaurant, L'Abbaye de Thélème, the motto of which, fittingly, was 'Do what you will.' The place was awash with joviality, as figures toasted Lindbergh's success. But then an American seated with his wife at a nearby table was heard to say, loudly: 'At home a n***** woman belongs in the kitchen.'[29]

A stunned and horrified hush settled over the room. The restaurant manager went to investigate. The American repeated the remark. 'You are in France,' the manager told him, 'and here we treat all races the same.'[30] Still, Josephine was mortified. It was a painful reminder of all that she had fled from, finding in Europe a kind of sanctuary and freedom that she had never imagined possible. Yet a little over a decade later, with the relentless rise of Nazi Germany, all of that – all that she held dear and all that she cherished – seemed to be falling into shadow once more.

The next communication from the mystery traitor, 'A', popped into the Dublin mailbox, this one announcing that he was ready to deliver a very large cache of documents. Still there were no decisive clues. Then, in mid-August 1938, Dunderdale retrieved a fourth missive from the Dublin PO Box: a postcard, also mailed by 'A', but this time dispatched from Antwerp. Several things struck the Paris spy-hunters most powerfully. Antwerp was in Belgium, a neutral nation, and as a neighbour of both Germany and France it was the perfect place for a French traitor to rendezvous with agents of the Abwehr.

Via contacts in Belgium, Paillole gathered all the Antwerp hotel registration cards for 16 August 1938, the date of the postcard from 'A'. There were hundreds of them, each of which required a painstaking study to compare the handwriting with that of the mystery traitor. But after a gruelling search by Jacques Abtey, plus a fellow agent, Major André Bonnefous, they scored a stunning breakthrough . . . although at first Abtey feared it was 'too good to be true'.[31]

He rushed over to Paillole's office, almost speechless with excitement. In his hand he clutched one of the hotel registration cards. It read:

Surname: Aubert
First name: Henri
Date of birth: 12 July 1914
Profession: Officer
Nationality: French[32]

The handwriting was a carbon-copy of that of the traitor hitherto known only as 'A'.[33]

The net closed quickly. While there were several individuals in the Mediterranean fleet named Aubert, only one fitted the description – a young officer serving on the destroyer *Vanquelin*, based out of the French port of Toulon. When a sample of his handwriting was acquired it proved the perfect match. The priority now was to uncover the full extent of Aubert's treachery. Ideally, Paillole's team would then take Aubert's place, so as to feed the enemy false information, in an attempt to undo whatever damage he had wrought.

It was vital to confront Aubert in absolute secrecy. If word leaked to the Abwehr, the game would be up. They decided to arrest him on a Sunday when he was scheduled to be on guard duty, but the *Vanquelin* otherwise largely deserted. A cover story was concocted, to explain what was likely to be a long absence. On the allotted day, several Deuxième Bureau agents, all dressed in civilian clothes, headed for a rendezvous with the ship's captain, who was in full uniform complete with white gloves and sword.

Together, they headed for Aubert's cabin. The captain knocked, a well-built individual answered, at which point the agents shoved him inside and closed and bolted the door. Aubert stared at the men in ashen-faced silence – a rabbit caught in the headlamps. One glance at his desk betrayed exactly what he had been up to. The French naval codebook lay open, and Aubert had been painstakingly copying the details into yet another exercise book.

'Aubert, you have dishonoured the Navy,' the *Vanquelin*'s captain declared, aghast. 'All you have left to do now is atone for your crimes.'[34]

'Honour and Homeland' was the motto inscribed in gold lettering on every French warship, but Aubert had sold out 'his comrades, his brothers, his country', Abtey noted, in 'a most horrible crime'.[35] For those wondering what on earth Aubert's motive might be, the answer was to be found in letters scattered across the young naval officer's desk, hailing from a certain lady. While Aubert remained tight-lipped about his treachery, on her identity he was immediately forthcoming.

'She is my friend,' he protested, as the letters were siezed. 'This matter is none of her business.'[36]

Having made a note of her name – Marie Maurel – and address, Paillole's men paid her a visit. It turned out that Marie Maurel, Aubert's mistress, lay at at the root of his betrayal. Under her avaricious influence the besotted young naval officer had turned traitor, and all so that he would have enough funds to set up a love-nest.

Under interrogation Aubert revealed the breathtaking scope of his treachery. At their 18 August rendezvous in Antwerp, he had met with seasoned Abwehr agent Fritz Gibhardt. Gibhardt, a captain in the German Navy, had been a very deliberate choice: the meeting was to be navy man to navy man, a none-too-subtle attempt by the

Abwehr to forge some easy 'camaraderie'. In truth, they need not have worried greatly. Aubert was accompanied by Marie Maurel, and once she smelled the money there was no turning back. Gibhardt himself would go on to describe her as being 'cold as a fish . . . He was under the law of this girl. We owed this choice recruit to her.'[37]

Incredibly, Aubert handed Gibhardt two suitcases stuffed full of documents, including reams of technical reports stamped TOP SECRET, detailing the warships of the French fleet and their armaments. Gibhardt could barely believe his eyes.[38] Among many other highly sensitive papers, there was a detailed report concerning the *Surcouf*, a state-of-the-art French submarine then viewed as being the most advanced such design in the world.[39]

When Admiral Wilhelm Canaris, the head of the Abwehr, heard of the incredible haul, he summoned Gibhardt to his Berlin headquarters. 'Let's congratulate ourselves that this woman exists,' Canaris enthused, referencing Aubert's lover, 'for without her this boy would never have come to us.' Knowing what a hold this gave them over Aubert, they set upon seizing the greatest prize of all: the key to the French Navy's encrypted codes, which would prove 'invaluable to the German Navy'.[40]

Sure enough, Aubert proceeded to send the Abwehr copies of the French naval codebooks, via which their wireless telegraph (radio) messages were encrypted, before transmission between vessels and headquarters. 'Possessing this code, the Germans were able to decipher all movement orders concerning our ships,' Abtey would write of Aubert's treachery.[41] The head of the Deuxième Bureau put it even more starkly: 'Had we been at war, the enemy would have read our manoeuvres like an open book and we would have faced disaster.'[42]

In light of Aubert's revelations, many wished to change the French naval codes immediately, but Paillole argued otherwise. To do so would alert the Abwehr. Instead, they should continue to use the 'burned' codes, while they worked up a plan to turn Aubert's treachery back on their adversaries.

A new missive 'from Aubert' was penned by Paillole's team. The message was typeset, the author claiming that he was worried about surveillance, hence the extra precautions. With Dunderdale's help, it was slipped into the Dublin PO Box, as if Aubert were still very much in action. The Abwehr's response was entirely as intended: they congratulated 'Aubert' on his precautions, and on the excellent intelligence he was providing. Money was dispatched, the banknotes secreted between the pages of a novel, which was posted to the address of Aubert's mistress.

The woefully underfunded Deuxième Bureau pocketed the cash. It went into a special fund, which also banked the proceeds from several other double-cross operations targeting the cash-rich Abwehr. Mostly, these involved so-called 'penetration' agents that the Abwehr believed were providing high-quality information, but which were in truth feeding them false intelligence. The Abwehr's generous pay-offs went straight into the Deuxième Bureau's slush fund. It was money for a rainy day, and few doubted that dark and stormy days were coming.[43]

The book posted to Aubert's mistress also contained his next instructions, painstakingly rendered into 'micro-dots' – tiny, condensed lines of text, which could be hidden beneath full stops. Once removed, they were legible under a microscope. For months Paillole's team continued to play the Abwehr, feeding them false intelligence, during which time the French Navy were able gradually to readjust their codes, undoing the worst of Aubert's treachery. At the beginning of December 1938, 'Aubert' warned his Abwehr handlers that his payments had to be doubled, as a 'Christmas Bonus' was very much in order. Even as Paris prepared to celebrate the festive season, more Abwehr cash flowed into the Deuxième Bureau's slush fund.

But all good things must come to an end.

At dawn on 8 March 1939, Ensign Henri Aubert was executed by firing squad. He died more bravely than he had lived, sincerely expressing his regret.[44] His mistress was sentenced to three years' imprisonment, seeming callously indifferent to the fate of her erstwhile champion. Aubert's mother had begged the authorities for clemency, but to no avail. Aubert was the first to be sentenced to death for treachery in France for many a year. There had been other traitors, yet they had received lenient custodial sentences, for the law had only recently been changed to allow fitting punishment for selling one's country to the Nazis.

Paillole and Dunderdale worried it would all be too little, too late. They were shutting the door after the proverbial horse had bolted. They feared that Hitler's rise would prove inexorable, the spread of his poisonous ideology unstoppable. Paillole was convinced that Germany was already too powerful militarily, and that France would not be able to stand against the onslaught, and that the only hope of their – and Great Britain's – salvation lay across the Atlantic, in the USA.[45]

Under Hitler, Germany had become a one-party state ruled by a sinister personality cult. The SS permeated the Nazi party, and chillingly every member swore an oath 'to obey Hitler unto death'. Ninety-five per cent of German children had joined the Hitler Youth – *Hitlerjugend* – and were brainwashed in Nazi ideology: reunification of all Germanic peoples, seizure by force if necessary of *Lebensraum* – land for the Aryan elite – and virulent antisemitism. The Gestapo and all security services were firmly under Nazi control, and a terrible fate awaited any who tried to stand against them. They were to be sent to the concentration camps, like Dachau, which was ruled with extreme brutality by the SS Death's Head – *Totenkopfverbände* – units.[46]

Under Goebbels, Minister for Total War, the line pumped out from Berlin, backed by massive budgets and masterly propaganda, was that Germany's sole aim was to defeat the threat from the east. Hundreds of thousands of copies of the Hitler Youth magazine, *Wille und Macht* – Will and Power – flooded France, driving home that same message: there was nothing to fear from Berlin, which was the much-needed bulwark against communism. In Paris there seemed neither the will nor the means to resist, especially as the memory of the terrible bloodshed of the First World War still lay heavy on people's minds. Senior French figures even made proclamations like: 'German influence fertilises the French spirit!'[47]

For those who knew the truth, it was all so disheartening.

*

As Berlin cranked out the propaganda, so the enemies of the Nazi state began to be targeted. Josephine Baker was one: she would find herself the subject of Goebbels' personal vitriol. In 1937, a new and ground-breaking show, *En Super Folies*, had opened in Paris, with the express aim of promoting the city's upcoming Exposition Internationale des Arts et Techniques dans la Vie Moderne – a six-months-long festival showcasing global art, culture and technology. Among others, there would be a British Pavilion, a Spanish Pavilion, a Soviet Pavilion and, of course, a German one, too. The headline performer of *En Super Folies*, which was designed as a prelude to the Exposition, was Josephine Baker.

By now she had starred in two movies, for the first of which, *Siren of the Tropics*, she'd been signed up aged just twenty-one. She'd also performed *La Créole*, a comic opera by the German-born French composer Jacques Offenbach. Her star was at its zenith, and the producers of *En Super Folies* commissioned a giant painted frieze to publicise the show, depicting Josephine draped in jewels and feathers, drinking a toast with a top-hatted gentleman. The Exposition was defined by a global theme and the show echoed that. It opened with a series of distinct routines, each set in contrasting regions of the world. One, 'La Jungle Merveilleuse', was set in the jungle, complete with a massive stage-elephant. Another was set in the snowy wastes of the North Pole, with Josephine cast as 'the Queen of the Far North', complete with sled and huskies. A third was set firmly in Africa, from where Josephine's ancestors would have hailed.

Josephine's dear friend, the acclaimed writer Colette, was there to see one of the earliest performances. 'We love her assured, pene-trating, emotional voice . . . and we do not tire of the gentleness, that affecting desire to please,' Colette wrote. But she was most struck by the 'African Josephine . . . covered by a white woollen oriental cape, and swathed in veils,' the stage bedecked 'in colours both fiery and pure blue, the delightful entrance to the Oudayas garden in Rabat . . . Her eyes huge, outlined in black and blue, gaze forth, her cheeks are flushed, the moist and dazzling sweetness of her teeth shows beneath dark and violet lips . . .'[48]

As Collete's review foreshadowed, Josephine's performance in *En Super Folies* was a sensation. But not with everyone. As the grand pavilions rose above the Paris skyline, many built in stark, modernist style, that of Nazi Germany seemed the biggest and the brashest, dwarfing Great Britain's. Its design by Hitler's architect, Albert Speer, sought to embody the power and potency of the new Germany. Above the pavilion thrust a rank of flagpoles, on each of which flew the signature emblem of the Nazi state, one co-opted from ancient history – the Swastika. It was a grim portent of what was to come.

Ironically, the German pavilion lay just a short walk from Josephine's iconic club, *Chez Josephine*. If anything, the Spanish pavilion struck an even more controversial tone, as it featured Picasso's shocking, chaotic and tortured painting, *Guernica*, whose screaming faces and dismembered limbs commemorated the bombing of the Spanish city of that name. Just a few months earlier the Luftwaffe had levelled that Basque city, killing over two hundred civilians. Italian warplanes had also taken part in the raid, some 75,000 troops from fascist Italy joining German forces fighting on the side of the Spanish leader General Franco in the Spanish civil war.[49]

Not content with such provocations, Goebbels issued a propaganda leaflet, which denounced the 'decadent' artists of the day, who were declared to be the enemies of all that Berlin stood for. On the front cover, in pride of place and epitomising all that Goebbels and Nazism abhorred, was an image of Josephine Baker. Jumping on the bandwagon, Benito Mussolini, Italy's fascist dictator, proclaimed that Josephine was henceforth banned from visiting Italy. The Italian Pavilion – which vied to rival Germany's – nestled beneath the Eiffel Tower, in the heart of Paris, gazing out over the river Seine. Presumably, she was not welcome there either.[50]

The lines were drawn. It was not even a case of *if you are not with us, you are against us*. If you hailed from the *Untermenschen* – the subhumans – you were precluded from membership of the *Übermenschen*, the Nazi master-race, by the very essence of your being: your colour, your ethnicity, your religious beliefs or your political views ...

You were condemned by the blood or the convictions that ran through your veins. If Jew, black, Gypsy or Slav – indeed, simply for nurturing a belief in freedom and democracy – you were by definition an enemy of the state. Immutably so. And on any number of those counts Josephine Baker was first and foremost a high-profile – and reviled – adversary.

Of course, Josephine knew this. She railed against the tide of hatred, intolerance and totalitarianism emanating from Berlin. That autumn she was to fall for and marry a French industrialist, Jean Lion, who just happened to be Jewish. It gave her double the reason to abhor – and to fear – the ascendency of Hitler and his ilk. But other than speaking out and posturing, the question was – what could she do about it? With the clouds of war gathering ever more thickly, what else could a high-profile superstar – and a natural-born enemy of the Nazi state – do to stop the seemingly inevitable?

Shortly after Aubert's execution, another parcel arrived at the Deuxième Bureau's headquarters. Paillole opened it, only to find an espionage thriller by the French author Robert Dumas. But this book contained no hidden banknotes or micro-dotted messages. Instead, a slender sheet of paper fluttered out, on which was written the one word, in French: 'Congratulations'. It was the Abwehr's way of letting Paillole know that his adversaries had discovered the double-cross.[51]

While Aubert's trial had been held in the strictest secrecy, word had leaked out. Unsurprisingly, the Abwehr had been watching and listening, and they'd realised then how they had been played. But what the Aubert affair had proven most powerfully was the vital importance of close, almost seamless cooperation between those Allied intelligence agencies facing a common and powerful enemy, such as Germany then constituted.

In the spring of 1938 Paillole travelled to London to meet with senior figures in British intelligence, including Sir Stewart Menzies, chief of the Secret Intelligence Service, otherwise known as 'C'. Two years earlier, Dunderdale had first brought Paillole to the British capital, for a round of high-level talks. As the Americans had no foreign intelligence agency, that left the SIS as France's natural ally.[52] In terms of the double-cross served on the Abwehr, the Deuxième Bureau had more than shown its worth. London offered fulsome praise. In that department, certainly, Paillole and his colleagues had proved to be the 'masters'.[53]

But in many other respects the French intelligence services were woefully lacking. Aubert should have been caught far earlier. A string of clues had been missed, a clutch of errors made. If it hadn't been for American vigilance, and British brotherhood and tradecraft, Aubert might never have been unmasked. Of course, it all boiled down to a lack of manpower; of agents. Paillole had just a handful for the entire German Desk. But the moribund French Government remained implacable: there was little appetite to increase funding or to boost the Deuxième Bureau's numbers.[54]

Sadly, the SIS wasn't in a great deal better shape. The British, labouring under an appeasement-minded administration, had refused to boost the coffers and manpower of that nation's secret agencies. Quite the contrary: to Churchill's horror, the budget of the SIS had been slashed during the interwar years. 'With the world in its present condition of extreme unrest and changing friendships and antago-nisms, and with our greatly reduced and weak military forces, it is more than ever vital for us to have good and timely information,' he had railed, but to very little effect.[55]

As a result, SIS's French operations were stretched to breaking point. While Paillole viewed Dunderdale as a past-master of espio-nage – *'un camarade séduisant, d'une élégance raffinée'*; a seductive comrade of refined elegance – even the poise of this long-lived Paris spymaster seemed in jeopardy.[56] With war threatening, SIS headquar-ters worried that Dunderdale was at risk of burnout, especially with the impossible burdens he was forced to shoulder – liaising with his French counterparts, hunting traitors, running agents and gathering much-needed intelligence.[57]

After the Aubert affair, it was obvious that the Deuxième Bureau had to find more recruits, but how? There was in fact an alternative to hiring full-time agents: volunteers could be called for. Traditionally, such individuals were known as 'Honorary Correspondents' (HCs). They tended to hail from all walks of life, as long as their daily business took them into situations that could yield useful intelligence. The key qualities sought were a certain independence of means, for no one could afford to pay them; an unbending moral rectitude, and a heartfelt patriotism. A dash of abhorrence for Nazism wouldn't go amiss, but frankly the HCs would need to be recruited from a broad spectrum.

And of course, they would need guts, front and daring in spadefuls. The risks involved were legion, for the Abwehr would draw little distinction between a professional and a voluntary spy. Indeed, Nazi Germany had shown far fewer qualms than the French when it came to punishing their traitors. In recent years, two high-society ladies, Benita von Falkenhayn and Renate von Natzmer, had been seduced into spying on their country. A dashing Polish Army officer, Jerzy Sosnowski, who worked for Polish intelligence, had sought them out because they worked at the German War Ministry. But once their treachery was uncovered, they were taken to a Berlin prison and each beheaded by an axe.[58]

Beheading – as far as Berlin was concerned it was perfect *pour encourager les autres*. An axe-blade cleaved to the neck – that had become the default punishment for treachery and espionage. Horrifyingly, the Gestapo would add their own macabre twist to the method of beheading – head facing upwards on the block, so the condemned man, or woman, could see everything, including the axe-blade flashing down.[59] Despite such risks, the Deuxième Bureau was in desperate need of HCs. They would need to be sought. Those ready to take the plunge regardless of the dangers would need to be found, forming a coalition of the courageous and the willing.

That would draw into the Allies' sphere one of the most unusual candidates ever to have played the espionage game.

CHAPTER TWO

An Honourable Spy

Not long after the conclusion of the Aubert affair, the suggestion was made to Jacques Abtey that he should recruit as an Honorary Correspondent one of the foremost superstars of Europe. The recommendation was not without a degree of controversy. Firstly, the nominee was a woman and in the distinctly chauvinistic atmosphere of the late 1930s, women were not looked upon very kindly across the world's intelligence agencies. After the Aubert affair, Admiral Canaris had reiterated his strong opposition to using female agents.[1] Likewise, Britain's SIS had few women in its ranks.

Abtey remained undecided. On the one hand he cited the infamous case of Mata Hari, the cabaret dancer of supposedly Asian descent, but who was in reality Dutchwoman Margaretha Zelle. Recruited as an Honorary Correspondent during the First World War, she was found guilty of being a double agent and of selling secrets to the Germans. She was shot as a traitor, and few in the French espionage milieu had ever forgotten.[2]

On the other hand, Abtey had little option but to resort to 'people acting voluntarily out of pure patriotism . . . *gratis pro Deo*' (free of charge), and some of those who stepped forward were bound to be women.[3] As far as he saw it, a woman could be 'as brave as a man, have as much tenacity, as much willpower and could be counted upon to be discreet'. In some ways he believed a female agent could be 'superior', being more innately intuitive and also being able to fly under the radar.[4]

Even so, the present, world-famous nominee was clearly no spy by nature. How could someone with such a high profile possibly serve as an undercover agent, operating in the shadows?[5] For any such individual the 'ability to go unnoticed' was key. Surely, the very fact of her stardom – her notoriety – ruled her out.[6]

HCs were required to have a keen intellect, a razor-sharp memory, so as not to get ensnared by one's own lies, an ability to make people talk, plus the self-possession to retain a cool head when all around were losing theirs. The very best such agents never carried a weapon. They had no need. They got out of the direst of situations by relying upon their mental faculties, their composure and an iron-willed self-control. As far as Abtey knew, this star of stage, screen and song was hardly renowned for her powers of discretion, and as any trawl of news-clippings would reveal, she had contradicted her own life story several times over.[7]

But Abtey's single greatest objection was based upon patriotism. First and foremost, any credible HC had to be a true French patriot. Without a burning love of country, there was no heart; no iron core of principles from which to keep taking risks. Abtey wasn't sure if this woman was even French. She certainly hadn't been born in France. She hailed from across the Atlantic, and while she had spent the best part of two decades resident in Paris, for much of that time she had been touring the world's capitals, giving sell-out shows. Admittedly, her ability to travel widely offered the perfect excuse to spy, but even those performances weren't without their controversies.

The prevailing image of this icon was of her stalking the Paris streets, together with her cheetah, Chiquita, held on a diamond-studded leash, and of her near-naked stage shows. Rumoured to be one of the wealthiest women then alive, even her ethnicity was clouded in mystery. While her mother, Carrie McDonald, was a black American, she had variously claimed that her father was a famous black lawyer, a Jewish tailor, a Spanish dancer, or a white German then resident in America.[8] Whatever her father's true identity, what was not up for debate was her Native American heritage: one of her grandmothers,

Elvira, was descended from the Apalachee, a fierce warrior tribe originating from the southern United States.[9]

All things considered, Abtey remained sceptical. But Daniel Marouani, the foremost champion of this superstar, would brook no dissent. Marouani certainly had form, for he served as a part-time HC, while also managing a top casino in Cannes. His younger brother, Félix, worked as the impresario – the theatrical agent – for this famous individual, and he too recommended her. She might well be an exceptional artist, Abtey argued, but she was 'a little eccentric', not to mention '*une grande amoureuse*' – a seductress. Well, Daniel Marouani countered, who in the world of espionage wasn't?[10] More to the point, she was actually 'more French than the French'.[11]

She had more reasons than most to abhor the Nazis, and to want to fight them with every essence of her being. That she was a woman of singular courage was beyond doubt. A few years back, she had been returning from a tour of Europe when a bomb had exploded beneath the train she was travelling on. The attack was deemed to be the work of terrorists with communist leanings. It proved mightily effective: the locomotive and nine carriages were blown off the tracks, tumbling into a ravine. Dozens were killed and injured. As the survivors sat in the carriages 'frozen with fear', our heroine did the only thing she could think of to bolster everyone's spirits . . . she began to sing.[12]

Faced with Marouani's relentless badgering, Abtey finally relented. After all, nothing ventured, nothing gained. Having persuaded Abtey to make the journey across Paris to meet this superstar, Marouani volunteered to drive. So cash-strapped was the Deuxième Bureau that the agency boasted not a single motor car. As befitted a superstar of the era, she had made her home in a beautiful neo-Gothic mansion set amid the rolling parklands and lakes of Le Vésinet, a suburb on the city's western outskirts cradled in a bend of the Seine, and favoured by the wealthy of Paris.

Despite the favour Marouani was doing him – 'an extremely resourceful boy, burning with the desire to do well' – Abtey kept a scowl on his face the entire journey, feeling sure this was a complete waste of time.[13] The car pulled through the imposing gateway of Le Beau Chêne, the grand, turreted villa, whereupon Abtey heard a cheerful and unaffected cry ring out from the direction of the gardens: 'Hello.'[14]

He turned, only to spy an unmistakable figure emerge from the bushes, her face shaded by a battered felt hat, one hand thrust into a pair of old gardening trousers and the other clutching a dented tin can brimming with snails. Despite the wholly unexpected attire – Abtey had supposed he'd find her draped in a designer gown and dripping with jewels – there was no mistaking the striking features or the dazzling smile.

Josephine Baker, superstar, was bidding him welcome.[15]

Abtey had come bearing an assumed identity, as any spy should, and Marouani introduced him as an Englishman, 'Mr Fox'. For an instant, Josephine Baker threw a shrewd glance in his direction, and he realised in that moment that he was as much on trial here as was she. They turned towards the sumptuous residence, at the entrance to which she deposited her can of snails – not to cook and eat, as one might imagine in France, but for feeding to her ducks – as a white-coated butler ushered them inside. There, a roaring fire and a bottle of iced champagne awaited.[16] Having filled their glasses, the butler quietly withdrew.

'It's a pleasure to meet you, Mr Fox,' Josephine declared, raising her glass. 'To France.' And so they toasted the mother country.[17]

As they talked, Abtey was struck by several things, perhaps best summed up in the phrase – *this was not at all what he was expecting.* The house impressed with its sombre, tasteful elegance. She impressed, with her simplicity and unpretentiousness; her almost childlike quality, at turns playful and pensive, and her schoolgirlish habit of wrinkling her forehead when lost in thought. Instinctive, innate, she tended to make up her mind about people almost instantly. Though he was only to learn this later, Abtey had made an unexpectedly favourable impression, for he too was up for judgement on this day.

Josephine had been anticipating an archetype of a security services agent as she saw it – someone in the vein of the fictional 1930s French detective, Inspector Jules Maigret; a gruff, downbeat individual, wearing a dark overcoat and sporting a pudding-bowl haircut, above a porcupine moustache, with clothes smelling of stale tobacco and grease.[18] She'd steeled herself to be speared by a bristly stare from beneath bushy eyebrows. Stylishly dressed, handsome, well-travelled, multilingual – Abtey spoke fluent German, French and English, plus some Arabic – her visitor was a far cry from all that.[19]

Who would ever have expected an officer of the Deuxième Bureau to be 'young, blond, athletic, bursting with life?' she would write of their first encounter.[20]

The surprise, on both sides, was complete. As they relaxed beside the fire, and Josephine chatted away, Abtey began to appreciate what had made her such a global sensation. This beautiful, bewitching woman possessed an almost unique ability to reach out from the stage and connect with her audience. As Jean-Pierre Reggiori, one of Josephine's youngest-ever dance partners, who she nicknamed 'Little Page', pointed out, this gift of Josephine's to touch her audience, to connect, was a truly remarkable and rare thing.

'Not only could she sing, dance and act wonderfully, but she always went one hundred per cent. *Always*,' Reggiori would remark of Josephine. 'Even in Paris, with its famously reserved clientele, she broke down barriers, and talked to and with her audience. She reached people. She gave herself to her audience. She made personal connections as almost no other performer was able to.'[21]

Little by little, Abtey outlined exactly why he had come, and what exactly was expected by the Deuxième Bureau of an Honourable Correspondent. Josephine's response left him almost speechless, and very close to awestruck. If what Abtey was hearing was genuine, Marouani had been fully vindicated, proving himself a fine judge of character.

'France has made me all that I am,' Josephine declared, simply. 'I shall be eternally grateful to her . . . I gave my heart to Paris, as Paris gave me hers. Captain, I am ready to give my country my life. Dispose of me as you will.'[22]

As Abtey studied her 'beautiful, slightly misty' eyes – the windows into the soul – he detected that this apparently fearless pronouncement seemed genuine. She burst out laughing, breaking the somewhat awkward silence that had settled between them.[23]

'I'm glad to be dealing with such a young, friendly man as you,' she declared, light-heartedly. 'You know how I had imagined you?' Playfully, she went on to describe a 'short, paunchy gentleman' with a grubby bowler hat, fierce eyes and a smelly cigar. But Abtey – Mr Fox – was quite different. 'You have an accent that is not French, nor is your name? Excuse me, but you are the first officer of the Deuxième Bureau that I have ever met.'[24]

Did this gentle inquisition betray a 'certain mistrust' towards him, Abtey wondered? The way she had turned the tables, putting the Deuxième Bureau agent in 'the hot seat', was remarkable. It boded well for Josephine's potential as an HC.[25] By way of answer, Abtey explained that he hailed from the border country – Alsace – making him an Alsatian, but that for now at least she should continue to call him 'Mr Fox'.

For a long moment the flames that sprang from the fireplace crackled and hissed, throwing tortured shadows across the ebony statue that stood in one corner of the room. Dusk had fallen, and in the dancing half-light Josephine Baker appeared to Jacques Abtey as a 'true goddess of the night'.[26] This was the moment when he somehow had to make her recruitment as an HC official.

'You will accept me to work for France?' she ventured, somewhat timidly.

'From now on, you are one of us,' Abtey confirmed, simply.[27]

Josephine seemed overjoyed. She demanded what the first task was that she might usefully perform. Abtey explained that he wanted her to work her magic at the Italian embassy. She was to befriend a certain individual there, an attaché, who Abtey hoped would prove a font of intelligence. France and Britain were desperate to learn of the Italian Government's intentions, should Germany declare war, and Miss Baker was known to have a particular 'in' with the Italians.[28] A while back she had endorsed Mussolini's 1935 invasion of Ethiopia, in East Africa, having fallen in love with the Italian nation and its people while on tour there, being struck most powerfully by the long history and striking beauty of this land of contrasts.[29]

Infatuated with the country and its swaggering showman of a leader, Josephine had publicly backed Mussolini over Ethiopia, to the horror of many. Unwisely, she had chosen to believe the Italian dictator when he had told her that he aimed to 'liberate' Ethiopia, stamping out slavery, which still existed there. Certainly, the Italian troops had freed some slaves, but then, as the Ethiopians had fought back with spirited defiance, Mussolini's forces had unleashed mustard gas on the nation's defenders.[30]

Foolish and impulsive though her support may have been, it should give her an edge now. As Abtey knew full well, Admiral Canaris – chief of the Abwehr – and General Mario Roatta – chief of the Servizio Informazioni Militaire (SIM), the Italian intelligence service – had held a series of meetings, as they sought to forge an alliance. Italy had also flooded France with 'diplomats' – thinly disguised spies – while at the same time somehow convincing the French government that they didn't trust Hitler and that all they sought was peace.[31]

What Abtey needed was proof otherwise, and due to her earlier indiscretions, Josephine should be well-placed to furnish it. While Mussolini had publicly repudiated her, in relation to the International Exposition, privately many Italian diplomats were known to have a soft spot for Josephine. Abtey charged her to use such connections now, for the good of the Allied cause. He left her with that mission – that singular challenge – and as he and Marouani exited the château, he noticed that the tin can was where she had left it, but that all the snails were gone. They had fled back to the garden, to escape the fate that Josephine had intended – dinner for her ducks.

As they made their way towards the car, Abtey was struck by the dichotomy of this superstar: her split life. On the one hand, she was the glamorous, glittering performer who lit up the stage at the Casino de Paris, modelled dresses by the city's top couturiers, and stalked the

Paris streets with Chiquita the cheetah to hand. On the other, there was the young woman he had discovered here at Le Beau Chêne – a down-to-earth individual with a simple, child-like charm, who loved France, her garden and its animals, Chiquita included.

Getting Chiquita for Josephine had been the brainchild of Henri Varna, a seasoned showrunner at the top music halls. In 1930, five years after she had hit the Paris scene, Varna had realised that while she was still rough around the edges, Josephine possessed true star quality, and under his tutelage she could be polished, like a fabulous diamond. He'd taught her how to properly receive the adoration of her audience – to take a stately bow. The cheetah, which he'd purchased from an exotic animal farm, was a canny gift, intended to be her personal and stage companion.

Though it was a male, Josephine had promptly named him Chiquita. Enchanted by him, Chiquita had quickly become her favourite pet, despite his habit of catching and eating the ducks that lived on her ornamental ponds, the ones to which she loved feeding snails. Milking the publicity – somehow, they seemed to make the perfect double-act – Varna decreed that Chiquita should be featured on the cover of the programmes for her shows, the cheetah offering Josephine a lavish bouquet of flowers.

The summer she had been given Chiquita, she'd treated him to a performance of the opera *La Bohème*, where he perched on her lap. At one stage he'd broken free, stalked down the aisle and leapt into the orchestra pit, with Josephine chasing after. The story made head-line news as far away as America, such publicity being just the kind of thing Varna intended. He schooled Josephine relentlessly to be a performer worthy of her destiny. He had her descend the staircase on stage again and again, with a heap of books balanced on her head, perfecting the erect and elegant poise which she had inherited from her mother, Carrie. Like Josephine a performer – though nowhere near as successful – Carrie had danced with a glass of water perched on her head, not spilling a drop.

Parisians liked to joke of Josephine and her cheetah that it was impossible to tell which was the more dangerous, Josephine or Chiquita.[32] For Jean-Pierre Reggiori, Josephine's future dance partner, the cheetah was a powerful symbol of her 'wild and irrepresible femininity'. Abtey, too, had seen a different side of her from the glamorous, bejewelled superstar: the simple, unaffected woman in the battered felt hat who liked gathering snails for her ducks. And he had bequeathed to her a third potential identity now – that of an Honorary Correspondent of the Deuxième Bureau. Should she prove up to the challenges of being an HC, it would be precisely by posing as Josephine Baker the glamorous, glittering superstar that she would be able to cast a veil over her clandestine activities. Her very stardom would be her cloak and her dagger.

'Well?' asked Marouani, as they pulled out of the gates of Le Beau Chêne. *What did he think?*

Abtey didn't answer. No response was necessary. Surely, it was obvious how he felt about his newest recruit.[33] As they drove through the darkened Paris streets, he wondered what Josephine might be thinking, now that he was gone.[34]

As Josephine had declared in her 1927 memoir, penned with French writer Marcel Sauvage, she abhorred the stereotyping of women and she cherished her freedoms.[35] But since then, a far greater challenge – a far greater menace – had raised its ugly head. In 1926, she had left Paris to tour Europe, her itinerary taking her finally to Berlin. Not yet a decade after the horrors of the First World War, there was a wild exuberance to Germany's capital city, and the bright, brash nightlife felt more like the America she had known in her youth – Harlem, or the Chestnut Alley district of her native St Louis – than it did the refined airs of a historic capital of Europe.[36]

This was Germany prior to the rise of Nazism, and there was a hectic decadence about the city, a need to hunt for sensation and thrills, as an antidote to the horrors of the Great War. Not only had Germany suffered during that conflict, but this was the nation of the vanquished and there was a need to party and forget. Raised in dire poverty in the city of St Louis, Josephine often had no uniform or even shoes to wear to school. Teased, rejected, mocked, she'd played the fool and had mostly hated school. She was far happier leading her street gang stealing coal from locomotives, to sell to rich white folks. She'd proved the fearless and the wild one, climbing onto the rail cars to throw down handfuls of the dirty black rock, so the rest could stuff their sacks full.

Often, the train would jolt into motion even as she was so engaged. Invariably, she would remain on her precarious perch, hurling down more coal, as the locomotive began to gather speed and her street pals yelled for her to jump. Typically, she'd push it to the very limit, throwing herself free just before the train had reached a speed at which the impact could have proven injurious or even fatal. Often she went barefoot, and during the coldest months she would resort to dancing along the streets in an effort to ward off the chill.[37]

Unsurprisingly, she thrilled to the wild excess of Berlin in 1926. Fearful that her stardom and good fortune might prove transitory – that she might sink back into the abject penury and hard grind of her youth – she chased fame and fortune relentlessly, lest it slip away.[38] She also, unashamedly, rewrote and recast her origins, her parentage especially. 'I don't lie. I improve on life,' she once told a reporter, who had commented pointedly on the contradictory versions of her family history that she had told.[39]

During her first Berlin tour, Josephine's performance in *La Revue Nègre* – the show that had brought her from New York to Paris, in 1925 – proved a sell-out hit. In Germany, the concept of the 'noble savage' – supposedly a more primitive and natural form of human existence, one that predated modern, mechanised existence – was all the rage. Josephine's headline act in *La Revue Nègre* was seen to embody all of that, her near-naked dances – she believed she was born to move, rhythm hard-wired into her soul – captivating audiences, just as the *nacktkultur* (nudist) movement was taking Germany by storm.[40]

But at the same time there was an extreme right-wing ideology starting to take hold, which aimed to purge the country of such 'immorality', and to build a nation that was 'healthy, fit and strong'. This was the nascent Nazi movement, and its storm-troopers at the time were the so-called Brownshirts. They condemned Josephine Baker and her shows vociferously. In their warped mindset she was not only a symbol of the decadence they abhorred, she also epitomised the 'racial impurity' they despised.

With the Brownshirts then viewed largely as a lunatic fringe, Josephine proved more than able to counter their criticism. 'I'm not immoral,' she objected, pithily, 'I'm only natural.'[41] With most in Germany, her tour had gone down a storm.

But when she returned two years later it would prove a very different story. Long before she got there, her detractors were ready. She travelled first to Austria, only to be greeted with screaming headlines – she was the 'Black Devil' and 'Jezebel', the biblical female pariah and false prophet. Armed guards had to escort her through Vienna, as leaflets decried the 'brazen-faced heathen dances' she would perform. With many Austrians embracing the proposed union with Germany, Hitler's rantings in *Mein Kampf* – including that black people were inferior 'half apes' – had found a ready readership.[42] The very worst coined the phrase *negersmach* to greet Ms Baker, meaning that her performances and her very existence were an insult to the Nazi cause, and especially that of breeding the so-called *Übermenschen*, the much-vaunted Aryan master-race.[43]

By the time Josephine's show opened in Theater des Westens, one of Berlin's most famous opera houses, the agitators were there in force, drowning her out with hoots and catcalls. A review the following day, in a pro-Nazi paper, screamed: 'How dare they put our beautiful, blonde Lea Seidl with a Negress on the stage.' (Lea Seidl, an Austrian actress, had actually befriended Josephine and was mortified at how she was being treated.)[44] The show was scheduled to run for six months. It lasted three weeks, before Josephine – haunted, harangued, abused – was forced to flee.

Moving on to Dresden, the press decried the 'convulsions of this *coloured girl*'. In Munich, Josephine faced even worse. She was banned outright, for her performances would offend the city's sense of self-respect, she was warned.[45] She faced mobs who seemed to hate her and she sensed that they would like to see an end to her life.[46] In truth her instincts – her palpable sense of the threat – were far from over-blown. Her Berlin tour had been booked by the Rotter brothers, who happened to be Jewish. Facing vitriolic criticism and denigration, they would be forced to flee to Czechoslovakia, leaving behind them the foremost Berlin theatres that they had run. Even there they were still not safe from the long arm of the Nazi state. Tracked by the Gestapo, the Rotter brothers would be hunted down, arrested and murdered.[47]

After the shock of that tour, Josephine kept her distance from Germany and those other nations falling under Hitler's sway, even as the dark horrors of Nazism suddenly grew clearer for all to see. On 9 November 1938, in a terror that foreshadowed the Holocaust, *Kristallnacht* – the Night of Broken Glass – convulsed Austria and Germany. Jews were dragged from their homes and synagogues were put to the torch, as men, women and children were clubbed to death. Of course, by then Josephine was married to the wealthy Jewish industrialist Jean Lion, so she felt this horror most personally. As nothing else, *Kristallnacht* crystallised her abhorrence of Hitler and all that he stood for.[48]

Ironically, this was the year that Josephine's existence would come to Hitler's attention most personally. Visiting Austria following the *Anschluss* – the takeover of that nation by Nazi Germany – the Führer chose to commandeer Vienna's historic Weinzinger Hotel. Typically, he took the best suite for himself, having failed to notice before retiring to bed that none other than Josephine Baker's portrait was gazing down at him from the wall. Needless to say, he was not best pleased.[49]

By the time Jacques Abtey had come calling at Le Beau Chêne, Josephine was acutely aware of the need to stand up to bullies like Hitler and all he espoused. Nazi Germany's actions were 'criminal', she would write and 'criminals had to be punished'.[50] As war engulfed Europe, she would declare herself willing to kill Nazis with her own hand, if the need arose. Of course, her recruitment as an Honourable Correspondent gave her the means to strike back, without necessarily ever needing to draw blood.[51]

Josephine would become 'emblematic of many things,' as Géraud Létang, of the Service Historique de la Défense, the Defence Historical Services of the French military, would declare: 'of the engagement of women during the Second World War, of the engagement of foreigners in the French Resistance . . .' In truth, the coming conflict would bring her face-to-face with herself, as she 'refused defeat', requiring her to master the greatest performance of her life in which her very survival would hang in the balance.[52]

But first, she would have to prove herself in the cut and thrust of espionage.[53]

It was six days after Abtey's visit when he and Josephine next spoke, this time by telephone. Nothing remotely sensitive could be said over a phone line, but he was aware that her voice was taught with tension.

'Come quickly,' she urged, 'I would be so happy to see you.'[54]

That was easier said than done, for Abtey was at the very apex of one of the longest-running spy-hunts of his career. Almost a year earlier the head of the Deuxième Bureau's telephone tapping service, Cazin d'Honincthun, had burst into his office, throwing a transcript of an intercepted phone call onto his desk. 'Here, Petz!' he'd cried – for some unknown reason Abtey was known as 'Petz' by his colleagues – 'get excited about that.'[55]

The transcript was of a call made to a Herr vom Rath, at the German embassy in Paris, by a French-speaking individual known only as 'Georgette'. What made it especially noteworthy was how vom Rath and Georgette, knowing full well that the Deuxième Bureau would be listening, had taunted them with the bare-faced treachery then in play. Abtey had spent the next several months hunting for Georgette. While the Deuxième Bureau made sure to photograph all individuals entering or leaving the German embassy, he was still none the wiser. But the day after his first meeting with Josephine, Abtey had been passed a fat file on a French-speaking agent of the Abwehr. A careful study of the contents confirmed it: 'Finally, we had Georgette.'[56]

With that, Abtey arranged for a special switching device to be inserted into the German embassy's telephone system. When Georgette next tried to speak to vom Rath, Abtey flicked a button which put himself on the line instead. In his fluent German he explained that vom Rath was not there, but that he'd been given instructions to meet with Georgette. They arranged a rendezvous in front of La Madeleine, an imposing Roman-style church in the 8th arrondissement. Georgette told Abtey he would recognise him by his 'navy blue mackintosh and beret', plus he would be accompanied by a female friend carrying an umbrella.[57]

Sure enough, Abtey had just managed to arrest a man dressed in a blue gabardine mac, and drag him into the Deuxième Bureau's cells. There the interrogation had begun. And now he had Josephine Baker demanding to see him. All he knew was this had better be good. Things being as hectic as they were, they agreed to rendezvous in central Paris, with Josephine at the wheel of her long, graceful, black-and-white Delage, then one of the world's most exclusive motorcars, with the interior upholstered in a riot of snakeskin.[58]

Abtey, however, was mostly worried about Josephine's driving. Famously erratic at the best of times, with her present, flustered state of mind Abtey feared for his safety, not to mention that of those who thronged the streets. Josephine had passed her driving test in June 1927, the Paris driving school using her photo to trumpet their credentials. But from the very start her driving was defined by a certain 'recklessness' and had proved something of a 'nightmare'. Once, she had crashed into a lamppost near the Paris Grand Hotel, got out of the car seemingly unperturbed, signed some autographs for the crowd that had gathered and caught a taxi home.[59]

Now, as she drove, Josephine spouted out a 'furious torrent' of words, all concerning what she had learned from the attaché at the Italian Embassy. She'd realised the best way to pump him for information was to provoke and contradict him, in response to which he had fallen into the habit of whispering reassurances into her ear. In this way she had extracted from her unsuspecting target some very useful material, during this, her first assignment for the Deuxième Bureau. She'd paid very close attention, so she could report all to Abtey.[60]

As Abtey listened, he could well appreciate Josephine's excitement: the intelligence she bore was 'choice'. When all the leaders of the free world were trying to second-guess Mussolini's intentions, Josephine had discovered the bitter truth: *Il Duce* – The Leader – as Mussolini styled himself, 'had just decided to play Hitler's game against France', one that he was determined to 'play to the end'.[61] In short, Mussolini fully intended to strike an alliance with Germany, joining forces against the Allies.

Frustrated at the extent to which she had been duped by *Il Duce*, Josephine slammed her fist onto the steering wheel of the Delage, at which point it veered alarmingly, causing panic among other road users. 'A long, shrill whistle' rang out. Josephine brought her car to a halt, as a gendarme stepped into the road, fully expecting to find some drunk behind the wheel. Once Josephine treated him to her trademark smile – and the gendarme recognised just who it was behind the wheel – he waved her on, but with words of caution ringing in her ears. Abtey also made a 'discreet appeal for calm', but this just seemed to inflame Josephine all the more.[62]

Her state of 'unbelievable nervousness' unsettled him.[63] Sure, she had delivered some fine intelligence and in record-breaking time, just as he'd asked. Her potential as a special agent was very real. But Abtey was beginning to doubt if he could ever impart to this impetuous recruit 'the very special training' and the cool, calm powers of discernment that would lead to 'success in our kind of work'.[64] 'Will I ever manage to discipline my tumultuous collaborator?' Abtey wondered.[65]

In light of the revelations about Mussolini's intentions, the greatest worry of the Allies was that if fascist Italy and Germany did strike an alliance, Spain would follow in a 'domino effect', whereupon the entire Mediterranean would be rendered hostile to Allied shipping, with calamitous results.[66] Accordingly, Britain's War Cabinet gathered, with Neville Chamberlain, Winston Churchill, Clement Attlee and other key figures in attendance, to formulate a proposal that US President Franklin D. Roosevelt 'should be asked to make an . . . approach to Signor Mussolini,' to dissuade him from joining forces with Berlin.

When Roosevelt did as requested, Mussolini's response was that the American president should keep his nose out of Italian affairs.[67] The Allies could go hang. Still, at least now the leaders of the free world knew the worst.

Even as she'd delivered on her first Deuxième Bureau assignment, Josephine had been skittish, unsettled, unnerved even. On one level it was surprising. Josephine was a chameleon, a rebel, a warrior and rule-breaker at heart. She was undeniably at her best when she had an over-arching cause to fight for. For that – for those things she cared passionately about – she could prove tireless, resolute, unbreakable.

Once, when performing at the Lucerna Theatre in Prague, she had danced until she'd fainted with exhaustion, bleeding onto the stage. The conductor had directed the orchestra to play too fast, but she had refused to be beaten by him, even as he kept upping the tempo. Fighting the waves of exhaustion and pain that assailed her, she had pirouetted, whirled and spun, right until the final curtain, and even as the audience clamoured for more. There would be no encore. That night in the Prague auditorium she had given her all to the dance, until her knees were raw, the blood running down her calves. She had shown she would never give up. She would rather die than suffer such an indignity; such dishonour.[68]

She would display the same total commitment to the spying game, but no one could pretend that the journey ahead wasn't daunting. If things went badly, she could end up losing her head. Literally.

And very soon now the stakes would be increased many-fold, for the world would be at war.

CHAPTER THREE

From Paris With Love

On 23 August 1939, Nazi Germany and Soviet Russia signed the Non-Aggression Pact, also known as the Hitler–Stalin Pact or the Nazi–Soviet Alliance. Not only did it preclude hostilities breaking out between Germany and the USSR, but under a Secret Protocol it allowed for the carve-up of Poland. The day before the sealing of that alliance, Britain's ambassador to Germany, Sir Neville Henderson, had a meeting with Hitler to warn him that Britain would stand firm at Poland's side. The French Government declared that it would also remain steadfast with its Polish allies.

At the same time, Menzies, the SIS chief, headed to Paris, to meet with his counterparts in French intelligence, including Paillole, and with Dunderdale very much holding court. All in attendance agreed that the British and French pledges regarding Poland were unlikely to save the day. Paillole outlined the extent of the tsunami of Nazi propaganda that was inundating France, and his fears about how greatly it had sapped the nation's will to fight. The two intelligence services would need to work ever more closely, in an effort to prevent war.[1]

Paillole would write in glowing terms of 'the friendship and trust' that had grown between the French and British intelligence services, even as war threatened. They were determined to work together 'until we win, faithfully, putting all our cards on the table'. He would describe his British counterparts as being steadfast, efficient and always tactful, qualities which could never be praised highly enough.[2] In light of what was coming, that alliance was to be tested beyond all measure and unto the bitter end.

All present at the Paris meeting knew the folly of France's defensive strategy – stubbornly clinging to the Maginot Line, the string of massive fortifications lining the nation's border with Germany. Unfortunately, few among the political hierarchy seemed willing to listen. Indeed, it was far easier to gather intelligence, than it was to get those in power to act upon it. This was especially so in France, where the chiefs of the intelligence services tended to lack the direct access to their political leaders that their British counterparts enjoyed.[3] By contrast, Churchill was famous for his hands-on approach, and long before he became Britain's prime minister.

Dunderdale and Josephine would certainly have met, long before the outbreak of war. For more than a decade, they had moved in the same high-society Paris circles. In fact, Dunderdale deliberately cultivated such a refined milieu and largely for the espionage contacts and opportunities it afforded, which was all part of his genius. With Josephine's recruitment as an HC their acquaintance would have blossomed, for they could then make common cause. As Dunderdale, Paillole and Abtey plotted what measures to take upon the fall of France – an outcome which they feared was all-but inevitable – Josephine lay at the heart of their intentions. Once the forces of Nazi Germany invaded, in terms of the fight-back in the intelligence war, Josephine would take centre stage.[4]

The utter futility of the static defences of the Maginot Line became blindingly obvious, once Hitler's *blitzkrieg* – lightning war – steamrollered into Poland, his armoured legions crushing that nation's spirited defenders. Paillole had had forewarning of Berlin's intentions, and even of the exact timings, from one of his foremost penetration agents. Hans-Thilo Schmidt was the spy at the heart of Hitler's inner circle, furnishing intelligence hot from the German Cypher Office. Schmidt was 'one hundred per cent reliable', and he had provided a detailed account of Hitler's plans and intentions.[5]

On the evening of 31 August 1939, Berlin had launched its 'most disgusting plot' yet, as Paillole would describe it. An Abwehr commando, under the leadership of SS officer Alfred Helmut Naujocks, attacked the German radio transmitter at Gleiwitz, on Germany's then border with Poland. The attackers, who were dressed as Polish troops, left a bloodied corpse slumped in a doorway, but it was a body that had actually been furnished by the Gestapo. Cast as an unprovoked attack on Germany, but in truth a 'false-flag' operation by the Nazi state, the Gleiwitz incident was used as a pretext to condemn so-called 'Polish aggression'.

The very next day Hitler's tanks and warplanes bludgeoned their way across the Polish border. Two weeks later Soviet troops followed suit, and by then Britain and France had declared war. Even as Warsaw was overrun, the SIS station chief, Major John Shelley, and Sophie, his wife, evacuated the city, but in the process Sophie was killed in a German air raid. Using his secure SIS wireless, Major Shelley radioed London, reporting that 'matters here now look like . . . sauve qui peut and this place will become extremely dangerous.' In fact, Shelley got all of his staff out, and by 28 September they were reporting for duty at SIS's headquarters in Broadway, central London.[6]

A few days earlier two steamships, the *Clan Menzies* and the *Robur VIII*, had been dispatched from Britain to Poland laden with arms, and with the War Cabinet's blessing. They would fail to get there in time to be of any assistance.[7] Within the month the Polish nation had been crushed, with the capital Warsaw being terrorised. Hitler had ordered that all resistance be annihilated, and Poland's Jews be rounded up and exterminated.[8] That would pave the way for the Führer's next great project – the assault on France and Great Britain.

At the 19 September War Cabinet meeting that had green-lit those arms shipments to Poland, the issue of Japan's allegiances was very much in the spotlight. Japan's ambassador to London had called at the Foreign Office, in an effort to assure the British Government that there was no 'fresh orientation of Japanese policy' – in other words, that Japan had no intention of joining Germany and declaring war. But of course, words are cheap.

There was a world-wide jockeying for power and little reliance could be placed upon any such easy assurances.[9]

In Paris, Jacques Abtey headed for a meeting with Josephine Baker. While the world might be at war, for now it remained mostly empty of action; a battle of words alone. The Allied and Axis forces remained in their bunkers and their trenches, engaged in what would become known as 'the Phoney War'. Real hostilities were months away. Yet even so, the shadow conflict was becoming ever more intense, cut-throat and bloody, as Berlin's spies flooded ever more thickly into France.

'We were seeing them everywhere, even where they had never been before,' Abtey remarked. 'We thought we recognised them in the cassock of a priest . . . We were suspicious of the stationmaster and the maintenance man . . .'[10]

With agent Josephine being such a recent recruit, Abtey felt the pressing need to school her in the subtle, many-layered art of spycraft. As war quickened her spirit and her focus, she turned out to be a fast and precocious learner. 'I soon glimpsed the exceptional qualities that she unwittingly possessed,' Abtey wrote, 'and which would later mark so profoundly the success of her career in intelligence.'[11]

That Josephine was proving something of a natural was fortunate, for Abtey had a new mission in mind. As with the Italians, she was known to have a special 'in' with the Japanese, and he wished her to discover the true allegiances of *Nippon* – the Land of the Rising Sun. As luck would have it, one of Josephine's greatest fans was Miki Sawada, granddaughter of the founder of the Mitsubishi industrial empire. Over the years they had become close friends, and Miki just happened to be married to Renzo Sawada, Japan's ambassador to France.[12]

Miki and Josephine's friendship had been forged in the most unlikely of places, given their rarefied lifestyles – the Paris slums. One day Miki had overheard Josephine describe how she was in the habit of visiting the city's ghetto, taking alms to the poor. Miki declared that she would like to accompany her on one of those excursions.

Josephine had warned that she would be shocked when she saw how the dispossessed of Paris lived. Miki was not to be discouraged.

In due course Josephine had driven her into the city's underbelly, and upon reaching a tall tenement block she had honked her horn. Pinched faces appeared at the windows, and moments later the Delage was surrounded in a sea of need. Josephine's response to being mobbed was to cheerfully dole out the boxes piled high in the car, each tied with a colour-coded ribbon denoting medicines, food, clothing, toys. 'The sight of Josephine picking up the little ones, stroking their heads, made tears come to my eyes,' Miki would declare.[13]

Having grown up in conditions not dissimilar to these, Josephine was utterly unfazed. In truth, it was because she had suffered such poverty herself that she felt compelled to help. St Louis could be bitterly cold, especially in the winter, and Josephine would always remember it as a freezing city. She had lived in a series of run-down dwellings with no gas or electricity, heated by a fire kindled in a metal barrel, and with wads of newspaper stuffed into cracks in the walls.

As Miki Sawada's husband was the Japanese ambassador to France, getting access to the Japanese embassy in Paris should prove easy enough. But it would mean taking advantage of their friendship, which was a special one. For good reason, Josephine referred to Miki as her sister. In October 1935, Josephine had sailed to New York, a full decade after she'd left the USA for France, on what was supposed to be her American comeback tour. At the time Miki Sawada's husband was working as a diplomat in the States, and she had met Josephine at the New York docks in a Rolls-Royce flying the Japanese flag. They'd driven to the hotel in which Josephine had a reservation, but when the manager realised Miss Baker was a black person she was refused a room.

Miki had their driver take them to several other hotels, but at every one they were turned away. To make matters worse, the chauffeur began to complain that he didn't want to be seen at the wheel of a car carrying a black woman. In desperation, Miki took Josephine to the New York apartment that she used as an artist's studio (she was a keen painter). Once safely inside, Josephine broke down in tears, lamenting how the country of her birth had refused to welcome home its daughter. As she curled up on the floor, weeping, Miki was mortified, unable to believe this was the same woman she had seen showered with flowers and gifts on the Paris stage.

In the crazy dichotomy of America at the time, Josephine was welcomed with open arms by New York high society, while being ostracised at its hotels and other public spaces. She was invited to the Broadway premier of *Porgy and Bess*, the opera by celebrated American composer George Gershwin, which tells the story of Porgy, a black person and a street beggar, and his love for Bess, whose life is plagued by violence and drugs. At the after-show party, thrown in a plush apartment on Park Avenue, Josephine was feted by the great and the good of New York, who sought to rub shoulders with this woman who was the toast of Paris.

She frequented the Cotton Club, which starred such famous names as Duke Ellington, Louis Armstrong, Fats Waller, Billie Holiday and Judy Garland. She founded a New York version of her Paris club, Chez Josephine, on East 54th Street. It proved a runaway success and was far better received than her Broadway shows, which got scathing reviews. At Chez Josephine she was hailed as a 'bewitching performer'. Her regular guests included Cole Porter and Fred Astaire. But despite such triumphs, when she sailed again for France in May 1936, she was overjoyed to be heading home.

Josephine had never forgotten how Miki Sawada had tried to shield her from rejection in America. It had cemented their friendship. Miki was no longer just a wealthy high-society fan. She was her 'sister'. Yet now, in the winter of 1939, Abtey's new mission would mean pursuing espionage via her dear friend's good offices.[14] Regardless, Josephine accepted the task. As an HC she was expected to make use of – to deceive – her high-level connections, no matter that they might be friends. In the overarching fight against the enemy, such sacrifices would have to be made.

Thanks to wiretaps planted by Cazin d'Honincthun – the same individual who had alerted Abtey to the spy known as 'Georgette' – the fiendish espionage games being orchestrated out of Japan's Paris Embassy had been partially exposed. In 1938, a prominent Paris figure had been persuaded to provide blueprints of a new French fighter aircraft to a Japanese contact. At the last minute Paillole's team had been able to intercept those classified documents, so preventing a rerun of the Aubert affair, only this time betraying the secrets of the French Air Force. The man carrying those blueprints was stopped by Paillole's agents, even as he was about to board a train at Gare de Lyon station.

Invited into a side room, he protested that he had diplomatic immunity, but Paillole's men demanded that he open his case regardless. Diplomatic immunity was all fine and dandy, but not for stealing state secrets and especially ones such as these. The Japanese diplomat and his purloined blueprints were hustled into custody. The man who had leaked this priceless intelligence turned out to be none other than the boss of one of France's foremost aviation industries. The case was so serious it was raised with the French prime minister. Even so, when Renzo Sawada duly extended his apologies, the French Government agreed to forget the unfortunate matter. Worse still, the French industrialist – the traitor – was allowed to walk free. The entire affair was hushed up, to Paillole and Abtey's disgust and despair.[15]

But stealing French state secrets didn't amount to an alliance with Germany. Japan's seeking military advantage by any means didn't constitute a pact with Nazism. Hence Josephine being tasked to find out the true intentions of those based at the Paris embassy, and of the wider Japanese nation. Working her high-level contacts, she soon winkled out the truth. Japan's leaders had no intentions of maintaining a coalition with the Allies, as they had during the First World War, when Japanese forces had played a key role in containing the German Imperial Navy in the Pacific and Indian Oceans. In 1936, Japan's prime minister, Koki Hirota, had signed an 'anti-communist' pact with Hitler, much of which remained cloaked in secrecy. It was a thinly veiled first step to a formal alliance and as Josephine discovered, Tokyo was determined to march firmly in step with Berlin.

She reported her findings to Abtey, who immediately passed her warnings up the chain of command. When intelligence was shared with political taskmasters, invariably the source was treated as sacrosanct. It was often graded as to quality and reliability. With British intelligence, the very lowest quality was from a 'New and Untried' source. More proven sources were graded from 'C.3' through to 'B.0', with the very highest reliability occasionally straying into the 'A' range.[16] Material gathered directly by agents of an intelligence service – including HCs – generally fell into the higher-grade category.

In London, the War Cabinet gathered. It was 13 November 1939, and Neville Chamberlain was still prime minister, Winston Churchill was First Lord of the Admiralty, and Sir Dudley Pound was Admiral of the Fleet. As they studied the shifting patchwork of global alliances, things seemed to be growing ever darker for the Allies. The Dutch royal family was seeking sanctuary in Great Britain, should Germany invade Holland. Of far more concern was the rising power of Japan and her hostility to Britain and the USA. 'If Japan began to expand outside the China sea zone [sic],' the War Cabinet noted, Britain and the USA would need to mount 'a powerful movement to stop her'.[17]

Two weeks later, the War Cabinet met to discuss Russia's invasion of Finland, a hugely worrying development. If Russian aggression expanded still further, the British Government 'might be forced to declare war upon her . . .'[18] And if Japan struck a treaty with Russia, just as Germany had done, it would cement the Axis still further.[19] In due course, the War Cabinet circulated a memo, marked 'SECRET: TO BE KEPT UNDER LOCK AND KEY', and headlined 'COMPARISON OF THE BRITISH AND JAPANESE FLEETS'. Its preparation had been overseen by Winston Churchill, and in it he suggested a high-stakes gamble to free up British naval power, in an effort to counter the growing threat of Japan, leaving the French fleet to safeguard 'Home Waters'.

By now Japan's true allegiances were crystal clear. The lines were drawn.

Josephine's intelligence had proven most useful, but in Paris she was far from done. Empowered via her HC role, fired up by Hitler's meteoric ascendency, Mussolini's perfidy and Japan's growing hostility, she was busy like a whirlwind. Hobnobbing at the Portuguese embassy in Paris, she learned of Berlin's plans to occupy that neutral nation. Its ports would serve as prime U-boat bases, from which to paralyse shipping across the length and breadth of the Atlantic, placing a stranglehold on Great Britain and ultimately on the USA.[20] Working her high-level contacts without let-up, she tracked Abwehr agents across the length and breadth of the City of Light.

Despite their lack of proper funding and staff, Abtey and Paillole were aware that their recruitment of the Honourable Correspondents was paying dividends. The Deuxième Bureau had upped their arrest rate ten-fold – from a paltry few dozen enemy agents in 1935 to over six hundred in 1939–40.[21] But still it proved a zero sum game. The more adversaries they took off the streets, the more the Abwehr recruited and the more they pumped in. They had money to burn, and the financial rewards on offer were generous indeed. For everyone involved, the work of tracking, tracing and breaking those enemy agents proved relentless and fraught.

The citation for one of Josephine's war decorations would state of her work at this time: 'Provided valuable information, notably on the possibility of Italy's entry into the War, on Japanese policy and on certain German agents in Paris.'[22] Echoing such sentiments, French General Pierre Billotte, a notable war hero, would write that Josephine was 'an ardent patriot', who put her 'great talent' at the service of the Allies. 'She has, moreover, with exceptional intelligence, used her very numerous international relations to send highly valuable information to qualified organisations for National Defence.'[23]

For such a recent recruit this was praise indeed. But there was one slight impediment to Josephine Baker's and Jacques Abtey's burgeoning espionage partnership. They were fast falling in love. It was perhaps not the ideal relationship for a spymaster to forge with his newest recruit – especially as both of them were still married.

In April 1928, when he was twenty-two years old, Abtey had tied the knot with Emma Kuntz, at Bourbach-le-Haut, a village lying on

France's north-eastern border with Germany.[24] They had the one son, Jean Louis, born a year into their marriage. But when war was declared Abtey had sent his family to the countryside, on the strong advice of his superiors at the Deuxième Bureau. 'My duty, I was told, was to get my wife and child away from the capital, without delay.'[25] Paris was vulnerable to bombing by the Luftwaffe, hence such precautions.

But that had left Abtey distanced from his wife of ten years, even as he grew close to his newest recruit. As for Josephine, her marriage to Jean Lion had almost never stood a chance. When Lion had first announced the engagement, his Jewish parents had practically had a heart attack, but over time they had warmed to their singular daughter-in-law. In many ways the newlyweds had seemed the perfect match. Theirs had been a whirlwind romance – a *coup de foudre*, as the French call it. Lion had taught her to fly, and it was during one of those lessons high in the air that he had proposed. It had been a fairy-tale romance and they had been the toast of Paris.

The chief problem had lain in their competing – some would argue towering – ambitions, his mostly in business and politics, hers in showbiz. Neither had seemed willing to play second fiddle to the other, and over time they had drifted apart. That was the first nail hammered into the coffin of their relationship. The second was when Josephine had become pregnant – she had long dreamed of having a child – but had sadly miscarried. The final nail was when she had discovered that her husband was having an affair.

Feeling hurt – wounded deep in her soul – she had left Paris for the French countryside, ending up in the captivating Dordogne region. There she had stumbled upon a stunning if rundown fourteenth-century edifice, one steeped in history and legend – the Château des Milandes. As luck would have it the place was up for rent. Le Beau Chêne had been her Paris home with Jean Lion, and she felt temporarily alienated from the place. Spontaneous as ever, she decided to rent Milandes. It was a decision that would have deep ramifications for her fortunes throughout the war years and beyond.[26]

On some levels Josephine was famously needy; she craved love. But at the same time she was fiercely independent and determined to rely on no man; to trust no one but herself. She used to say that her closeness to animals was driven by similar sentiments; far less complex than humans, they were so much more ready to offer unconditional love.[27] She had always had a special connection to the animal kingdom. As a young child she had been kicked out of the family home for filling the bedroom she shared with her three siblings with hordes of pets.

Sent to work at the age of eight as a maid in the home of affluent white folks, the lady of the house, Mrs Kaiser, proved cruel. Beaten on a whim, Josephine was made to sleep in the cellar with the dog. She took to sharing her food with him and he became her confidant. She nicknamed her canine companion 'Three Legs' for he had been injured in a car accident. Her other friend was a white rooster who lived in a cage in the house. She named him 'Tiny Tim' and fed him devotedly. His small round eyes seemed full of love for Josephine, though they struck her as having a faintly mocking air too.[28]

One day Mrs Kaiser weighed Tiny Tim and declared the time had come for him to die. Josephine must kill him. Mrs Kaiser threatened to stop her pay unless she ended the life of her feathered friend, and there were her younger siblings at home to look out for. Numbed with shock, she forced herself to grip the rooster between her knees and cut at his neck with some scissors, as she held back her tears and begged his forgiveness and his hot blood drained into a bowl.[29]

That had proved the final straw with Mrs Kaiser. Josephine ran away, yet even then she could still feel Tiny Tim's life and horrible death weighing heavy on her soul.[30] A decade or so later she'd chosen to turn her Paris theatre dressing rooms into a veritable zoo, just as she had with her childhood bedroom. Snakes, a piglet, parrots and parakeets slithered, oinked and squawked at every turn, until her fellow performers complained of the unbearable stench. Despite their wayward toilet habits, Josephine's love for her animals remained undimmed. When filming one of her movies, she was directed to stroll along arm-in-arm with a sailor, only to pause to admire a flock of caged songbirds. Heedless of the director's instructions, she had unlatched the cage to let them fly free. It seemed to Josephine that if she were made to repeat the scene several times over, so many wild animals would earn their freedom at her hand.[31]

In the aftermath of losing her baby and then her marriage to Jean Lion, Josephine was hurting and she was hungry for love. By coincidence, Jacques Abtey looked remarkably similar to her husband – athletic, blond and with a vibrancy and energy – plus he was about the same age. With several marriages and love affairs behind her, Josephine hated to be alone, without closeness and affection. She found it preferable to 'live without food than deprived of love'. Life was 'richer, surer, deeper' with a partner to share it with, she would write, 'a trusting heart'.[32] Her attraction to Abtey, fuelled as it was by the heightened tensions and emotions of war, proved irresistible.

She commissioned a special present for him, from the luxury jewellers Cartier (the same as Dunderdale favoured). It was a military-style ID bracelet hand-crafted in silver, with his name inscribed upon it. Misspelled, as it happened, but as Abtey was using the cover name 'Fox' that was hardly surprising. On the inside was engraved the acronym 'PFQA'. *Plus fort que l'amour.* What exactly was 'stronger than love' remained open to interpretation. Their relationship? The coming struggle? The cause?

Abtey had laughed good-naturedly upon receiving the gift, declaring, 'You cannot expect me to wear that with my name upon it. I'm a spy!'[33]

Regardless, the die was cast. Even as the spying game grew deadly serious, the handler and his special agent became lovers. Theirs would prove an intense and tumultuous affair, but one with a special magic all of its own. Whether it was professionally healthy and conducive to getting results remained to be seen. As Abtey himself would say, 'Espionage is such an ugly thing, it should only be entrusted to gentlemen.'[34] Was this love affair gentlemanly behaviour? Or would it fatally compromise their clandestine activities?

One thing was for sure, Josephine Baker was tough and resolute: it would take a great deal to stop her.

CHAPTER FOUR

A Most Sensational Woman

When Josephine Freda McDonald – to use her full name at birth – was still just an infant her mother, Carrie, had split from Eddie Carson, a man who was both her on-stage and her life partner before then, and very possibly Josephine's father, too. With Carrie – tall, elegant, striking looking – working in a struggling song-and-dance act, interspersed with waitressing and cleaning jobs, and with Josephine and her younger brother to feed, the family were forever moving home, and often getting evicted due to unpaid rent.

Since anyone could remember, 'Tumpy' was the young Josephine's informal name. She had been nicknamed 'Humpty Dumpty' due to her being a decidedly chubby baby, which had been shortened to 'Tumpy'. Somewhat on the rebound after the Eddie Carson split, Carrie had married Arthur Martin, a powerfully built black man who worked as a labourer. Arthur had adopted Tumpy, and her younger brother Richard. The family lived in the poorest part of St Louis. It was little better than a disease-riddled slum, tenements crammed between stinking factories churning out shoes, carpets, coffins and carts, plus one of the few products that St Louis was then famous for – 'German' beer.[1] Their quarters became even more crowded when Carrie gave birth to two more children, Josephine's younger sisters Margaret and Willie Mae. Willie Mae was a lot like Josephine – feisty, quick to talk and to learn – and they became close.

St Louis was a city founded by immigrants – waves of Germans, Spaniards, Italians, Greeks and Syrians were intermingled with former slaves, those freed from the Southern states of the USA. It was a natural melting pot, awash with a mix of cultures, languages, music and dance. Despite the poverty, it had a vitality, energy and drive, but the family's shiftless, rootless existence left an indelible impression on Josephine. The four children had to share the one mattress on the floor of their parents' bedroom. During the coldest months her adoptive father would trudge off to work with old newspapers tied around his shoes. At five in the morning, Josephine and Richard would race down to the nearby market to collect any vegetables or fruit that might have tumbled from the stalls.

For Richard, Tumpy was a fantastic big sister. Ringing on rich folks' doorbells and offering to sweep their steps, she didn't exactly make a lot of money, but what little she did she'd share with the family. As the oldest child, Josephine was responsible for their welfare, too. After the deprivation of her childhood, it was not surprising that she cherished the comfort and security of her French home, which would take on a totemic significance for her. However fragile, it was a fortress in an often hostile world. With war coming to Europe, the Nazis threatened to take away the country and the city that she had come to love; France and Paris, *her home*. The onslaught from Berlin would need to be resisted with every essence of her spirit and her soul.

Born and brought up on the harsh but vibrant streets of St Louis, Josephine had learned to weather the hard knocks of life. From her earliest years, she'd hungered to sing and to dance. When she was aged seven a small music hall, The Booker T Washington, had opened near her home. Every week it ran a different-themed act – cowboys, Egyptians, Africans and the like. Inspired by the shows, Robert McDuffy, an older brother to one of Josephine's friends, decided to open his own theatre. He fitted out the family basement with old fruit cases for seats, candles for lighting and a curtain cobbled together from cast-offs. He had two chorus girls – one, his sister Joyce, and the other, her best friend Josephine.

They called the theatre 'McDuffy's Pin And Penny Poppy Shows'. It cost a penny to enter and was for the neighbourhood kids. Soon,

Josephine was running her own version in the family basement, making a 'dramatic' entry down the cellar steps. Then, in 1916, when she was aged ten, a travelling medicine man drove his rainbow-coloured wagon into her part of town. Such amateur 'doctors' were a common enough occurrence in impoverished communities, where proper medicines were beyond the reach of most. A white guy sporting a smart grey beard, a Stetson and a waistcoat groaning with 'medals', the medicine man tried to adopt the air of a wealthy Southern gentleman. For Josephine his arrival was extra-special, for he carried with him a mobile theatre of sorts.

The street theatre was a cheap and easy way to attract customers to his 'medicines'. Setting it up at dusk, with the scene lit by kerosene lanterns, he invited any would-be stars to perform. Josephine sat in the audience entranced, as the medicine man announced the high-light of the evening – a dance competition. A makeshift band began to play, and before she knew it Josephine was up on the stage, throwing her arms and legs about just as the rhythm dictated. The audience roared and clapped with delight. When she was done, the 'gentleman' gave her a celebratory pat on the head and presented her with the winner's prize – a dollar bill. Josephine raced home and presented it proudly to her mother.

In that instant she realised something of huge significance: by dancing, she could possibly earn a living. It sure beat sweeping steps or stealing coal. When she was fourteen Josephine joined a travelling song-and-dance troupe and left St Louis on tour. A natural and a gifted performer – many of her routines were inspired by the moves of her pets – she adored being on stage. But being on the road at such a young age proved unsettling and bewildering. She felt like an orphan. In time she realised that getting a part on Broadway was the only way to break through, and she managed to blag an audition as a chorus girl for the hit New York show *Shuffle Along*. But while those running the show loved her moves, they figured she was far too thin and small to be a chorus girl.

As they questioned her age, Josephine told them, defiantly, that she was all of fifteen years old (in fact, she was still just fourteen). New York law decreed that chorus girls had to be sixteen or over to take to the stage, so she was summarily rejected. Josephine wandered dejectedly out of the theatre, her shoulders hunched against the rain as her sobs rang out through the alleyways. But a few months later she was back. She auditioned again, this time for a new line-up. In many ways this was make-or-break for her. She'd been sleeping rough on park benches, she was so destitute. Telling all who would listen that she was seventeen years old, she finally got herself hired.

She joined the *Shuffle Along* chorus as the 'comedy girl' – the one last in line who tripped over her own feet, went all knock-kneed and cross-eyed, but all the while somehow managing to dance wonderfully to the beat and rhythm. The audience loved it. Touring with *Shuffle Along* Josephine would get to perform in St Louis, in front of her family – the dream coming home. Highly paid by their standards, she vowed to cover her siblings' school fees. But after four years mostly spent in New York, by her own account she had failed to make it big. In segregation-plagued America she could only ever get so far.

By contrast, she had heard all about the freedoms and opportunities to be found in Europe. When the American show-manager, Caroline Dudley Reagan, offered her a star role in *La Revue Nègre*, a Paris show she was putting together, Josephine figured she should take the plunge. In 1925, aged nineteen, she had sailed for France, and fortune and fame had beckoned. She'd rarely been back to her home city, although she sent regular money, letters and well-wishes to her family. Even so, from her St Louis years she'd acquired an inner core of iron, plus she had an outer shield of steel. She'd had need of both, even in the refined airs of Paris, and even as her star seemed to be firmly on the rise.

Josephine was feted by the American novelist Ernest Hemingway, then resident in Paris. He famously wrote of her that she was 'the most sensational woman anybody ever saw. Or ever will.'[2] Picasso loved to paint her, and Jean Cocteau, the poet, writer and film-maker, would help her vault to stardom. A year after her arrival in Paris, Josephine was reported to be the most photographed woman in the world. It was hardly surprising that some were miffed.

Her fiercest rivalry was with the famous stage performer Mistinguett – real name Jeanne Bourgeois. Well into her fifties by the time a twenty-something Josephine was taking France by storm, the long-reigning queen of the Paris music hall wasn't happy. She'd taken to referring to the young upstart thus: 'How is – I forget her name – that coloured girl, my substitute?'[3] One evening, when an elegant Josephine attended a movie premiere dressed to kill, Mistinguett called over: 'Well, Pickaninny, why don't you come up and salute me?' In a flash, Josephine the street-fighter was back. She stalked across, sank her nails into Mistinguett's arm and spat in her face.[4]

Their rivalry played out in the Casino de Paris, one of the city's most prestigious music halls (despite its name, it is a performance venue). Owned by top theatre director Henri Varna, his first show at the Casino, as it is known, was entitled *Paris Miss* and starred Mistinguett. But by the following year, 1930, Josephine had replaced her. In part this was a deliberate ploy. Varna figured the rivalry between the long-lived music hall diva and the young upstart would make for great publicity. He was right. Upon starting her rehearsals Josephine was seen as 'stealing' the 'real star's' dressing room, the one that 'belonged' to Mistinguett. The latter hadn't exactly helped matters. She'd let all in the theatre company know that she didn't want 'that little black girl' using her room.[5]

Josephine opted to defuse the situation by having a tent erected for her use as a suitably 'exotic' kind of dressing room. But she faced a further challenge in that one of the show's chief choreographers was the American Earl Leslie, who also just happened to be Mistinguett's dance partner and lover. Leslie worked on undermining Josephine, letting it be known widely that she didn't have the voice or the dance skills for a venue of the Casino's standing. Finally, he challenged Henri Varna directly: did he really intend to let Josephine walk down the same staircase as Mistinguett? Why not, Varna countered. Of course Josephine would enter via the Casino's grand stairway.[6]

Though Josephine was not yet twenty-five years old, Varna believed that she was ready, or very nearly. Varna, who had taken over the role of being her mentor, knew exactly what he was about here. Her star was in the ascendant, while Mistinguett's was going very much in the opposite direction. He also knew that Josephine had the hunger and the energy to conquer. Her Casino show, entitled *Paris Qui Remue* – Paris Who Stirs – proved a smash hit. Inspired by Chiquita, but coached by Varna, Josephine's self-assured walk onto the stage – the 'Josephine Baker strut' – was acclaimed by many as being 'panther-like'. 'We said goodbye to a perky and amusing ...' Josephine, ran a review in the newspaper *Paris-soir*. 'An artist, a great artist, comes back to us.'[7]

The show ran for 481 performances, and on average Josephine drew larger audiences than Mistinguett. A year or so later she would be invited to open the Tour de France, something so quintessentially French it represented a real accolade. With the bicycles bedecked in flowers, Josephine cut the ribbon in front of her home, after which she invited the Tour officials into Le Beau Chêne for a celebratory glass of champagne. In short, she had been taken to the nation's heart, by her own efforts conquering Paris and her fiercest rivals. But then had come the rise of Nazi Germany and all that that signified.

That Christmas of 1939 – four months into the Phoney War – Josephine insisted she should do more for the cause. Possessing a pilot's licence, courtesy of Jean Lion's flying lessons, unlike many wealthy show-business stars she insisted on putting herself firmly in the pilot's seat whenever the need arose to take to the skies. 'I tell you how I fly the plane, how I have learned to loop-the loop,' she enthused, when speaking to an American reporter. 'I love it. I thrill to it.' But during that winter of 1939–40 she would volunteer her aerial skills for far more desperate purposes – flying aid to the thousands of refugees then flooding into the Low Countries.[8]

For some, of course, the war had proved anything but phoney. Indeed, it had been savage and life-shattering. A vast swathe of

Europe – Germany, Austria, Czechoslovakia, Poland – was being brutally purged of the *Untermenschen*. For the Jews, gypsies, communists, Slavs, homosexuals – anyone seen as being an enemy of the Nazi state – it was a case of flee or die. Bearing in mind the risks Josephine began to take with her mercy flights, Abtey persuaded her to sign up with the Infirmières-Pilotes Secouristes de l'Air (IPSA), the aviation section of the French Red Cross. That way, if she did somehow fall into enemy hands – crashlanding, straying off course, or heaven-forbid being shot down – she would at least have some kind of official cover.[9]

As the winter of 1939 ground into 1940, the key problem for the Allies became one of keeping up morale. With barely a shot being fired on the front lines, the French and British troops shivering in their bunkers began to wonder what on earth they were there for. Again, Josephine volunteered her services, and in this instance she felt she could make a major difference; a step-change. She was born to perform. She pledged to do so now on the front lines, to truly lift the fighting men's spirits. But first she needed a fitting repertoire – a show fit to light up the trenches.

In the aftermath of Josephine's bleak 1928 tour of Austria and Germany – in which she'd first come face-to-face with the vile reality of Nazism – she'd premiered a song that would become her anthem. She would sing it at just about every performance for the rest of her life. Written especially for her by the composer Vincent Scotto, it was entitled 'J'ai Deux Amours'. She'd sung it first at the Casino de Paris and it had gone down a storm. Everyone seemed to understand its meaning and symbolism. The 'two loves' she sang of were Paris and 'her country', the USA, and few doubted that the transatlantic alliance was more essential than ever with the enemy on the march.[10]

Doubtless, 'J'ai Deux Amours' would play well in the trenches, but Josephine wanted more. She headed for the studios, recording songs aimed to boost the morale particularly of the British troops, who were serving far from home (she had toured Great Britain several times before the war). She sang the classics 'Oh, Tommy' and 'London Town', plus a collection from the First World War, including 'Tipperary' and 'If I Were the Only Girl in the World'. She began rehearsing intensively for her show for the troops, fittingly entitled *Paris–London*. Its theatrical director was Henri Varna, and he believed fervently that in wartime people needed an especially uplifting, fast-paced performance, full of 'charm, rhythm and beauty'. To deliver it, he'd brought in 'the two greatest stars of song and dance' – Josephine, plus Maurice Chevalier.[11]

With his trademark attire of a straw boater hat and tuxedo, Chevalier was arguably France's foremost male star. Nominated in 1930 for an Academy Award as Best Actor for his performance in *The Love Parade*, he was a household name across America and Europe. Now in his fifties, he had been making waves in showbusiness for decades, and he fully expected to top the bill in *Paris–London*.

He insisted on appearing after Josephine, in the show's second half – traditionally the leading star's role. Josephine agreed with surprisingly little fuss. She had a greater cause to fight for. But it was not to work out quite as Chevalier had intended.

For the bored and homesick soldiers manning the Maginot Line, Josephine's appearance was like that of a goddess or an angel. For her grand finale she stepped out in one of her briefest costumes, fashioned by top Paris designer Rosevienne. A glittering skeleton of rhinestone-studded ribs barely covered her body, while from each hip hung a fan of dazzling plumes, intertwined with tulle – a lightweight, chiffon-like material – which swung deliciously as she swayed, spun and twirled. Her final song, 'Mon Cœur est un Oiseau des Isles' – My Heart is a Bird of the Isles – was one of her best ever.[12]

Her performance proved enthralling. As always, she somehow managed to make every man among her audience feel like an emperor; as if he were her knight in shining armour. The French and British soldiers were enraptured. They yelled for more, demanding encore after encore. Josephine could hardly say no: these were the men who would fight in freedom's cause; in her fight; in Josephine's war. She could not deny them. By the time an enraged Chevalier made his appearance, his half of the show had to be cut short. In a fury, he threatened never to perform for the troops again. Josephine had to remind him, quietly, just why and for whom they were gracing that stage.

But the seeds of dissent had been well and truly planted. Josephine would nurse a lifelong contempt for Chevalier, which would quicken as the war progressed. It was hardly helped by the fact that Chevalier and Mistinguett had been lovers. For his part, Chevalier complained to the press about Josephine's front-line performances: 'All she does is get up there and wiggle her rear end.' Regardless of whether this was true or not, it had proved mightily effective. Josephine herself was not proud. 'I wasn't a great dancer or singer,' she would tell Jean-Pierre Reggiori, one of her later dance partners, with disarming modesty, 'but I had the body and a nice butt and I could smile.'[13]

Along the Maginot Line in the winter of 1939–40, she would prove that time and time again, much to Maurice Chevalier's chagrin.

The grim reality of the war kept being driven home. Through her connections with the Red Cross, Josephine volunteered at a Paris feeding centre. It lay within an ancient, twisting alleyway in the shadow of L'Église de la Sainte-Trinité, a place that was a haunt of the homeless. As more and more refugees flooded into the city, she found herself there every day helping feed and comfort a biblical multitude. Despite their parlous state, many recognised her immediately: 'Look, it's Josephine!'[14] Like magic, just her very presence put a smile on the pinched, gaunt, war-weary faces.

Josephine was lifted up, but also mortified and moved to tears. 'War was an anonymous, brutal machine,' she wrote of this time, spawning a world of pain and hurt.[15]

She worked tirelessly, relentlessly, driving herself to help those 'broken body and soul by defeat'. On all sides were elderly couples, mothers, young children, whose bodies and minds were in torment.[16] But even amid such suffering, the Honourable Correspondent side of her – her vigilance – never rested. Abtey had warned her that hiding among the refugees there might well be agents of the Abwehr.

She should be alert for any fit and able-looking young men, who should be away manning the front lines. Several times she telephoned him, so he could come and investigate and, if need be, make arrests.[17] Several times he did just that, but in truth the Deuxième Bureau was inundated with suspects. There just wasn't the time to lock them all up.

The horrors of war lurched closer still. Jean Lion, Josephine's estranged husband, himself became a victim. Dispatched to the Maginot Line as a French Army pilot, he was involved in a nasty jeep accident and ended up in hospital. Josephine went to visit, but soon realised how irrevocably they had drifted apart. 'I can't believe it,' she confessed to a mutual friend. 'I've lost him forever.'[18] She decided she had no option but to file for divorce. Yet the French courts would not get to hear the case for many a year.

Shortly, the enemy would be on the march and most of Western Europe would be cloaked in darkness.

CHAPTER FIVE

The Darkness Descends

Paris had fallen ominously silent. Across the ancient city the streets appeared as empty as the grave. Along the wide, leafy boulevards and among the grand monuments and the cobblestone cafés, all life seemed to have been snuffed out. A blizzard of charred paper drifted over the Seine, only to be snatched into the current, as heaps of sensitive documents were left to burn. Those who had not fled had gone to ground; all across Paris, the cowed inhabitants of this benighted city were in hiding.

To the south, the roads were clogged with millions of the city's evacuees. In a confusion of curses, groaning engines, grinding gears and choking exhaust fumes, terrified Parisians joined with shellshocked refugees from across the vanquished nations of Europe, all fleeing the advancing German war machine.[1]

It was 13 June 1940, and barely a month earlier Hitler had made his move, his armoured legions punching into Holland, Luxembourg and Belgium, as his squadrons of warplanes weaved and dived overhead, unleashing mayhem. Dummy parachutists were dropped to terrorise populations, while sabotage parties wreaked havoc at key targets. At the very vanguard the Abwehr sent their special commandos, charged to seize their enemy's secret archives and to capture those individuals who worked for their intelligence services. In short, it had been a carefully planned, pin-point accurate and lightning-fast assault – warfare as it had never been waged before.[2]

The Wehrmacht – the German armed forces – had struck just as

Paillole, Dunderdale and others had warned they would, advancing via the rolling hills and forests of the Ardennes region and circumventing the Maginot Line.[3] While the British, French and Allied troops had fought bravely – often to the last round; sometimes to the last man – they had been outmanoeuvred and routed by a foe of far greater technological and tactical superiority. As the War Cabinet in London was forced to acknowledge, French and British resistance had been 'shattered' by the fearsome combination 'of dive-bombing and tanks'.[4]

Even as Paris emptied, well-over 300,000 mostly French and British troops had been plucked off the beaches at Dunkirk, as a makeshift fleet of 800 vessels whisked so many across the Channel to comparative safety.[5] Even so, in late May and early June 1940 War Cabinet meetings, in London, the fears of the British public of an imminent German invasion were palpably clear. Morale, it was feared, was in freefall and in danger of out-and-out collapse. It was left to Winston Churchill – just weeks into his new role as Britain's prime minister – to buoy up the nation.[6]

For years Churchill had been an implacable opponent of the unchecked rise of Nazi Germany and of Hitler. Having been ignored for so long, he was able to promise little but a brutal, grinding, interminable struggle. 'I have nothing to offer but blood, toil, tears and sweat,' he told Parliament. 'We have before us an ordeal of the most grievous kind. We have before us many, many long months . . . You ask what is our aim? I can answer in one word: it is victory, victory at all costs, victory in spite of all terror, victory, however long and hard the road may be; for without victory, there is no survival.'[7]

Those had proven hugely insightful and prophetic words. They had rung out from London, stiffening the nation's morale. But in Paris all seemed lost. The French Government – even the mayor of Paris – had fled. At the cathedral of Notre-Dame on 13 June a few remaining diehards gathered to pray for the nation's salvation. In the front pew, William C. Bullitt, America's ambassador to France, was in tears. Rousing himself from his knees, he took the unprecedented step of declaring himself the city's stand-in governor.

Finding one of the few telephone lines still functioning that day – all outside communications were supposed to have been cut – he managed to get a message through to Berlin. 'Paris has been declared an open city . . . all possible measures are being taken to ensure the security of life and property.'[8] By announcing that Paris was an 'open city' – meaning that the Wehrmacht were free to march in unopposed – he hoped to spare the French capital from devastation and ruin, but of course there were no guarantees.

For several days as the streets had emptied under a burning summer sun, the United States embassy on Avenue Gabriel had been inundated with desperate American citizens, seeking to secure last-minute papers to get them out of Europe, to the USA and safety. Amid such confusion and chaos, the embassy's most sensitive papers and their codebooks had been burned. That evening – the last upon which Paris would be free of Nazi occupation for several long years – the embassy staff walked the deserted, ghostly streets, lost in thought and with heavy hearts.

One such figure was Bullitt's political counsellor, the seasoned diplomat Robert Daniel Murphy. Murphy had been taking calls from panicked French ministers, while trying to dispatch some kind of meaningful update to Washington. But in truth, all was chaos and confusion. As he paced the silent streets, not a light glimmered anywhere. Not a soul moved. All had fled or were locked in dark cellars and basements. To the south of the city, he could make out the occasional flash of heavy artillery fire. The enemy were coming, and many feared the City of Light would be ground into rubble and ruin. But at least Murphy and his fellow diplomats had got a good number of American citizens away to safety.[9]

One American who had opted not to run was Josephine Baker. In fact, arguably she was no longer a US citizen, for with her marriage to Jean Lion she was supposed to have given up her US citizenship, in order to become fully French. But at the same time she was very likely still married to Willie Baker, the American husband she had left behind in 1921, when she had sailed for Paris at the age of nineteen

63

seeking fame and fortune. Having tied the knot with Willie Baker – a former jockey and railroad porter – four years earlier, following a whirlwind romance, she had opted to retain his surname, for that was how she was known on the stage. As with so much in her personal life, her marital status was all a little uncertain and unclear.[10]

But for an American-born individual of such high standing and renown, the right papers could have been sought. As a global superstar, Josephine would have been a top priority for Murphy, Bullitt and colleagues. Yet true to her promise to Jacques Abtey et al., she chose to remain in France. The inexorable march of the enemy had to be resisted. The trouble was, with the whole of the nation in tumult and turmoil – thrown into the dark shadow of defeat – no one seemed to have the slightest idea how to stand firm or to strike back. And of course, no one – not even Josephine's seasoned comrades, normally so blessed with foresight – had envisaged a rout as rapid and cataclysmic as this.

Those in command at the Deuxième Bureau thought they had taken appropriate measures. They were wrong. 'We knew the power of the Wehrmacht . . .' Paillole would write of this moment. 'We knew that despite our warnings, the defences installed at the mouth of the Ardennes were insufficient . . . That alone should have led us to consider the worst: the occupation of France . . . We never imagined the rout of the Army could be so decisive. It was frightening!'[11]

Neither had agent Josephine. In recent weeks she'd walked the fifteen kilometres from her Paris home to L'Église de la Sainte-Trinité, to ensure that she could continue to make the journey to the Red Cross feeding centre on foot if need be. Petrol supplies were running short, and the Paris hospitals had been inundated with wounded. Josephine's response was to make the rounds of the wards, during her breaks from performing *Paris–London*, so she could sing for the injured troops. In such an unprecedented crisis, she had proved undaunted, unbreakable. Each night after her performances she would rush to help – making beds, bathing the wounded, whispering encouragement and everywhere finding a moment to sing.[12]

It wasn't until the second week of June 1940, when Henri Varna announced to the *Paris–London* cast that they had just performed their final show, that Josephine began to accept the terrible truth: Paris, the city that had stolen her heart, seemed lost.[13] If the City of Light fell into darkness, she would need a base from which to continue the fight. But the role that she had started to own, that of the Honourable Correspondent, felt largely redundant now. No one seemed to have made any plan to resist. No one had stashed any weapons or explosives. No one had thought to properly safeguard the means to gather and transmit intelligence.[14] As with so much else, the Deuxième Bureau had been thrown into disarray.

As Paillole well appreciated, they should have established a 'rear-guard' – a secret base at which they would have assembled the means to continue the 'clandestine fight against the invader'.[15] Chiefly, that would have consisted of teams of agents, their precious files, plus secure communications facilities. It wasn't as if they hadn't had ample warning. On 3 June 1940 the Luftwaffe had bombed Paris, chiefly targeting the airfields and the Citroën and Renault factories. There were over nine hundred casualties, and the French Air Force had seemed able to offer only token resistance. Paillole, Abtey and colleagues had taken to the concrete air-raid bunker at their Avenue de Tourville headquarters, where they commented 'bitterly about [their] impotence'.[16]

Yet it wasn't until a week later, late on the afternoon of 10 June, that the decision was finally reached to evacuate the Deuxième Bureau's offices, and to burn all non-vital papers. As it was, the main body of their precious archives was crammed onto a convoy of trucks, which was ploughing south on roads clogged with refugees. If those files fell into enemy hands, the results would be little short of catastrophic. If that happened, Paillole, Abtey, Josephine Baker, plus countless other agents would be unmasked, at the risk of losing their heads.[17]

The danger was very, very real.

Abtey warned his prize special agent that they were evacuating Paris, and that she too should flee. Identified by Goebbels as an enemy of the Nazi state, Josephine was in danger, regardless of whether or not her role as an HC was blown. In recent months, Goebbels had upped the rhetoric and vitriol, declaring that: 'Hatred against France must be rekindled; it must be shown how this nation in demographic decline is trying to defeat Germany with, yellow, black or brown people.'[18] Fortunately, Josephine had the perfect bolt hole – her medieval château in the Dordogne, from where so many of the wars of the previous centuries had been orchestrated.

Shortly before the polished jackboots marched down the Champs-Élysées, Josephine began to motor south, her car piled high with old champagne bottles in which she'd hoarded petrol, in preparation for a long journey on roads clogged with the desperate and the dispossessed. Travelling with her were those fugitives from Nazi oppression that she had welcomed into her Paris home – Mr and Mrs Jacobs, an elderly Belgian Jewish couple, among them – plus, of course, her menagerie of animals.

Hundreds of thousands of refugees jammed up the roads. They were crammed into anything that would move: horse-drawn carts, buses, bicycles, tractors, trailers, bakery vans – even hearses. Low-flying Heinkels thundered across at tree-top height, shooting up and bombing the snarled-up, helpless multitudes. The pilots unleashed murder and terror on the largely defenceless civilians, aiming to clog up the roads with burning vehicles, the wounded and the dying, so preventing the French military from being able to move; to ensnare it still further.

'Civilian refugees were trapped and helpless in the traffic jams,' wrote American scholar and author Louis Snyder of the helter-skelter retreat. 'Bombs and bullets burst among automobiles, carts, farm wagons and bicycles, catching humans and horses in a deadly melange of flame and smoke . . .'[19]

After braving the exodus, Josephine finally made it into the lush, rolling farmland of the Périgord region, which is cut through by the River Dordogne, the fine black earth to either side lying thick with crops. At every turn, historic castles and manors clung to cliff-faces and ravines, while to their rear labyrinths of tunnels dating back to prehistoric times honeycombed the limestone cliffs. Ancient and timeless, these fields, forests and rivers had played host to a plethora of armies and seen wars come and go. What better place from which to wage resistance, should such a thing be possible.

Josephine turned onto a narrow, twisting lane – little more than a cart-track – nosed across a stone bridge, and there lay the village of Castelnaud-Fayrac, while above it, perched on a rise, was the Château des Milandes. Driving up the hill she passed a wood and a cemetery – 'like a secret garden' – and pulled to a halt at the château's massive wooden gates, studded with iron – suitably war-like – barring the way. Fortunately, Eli Mercer, the son of a local farmer, was there to meet her and to swing the gates wide.[20]

Though Josephine had spent precious little time here, the château's world-famous occupant could hardly keep a low profile. She'd made friends among the locals, who had made her suitably welcome. Georges Malaury, the village blacksmith, lived opposite. He nursed a burning hatred of the German invaders; it smouldered over his fiery furnace and anvil. Josephine had taken to driving his young children, George and Georgette, to a nearby patisserie, to treat them to cakes. Malaury would become one of her staunchest allies. A future Resistance fighter, he would operate a clandestine radio transmitter from the château's tower with direct contact to Britain.[21]

With war engulfing Western Europe, Josephine needed the camaraderie of the locals as never before. But for now, the château, set in thickly-wooded countryside overlooking the Dordogne, seemed a small slice of rare and precious peace. Here, it was almost possible to believe that the suffering and death that had engulfed France could not be happening.[22] So tranquil was it that she had never once imagined fleeing here, to seek refuge. The ancient building with its secret nooks and crannies, its deep cellars, twisting stone staircases and soaring towers, seemed to offer the perfect hideaway.

Here, Josephine drew to her those like-minded souls who hungered to resist – 'a Naval officer, an Air Force captain, a Pole, my Belgian friends'.[23] That Polish man, François Dudek, would work as a farmhand at the château. Healthy, young – in his early twenties – and as strong as an ox, this refugee from the Nazi blitzkrieg would fall for Paulette, Josephine's striking-looking maid, known to all as Libellule – the dragonfly.[24] Love springs eternal, even in the midst of war.

Later, as the horror bit deeper, the château's cellar would be filled with weapons – a hidden cache for the burgeoning local Resistance.[25] When he was caught running messages for the very same Resistance group, François would be held as a hostage by the Germans. His captors would shoot him dead.[26] The local station master would suffer a similar fate. 'I was in the First World War against your country,' he would tell his German captors. 'I have a wooden leg. Fuck you.' So they shot him too.[27]

But all of that lay sometime in the future.

Just after dawn on 14 June 1940, the advance units of the Wehrmacht rolled into Paris. At the forefront went the Abwehr commandos, seeking to seize the documents and personnel that would unlock the world of the French, and Allied, secret services. The Abwehr commandeered the city's luxurious Hotel Lutetia, tore down the French tricolour and ran up the Swastika in its place, before dispatching agents across the city . . . hunting. Meanwhile, to US diplomat Robert Daniel Murphy, a fluent German speaker, fell the unenviable task of paying a visit to Lieutenant-General Bogislav von Studnitz, one of Hitler's ace panzer commanders and now the military chief of occupied Paris.

With dark irony, von Studnitz commandeered the Prince of Wales suite at the sumptuous Hotel Crillon. Sporting a monocle and clipped moustache, he looked every inch the German cavalry officer. Once he was done describing exactly how the forces of Germany had routed the British and the French, he outlined to Murphy what came next. Mopping-up operations would take a matter of days: 'Further resistance is impossible.' With the British exhausted and defeated, German forces would cross the Channel shortly. The war would be over in six weeks, and by no later than the end of July, he concluded.[28]

In a sense, von Studnitz had every right to be so arrogant. By taking Paris, the Germans had succeeded in doing in thirty-eight days what they had failed to achieve in the entire First World War, which had lasted four years and cost two million lives. Von Studnitz was known to have the ear of Adolf Hitler, and Murphy appreciated how he needed to get a full report on all that he had said to Washington. But there was simply no way of doing so. The US embassy had burned its code books, and in any case the Germans had cut all communication out of Paris, save via Berlin.

Ten days after German troops had taken the city, Hitler would arrive to survey his newest conquest. All of Paris lay at his feet and a Nazi flag flew from the topmost heights of the Eiffel Tower. That same day, seventeen death sentences were handed down by the Wehrmacht's mobile military courts. The occupier's justice proved swift and brutal – 'judgements' were reached in a matter of hours. Three of those sentenced to die were French secret service agents who'd been captured during the rout. The hunt was fuelled by those the Abwehr had been able to spring from prisons all across France, including many of the spies that the Deuxième Bureau had put behind bars.[29]

Even as those first agents were executed, so Paillole, Abtey and colleagues were trying to salvage something from the ashes of defeat. Forty tonnes of Deuxième Bureau files had been shipped south, in a series of horribly disorganised 'backwards leaps'. On the Loire, around a hundred kilometres from Paris, a temporary HQ had been established, in the 'mad hope' that the German onslaught might be halted.[30] It had held for a matter of hours. Having returned their trucks to the French military, Paillole and company were forced to beg, borrow and steal whatever transport they could.

Some three hundred kilometres further south they called a fresh halt, at the military camp of La Courtine, in the remote Massif Central – a mountainous region of central France. That proved all too temporary. As they retreated still further on roads jammed with refugees, they were strafed and bombed by low-flying warplanes, which turned out to be Italian. On 10 June Mussolini had revealed his hand, joining Hitler in declaring war. Under such desperate circumstances, the burden of the archives – the Deuxième Bureau's Holy Grail – proved unendurable. 'We burned tonnes of files,' Paillole wrote of this time, targeting the oldest to reduce the load.[31]

They kept crawling south, 'mute and hurting,'[32] as Paillole would describe their helter-skelter retreat, 'step-by-step losing contact with command and the government a little more each time.'[33] But at least the further they fled, the better the chance of saving their precious files and with them 'hundreds of patriots' lives', and chiefly those of 'the Honourable Correspondents . . . those brave people' who had risked all and faced torture and execution if caught.[34] How was anyone to warn them of the danger? By now, agents and HCs alike had been scattered to the four corners of France.

In desperation, the ragged convoy alighted upon the ancient monastery of Bon-Encontre, at Agen, some six hundred kilometres south of Paris. It offered far from certain sanctuary. The father superior of the monastery was singularly unimpressed that his house of God was being requisitioned. 'I invite you to leave this seminary immediately,' he told Paillole, making it clear he wanted nothing to do with the struggle, and that their presence there was somehow a desecration.[35] His protests were ignored and the precious files were unloaded, whereupon the search for a proper place of hiding began all over again.

Paillole had had grim forewarning of the likely terms of the armistice – the price of peace that Hitler would extract from France. Three years earlier, his arch-agent Hans Thilo-Schmidt had provided a detailed outline, based upon Hitler's briefings to the highest echelons of the Nazi party. Under draconian terms the German Army would occupy much of France, setting up a puppet administration to govern the remainder. But as far as Paillole was concerned, an armistice did not signify the end of the war. It could be broken at any time. The enemy remained the enemy. They would have to find the means to save their precious files and continue the struggle.[36]

He turned to one of the few remaining individuals who could help – an HC who offered to hide the bulk of their files in the Roquefort cheese dairies. Roquefort-sur-Soulzon lay a little south of the Bon-Encontre monastery, so marginally further away from the enemy. But as Paillole fully recognised, 'We could not stay there for ever.' Tonnes of top-secret information – some 100,000 card indexes plus 25,000 in-depth files, detailing the identities of all the Deuxième Bureau's agents and contacts – could not be hidden indefinitely in the insecure confines of a cheese dairy.[37] While much of the information was encoded, with the number of spies and agents the Abwehr had rounded up they were sure to have the means to crack those codes.[38]

But if not hidden in that dairy, then where? Where in all of France was secure from the predations of the Gestapo, the SS and the Abwehr?

As if to underline the threat, on 22 June 1940 Paillole received shocking news: the forces of the enemy had seized a vast cache of files of the French High Command. The train which had been carrying them was forced to a halt two hundred kilometres to the south of Paris, at the town of La Charité-sur-Loire, due to a series of wrecked bridges blocking its path. A unit of Wehrmacht troops were looting a nearby railway station. By accident more than design, they stumbled upon the train with its priceless booty. In political and diplomatic terms, the value of those files was incalculable, as was their military worth. It was a gift to Goebbels and to the Führer.[39]

Three days later, Paillole, Abtey, Bonnefous and comrades gathered at the Bon-Encontre war memorial, in sombre silence. The Armistice negotiated by Marshal Philippe Pétain – a hero of the First World War, who had recently taken over as the prime minister of France – had come into effect. More than half of France – the north – had fallen under occupation, while the remainder would be under Pétain's government, banished from Paris to the south-central spa town of Vichy. Pétain had spoken by radio to the French nation, 'with a heavy heart', declaring that the deal he had struck with Berlin was 'in honour, the means to put an end to the hostilities'.[40]

The terms of the Armistice were draconian in the extreme. With 92,000 French soldiers dead, 200,000 wounded and 1.5 million set to become prisoners-of-war, France was to free all German captives and to turn over all refugees with known anti-Nazi sympathies. The French nation was to pay 400 million francs a day to the occupying power, and anyone with the temerity to start any kind of a resistance movement was to face the death penalty.[41]

Even as the Armistice came into effect that 25 June morning, Paillole, Abtey and comrades swore an oath to continue the struggle against the invaders.[42] But how on earth were they to do so? The task that lay before them was daunting, especially as the vast majority of the French people backed Pétain: anything to save the country from further death and ruin. That meant the Deuxième Bureau would be operating among a largely hostile population, pitting Frenchman against Frenchman.

Chillingly, the Armistice was to be policed by the *Waffenstillstands-kommission* – the Armistice Commission – based in the city of Wiesbaden, a hundred kilometres the German side of the border. Its agents – including Gestapo and SS – would flood into the newly conquered territory. In Paris, SS Commander Karl Boemelburg, the Chief of the Gestapo in France, declared: 'This country must be bound and gagged. We need 30,000 agents here in the shortest possible time.' Daily, the stranglehold tightened. This was the start of the 'long night' for France, as the nation was sucked into a web of darkness.[43]

Not only was the Deuxième Bureau fragmented and broken, but Paillole and his colleagues had lost all contact with their closest allies, the Secret Intelligence Service. The British 'remained alone in the struggle', Paillole would write, and somehow a means needed to be found to reach out to them and to forge the partnership anew.[44] Under the terms of the Armistice, the French security services were supposed to answer to the Vichy state. Officially, that left agents of the Deuxième Bureau allied to their erstwhile enemies. Unofficially, things were quite different.

'We are and remain at war with Germany,' Paillole insisted. Regardless of the position of the Vichy regime, the struggle would continue. Paillole and his comrades would have to act beyond the rules, subverting their own leadership. Their only guide would be their consciences, as they stepped outside the law of the land, truly becoming 'rebels'.[45] Fortunately, they had a secret fund from which to bankroll such shadow operations. Thanks to the Abwehr's payments made to Aubert, the French Navy traitor, plus dozens of other special agents, they would use Germany's own money to fight it.

Anyone engaged in this battle was playing a deadly game. The chances of getting caught were all too obvious, for they would be operating under the enemy's very noses. Even so, the HCs – at least, those who remained steadfast, courageous and committed – would have to be reactivated. They would need to be truly exceptional individuals, for now they would be forced to operate in a world of fractured allegiances, plagued by betrayal, deception and mistrust. They would need to be blessed with iron nerves, unimpeachable moral standards, and be willing to risk all for the cause.[46]

Upon first being recruited as an Honorary Correspondent, Josephine Baker had been promised by Jacques Abtey: *From now on, you are one of us.* It certainly didn't feel that way in late June 1940, as she licked her wounds and tried to regroup in Château des Milandes. She had been sucked into the nightmare that had engulfed France, losing all contact with her unit; her band of brothers; her Deuxième Bureau comrades. Yet she remained determined to fight on.

In many ways the Château was a natural setting from which to plan for insurrection. The name itself, Milandes, is steeped in myth. It is formed from two medieval words, 'mi', meaning middle, and 'lande', meaning wooded countryside; the château set in the midst of dense woodland. The family of François I de Caumont – the Caumonts were a legendary French warrior dynasty – had built the castle and bequeathed its name. Above the window beside the ornate entrance they had carved a Latin inscription: 'LAN MCCCCIIIIXX ET IX FUREN COMENSADES LAS MILANDES DE CASTLENAU' – in 1489, the castle was founded and named Milandes of Castlenau (presumably an archaic spelling, for the local commune is called Castelnaud-la-Chapelle).[47]

François I de Caumont was a foremost landowner, lord and knight. In 1542 he was assassinated at Milandes by rival French noblemen, part of a long history of religious wars, assassinations, poisonings, kidnappings and associated skulduggery which were rife. Variously a seat of both Catholics and the Huguenots – protestant reformists – the château had played host to some of the nation's wealthiest families. In 1622, Jacques-Nompar de Caumont, then Milandes' owner, was appointed Field Marshal of all of France by King Louis XIII. Fifteen years later, the French king still hailed de Caumont – then all of seventy-nine years old – as 'the most experienced and able captain of the realm'.[48]

Yet de Caumont would also be criticised – in verse – for supposedly betraying the Huguenot cause: 'God saved you by grace, and maybe for reproach . . . Reproach by making you the slave of your foes.'[49] *The slave of your foes* – those were sentiments that resonated powerfully in a France reeling under Nazi occupation. Fittingly, Milandes bristled with fearsome gargoyles – intricately carved dragons, demons, hunting dogs – plus the heraldic shields of the Caumont family. The venerable château seemed forged in implacable stone . . . for war. Now, it was home to the world's most famous woman of colour, who hungered to fight.

Josephine had studied the castle's martial traditions and the centuries of rich history.[50] She would add her own deeply personal touch, a nod to the roots of her ancestors' long history of struggle in the USA. Her grandma, Elvira, had been born into slavery on a tobacco plantation, in Holy Springs, Arkansas. Tearfully, she'd told an infant Josephine stories about the slave days. 'I adored Grandma,' Josephine remarked. 'The songs she sang as she rocked me to sleep . . . told of freedom that would someday come.'[51]

As a child Josephine had been ostracised by her mother, who resented the fact that she had become pregnant with her at such a young age. Carrie had conceived when she was just nineteen years old, and she blamed Josephine for bringing about a premature end to her dancing career. As Josephine would remark later in life, her mother had sometimes told her that she wished she hadn't been born. The young Josephine was foisted onto her grandmother, with whom she was close. Each Sunday, Elvira would pull on her best flowery dress and a huge hat with a hole in the top, through which her bun was supposed to poke, and they'd set off for church. Josephine loved those outings, for grandma was so cheerful she made everyone smile.

It was from Grandma Elvira that Josephine received what love there was to have. Elvira was forever baking cornbread – an easy-to-make corn-based recipe, popular in the Southern USA, whose origins are rooted in Native American culture. She'd spread the fresh-made cornbread thick with jam, so Josephine could munch away while she told stories. Elvira loved relating them just as much as her granddaughter loved listening. She'd cover all the classics – the Three Little Pigs, Snow White and Little Red Riding Hood – but Josephine's standout favourite was Cinderella. The image of Cinderella, sweeping up the ashes and tempering her grief and loneliness with the conviction that one day she would win through by her own efforts, struck a powerful chord.

But at times, Grandma's tales would become emotional, as she reminisced about her great-great-grandparents, who had been brought to the USA from Africa to face a life of slavery. She'd round it all off with uplifting Bible stories and songs, telling of freedom after oppression, of happiness after grief, of sunshine after rain. In memory of her Grandma Elvira and of her family's long history of emancipation, Josephine would grow a tobacco plant just by the entrance to her château. It was a nod to another struggle in freedom's cause: the summer of 1940 fight against the Nazi invaders.

As if drawn to her need to wage battle, a makeshift crew of would-be resisters coalesced at Milandes. There was Joseph Boué, a French Air Force captain, his uniform discarded but his hunger to battle on undimmed. There were the elderly Laremie couple, whose sons were being held as POWs behind German barbed wire. There were the Jacobs, the Belgian Jews rescued by Josephine from the shelter beneath L'Église de la Sainte-Trinité, who offered thanks to God that France had been their saving grace ... so far. Most interestingly, there was Emmanuel Bayonne – dark-haired and dark-eyed, officially an officer in the French Navy, but secretly an agent of the Deuxième Bureau, and a close colleague of both Abtey and Paillole.[52]

All they needed – all they hungered for – was the means to wage war.

CHAPTER SIX

It Can't Always Be Caviar

One man had managed to get out of Paris carrying with him with the ultimate prize, in terms of securing the means to continue the fight against a seemingly invincible foe. In doing so, Wilfred 'Biffy' Dunderdale had pulled off one of the greatest intelligence coups of the entire war.[1] Once hostilities had been declared, Britain's Paris spymaster had been given a very particular set of orders: 'Establish and enhance contact in future occupied countries, prepare for guerrilla warfare, foment insurrections and develop destructive devices . . .'[2] Dunderdale certainly had prior form.

In 1918, he'd helped investigate the killings of Russia's Romanov Imperial Family: the emperor, his wife and five children had been shot and bayonetted to death.[3] In Turkey, he'd managed to spirit the Turkish ruler, Sultan Muhammad VI, into exile, aboard the British battleship *Malaya*, prior to which he'd had to pay off the sultan's harem in gold sovereigns.[4] Later, in Paris, he'd debriefed the first high-level defector from Soviet Russia, Boris Georgiyevich Bazhanov, one of Stalin's assistants. Bazhanov had provided such a trove of intelligence that Moscow had ordered him eliminated.[5]

Germany relied upon a top-secret device of ground-breaking technology to encode its communications – the Enigma machine. Looking something like a typewriter crossed with a rudimentary computer, the Enigma relied upon an electromechanical rotor mechanism to scramble the twenty-six letters of the alphabet, plus a series of codebooks to interpret cyphered messages. It was used by all branches of the German military, and Berlin believed it to be so secure as to be unbreakable. The Polish had felt otherwise, and at their top-secret cypher school they'd managed to build an exact replica of the Enigma, and to partially break Nazi Germany's codes.[6]

With the fall of Poland, their cypher teams had fled to Paris, taking their precious technology and codebooks with them. They had been welcomed as guests of French intelligence, and with a permanent SIS liaison officer on hand, plus a 24/7 teletype link – a hotline – to London. During the long months of the Phoney War, the Polish cypher team cracked 'hundreds of messages', which were 'intercepted day and night'.[7] But when France looked set to fall, the Polish team and their Enigma machines were in dire jeopardy.

Dunderdale had convinced his French colleagues that only one course of action lay open to them: somehow, they had to spirit the precious technology and codebooks to London. Employing a good dash of skulduggery, Dunderdale had masterminded an operation described by Gwido Langer, chief of the Polish Cryptographic Service, as 'one of the most significant SIS actions during the war', though Dunderdale, typically, would describe the mission as 'peanuts' compared to some of his later wartime exploits.[8]

In his Paris rooms Dunderdale had had a special French safe fitted into one wall, which was manufactured by a famous firm of safe-makers and which could only be opened by a 'unikey' – a solitary key unique to that device. Dunderdale persuaded his long-standing colleague, Gustave Bertrand, Chief of the Deuxième Bureau's Section des Examens, its cryptanalytical unit, that the Polish Enigmas and their codebooks should be secreted there, for safekeeping. He would give Bertrand the unikey, as a guarantee that they were inviolable and secure.[9]

Dunderdale had worked closely with Bertrand for nigh-on a decade, visiting both London and Warsaw on the trail of the Enigma secrets. In truth, his safe was actually a SIS replica made to order in England, with a secret back door lying on the far side (actually, a redoubt-able piece of equipment not uncommonly used by agencies like SIS). Having accessed it via a staircase, Dunderdale was able to extract the

Enigma machines and the codebooks, place them in a suitcase – now a 'diplomatic bag', of course – whereupon he caught a train post-haste to London. He would arrive triumphantly at King's Cross station, to be met by the chief of SIS, Stuart Menzies himself.

Once the precious booty was delivered to Bletchley Park, headquarters of the Government Code and Cypher School (GCCS), it provided 'an astounding breakthrough' which 'shortened the war – and saved countless Allied lives – by perhaps three or four years.'[10] Having escaped France with his diplomatic case stuffed full of priceless booty, Dunderdale was determined to return. Sure enough, during the dark summer of 1940 he would stand shoulder to shoulder with his French comrades, and he would only leave for Britain at the last possible moment, when Menzies ordered him to do so, and no excuses.[11]

Some accounts of this incredible episode have Dunderdale sharing with Bertrand the dramas of the Enigma coup, and of them both spiriting the booty to London. One thing is for certain: despite his piratical streak, Dunderdale was renowned for being a true and constant friend, and he very likely had brought Bertrand in on the whole thing (in which case the deception involved in the rear-door trickery with the safe may not have been necessary). Either way, by summer 1940, from Norway in the north to the tip of Italy and France in the south, the Axis were triumphant. With Denmark, Holland, Belgium, Luxembourg, the Channel Islands, Poland, Czechoslovakia and France having fallen, a shroud of darkness had descended over Western Europe. While the Enigma success would enable a beam of light to be shone into that void, it would remain so secret that very, very few would ever know.

To all appearances the darkness – the evil – reigned complete.

A few days after Josephine and company had gathered at Château des Milandes, the first signpost on the road to resistance materialised, beamed across the airwaves via their wireless set. On 18 June 1940, via a BBC broadcast from London, a relatively obscure army officer spoke to the French nation. At the time General Charles de Gaulle was little-known, even in France. An arch-proponent of armoured warfare, ironically his writings and theories on the use of tanks had been read by Hitler, inspiring the Führer's concept of blitzkrieg, even as they had been dismissed by de Gaulle's superiors in France.[12]

A matter of days before making his historic broadcast, de Gaulle had managed to spirit himself aboard an aircraft bound for Britain, knowing that Pétain's rise to power only boded ill. By the time he took to the airwaves in an impassioned plea for the people of France to rise up and fight, he had the full backing of Winston Churchill. Indeed, the British prime minister and the leader of what would become known as the Free French had much in common, despite the differences – the deep well of rancour – that at times lay between them.

On one level a brilliant and inspirational visionary, de Gaulle abhorred the fact that France had fallen so spectacularly, forcing him to fall back on the charity of the old enemy, Great Britain.[13] As he made his historic speech, he was well aware he was exhorting a divided population to fight. But as Churchill put it, de Gaulle was now the torchbearer of 'the honour of France'.[14] Even before de Gaulle's arrival, Britain's wartime leader had hatched a most incredible plot to enable the French to continue the struggle.

On 16 June 1940 – just days after the fall of Paris – Churchill had put before Parliament a proposal entitled the 'Franco-British Union', something that had been under consideration for many months.[15] As Churchill put it: 'In this crisis we must not let ourselves be accused of lack of imagination.'[16] This seemingly unimaginable deal would see the two countries – or at least the unconquered parts of France, including her extensive colonies – merge politically, economically and defensively, in order to prevent them from falling under Nazi dominion, which would mean 'subjection to a system which reduces mankind to a life of robots and slaves'.[17]

Britain's Parliament voted overwhelmingly in favour of the Franco-British Union. To succeed, 'the gesture must be immediate,' de Gaulle had counselled. He telephoned the French prime minster, Paul Reynaud, who refused to believe that such a proposal was even under consideration, until de Gaulle passed the receiver over to Churchill.

The two leaders rushed to board a train and then a ship bound for France, to sign the deal into law, but the proposal would die a sudden death before the French legislature. Pétain's damning reaction was to declare that Britain was finished, and that any Franco-British Union would be a 'fusion with a corpse'.[18]

Churchill was left downhearted but unbowed. 'Whatever you may do,' he told the French leaders, 'we shall fight on forever and ever and ever.'[19]

It was in similar spirit that de Gaulle seated himself before the microphones in that BBC studio, to make his 18 June 1940 call to arms. Britain's newspapers would acclaim the extraordinary prescience of de Gaulle's words. 'Nothing is lost,' he intoned, 'because this war is a world war. In the free universe, immense forces have not yet swung into operation. Some day these forces will crush the enemy. On that day France must be present at the victory. She will then regain her liberty and her greatness. Such is my goal, my only goal.'[20]

At Château des Milandes, twelve chairs were arranged on the terrace, facing the radio, as those stirring words rang out. Whatever jamming methods the Nazi occupiers might have employed, they were not yet powerful enough to stop the BBC from getting through. In a direct appeal to the hearts of French men and women everywhere, de Gaulle declared that honour demanded they fight. 'France has undertaken not to lay down arms, save in agreement with her allies. As long as the Allies continue the war, her government has no right to surrender to the enemy.'[21]

'A medieval castle at the gates of the enemy,' is how Jacques Abtey would describe this watershed moment at Milandes. 'There were a dozen there listening, faces grave, faces determined, and when . . . the wireless had fallen silent, the voice still spoke: it spoke in their souls, it spoke through their hearts . . . and it worked miracles.' De Gaulle's call to arms 'settled everywhere, haunting the castle, mingling with the crackling logs in the medieval chimneys, resounding in the spiral staircase . . . the spirit of France sang the old, glorious song of its eternal Freedom.'[22]

Abtey wasn't present at Milandes that day, but he would be shortly.

De Gaulle's words roused him to action, and he decided that the only place from which to resist was at Josephine's side, at Château des Milandes. Her reaction to the broadcast was ecstatic. It had been truly cathartic, a powerful vindication of all that she held dear. She had been 'deeply moved' by the speech, especially as those were sentiments she had so long 'despaired of hearing, phrases that touched our innermost being'. To Josephine, de Gaulle's words reflected the true spirit of France, and from now onwards 'everything seemed possible'.[23]

Even so, the route ahead, the path of the struggle, remained uncertain. Few in France had heard, and fewer still would heed, de Gaulle's call to arms. That summer of 1940 his was truly a lone voice in the wilderness. It mattered not to Josephine. 'I never took the easy path, always the rough one,' she would write. 'But you know, when I took the rough path, I wanted to make it a little easier for those who followed . . .'[24]

Right now, her chief 'follower' would be Jacques Abtey. By the time Abtey would reach Château des Milandes, somehow Josephine wouldn't find it at all surprising that this warrior of the shadows had found his way to her door. He was her foremost comrade in arms, one whom she believed fate had sent her to serve as a constant companion throughout the war.[25] But she was to be more than a little amazed by the tales of Abtey's daring and piratical adventures over the weeks that the two had been apart.

Jacques Abtey hadn't seen his Honourable Correspondent for a good two months, but he knew well where she had taken refuge. As he made his way towards Milandes, uppermost in his mind was avoiding enemy patrols and checkpoints, plus the crying need to re-establish contact with London and the Secret Intelligence Service.[26] He had a sense how they might do so. A plot of sorts had been hatched, with the help of a most extraordinary character, a German national with a distinctly chequered past, including serving as a sometime agent of the Deuxième Bureau.

A few days after the Armistice had come into effect, Abtey had run into Hans Müssig – alias Thomas Lieven, among many other cover names – seemingly by chance. If there was a Teutonic equivalent of James Bond, Müssig was it. Indeed, a thriller would be written based upon Müssig's life story, *It Can't Always Be Caviar*. The book's subtitle gives a flavour of its subject: 'The fabulous daring adventures and exquisite cooking recipes of the involuntary secret agent Thomas Lieven'.[27] Müssig's story, in brief, was of a once-enthusiastic Hitler Youth leader with high-born family connections, who had woken up to the true evils of the Nazis – the 'bastard gang' – before the outbreak of war, and fled Germany. Perhaps unwisely, he had emptied the bank account of his local Hitler Youth branch, taking the funds on a round-about journey, ending up in London, and in the process earning a death sentence in absentia from Berlin.[28]

In Britain, Müssig had befriended the high-society London crowd, and had even managed to found an investment bank. Things had gone swimmingly, until his past had finally caught up with him, at which point he'd abandoned Britain for France. In Paris he'd obtained a genuine-seeming, but forged, passport, which soon brought him to the attention of the French security services.

Müssig was duly arrested, whereupon he declared his anti-Nazi sentiments and volunteered to work in the cause of France. At that point Abtey had been called in to 'probe his heart and his kidneys' – in other words, to grill Müssig, in case he was an Abwehr plant. Tall, striking-looking – 'a knife-bladed face, steel-grey eyes' – and dressed with the 'sober elegance' of a proper English gentleman, in Hans Müssig, Abtey had met his match.[29] His report would stress Müssig's 'extraordinary assurance, self-control and irony. Hardness too, a hardness that later proved to be firmness . . . An explosive mixture . . . To be handled with the utmost caution.'[30]

Despite Abtey's warnings, individuals like Müssig were in very short supply in Paris at that time: a 'very clever, very skilful' German keen to work for the Allied cause. Recruited as an agent, he'd masterminded a highly profitable currency-smuggling operation, in an effort to boost the coffers of the Deuxième Bureau. With the French government having banned the taking out of French francs from the country, Müssig was given carte blanche to fly to Belgium carrying suitcases stuffed full of cash, so as to purchase US dollars at a highly preferential rate, which he re-imported to France. The profits so reaped went into the coffers of the French intelligence services, where they were much in need. They also helped Müssig rent a luxurious apartment on the Boulevard Malesherbes, an exclusive district of Paris. But with war being declared, Müssig was imprisoned as an 'enemy alien' just prior to the fall of France.[31]

Typically, Müssig had talked his way out of the internment camp where he'd been held, after which he'd made his way into Vichy France. It was there that he and Abtey had stumbled across each other and rekindled their former acquaintance.[32] At first, Abtey had been suspicious: here was a German Aryan-archetype whom the French had imprisoned, and who was now somehow at liberty in the Vichy zone, and seemingly keen to ask a lot of probing questions. But as the two talked, Abtey began to realise something about Müssig that he had missed the first time around. A highly unusual character, the German was 'a spy in spite of himself'. Müssig 'hated war as he hated the stupidity of men'. Above all, Abtey concluded, he 'hated those who violated the freedom of others, and that is why he became my friend'.[33]

Indeed, he became much more than simply Abtey's friend. Together, they began to hatch a plot which would help turn the fortunes of the war. At the urgings of Paillole, Abtey had determined that the surest way for making contact with London lay well over a thousand kilometres and two international borders away. In Lisbon, the capital of the neutral nation of Portugal, the British embassy was known to double as an outpost for a small crew of Secret Intelligence Service agents. Portugal was also Britain's longest-standing ally, an alliance that dated back to the time of the Crusades.

If an agent of the Deuxième Bureau could somehow make it to Lisbon – running the gauntlet of Gestapo and fascist Spanish checkpoints along the way – then maybe contact between the shadow French intelligence service and Britain's SIS could be re-established. As it happened, Müssig was hell-bent on getting to Lisbon, for it offered a rare refuge from occupied Europe. Abtey agreed to help secure Müssig a passport, complete with genuine exit visas, in exchange for which he was to lay the groundwork for that vital Lisbon intelligence connection.[34] As an added bonus – of sorts – Müssig was known to British intelligence already. Not for all the right reasons, but at least it gave him a kind of an 'in'.

Never once would Abtey regret forging this unique partnership, one made in extremis. Müssig would prove 'loyal in all circumstances', even when he was captured by the Gestapo, whereupon he could have sold out Abtey and his Deuxième Bureau comrades, Josephine Baker included.[35] But typically, Müssig's altruism was blended with the desire to make a quick buck. When he'd talked his way out of the French internment camp, he'd taken with him a wealthy Jewish banker, along with his wife and children. As that man was 'rich to the bone', and Müssig was 'penniless', he was charging him for a safe passage to Portugal, and from there to the USA.[36]

As part of that process, the Jewish businessman and his family were about to convert to Catholicism, and they were short of a witness for the ceremony. 'Why not you?' Müssig suggested to Abtey. 'Surely, you won't spit on a good meal.' The next day, Abtey duly helped officiate at the 'baptismal font of the medieval church', as the Jewish banker and his family converted to Catholicism in a desperate effort to save themselves from the Nazis.[37] It was a last act before he and Müssig went their separate ways. Temporarily, at least. Abtey was off to Milandes, Müssig to Lisbon. Their intention was to meet there in due course, with the task of defeating the enemy foremost in mind.

In essence, Müssig was now an Honourable Correspondent. How honourable he would prove himself to be was up for debate; it was all a matter of perspective, really. In effect, both Abtey and Paillole were willing to do a deal with the devil, if it would help defeat Nazi Germany, and while there were distinctly devilish traits to Müssig, there were equally angelic ones too. Either way, for now at least he would serve as Jacques Abtey's – and Josephine Baker's – HC in Lisbon, that's if he made it there safely. As a last act before they parted, Abtey and Müssig decided on a coded phrase that the latter would mail to Château Des Milandes, if all went as planned.

He was to report that there was 'good sunshine' in Lisbon.[38]

It was late June 1940 by the time Abtey reached the Dordogne. There, he discovered Josephine Baker holding court – the seasoned chief of the vagabond crew of resisters now headquartered at Château des Milandes.[39] He was struck immediately by how much she had changed; grown; matured. Already, she was far from being the flighty, nervous, unpredictable HC delivering on her first espionage assignment, and almost crashing her Delage in the process. But in truth, in terms of the spying game, they hadn't even got started.

'Fox of misfortune, where the hell did you come from?' Josephine threw out a greeting, eyes flashing a challenge as she looked him up and down. 'I thought you were dead, buried with a kilo of buckshot in your back. Come on! A quick trip to the barbers, a brush of your boots, and you'll be fresh and ready.'[40]

Before they could go anywhere, there was a little Deuxième Bureau housekeeping to take care of, Abtey explained. First off, he was no longer 'Mr Fox'. That man had perished on the very day that Pétain had cut a peace deal with Germany. In his place had risen, phoenix-like, Mr Jack Sanders, conveniently the citizen of a supposedly neutral country, the USA. Abtey even had the passport to prove it.[41]

'Hello, Mr Jack Sanders!' Josephine declared with a laugh.

Had she possibly heard of a city called London, Abtey ventured, and a certain General Charles de Gaulle?

Josephine feigned ignorance. 'The general of what? You forget I'm an artist and I didn't do my military service.'

She took him by the arm and steered him towards the château. It was time to introduce Abtey to the rest of her Resistance crew – her menagerie of animals included. There was Bonzo, the Great Dane, Glouglou (Gobble-Gobble), a young monkey, Mica, a golden lion tamarin – a tiny primate whose long fur is an explosion of orange – Gugusse (Clown), a moustachioed marmoset – a squirrel-sized monkey with a striking white beard and moustache – plus Bigoudi and Point d'Interrogation (Curly and Question Mark), two white mice.

She leaned closer to Abtey as they walked, feet scrunching through the gravel. 'Tell me,' she whispered, mischievously, 'when are we going to see him?'

'Who?' Abtey asked, momentarily thrown.

'Our General de Gaulle!'[42]

There and then the two of them resolved that come what may, they would head for London to meet with the Free French leader, from where they would join the battle to liberate Europe.

Having met with the decidedly colourful Milandes Resistance company – two- and four-legged varieties included – Abtey sought out the river, for he was desperate for a quiet moment to himself. The last months had been exhausting, nerve-racking and traumatic. No one had foreseen what was coming, and Abtey had had barely the briefest of moments to rest or recuperate. At Milandes he'd spied a kayak and the river lay barely a stone's throw away. Since his earliest days he had loved to canoe, as a boy on the Rhine, 'this majestic river', its 'deep green waters . . . a gush of foam, eternally young and beautiful'.[43]

As he struck out on the lazy expanse of the Dordogne, Abtey let his canoe and his thoughts drift, deliciously, luxuriating, until he almost 'seemed to have forgotten the war'. Gliding along the fastest sections of the magical river – the boat's shadow flitting across the golden sands, the waters gushing through dramatic gorges, channelled between deep, sculpted cliffs – he searched for the perfect spot to fish. At sunset he returned to Milandes, presenting Josephine with a frying-pan's worth of roach and perch.[44] While canoeing together on the Dordogne their love affair would flourish anew, but only until the enemy came calling.

Matters began to move swiftly now. Through the intermediary of one Captain d'Hofflize, a long-experienced Deuxième Bureau hand, they began to put flesh on the bones of the plans that had first been hatched between Abtey and Paillole, and expanded with the help of Hans Müssig. Shrewd, rebellious, single-minded in the extreme,

Paillole – now known as 'M. Perrier' – had gone deep underground to establish a shadow intelligence network, adopting the most imaginative of disguises.[45]

He'd set up base in the southern French port city of Marseilles, a place with which he was very familiar, having been raised and schooled there. As cover for what he intended, he'd created the Entreprise Générale de Travaux Ruraux (TR) – the Rural Works Company – supposedly an agricultural development bureau.[46] Bankrolled out of the Deuxième Bureau's slush fund, overnight his agents became rural development workers.[47] From his Marseilles headquarters, based at the seaside Villa Eole, to substations across France – in Limoges, Clermont-Ferrand, Lyon and Toulouse – Paillole's 'rural engineers' quartered the country under perfect cover, with a two-fold mission.[48]

The first was to gather intelligence on Germany's intentions, and especially concerning Great Britain, for that was the only dog left in the fight any more. Paillole felt confident in the British, who would 'never let us down'.[49] With the Battle of Britain raging over the skies of southern England, it was crucial to gather intelligence to enable London to win the war of the air. Hitler had decreed that the Royal Air Force (RAF) had to be smashed by the Luftwaffe, earning Germany total air superiority, before his invasion fleet could set sail across the Channel for British shores.[50]

On 18 June 1940, Churchill had underscored the import of the Battle of Britain, even as Luftwaffe warplanes prepared to attack airfields across Britain. 'The whole fury and might of the enemy must very soon be turned against us. Hitler knows he will have to break us in this island or lose the war.' Days later he turned up the rhetoric. 'We await undismayed the impending assault. Perhaps it will come tonight, perhaps it will come next week . . . We must show ourselves equally capable of meeting a sudden violent shock, or . . . a prolonged vigil.'[51]

The Wehrmacht's invasion fleets gathered at French ports. Flights of Luftwaffe bombers lifted off from French airfields, together with their fighter escorts. Furnishing intelligence to frustrate and confound those operations was the foremost mission of Paillole's TR networks. But no one underestimated the challenges of getting such information to where it was needed. Just as Paris had been wrong-footed by the speed and scope of the Nazi victory, so had London. Across the length and breadth of France, the Secret Intelligence Service's networks had been obliterated. London had been blinded. Her eyes had been gouged out. Incredibly, not one active SIS agent or wireless station was known to be operational in France any more.[52]

Churchill had been appointed prime minister on 10 May 1940. On 3 June he had called a meeting of his intelligence chiefs, demanding of them how they intended to reorganise after the precipitate fall of so much of Europe. Though there were no ready answers, Churchill demanded that information be winkled out of France.[53] Dunderdale, only recently back in Britain, was duly appointed SIS Chief of Operations for all of Vichy France, which crucially included her extensive North African colonies. His SIS colleague Kenneth Cohen, a man of long experience, was made Chief of Operations with the Free French – de Gaulle's people, and encompassing all French territoy that had been occupied by Germany.[54]

Paillole, of course, knew none of this. Nonetheless, he was determined to reach out, to break through, to make connections and to forge the alliance anew. Without 'official cover or contacts with our allies,' he would write, and deprived of 'sure connections between us . . . it is impossible to use the intelligence that is being harvested.'[55]

He decided it was time to risk moving the Deuxième Bureau's precious files. In fact, officially the Deuxième Bureau had ceased to exist. With the signing of the Armistice, it had become an organ of the Vichy state, being renamed the Bureaux des Menées Antinationales (BMA) – the Bureau of Anti-National Activities. Not that Paillole gave a damn. No way was any such upstart agency about to get its hands on his files. The remaining twenty-five tonnes of documents were loaded onto a convoy of cheese lorries and trucked to Marseilles, where they were delivered to the Villa Eole courtyard.[56]

Twenty-four hours later, Paillole's archivist had got the files sorted and the shadow-agency was truly operational. For their courageous wartime efforts, sadly any number of Paillole's TR agents would pay the ultimate price, ending their lives in Nazi concentration camps or the Gestapo's torture chambers. Paillole knew the stakes he was playing for. This was life or death stuff. Likewise, he could be utterly ruthless – murderous – when the need arose.

In Marseilles he would forge links with the city's foremost crime groups – its 'honourable gangsters' – to rub out enemy agents and collaborators, those hunting his TR teams. Such extrajudicial executions were dirty, violent and bloody. They involved taking the law into their own hands, but as Paillole knew, 'sooner or later, we will be obliged to put the enemy's agents out of action ourselves without the possibility of resorting to legal means.'[57]

His two key enforcers were 'Big Louie' and 'Little Pierre', the former as massive as the other was diminutive, but both equally lethal. Long-standing Marseilles mobsters, their motives struck Paillole as being no less honourable than those of many embroiled in this war. As Louis Raggio – Big Louie – confessed to Paillole, he'd done a lot 'bad things' in his life. His mother was getting old, and he wanted to prove to her that he deserved her forgiveness. 'I'll do anything you want against the Krauts,' he promised. 'Before she dies, I want to bring her back a Croix de Guerre or some other proof that I did my duty properly as a soldier in this dirty war.'[58]

Paillole appreciated such 'patriotic feelings'. He and Big Louie would become lifelong friends, especially once Big Louie proved 'what a repentant crook could achieve, with will and courage'. At Big Louie and Little Pierre's hands, and on Paillole's orders, German and Italian agents, plus French collaborators, were destined to die.[59]

Despite the obvious risks, Paillole needed volunteer agents. All-comers were welcome, as long as they had the will and the moral rectitude to fight. The other key priority of his earliest TR recruits was to rally the troops – those still willing to engage in the shadow war. To that end, Major Bonnefous signed up to run a TR substation in Bourg-en-Bresse, a town in eastern France. Scores more would join Paillole, and they would start to create hidden weapons dumps in preparation for the coming uprisings.[60]

It made perfect sense for Château des Milandes to double as a TR outpost, set as it was amid the rich Dordogne farmland. More to the point, at several locations just a few minutes' drive away – the hamlets, villages and towns of Griffoul, Saint-Cyprien, Saint-Geniès et Calviac, Sarlat and others – Paillole and his people were helping to set up the Camouflage du Matériel (CDM), the Material Camouflage Company, a central weapons hide for would-be Resistance fighters.[61] Milandes lay at the hub of a nascent network for armed resistance, and via his couriers – chiefly Captain d'Hofflize – Paillole made it clear what needed to be done.[62]

Abtey would serve as a TR agent, and so too would Emmanuel Bayonne, the French Navy officer and former agent of the Deuxième Bureau now resident at Château des Milandes. As for Josephine Baker, Paillole had a far more singular mission in mind for his standout Honorary Correspondent, one whom he was starting to realise had the ability to remain 'admirably self-possessed' whenever danger threatened. He was struck by Josephine's sheer optimism; her unshakable faith that the United States would join the war and that victory would be assured. She remained resolute, he would observe, 'even when the rest of us despaired of the immensity of the task ahead'.[63]

If any agent – Jacques Abtey included – were to stand a chance of reaching Lisbon without being unmasked, he would need an impeccable, unimpeachable cover. Clearly, French rural development workers had no need to partake of international travel, so the TR cover would not wash. But globally famous superstars certainly did. With the coming of the war, the world hadn't stopped and neither had the business of showbusiness. While Josephine Baker had vowed never to perform in France until it was purged of the Nazis, others had been far less principled, far less resolute.

In Paris, where signs in Nazi Gothic script had been pinned up at theatre entrances declaring 'ACCESS FORBIDDEN TO DOGS OR JEWS', many of the stars chose to turn a blind eye.[64] Maurice Chevalier and Mistinguett were among those now performing for the occupiers. Paris fashion houses, cinemas, theatres and cafés were reopening, and once again they were packed with customers. Menus were now printed in German, with 'Forbidden to Jews' stamped across them, but much of the Paris glitterati seemed happy enough with '*la paix honteuse*' – this shameful peace.[65]

Josephine begged to differ. To her all humans were created equal. She feared no one and wasn't intimidated by anyone; this was a matter of principle.[66]

As a global superstar Josephine remained in high demand, and Paillole argued that surely she could perform *outside* occupied Europe, in neutral countries such as Portugal. She had high-level contacts with those nations, having toured them prior to the war to great acclaim. If anyone, Josephine Baker could secure the proper travel permits, and very possibly she could use her stardom as the cloak and dagger to spirit a man like Abtey – Paillole's man – through.

That was the plan being hatched at Milandes in summer 1940. It was all done very quietly, under intense secrecy. It was whispered closely between Jacques and Josephine, as they paddled in the waters of the Dordogne, for there they could rest assured that no one – no hostile ears – were listening. As for Paillole, he understood that 'any slip-up could wreck everything.' He'd been warned: 'We must avoid increasing the risks by multiplying the contacts with our friends.' 'Our friends' equalled London.[67]

Abtey cautioned Josephine to take great care, to be extra vigilant. Any 'refugee' or 'Resistance volunteer' who arrived at the château gates could well be a Gestapo agent. The enemy might even arrive at Milandes in full view, having been tipped off about the 'suspicious' activities being organised there. As he'd feared she would, Josephine had seemed to laugh off such warnings, apparently teasing him for being so paranoid. But as matters transpired, she had been listening and she had paid proper heed.

Which was just as well, for the enemy was about to arrive at their very gates.

CHAPTER SEVEN

The Enemy At The Gates

All the danger signs were there to read. The Milandes crew should have seen it coming. Jacques Abtey had long known the Abwehr was hunting down the ranks of the Deuxième Bureau. By now, surely they would have worked out his and his fellow agents' true identities. In early September 1940 his Paris apartment was searched, proof positive that they were onto him. As Abtey feared, the Abwehr had identified most Deuxième Bureau operatives and was 'already looking for us'. He had been well-advised to get his family out of the city and to adopt a new identity. Had he failed to do so, even now he could be chained in some cellar, facing the very worst.[1]

Paris, of course, lay in the zone of France fully occupied by German forces. By contrast, Château des Milandes and TR Central, in Marseilles, lay in the Vichy sector. But that meant little: they were only marginally safer, for the Germans were flooding the so-called 'Free Zone' with agents. Both the Abwehr – under Admiral Canaris – and the Gestapo – ruled by Heinrich Himmler, *Reichsführer*-SS and head of the Gestapo – were dispatching teams into the Free Zone, for it stood to reason that many of those they hunted had taken refuge there.

Then there was the Armistice Commission, which had free run of the Vichy zone, where it was supposed to ensure compliance with the terms of the ceasefire. It had set up headquarters at the imposing Grand Hotel Roi René, in Aix-en-Provence, ironically just a short drive from Paillole's Marseilles HQ. Typically, Paillole was determined to penetrate their operations. That autumn, one of his TRs would 'denounce' a supposed arms cache concealed in a nearby quarry. There, Paillole and his men had hidden some old weaponry – machineguns and cases of ammunition – just so they could be 'unearthed' by the enemy. Once the Germans had seized that cache, Paillole's 'snitch' became their man, and he had a spy on the inside of the Armistice Commission.[2]

But that breakthrough would be some months in coming. Right now, operating unchecked within the echelons of the Armistice Commission – on paper at least, it was supposed to be wholly a Wehrmacht (German military) operation – were Gestapo officers and SS fanatics 'seeking to intimidate, or apprehend anti-Nazi refugees or to reveal nascent resistance groups'.[3] As Paillole well knew, the Abwehr had also scattered its agents among the Armistice Commission's rank and file.

It was around lunchtime at Château des Milandes and there were a series of resounding raps at the heavy oaken doors set in the main tower, beneath the imposing heraldry of the Caumont family, which includes an ornate pair of *chimeras*, a lion-like fire-breathing monster of Greek legend. Right at this moment the château's occupants were in need of all of the chimeras' mythological powers of protection, for the group of grey-uniformed figures gathered at the entrance were to prove most predatory.

Josephine was seated in the dining room, deep in conversation with two visitors. Each was a former agent of the Deuxième Bureau, and they had come to Milandes on a two-fold mission. The first was to discuss the plans being hatched at TR Central about how to forge an intelligence link with the SIS in London; the second was to provide the means to wage war. They had brought with them a stash of weaponry to add to the château's underground armoury, but of far greater import were the documents they carried – plans for the total occupation of the Free Zone by the Wehrmacht.[4]

If, in the eyes of the Armistice Commission, the Vichy regime was seen not to be adhering to the terms of the ceasefire, then the Free Zone would cease to exist. The German Army would march in, and all of France would fall under occupation. If that happened, it boded ill for operations like Paillole's shadow TR network and so much more.

As luck would have it, Abtey was out on the river at that moment, enjoying a spot of fishing, though someone had been sent to fetch him. So it was that Josephine would be left to hold the fort more or less alone. Following that series of sharp raps – terrible thumps as if intended to smash open the château's doorway, as Josephine would later describe them – her redoubtable maid, La Libellule came rushing in; out of breath; flustered.[5]

'There are six of them!' she warned. 'An officer, a non-commissioned officer, and four soldiers. All the doors of the château are already guarded.'[6]

Seeing as though the enemy were at the threshold and there was apparently no escape, Josephine ordered the chief *résistantes* – Joseph Boué, the forty-year-old former sergeant in the French Air Force; François Dudek, the twenty-something Polish farmhand and refugee; Georges Malaury, the grizzled blacksmith and stalwart of the local Resistance – to slip into the château's furthest recesses. They were to take the two visitors – the TR agents – with them and do their very best to hide.

As the agents gathered up their sensitive papers and hurried away from the dining room, Josephine turned to her maid. 'Bring the officer into the library.' It was her favourite room in the entire château. The ancient shelves, thick with weighty tomes, fascinated her, drawing her to its bookish calm and somehow tending to settle her nerves.

Outside, a German soldier – a Feldwebel; a sergeant – stood at the Château's entrance. He'd knocked on behalf of his commanding officer, who wore the uniform of a colonel in the Wehrmacht, though that meant very little. In truth he could very easily be Gestapo or Abwehr, the military uniform serving as *his* cloak and *his* dagger. The colonel's dress was redolent of all that Josephine despised: polished black leather boots under baggy jodhpurs, a tunic bedecked with the distinctive Wehrmacht collar flashes and the unmistakable symbol of Nazi Germany – an eagle grasping a swastika in its outstretched talons – topped off with a thickly braided officer's cap.

Behind him were ranged his men-at-arms standing guard, weapons at the ready.

La Libellule led the colonel up the wide stone staircase, off which branched the narrow servant's stairways and passages, until they reached the imposing library. The German officer was undeniably handsome, in that Hans Müssig, *knife-bladed-face-to-be-handled-with-the-utmost-caution* kind of way. Upon spying the lady of the house – the chatelaine, as female château owners are known in France – he bowed stiffly, before clicking his heels and making the Nazi salute.[7]

'Heil Hitler.'

Heil Hitler indeed: not in Josephine Baker's château you don't.

'Madame,' the colonel began, with rigid formality, speaking impeccable French, 'I am a member of the Armistice Commission, and I have special responsibility for controlling arms depots in the unoccupied zone.' He reached into a pocket and pulled out a folded sheet of paper, offering it to Josephine to inspect. 'Here is my search warrant.'[8]

Josephine didn't flinch. Now was not the time to show the slightest weakness or vulnerability. Now was the time for nerves of steel. Now was the time to give the greatest performance of her life; to dance and dance until the blood flowed down her shins, but never to falter, until the final curtain-close. She reminded herself that this man – this colonel – was here illegally; an illegal invader, here by force of arms alone. She abhorred all that he stood for and she was determined not to give him the honour of a name, let alone a welcome, or any kind of legitimacy.

'The officer cannot be speaking seriously, if he thinks I am hiding weapons here,' she countered, icily, deliberately addressing him in the third person. 'It is true that I have Native American Indian grandparents, but they left the warpath a long time ago. As for me, I think I know all the dances, except for one: the scalp dance.' The age-old scalp dance, said to be performed by Native American men and women circling a totem pole, with the scalps of vanquished enemies suspended on ceremonial staffs – the inference would be clear to anyone but a fool.[9]

The colonel smiled, thinly, acknowledging the barbed jest. No one could pretend not to know who this famous woman was. The thrust – her cool, cutting poise – had struck home. He folded the search warrant back into his pocket.

Despite the officer's somewhat conciliatory gesture, Josephine didn't believe for one moment that this was the moment to drop her guard, or that this was the end of the matter and that she was somehow in the clear. This was no passing visit. The colonel had to be acting on some kind of tip-off, or worse still on concrete intelligence. She was face-to-face with her adversaries, at last, as Abtey had warned her would happen.

'You were taking coffee?' the colonel asked.

'Not yet.'

'My apologies, but do you have any coffee?' he persisted. The verbal fencing was far from over, even less the inquisition. The test – the hunt – was very much on.

'We have a little,' she conceded.

'And some sugar to put in it?'

'Very little sugar.'

'Ah, this war is terrible,' the colonel ventured.

Her eyes flashed. 'If it were only a matter of sugar and coffee . . .'

The colonel changed tack. 'You must miss the theatre a lot, madame.' He knew exactly who she was; what she stood for. Why she was no longer gracing the Paris stage and what that had to signify. The City of Light was thronged with his kind, yet she had chosen to give Paris a very wide berth.

'I would not have the heart to go on stage when there is so much suffering,' Josephine countered. Words chosen very carefully, yet unbending; staunch; resolute.

For a moment the colonel seemed to let his guard drop. He sighed. 'We did not want this war—'

'So, let the German Army leave France!' she cut in.[10]

The colonel laughed. Such impertinence; such bare-faced defiance. It bordered on disrespect. Surely, if there were any weapons hidden in this château, the chatelaine would be acting very differently.

'I see you favour simple solutions,' he suggested. She was doubtless brave, but a fool. Of course, her suggestion – that the Wehrmacht leave France – was hopelessly naïve.

'I think they are always the best.'

He fixed her with a searching look. 'Are you telling me you have no weapons here? To tell the truth, madame, we received a denunciation.'

So, someone had talked. Some snitch had gone to their local Nazi contact, and whispered details about the Milandes Resistance crew, no doubt in an effort to curry favour with the enemy.

'What is worse,' Josephine countered, pointedly, 'to denounce, or to believe those who denounce?'

'This is war, madame.'

'Then long live peace.'

The colonel laughed again. In this verbal fencing match, at least, Madame Baker was proving his match. Clearly, there was no coffee on offer here, and very likely never would be. 'I will not trouble you any longer,' he told her. Then, that look again. 'But be careful.'[11]

He stiffened, saluted in the Nazi style and turned to leave, stalking out of the library, his boots echoing down the stone staircase until they could be heard no more.

When Paillole was informed of this steely confrontation, he would remark of his HC that she had performed with 'remarkable sang-froid'.[12] After the war, as part of the high honours bestowed upon Josephine, this episode would be singled out as one deserving special mention: 'Suspected by the Germans of hiding weapons, a search is carried out of her property, and she shows remarkable courage and composure.'[13]

Praise indeed, but just then it didn't exactly feel that way. The colonel – cold and rigid as a corpse, but somehow still exuding power and menace, as Josephine would later describe him – had placed guards everywhere around Milandes.[14] He had shown every sign of fearing that armed resistance might burst forth at any moment from the château's ancient towers and walls. His men had poked around, delving into nooks and crannies. They may have left, but she didn't doubt for one moment that they would be back. When Abtey returned from the river, he was of the same conviction. Never mind that Josephine had 'nerves of steel', even without a denunciation there was every reason for the enemy to suspect this chatelaine of deception and malfeasance.[15]

Josephine's bare-faced defiance – her unbending words and attitude – was a rare thing in the autumn of 1940. Across occupied Europe, the vast majority believed the war was lost; that total German victory was at hand. In Berlin the Führer was preparing to celebrate, his architects constructing a grand display through which he would parade in triumph, once Great Britain was crushed. As *Reichsmarschall* Goering boasted, the British people were cowering under the ferocious assault of the Luftwaffe. The mass bombing of London and other cities – the blitz – would force Churchill's resignation, after which the British government would sue for peace. If not, the invasion fleets would set sail and the British nation would face annihilation before the month was out.[16]

That day at Château des Milandes, Josephine had played her part with amazing cool. She had foiled a search party of the Armistice Commission, who had come with good cause, and all due to her consummate abilities as an actress. She was proving a fine student of spycraft – intelligent, agile, intuitive, but most of all, her steely fortitude shone through. 'I never saw anyone with such fire,' Abtey would remark.[17] Even so, the experience had left them shaken. More to the point, such rare defiance could not go unanswered. The Armistice Commission – or its agents – would be back. Of that there was no doubt.

As if to bear out such fears, barely twenty-four hours after Josephine's confrontation with the colonel, there came a second unexpected visitor at the château's gates. The timing of this new and surprise arrival – two in as many days – seemed far too suspicious.

Once again, by chance Abtey was out – this time on TR business – so it was left to Josephine, the rookie agent, to face the challenge alone.

The stranger demanded to be given an audience with Madame Baker. While there was no official security apparatus at Milandes, Josephine's crew were forever vigilant. After the previous day's confrontation, everyone was on edge. Under the fierce glare of the gargoyles that gazed down from the château's towers, the visitor was asked to wait in the gatehouse, while Josephine's maid was fetched.

La Libellule came bustling out, appearing most formidable and business-like as she scrutinised the stranger. He looked to be in his late teens or early twenties, smartly dressed, with a khaki raincoat draped over his left arm, while in his right he held a small leather suitcase. She demanded he explain the nature of his business, and at least give his name, for the chatelaine was a person of some standing who did not entertain all-comers.

'My name will not mean anything to her, because she doesn't know me, and I don't know her personally,' the young man explained, somewhat guardedly. 'But please, tell her I have come on a matter of the utmost importance.'[18]

Politely but firmly La Libellule announced that she would put forward his case, but there were no guarantees that Madame Baker would see him. 'Sir, please have a seat. I'll inform Madame.'[19]

Josephine told her maid that they needed an absolutely compelling reason to let this young man in. Otherwise, and especially after yesterday's unwelcome scrutiny, he should be sent packing. La Libellule returned to the gates, and passed across her sentiments. 'Madame asks you to let her know the reason for your visit. Madame is very busy.'[20]

The young man clasped his case ever more tightly. 'Please, tell your mistress that I must speak to her at all costs.'

'Come on, sir—'

'I won't leave this place without seeing her,' he cut in, passionately. 'If you tell me to leave, I will just find a way through the window!'[21]

Come what may, the young man would not be turned away. He was duly led in. No sooner had he laid eyes upon the distinctive figure of the chatelaine-superstar than he gave a solemn bow . . . and began to talk, the words pouring forth in a seemingly unstoppable flood.

'Forgive me, madame, for my approach, which must appear so impertinent to you, but you surely will understand right away my behaviour: I have some documents of great value for you to remit to the Intelligence Services.' With that he placed down his suitcase – Josephine had received him in the château's kitchen – and he pulled out a thick wad of documents from inside his jacket. 'This,' he declared, 'is only a first delivery. I will make another in a fortnight, and after that I will ask you to put me on the road to England.'[22]

Though intrigued, Josephine feigned disinterest, barely glancing at the weighty cache of papers that the young man had produced. After the previous day's visit, she didn't doubt that this was a further attempt to entrap her and all of her Milandes crew – although it did seem a remarkably clumsy and ill-disguised one. She had expected far more from the likes of a colonel of the Armistice Commission.

She shook her head. 'Good sir, I'm afraid you are mistaken. I have no idea what you are talking about.'

'But the Intelligence Services . . .' he spluttered.[23]

'I haven't the slightest idea what you are talking about,' she repeated. 'I don't know what this "Intelligence Service" is, and as for getting you to England – why, I would be at a loss. I am an artiste and I have only ever been concerned with my art.'[24]

At that moment Abtey burst in, having rushed back from his TR errand. Though playing her part with remarkable poise, Josephine was more than a little relieved to see him. 'Jack, would you check what this gentleman wants. I don't understand a word he's talking about.'[25] She turned back to the visitor and gestured at Abtey. 'You may speak with him as openly as you would with me.'[26]

The mystery guest repeated his story. By way of response Abtey replied in similar vein to Josephine – reiterating that neither of them had the slightest clue what he might be on about. The young visitor looked ever more downcast and troubled.

'This can't be true,' he exclaimed. 'I know that I can't be mistaken, because the person who sent me cannot have misled me—'

'Who sent you?' Abtey interrupted.

'The Reverend Father Victor Dillard. You must know him – he's in Vichy. For three weeks myself and a comrade searched for a way to join General de Gaulle . . . But we didn't want to leave empty-handed. Chance served us well, and we were able to get hold of the secret code of the Luftwaffe. Now, I'm handing it to you so you can get it to London.'

He glanced searchingly from Abtey's face to Josephine's and back again. 'It was Father Dillard who told me: "Go to Castelnaud-Fayrac, near Sarlat. Ask for the Château des Milandes. There you'll find the artiste Josephine Baker. Give her your documents and stay at the château until you leave for London."'[27]

Abtey certainly knew of Father Dillard and his burgeoning Resistance connections, but so too very likely did the enemy. Using that man's name didn't alter the fact that this was almost definitely a set-up.

He shook his head. 'I don't know this religious man whom you're talking about.'

'But I am sure he told me the truth,' the young visitor implored. 'Besides, you, sir, have an English accent—'

'Sir, please – calm down,' Abtey interjected. 'I'm sorry for your long journey, believe me, and perhaps I am sympathetic to your cause, but I'm not English. I'm American and a complete stranger to your war. Besides, I'm an artist, just like Miss Baker. Quite frankly, you have made a mistake. Keep your documents.'

'But—'

'I don't know who you are and I don't want to know,' Abtey cut him off. 'Have a strong cup of tea, some bacon and eggs and head home. There is a train at six p.m. – the only one before tomorrow. God speed – you'd best be on it.'[28]

Seeing no other option, the apparently despairing visitor took a lonely meal in the kitchen, after which he was sent on his way.

Two serious scares in as many days: what to make of it all? One thing was for certain – Abtey and Josephine needed a private moment. Neither doubted the loyalties of those who served in the Milandes crew, but during a life spent in counter-espionage Abtey had learned to trust only those he absolutely had to. Even the most loyal might break, especially if their loved ones – their wives, husbands or children – had been taken captive, and the Gestapo had ways of making just about anyone talk.

With the château set deep in the wild woods, there were countless quiet places in which to slip away. It was a beautiful day with barely a breath of wind. On one level the two of them wanted to forget all about that afternoon's bizarre visit, coming so rapidly as it had upon the heels of the German colonel. After all, it was here on the banks of the Dordogne in the midst of the struggle that their love had really started to take hold, and the temptation to indulge a few moments of intimacy was always present.

For Abtey, the war had separated him irrevocably from his family, thrusting him into the shadowy world of deep-cover espionage and Resistance work. Under his assumed identity – American Jack Sanders – he couldn't risk the slightest contact with his wife or son. He'd sent them away from Paris to a house in the French countryside. They were bound to be watched and it was better if they assumed he was dead.[29] For him – for all of the Milandes crew – capture, torture and death were only ever a whisper away, so what else was he to do but to seize the moment.

It would be wonderful to spend a carefree hour now, enjoying each other's company. But equally, they knew that today's visitor couldn't be ignored. As an Armistice Commission sting it was all so clumsy and ill-judged. While the young man had seemed so impassioned, his approach had been so amateurish. Who would ever believe that a man barely out of his teens had been entrusted with the Luftwaffe's secret code, which amounted to the Holy Grail in terms of intelligence? After all, being able to read the German Air Force's signals could have a decisive impact on the Battle of Britain and the blitz.

Who did he take them for? Even a child wouldn't try that. But then again, surely it was too far-fetched for the Armistice Commission to have chosen such an implausible set-up . . . so maybe that meant that it was all for real? The young man had seemed so sincere. Of course, double agents were forever striving to give that impression. It was their stock in trade. But it was the visitor's final words that caused them real pause for thought.

Father Dillard could not have misled me! Admit that you know him! You can't send me away like this . . .[30]

Well, who didn't know of Father Dillard?

Born in a château as one of seven children, Dillard had been decorated in the First World War. Hungering to be a man of the cloth, he'd gone on to train as a Jesuit, a Catholic religious order whose martial traditions were renowned, being known as 'God's soldiers', or 'God's Marines'. Long before the war, Father Dillard's revulsion at Nazism was clear to see. Widely travelled, he had dined with President Roosevelt in Washington and expounded on the virtues of American freedom and democracy.

He'd earned his priest's robes alongside Father Michel Riquet, a figure whose spirited opposition to the Nazis was whispered everywhere; in time, Father Riquet would help some 500 Allied airmen escape from France.[31] At the outbreak of war Father Dillard had become a hero once more, commanding an artillery battery during the bitter fighting in the Ardennes. There he had stood shoulder to shoulder with Riquet, until their guns fell silent, having fired their very last round. Taken prisoner, Father Dillard had remained undaunted, inspiring many with his talks in the POW camps.

Then there was Father Dillard the escapee, who had leapt from a train packed with POWs, even as it had steamed for Germany. Disguising himself as a French railway conductor – an officer of the Société Nationale des Chemins de Fer Français (SNCF) – he had slipped into the Free Zone. Finally, there was Father Dillard the Jesuit priest now based in Vichy, who preached openly to Pétain and his cohorts about the wrongs of Nazism and the evil it entailed.[32]

Sure, they knew of Dillard, but so too would a colonel of the Armistice Commission. By claiming such a connection, the young man's tale had apparent plausibility, but that didn't make it genuine. But the real question was this: should they have let him leave? Or should they at least have tried to get to the bottom of it all? The more they discussed it, the more Abtey – the seasoned operative – and Josephine – something of the upstart agent – became convinced that they had erred.

Whether the visitor was or was not an agent provocateur, surely they should have reported him, which is what any 'good' Frenchman was bound to do under the terms of the Armistice. On the face of it, that young man was trying to aid the British, the foremost enemy of Germany. By rights, Jacques Abtey and Josephine Baker were duty-bound to have had him arrested. In the unlikely event that the mystery visitor *was* genuine, what on earth was he doing running around the French countryside armed with such priceless intelligence? How could he possibly offer such documents to people he had never met, or had Josephine's reputation reached such levels that people would blindly entrust her with potentially war-winning intelligence? If so, was it any wonder that the colonel of the Armistice Commission had paid them that visit yesterday?

Either way, they had very likely made a mistake. The young man needed to be chased after and apprehended – at which stage he could either be handed over to the authorities, or quietly brought into the Resistance fold. As Josephine and Abtey were readying themselves to travel to London, via Lisbon, they could take the young man's documents with them, if they were genuine. In short, they needed to make hell-for-leather for the railway station, before he might disappear.

They would need one other companion if they were to stand any chance of success - M. Pierre Ruffel, the chief of police at Sarlat-la-Canéda, the nearest large town, and a secret friend of the Milandes Resistance crew. If the young man was an agent provocateur, M. Ruffel would be able to hand him over to the Germans, acting as if he were loyal to the Nazi cause. Conversely, if he proved to be genuine,

M. Ruffel would forget he'd ever laid eyes upon the fellow. Over the phone, Abtey begged the police chief to come. Shortly he arrived and declared himself in full agreement that they had to intercept the mystery visitor.

Without knowing the man's name, he was as good as gone if he managed to catch the evening train.

CHAPTER EIGHT

The Iron Resistance

The drive to the nearby train station was executed in M. Ruffel's police car, and at the double. They arrived, only to find no sign of their prey. He would very likely have to change trains at Siorac, M. Ruffel explained, and with luck they should be able to catch him there. They dashed back to the car.

'Go! For Siorac!' the police chief ordered his driver.

Upon reaching Siorac station they made a beeline for the platform, elbowing their way through the crowd. It was Abtey who spotted the mystery visitor, at about the same time as he spied them. He was standing at a rail-side bistro. Upon spying M. Ruffel in his gendarme's uniform, the young man turned and dashed inside the café, trying to get away.

They raced after him, yelling for him to stop. 'Police! You need to come with us! Police!'[1]

When finally they caught up with the young fugitive, they were struck by his contemptuous look. Presuming them to be collaborators who had reported on him, he gazed at them with an expression verging on pity . . . and without the slightest hint of fear. Clearly, he believed he had been betrayed and his reaction was one of undisguised scorn. Or maybe this was all because he knew he was untouchable. After all, this was just the way an agent of the enemy might be expected to behave.

They marched the young man to M. Ruffel's police car. There, they confiscated his case and overcoat.

'Get in the car,' M. Ruffel ordered.[2]

Sandwiched in the rear, the captive's interrogation began, as the police chief ordered his driver to make directly for his Sarlat headquarters.

'Now, give me your documents,' M. Ruffel demanded.

'Impossible,' the prisoner countered, with a distinct note of triumph. 'I do not have them any more.'

'Where are they?' the police chief demanded.

'Torn up and thrown away.'

'Where?' M. Ruffel barked.

'Near the château.'

'Driver – to the château!' M. Ruffel ordered.[3]

Tyres shrieking, the sleek black vehicle took to the twisting road that hugs the banks of the Dordogne, flitting through the shadows cast by the massive rock walls on either side. The scene was lit with the last rays of the setting sun, which burnished the sculpted limestone a reddish-gold. Abtey offered the fugitive a cigarette. He took it, settled back in his corner of the car, smoking quietly, and not offering the slightest hint as to who he was or why he had jettisoned his supposedly precious papers. The more Abtey got to see of the young man, the more he was starting to like him.

'What is your name?' he asked, breaking the silence.

'Le Besnerais,' the prisoner replied, curtly.

Abtey stared. Le Besnerais was not a particularly common French family name, but it was one that, by chance, he knew. 'Are you related to the head of the SNCF?' Abtey probed. It seemed unlikely, but he had to ask.

'He's my uncle,' the young man replied, simply.

What the hell? Abtey thought. No way was that man's nephew an agent provocateur.[4]

The Director General of the SNCF – France's state-owned railway company – was Robert Henri Le Besnerais, and both he and his deputy, Albert Jean-Marie Guerville, were key figures in the Resistance. They helped found the Cohors-Asturies Resistance network, part of the

108

Résistance-Fer – the 'Iron Resistance' – a group of mostly SNCF workers who would pioneer the secret war in France. Eventually, their network would girdle the length and breadth of the nation, spilling over into Belgium.[5] Guerville was codenamed 'P1' to those in the know and he would travel to Britain for training with de Gaulle's Free French. For much of the war he would be listed as being on a 'special SNCF assignment', as cover for his sabotage and espionage activities.[6] He would be hailed as a 'brilliant network chief', and there was no way that any individual associated with either of these people could be in league with a colonel of the Armistice Commission.[7]

Abtey studied the young man's features more closely. 'You know that you are risking a lot if you don't tell me the truth?'[8]

The prisoner reiterated his truthfulness, and Abtey was inclined to believe him. Either way, it was time to chance his arm. They had lied to him earlier, in the château, Abtey explained. For example, he was not an American performing artist, but an active officer with the security services, with the power to ensure that nothing bad would happen, as long as the young man told the absolute truth right now.

'I believe you!' the young man exclaimed, springing back to life. 'But I didn't tear up the documents or hide them near your castle. When I spied you at the station, I had an idea to get rid of them, so I slid them under the table in the bistro . . . You will find them there. But hurry, because they are very important!'

'Driver, to Siorac!' M. Ruffel yelled.[9]

If the drive so far had been hair-raising, that which now ensued would be heart-stopping, as they raced to secure the documents that young Le Besnerais had, in his disquiet, slid beneath the café table. After a dash around the station, the hidden case was retrieved. Though naïve in the extreme, like so many young men and women at the time, Le Besnerais had been ready to risk all in the cause of erasing the shame that had befallen France. The young man's courage – if not his street-sense – had them all in awe.

A close examination of his 'precious folder' mostly proved his claims, though the documents were not quite as he had described them. Rather than delineating the Luftwaffe's means for encoding their radio traffic, they comprised scores of transcripts of untranslated encrypted Luftwaffe signals. From a quick perusal, Abtey concluded they listed the locations of the main Luftwaffe airbases, and the formations, numbers and types of aircraft utilised. This constituted priceless intelligence for those fighting the Battle of Britain, but only in the right hands ... and that meant getting the documents to Britain.[10]

Le Besnerais also revealed how Father Dillard had come to direct him to Château des Milandes. The priest had been told by 'a reliable friend' that Josephine Baker was running a Resistance cell, with strong links to London.[11] While this was grossly overcooked – no link with SIS had been established, and they were a long way from doing so – it explained with shocking clarity why a colonel from the Armistice Commission had come calling. With loyalties in France proving shifting and treacherous, word of Josephine's supposed activities must have leaked to the enemy.

Le Besnerais stressed how time-sensitive was his mission. The documents had been secured by a high-ranking French military officer, posing as loyal to Vichy France and the Nazi powers, while in truth being all for London and de Gaulle. They needed to be copied and returned to that man's office, before their absence might be discovered. After a frenetic night spent copying them painstakingly by hand, a party set out from the château the following morning.

Their mission now was two-fold. First, they were speeding Le Besnerais back to Vichy, so he could return the papers from whence they had been borrowed. Second, and by coincidence, a telegram had just arrived from Paillole: 'Come to Vichy. Hotel George V.'[12] Presumably, Paillole's summons could mean only one thing: their planned Lisbon mission was imminent, and as far as they were concerned there was no better time to be getting away from the Château des Milandes.

Upon reaching Vichy, they found the pretty spa resort transformed into a hotbed of wartime intrigue. The boutique hotels had been press-ganged into accommodating a slew of Vichy government officials. With their influx had come all the associated foibles: casinos, gambling, prostitution. Regardless, the Milandes crew had urgent business to attend to. They had to return Le Besnerais and his papers to their source, but not before Abtey had managed to get the documents copied a little more professionally. And before meeting with Paillole, they had to check in with Father Dillard, in an effort to track down and silence his 'reliable friend'.

In recent weeks, Dillard had been bending Pétain's ear on the treatment of French prisoners-of-war – a fate he had narrowly avoided, by jumping from the POW train. Plagued by guilt, he feared he had abandoned his fellows to their doom.[13] But in his recent dealings with Pétain, Dillard had concluded that Vichy itself was little better than a POW camp. The 'Vichyites' had ensnared themselves in a pact with Nazism; a dark prison. Increasingly outspoken, he would earn praise from de Gaulle, whose radio broadcasts from London would hail the Jesuit priest who was a thorn in Vichy's side. But all of this drew him to the attention of the Gestapo, and eventually Dillard would be evicted from Vichy and face a dark end.[14]

Even in the autumn of 1940, any visitors to Father Dillard were bound to be watched. Upon meeting up, the Jesuit priest did his best to explain how he had come to recommend Château des Milandes so forcefully. 'Josephine Baker had set up an intelligence and recruitment service in her château,' he had been advised, 'for the benefit of the Intelligence Service and the Gaullist movement.' But Dillard was unwilling to reveal the source of the information. He was adamant that this was a man 'whose name I must not mention.'[15] As Abtey made clear, whoever that figure might be he had to be told that any further such talk could have catastrophic consequences.

There were several obvious candidates for Father Dillard's source. There was his close friend, father Michel Riquet, the Jesuit Resistance leader who would end up being sent to Dachau for his outspoken opposition to Nazism. Then there was Father Jacques Sommet, the man who had brought Dillard to Vichy, following his daring escape.[16]

Dillard himself would serve as an undercover Resistance activist with the Musée de L'Homme – Museum of Man – network.[17] Artfully christened after the Paris museum of that name, its very premises were used as cover for 'scholarly' meetings, which were in truth Resistance gatherings. They would help fugitives escape from France, circulate anti-Nazi propaganda and gather intelligence for the Allies.

With the likes of Father Dillard singing Josephine's praises, she was in fine company, but the dangers were legion, which made it all the more pressing that she and Abtey spirit themselves out of France. With that in mind, Paillole organised a dinner.[18] He was playing an ever more complex game of triple bluff now – officially serving as an officer of Vichy France, so working in partnership with his enemies, while secretly running his network of TR agents to spy upon those same adversaries. And on a deeper level he was using the likes of Big Louie to rub out anyone who seemed to be getting too close; whose activities simply could not be allowed to continue.

In part, the dinner was to thank Josephine for her standout role as an HC.[19] But it had a far more serious imperative behind it, of course. Paillole had made some hard and fast decisions. The plans concerning their mission to Portugal were now immutable, its vital importance for the war effort beyond contention. Right now, Paillole was about to entrust *all* of the intelligence gathered by the Deuxième Bureau, and that of his TR agents, to the two of them. On Abtey – but more on Josephine Baker – would ride Paillole and his team's entire hopes, not to mention the fortunes of France.

In Paillole's view, Abtey was the ideal person to entrust such a high-stakes mission, for he was blessed with having 'trustworthy friends in the [British] Intelligence Service'.[20] As for Josephine, she would furnish the perfect cloak. Her role was vital. The cover story was that the famous Josephine Baker was going on a showbiz tour, which would take her first to Lisbon. Crucially, any performer – any singer and dancer – of her standing would travel with voluminous luggage, which would be stuffed full of tour costumes, make-up and her musical scores – perfect for concealing secret intelligence.

On those copious score sheets, Paillole explained, Abtey would transcribe the most sensitive intelligence, using invisible ink. As it was Josephine's tour luggage, she would be squarely in the firing line should the subterfuge – the espionage – be discovered. The one other major challenge was timing. Lisbon was taking an age to issue visas, in part because of the flood of refugees trying to use Portugal as an escape route from occupied Europe. As Paillole stressed, their mission could brook no delay.

Typically, it was Josephine who volunteered a novel solution. 'I know the Brazilian ambassador very well,' she enthused. 'I'll tell him I'm planning a tour of his country. He'll be delighted. Once we have the Brazilian visas the rest will take care of itself.'[21]

She was right. In order to get to Brazil, she and her entourage would need to transit via Portugal, the departure point for liners steaming to South America. She could use her high-level contacts to secure the necessary travel permits, and as those for Lisbon would be transit visas only that should attract far less scrutiny or delay.

When first he'd heard suggestions about recruiting Josephine Baker as an HC, Paillole had been uncertain. He'd feared she would prove to be 'one of those shallow showbiz personalities who would shatter like glass if exposed to danger'. How far things had come since then. Still, this was some mission to entrust to Abtey and his voluntary partner in espionage. Equally, Paillole was keenly aware of how badly they needed to 're-establish ties with British intelligence'.[22] Making wireless contact was almost impossible. Only by human means could they achieve it.[23] Plus they needed a two-way flow – a secure means for Paillole and his ilk to send information to London, and for London to report back what was required, 'their wishes for common, joint action'.[24]

Secrecy was paramount. If the mission was unmasked, it could result in the Germans occupying all of France, with 'consequences you can well imagine', Paillole warned. It was 'absolutely necessary to succeed'. The SIS had to understand 'how sincere we are, and how serious is what we are doing'.[25] Across Europe, suspicion was rife.

Ally was turning against ally, friend becoming foe. So much hinged on this mission, if for no other reason than it would prove to the SIS that Paillole and his kind remained loyal, even while they apparently filled posts in the Vichy regime. Fighting the Nazis was one challenge, but so too was gaining the trust of one's supposed allies.

While some of the information could be transcribed in code and using secret ink, some of the documents were of such exceptional value they had to be carried exactly as they were. As just one example, Paillole produced a 'series of photographs of landing craft that the Germans are planning to use' in the invasion of Great Britain, which had been codenamed *Unternehmen Seelöwe* – Operation Sealion.[26]

In a sense, Paillole was the ideal handler for an agent like Josephine. He'd been educated at the Saint-Charles boarding school in Marseilles, where his 'classmates came from far and wide,' making him unusually cosmopolitan for the time. As Paillole writes, one of his closest friends was a boy from Madagascar who was black. 'We were very close,' Paillole would write of his 'protégé'. He admired how that 'brave' student had studied hard, while 'trying to adapt to our climate, our hectic life . . . our existence as Europeans'.

Paillole himself was no high-born individual. He'd never got to know his father, who had been killed in the First World War, after which his mother – 'a war widow with no fortune' – worked as a teacher to keep bread on the table. Regardless, he had been raised in the spirit of 'civility, honesty . . . moral vigour'.[27] Due to his humble roots, he'd often felt out of place at the elite Saint-Cyr academy. Only his prowess at fencing – he was a national champion – had evened things up a little. Paillole knew what it was like to feel out of kilter, and perhaps as a result he abhorred blind prejudice in all its forms.

Before his recruitment into the Deuxième Bureau, Paillole had been posted to North Africa with the 1st Algerian Rifle Regiment of French colonial troops. Serving as a lieutenant, he'd been assigned an orderly named Srir, a 'brave skirmisher, intelligent and kind'. The troops possessed 'exceptional physical stamina'. They'd march for 200 kilometres across the desert, in fifty-kilometre stages. One day

Paillole's feet had disintegrated. Upon spying their bloodied mess, Srir had declared: 'My poor lieutenant, what are we going to do?' He'd cleaned the wounds and dressed them with a 'miracle remedy' – a local antiseptic herb – and got Paillole back on his feet.[28]

'It was a hard school,' Paillole observed of his African posting, noting that his troops 'were used to walking. They went at a good pace, sometime barefoot. They sang as they marched.'[29] From them Paillole had learned discipline, toughness, brotherhood and an unbreakable *esprit de corps*. He would need it, for all that was coming.

In preparation for their Lisbon mission, Paillole handed Abtey a new passport, issued in the name of M. Jacques François Hébert, supposedly a former ballet master from Marseilles. Getting those fake papers had proven decidedly tricky – 'quite delicate' was how Paillole described it – but posing as Jacques Hébert, Josephine Baker's tour secretary, should furnish Abtey with the perfect disguise.[30]

'What about me?' Josephine ventured. Did she get a fake passport too?

'You are too famous, madame, to pretend to change your name,' Paillole demurred. 'And besides, you'll serve as cover for our friend here.'[31]

Abtey would need to age himself by eight years, for the new passport gave his date of birth as 16 September 1899. 'You know you have to be over forty to be able to leave France,' Paillole explained.[32] The restriction had been put in place by the Vichy regime, to prevent young men of fighting age leaving the country with the aim of joining the Allies. Abtey would age himself by sporting thick spectacles, and growing a bushy moustache of the sort the 'average cretin' might be seen wearing, as he would describe his new look.

Abtey seemed a natural at playing a part, Josephine would declare of her partner in espionage, whose ability to fuss around her, but to fade into the background when necessary, made him the ideal assistant for a touring superstar.[33]

The stakes could not have been higher for their coming mission. Both would need to be consummate actors if they were to make it through. Paillole declared that he had every confidence in them. He believed they made the perfect pairing. 'You look good together,' he remarked.[34] He offered Abtey a long embrace, before he turned to Josephine and gallantly kissed her hand.

'Bon voyage,' he called after them, trying to hide his emotions.[35]

They left on Paillole a striking impression – 'Josephine admirably self-possessed in the face of possible danger, Abtey intending to complete his mission no matter what the cost.' Of their Lisbon mission, and of the song that had been composed specially for Josephine, Paillole would remark that the fortunes of the Allies and of the Free French were 'written in part on the pages of "J'ai Deux Amours"'.[36]

Upon reaching Lisbon, Paillole had instructed Josephine and Abtey to make contact with the SIS at the British embassy, but somehow to do so without being noticed by the enemy.[37]

Specifically, they were to reach out to their former SIS comrade and long-time Paris spymaster, Wilfred 'Biffy' Dunderdale.

CHAPTER NINE

Stardom, Her Cloak And Her Dagger

That morning, an icy, cutting wind howled off the snow-clad peaks that reared to the south – the mighty Pyrenees Mountains, which straddle France's border with Spain. The two special agents waited, Abtey – or rather, Hébert as he was now known – huddled in his overcoat, while the famous Josephine Baker luxuriated in a 'magnificent fur coat like a bomb'.[1] Her tour luggage was heaped on the station platform: piles of trunks carrying the tools of her trade, plus the hidden, secret contents that might change the course of a war, that might help save an island nation which, under Winston Churchill, was holding out against all odds.

Come what may, Josephine had to play her part to perfection – glamour, glitz and stardom to the fore – even though the stark contrast to what was unfolding all around them was almost impossible to bear. They were at Pau, a French city lying some fifty kilometres short of the Spanish border and a major transit hub. A train had pulled in: battered, grey, wheezing steam from its rusting undercarriage like a tired and sickly beast. The human contents – freezing cold; crammed into inhuman conditions; crated worse than animals – spilled out onto the platform. They were refugees from Alsace-Lorraine, the region running along France's western border with Germany, an area claimed by both nations and fiercely fought over for centuries.

At the end of the First World War and the defeat of Germany, Alsace-Lorraine had been ceded to France. But in recent weeks Marshal Pétain had met Adolf Hitler, famously shaking hands,

Pétain confirming that France was 'entering the path of collaboration'.[2] Already, the Vichy regime was busy drafting anti-Jewish edicts, which would echo those spouted from Berlin. The first was issued on 3 October 1940, barring anyone 'of the Jewish race' from the civil service, the armed forces and many other key professions in France. Far worse was to follow.[3]

In London, Churchill had responded with an impassioned plea, imploring the French people to resist. 'Frenchmen! For more than thirty years in peace and war I have marched with you,' he began, mustering his best French. 'Tonight, I speak to you at your firesides, wherever you may be, or whatever your fortunes are: I repeat the prayer . . . "*Dieu protège La France*." Here at home in England, under the fire of the Boche, we do not forget the ties and links that unite us . . . Here in London, which Herr Hitler says he will reduce to ashes . . . we shall never stop, never weary, and never give in . . . We seek to beat the life and soul out of Hitler and Hitlerism . . .' He spoke of a glorious victory which, while still a long way off, was inevitable. 'For the morning will come. Brightly will it shine on the brave and true, kindly upon all who suffer for the cause, glorious upon the tomb of heroes. Thus will shine the dawn. *Vive la France!*'[4]

At Château des Milandes they had surrounded the wireless set, devouring those defiant words spoken by Britain's inimitable wartime leader, which had served to warm them amid the darkness. They marvelled at how Churchill could find such resolute, implacable hope, when all seemed lost. Of course, he was privy to a secret shared with precious few throughout the war: the Enigma secret.

The fact that Britain had acquired the technology and knowhow to read the Germans' most secret messages was dynamite. Since Dunderdale's Paris coup, the hunt for Enigma had intensified, as the enemy updated their technology and codes. It had drawn in Dunderdale's old friend, Ian Fleming, who served as a commander in Royal Naval intelligence. Fleming's father, Valentine, had been a close friend of Churchill, and through his position in Naval Intelligence Ian Fleming was ideally placed to pass the great man choice snippets of intelligence.[5]

In the summer of 1940, Fleming had alighted upon a daring – if incredible – plan, codenamed, appropriately, Operation Ruthless. It came about due to the capture of a Luftwaffe Heinkel He 111 twin-engine bomber, which had been forced to make an emergency landing. While the Paris Enigmas and codebooks secured by Dunderdale had enabled Bletchley to decode much of the German military's traffic, with the German Navy in particular the success was muted, largely due to the complexity of the *Kriegsmarine*'s encoding systems. Experts at Bletchley felt there was only one solution: to seize afresh the German Navy's codebooks and encryption machines.[6]

Cue Fleming and Operation Ruthless. Fleming proposed that a 'tough crew of five' should be assembled, all fluent German speakers, to be dressed in Luftwaffe uniforms and adorned with 'blood and bandages to suit'.[7] They should fly the captured Heinkel 111 – Werk No. 6853 – to midway across the Channel, ditch it and radio for a rescue. Once a German naval launch appeared, they were to 'shoot German crew, dump overboard, bring rescue boat back to English port'.[8] Fleming volunteered himself as one of the aircrew, but he was deemed to know too much.

That autumn, Fleming had taken his Operation Ruthless team to Dover, but conditions proved unsuitable, and the mission had been repeatedly postponed. Finally it was cancelled. The Bletchley hopefuls – waiting in tense expectation – had greeted the news 'like undertakers cheated of a nice corpse . . . all in a stew about the cancellation'.[9] Seven months later a German U-boat would be captured by the Royal Navy, complete with its priceless signals booty, ensuring that Bletchley would continue to have the edge.

The Enigma secret was known only to Churchill and a close circle of top military, intelligence and political figures. It offered them a spark of hope in their darkest hours. But regardless of their spirit of defiance, a victorious Germany was on the march. Across occupied Europe, Berlin was intent on seizing *Lebensraum*, and the deportations of the *Untermenschen* – the enemies of the Nazi state – were under way in earnest. The Nazi conquest had transformed millions of

Europeans into refugees, and as Berlin went about reclaiming – and 'sanitising' – Alsace-Lorraine, the dispossessed streamed into France.

Expelled from their homes by the Gestapo, those alighting at Pau station had been able to bring only what pitiful possessions they could bundle up and take with them. Ominously, 'there was not a single able-bodied man in their ranks,' Abtey observed.[10] The old, the sick, shivering children – they had been crammed onto cattle trucks for the interminable journey. Some still had straw embedded in their clothes. They gathered in long ranks, a 'sinister procession', their faces 'pale and undone', as the Vichy French authorities deliberated on the next stage of their terrible journey.[11]

For a moment, the two onlookers were struck by a scene as heart-breaking as it was tragic. An old man on unsteady legs, supported by two grey-robed nuns from the Daughters of Charity of St Vincent de Paul – a Catholic society dedicated to good works – tried to make his way into the line. Shrivelled, emaciated, what struck them most was that he wore a knee-length military capote – a hooded, woollen coat – very likely signifying that he was a French veteran of the First World War. Dangling on a string on his back was a chamber pot, while in his wake trailed a boy who could be no more than six years old, with his younger brother perched astride his shoulders.

Both children had their feet wrapped in sacking. Heartbreaking.

For Abtey, this was an especially poignant moment. He had rec-ognised the dialect that many were speaking, which was similar to that of his native Alsace tongue. Turning his face away, he felt himself choked by 'a dreadful anger'.[12]

'Come, Josephine,' he urged. 'Come quickly.'[13]

They were too conspicuous rooted to this rail platform, staring aghast at the suffering multitude. They needed to get on the move.[14]

They steamed south out of Pau station, the locomotive clinging to a track that snaked ever deeper into the mountains. Soon, they would hit their first international border, their first great test. With hordes of refugees and the hunted trying to flee war-ravaged France for Spain, a stepping stone on the road to freedom, this was one of the main crossing points, and it was bound to be intensively policed and watched.

Weeks earlier they had returned from Vichy to Château des Milandes, but right away things had felt different. How could they not be? They were no longer one crew united in the spirit of resistance. They had been given a very special mission, and Paillole had stressed the need for rigid secrecy. When they told the Milandes company that they had to go away, they could not, of course, explain why. Sadly, the secret of which they had become the custodians was a burden that they could not share.

Abtey had proposed a compromise of sorts. 'I know someone to whom we can entrust it without risk,' he'd suggested. 'Come with me.'[15]

He'd led Josephine towards the river, which was swollen after an autumnal storm had raged through the night. Although Abtey had pulled his kayak clear of the river, dragging it up into a neighbouring meadow, it was now drifting in the floodwaters. He waded in chest-deep, unhitched the mooring rope and turned the craft to face her.

'Sit in the bow,' he commanded.[16]

She did as instructed, and after a couple of strokes with the paddle he'd steered them out into the current and the kayak was tugged away and swept along. As the rush of the river filled their ears, blanketing the two of them from all possible watchers or listeners, Abtey began to mouth these fragments of verse.

> We are the Cadets of Gascony,
> Of Carbon, de Castel-Jaloux:
> Shameless swashbucklers and liars,
> Cuckolding all the jealous ones![17]

It was a somewhat bastardised rendition of the lines from the French playwright Edmond Rostand's *Cyrano de Bergerac*, which tells of the heroic defence put up by the Gascon Cadets – famed French knights – against the Spanish, and which is based upon the real-life story of the French nobleman after whom the play is named. In search of fortune, the Cadets of Gascony 'left for the battlefield with their swords at their sides and their courage as their standard . . . fearless and formidable soldiers wherever they went'. Cyrano de Bergerac was their standard-bearer, and the exploits of the Gascon Cadets had become legendary across France.[18]

In the knights' epic tale, Abtey took inspiration for what lay before him and agent Josephine right now. *Shameless swashbucklers and liars* they would have to be. In keeping with that swashbuckling spirit, there are accounts of Abtey training Josephine in the use of the pistol, the dagger, in martial arts and even to use a cyanide pill if in danger of being captured. But for what was coming, their future adventures were far more likely to be defined by the cloak, and far less by the dagger.[19]

'Who are you talking to?' Josephine cried, above the rush of the waters, once Abtey had finished reciting the verses.

'To my friend the river,' he yelled back. 'It is to her that I can say everything.'

From the Dordogne he had taken inspiration both in good times and in bad, he explained, learning to be both calm and courageous. Today, the grey and mud-hued current tore at the banks, swirling in violent, brown-foamed eddies. But then, seemingly miraculously, the sun broke through, the sky becoming blue and bright once more, the light washed clear by the rain, as if presenting a good omen for their coming journey.

Yet even as the two of them were readying their departure, a third unwanted visitor had arrived at the château's gates. Or rather, this one would creep into Milandes uninvited, to the very apex of the present intrigue. At the heart of the citadel, Josephine kept a private room in which she had fitted a safe. Its contents were both precious and sensitive, and even more so now. At well past midnight, Abtey awoke to a deafening crash from the direction of the garden. Leaning out of a window, he saw a light moving behind the shuttered glass of that holy-of-holies – the safe room.

Who could possibly have business in there in the depths of the night? Fearing the worst, Abtey hurried to wake Emmanuel Bayonne, fellow military man and a former Deuxième Bureau officer. Arriving at his bedroom, Abtey leant across Bayonne's prone form, pinching his nose to summon him from his slumber.

'Huh?' Bayonne exclaimed. 'What's the matter? What's the matter?'[20]

'Shhh . . . Bring your weapons,' Abtey whispered, 'and follow me.'[21]

Bayonne did as ordered, trying to shake the sleep from his head as they stumbled along the château's corridors. Barefoot, dressed only in their night clothes, they made not a sound as they approached the safe room. But upon reaching it, 'nothing disturbed the darkness or the silence.'

Wondering if he had dreamt it all, Abtey turned to Bayonne. 'I tell you, I saw a light . . .' he insisted. 'Someone is trying to break into Josephine's safe. We must wake her up.'[22]

It was *her* safe, after all, so she had to be warned. When alerted to the elusive intruder, Josephine leaned out of her bedroom window to check, and spied the mystery light glinting behind the shutters.

'Oh! Oh! Look! Look!' she gasped.

Without doubt the mystery intruder was back. With Josephine holding a candelabra, its faint light 'casting frightening shadows', they crept down the staircase 'in single file, mute, tense'.[23] In one hand Abtey grasped a grenade. He reached the entrance to the safe room, braced himself, before slamming the door open with brutal force, poised to roll the grenade inside. But the room appeared utterly dark. No one fired a gunshot. All was deathly quiet.

Abtey flicked on the light. The safe was there in the wall, seemingly unviolated. They proceeded to search the room from end to end – inside the wardrobe, under the bed, but nothing. They stared at each other in bafflement. Had they been seeing ghosts? Then, as if in answer, the bedside lamp seemed to flicker into life all of its own accord. A quick check, and there appeared to be a dodgy connection. A wiggle of the wires, and moments later the lamp had extinguished itself again.

Josephine started to giggle, and soon all three of them were sniggering. 'You'll wake everyone up,' she scolded, but her eyes were laughing.

'What about the noise that woke me?' Abtey demanded. Surely, that had been no dream.[24]

They headed outside to investigate. There they discovered a large flowerpot shattered into pieces. That would account for the crash. Could it be the work of some animal, prowling around in the dark? Would that, and a faulty electrical connection, explain away the entire incident? Either way, it was distinctly unsettling. It had underscored the need to get everything squared away and to get going on their journey.

The experience of that ghostly intrusion had been especially disquieting for Josephine. Tales of cemeteries and death had seemed to obsess her family and the wider community, when she was growing up in St Louis.[25] Likewise, Château des Milandes was steeped in a centuries-old history of warfare, skulduggery and murder, much of which was etched into its very stones. Of ghosts Josephine would write that these were the spirits of those who, though dead, were not yet finished with life, for there was still something vital to be done. She was drawn to the darkness and to shadows, yet at the same time she was frightened by it all.[26]

Josephine remained unsettled by the Château's mystery visitor. So were the rest of her Milandes crew. Had there even been anyone there? If so, what had he – or she – been after? Had they stolen away any precious secrets? What had they discovered? If only they could be certain, but there were no easy answers.

Either way, it had underscored the need to hurry. But in the world of espionage some procedures simply couldn't be rushed. Transcribing messages and documents to render them virtually invisible was a tried and tested tool of the spy's trade. The Abwehr had sent the arch-traitor, Aubert, instructions disguised as full-stops – microdots – but a careful examination could reveal their presence.[27] The use of 'invisible ink' was a further level of subterfuge, and a plethora of different types had been experimented with over the years.

The hunt for the 'perfect' invisible ink and the means to deploy it was never-ending. The Abwehr had experimented with women's underwear 'impregnated with ... chemicals from which the secret ink could later be reconstituted'. After all, what self-respecting agent would think to search a lady's underclothes? The SIS had gone several steps further, seeking an invisible ink that came from 'a natural source of supply'. They'd concluded that 'the best invisible ink is semen', which didn't seem to react to the main methods of detection. However, SIS had decided that the discovery had made life somewhat 'intolerable', for its agents, due to persistent 'accusations of masturbation'.[28]

As any Deuxième Bureau agent should, Abtey had long mastered the craft of invisible writing. Faced with the fraught and perilous journey that lay ahead, he had embarked upon his transcriptions with the greatest care. The sheer quality and quantity of the intelligence that Paillole had entrusted to them called for rigorous accuracy and attention to detail.

In addition to the *Unternehmen Seelöwe* invasion craft photographs, there were breakdowns of the Wehrmacht divisions massing in the north of France, including details of the armour with which they were equipped. There was a list of the known Abwehr agents who had been dispatched to Britain on espionage missions. There were details of key Luftwaffe airbases across France; material to corroborate Le Besnerais' haul of signals-intercept documents. And there was a breakdown of the elite airborne units – *Fallschirmjäger*; paratroopers – gathering on France's northern coast.[29]

As if that were not enough, there were copies of the plans drawn up by Berlin for the seizure of Gibraltar, the fortress-outpost at the gateway to the Mediterranean. Along the western coast of France, invasion craft were being readied and forces placed on standby, awaiting orders to set forth and lay siege to the Rock. If it fell, it would gift the Axis control of the Mediterranean, from Italy in the east to Gibraltar in the west. Heavy guns sited at the southernmost tip of the Rock could menace the Strait of Gibraltar, which was only 13 kilometres wide at its narrowest, closing it to Allied shipping. If Gibraltar were taken, it would be a calamity for Great Britain, a death knell.[30]

Paillole's dossier revealed how the Abwehr's Brandenburg regiment – its elite paramilitary commandos – were undergoing training in mountain warfare, readying themselves as 'shock-troops for an attack on fortress Gibraltar'.[31] Paillole's TR agents had picked up reports of German troops massing in the Pyrenees region, while General Franco had reportedly mobilised 100,000 Spanish troops. If, as Paillole feared, the Führer was now intent on taking the Rock, and drawing Spain in as a partner in that enterprise, the British needed to be furnished with warnings as quickly as possible.

Then there were the perfidious – but all too feasible – plans drawn up by the Abwehr to use the Republic of Ireland as the back door by which to invade Britain. In this truly global conflict the Dominions – Britain's colonies – had joined forces in declaring war. Canada, Australia, New Zealand, South Africa, the Indian Raj and Burma, plus fifty-odd other dependencies, protectorates, mandates and the like, had rallied to the cause, including distant Guyana and, much closer to home, Gibraltar. Only Eire, a self-governing dominion within the Commonwealth, had opted for neutrality.[32] As Paillole's intel dossier revealed, Britain's fears – expressed as early as September 1939 – that Ireland was ripe for a Nazi-backed insurrection, were all too real.[33]

Even before war's outbreak, the Abwehr had identified Ireland as Britain's Achilles heel. By January 1939 Abwehr agents had travelled to Ireland and Irish nationals to Germany, to train and arm themselves for clandestine warfare.[34] In Berlin, Dr Kurt P. Haller, the Abwehr agent in charge of Irish operations, recruited Irishwoman and actress Phyllis James, an ardent supporter of Hitler.[35] Abandoned as a young child, James had been fostered by an aristocratic English family, and she claimed to know her way around high society. She agreed to lead an Abwehr search squad once Britain was conquered, to guide them to Winston Churchill's home.[36]

In February 1940 the first German U-boat had dropped Abwehr

agents onto Irish shores; parachutists would soon follow. Then, the chief of the Irish Republican Army (IRA), Seán Russell, was recruited to the cause. In May, Russell was invited to Berlin, where he was wined and dined at the highest level of the Nazi party, before being dispatched for training in guerrilla warfare.[37] At a camp located in the Brandenburg region, in north-east Germany, the Abwehr ran a special school teaching the dark arts of clandestine warfare, including how to make high explosives from everyday household items.[38]

Russell was far from being alone: the Abwehr had raised files on 1,600 Irishmen and women whom they felt had potential.[39] At POW camps across Germany, they were screening Irish nationals, seeking further recruits. That July, *Unternehmen Seehund* – Operation Seal – had been launched, landing three more Abwehr agents in Ireland.[40] As Paillole's dossier revealed, 'Russell, the head of the Irish Republican Army', was slated to be 'dropped by submarine on the south-west coast of Ireland'.[41]

Russell had agreed to embark upon Operation Taube (Dove) – named after the iconic-looking Etrich Taube, the first ever mass-produced German fighter aircraft – seeking to foment revolt in the Emerald Isle. In fact, the Abwehr's plans for their Irish agents were three-fold: Russell and fellow recruits were to provoke unrest across Ireland, pending German landings; to launch uprisings in Northern Ireland, and to recruit Irish agents for sabotage and spying missions in Britain and the USA.[42]

If Operation Taube proved successful, Russell and his comrades had been promised top positions in a German-occupied Ireland.[43] In readiness for the Irish landings, Berlin had ordered 15,000 maps, 'copies of British General Staff Maps of Ireland'.[44] In fact, by the time Paillole's dossier had been assembled, Russell had embarked upon a German U-boat, but he would die on the journey while still a hundred miles short of the Irish coast. That would lead to Operation Taube II being developed, as others stepped forward to take Russell's place.

Irish agents were to communicate in coded messages using agony columns in the *Daily Herald* newspaper, and to identify fellow agents by whistling the tune of 'London Bridge is Falling Down'. As SIS concluded, the Abwehr were engaged upon a bold Irish gamble, conceived by a team who showed 'ability and imagination'. Those in Berlin orchestrating Irish affairs were 'men who had taken the trouble to think in terms of Irish – not German – affairs and traditions'.[45] Their chief, Dr Kurt Haller, was identified by British intelligence luminary Guy Liddell as being an enemy agent 'of [the] highest possible interest'. Haller was also responsible for Irish Republican sabotage and spying operations in the USA, cleverly seeking to exploit the large Irish-American community there.[46]

Working on the basis that 'the enemy of my enemy is my friend', the Abwehr had also recruited Welsh and Scottish nationalists. These 'British minorities', as the Abwehr characterised them, were trained in Germany for 'sabotage purposes'.[47] As Paillole's dossier warned, they were preparing to 'land on the Welsh coast west of Swansea', charged to 'take over the Welsh nationalist movement and Scottish separatist groups'.[48] Oxwich Bay, a remote sandy cove lying on the southern tip of the Gower Peninsula, had been identified as a landing point for explosives, to enable Welsh agents to wreak havoc across Britain.[49]

Perhaps of greatest concern was the Abwehr's *Unternehmen Walfisch* – Operation Whale – its plans to use Irish and Welsh nationals as 'pathfinders', helping to steer the German invasion fleet onto Britain's shores.[50] Those Welsh and Irish operations were linked to an ultra-shadowy Berlin agency known as the Jahnke Bureau. Formed in 1923, shortly after the founding of the Nazi party, the Jahnke Bureau had long been on the radar of the SIS. Named after its founder, a mysterious powerbroker named Kurt Jahnke, it was housed at a private address, Sedanstrasse 26, Berlin, and it acted 'with complete independence of any outside control'.[51]

While SIS had nailed the Jahnke Bureau as being an 'extremely high level political intelligence Bureau ... with sources in the UK, Belgium, Holland, France, Russia and further afield', frustratingly, Janke himself remained a figure of mystery, 'sedulously avoiding the limelight'.[52] Jahnke had reportedly served in the US armed forces during the First World War, before his conversion to the Nazi cause. He was said to be close to Rudolf Hess, Deputy-Führer to Adolf Hitler, and his power was such that he had been responsible for getting Admiral Canaris appointed as chief of the Abwehr.[53]

The Jahnke Bureau boasted high-level contacts among foreign politicians, civil servants and disaffected groups, including Welsh and Irish nationalists. Dangerous, dark and powerful, its aim was to raise pro-German fascist organisations, and its signature lay on the Abwehr's operations across Ireland, Wales and Scotland. It was a secret agency within a secret state, which aimed to spread the Nazi credo like a cancer targeting mostly Great Britain and the USA.

Such, then, was the breadth and scope of the intelligence that Paul Paillole had entrusted to Jacques Abtey and agent Josephine. Such were the details transcribed in invisible ink on the scores of 'J'ai Deux Amours'. Or, in the most extreme cases, carried as unadulterated, original documentation and photographs secreted deep in Josephine's tour luggage. It was a truly explosive – and damning – trove, were it to be discovered.

The train from Pau had pulled out of the station at eight a.m., leaving behind those desperate families to a dark and uncertain fate. Climbing ever higher into the Pyrenees, it wheezed along a series of dramatic knife-cut gorges, squealed and clanked across iron-girdered bridges, before being swallowed into a succession of tunnels which sliced through the very bowels of the mountains. Each shriek and jolt of iron wheels on iron track brought the carriages closer to the checkpoint, at Canfranc, just on the Spanish side of the border.

As never before, this would call for nerves of steel.

For Josephine, her head was triply on the block if she were caught. In the process of securing the Lisbon visas for her and Abtey, she'd opted to have stamped in his passport – the fake passport, rendered in Jacques Hébert's name – the following words: 'Accompanying Mrs Josephine Baker.' It provided an additional layer of seeming legitimacy to their cover story, but it meant that there was no way in which she could deny knowing her accomplice, if he were unmasked.

She had 'undertaken, of her own volition, to cover me to the very end', Abtey would remark, 'closing the door behind her and binding her fate to mine. I call that courage.'[54]

The train pulled into Canfranc, or more accurately Canfranc Estación, to give it its full name. In many ways, this remote outpost in its rocky, snowbound fastness was a wholly artificial construct: a settlement hacked out of the mountainside where none had previously existed, and solely to play host to the massive railway terminus that had been raised here. Just a dozen years old in 1940 – the line from Pau to Canfranc had only been opened in 1928 – all trains were forced to a halt, for the French and Spanish used different gauges of railway line.

There would be rumours of Nazi gold being run through Canfranc Estación. Certainly, it would be used as a wartime 'rat-run' by British intelligence, to get escapees and intelligence spirited from France into Spain and from there onwards to London. But right now it was about to play host to the world's most famous black female performer and her tour entourage. On one level, Josephine was fortunate in that she had visited Spain before, touring the nation in 1930 and falling in love with its people, its rich history and stunning landscapes. If she could conjure up that same magic now – forging that same connection – she could use it to mask the true nature of her present mission.

She stepped down from the train carriage, resplendent in her furs: apparently, not a trace of nerves; every inch a superstar. Abtey seemed happy to play the role of the grey man, lurking in her shadow, as she swept along the platform, giving directions for the unloading and reloading of her luggage. The effect was electrifying. French and Spanish policemen and customs officers stopped dead. Even the plain-clothes German agents seemed confounded. Railway workers gasped in star-struck amazement, before dashing to call wives and daughters. They crowded around Josephine, desperate to see, to feel, to touch; to bask in the radiance of that famous smile.

Laughing, chatting, everywhere flashing a welcome, she breezed her way through the border checks, charming all-comers. The awe-struck officials didn't seem inclined to trouble Josephine with a second glance at her mountain of luggage, less still at the unremarkable individual – this Jacques Hébert, tour manager – who hovered at her side.

At one moment, she turned to him, and whispered, teasingly: 'You see what a good cover I am?'[55]

As any good tour secretary should, Abtey did his best to keep a proper distance, adopting a 'shabby air', in sharp contrast to that of his 'elegant companion'. But even that proved quite unnecessary. When in the superstar Josephine Baker's company, 'no one would pay me the slightest attention,' Abtey was the first to acknowledge.[56] Even in the midst of a world war, the star-struck power of celebrity endured.

They slipped through that first checkpoint apparently unscathed, but neither was about to kid themselves that they were in the clear. On many levels, Spain was as hostile to their mission as was Vichy France. The Wehrmacht was intimately familiar with this country; their forces had soldiered here – killed here – very recently.

For three years the Spanish Civil War had ripped apart this nation, Germany sending 19,000 troops to shore up the fortunes of General Franco's Nationalists.[57] Forming the Condor Legion, it was in Spain that they had first proved the terrifying impact and power of blitzkrieg, the bombing of the town of Guernica being its bloodiest and most lasting legacy. The conflict had left Spain 'brutalised and impoverished', with half a million dead and hundreds of thousands imprisoned or forced into exile. With the outbreak of the Second World War, few doubted where Franco's true allegiances lay. He owed Nazi Germany and Hitler, and as everyone knew Spain was crawling with German agents, secret police and spies.[58]

It was late in the day by the time the border checks were complete and the train pulled out of Canfranc Estación, heading south towards the Spanish capital, Madrid, some five hundred kilometres distant. Josephine had bought tickets on the overnight express, and she and

Abtey were determined to keep a low profile; maybe even grab a little sleep. Apart from Abtey sneaking the odd cigarette break in the corridor, they dozed in their cabin, one eye on their precious luggage, doors firmly closed to the outside world.

Upon reaching the Spanish capital, they inquired about the Madrid–Lisbon Rapido, the fast train linking the two capitals. It was booked solid for several days. By chance, they decided to check with Iberia Airways, Spain's national carrier, which ran direct flights to Lisbon. Were there possibly any seats? By luck, two tickets had just been cancelled on an Iberia Airways Douglas DC3, the ubiquitous twin-engine airliner that would also see widespread war service, recast as the Douglas C47 Skytrain.

'You're in luck,' the Iberian desk attendant told them. 'It leaves in two hours.'

'Two hours? That's a bit quick.'

He shrugged. 'You can have those. Otherwise, there's nothing for another eight days.'[59]

Whether they flew or took the train, there would be checks along the way. On many levels, air passage might prove safer. On the train, there could well be interminable stops and checkpoints. By contrast, no one was about to halt a DC3 as it sped through the skies. With their precious luggage in tow, they dived into a taxi, ordering the driver to make haste to Barajas Airport. But as they pulled up at their destination, they began to regret their spur of the moment decision.

Out on the grass apron they counted a dozen aircraft, each adorned with the unmistakable symbol of a Nazi swastika etched in black on the tailplane. Around those flying machines swarmed mechanics in thick denim overalls, while groups of men in dark trench coats milled about, smoking, and everywhere keeping a watchful eye. 'The Spanish airfield could just as easily have been a German base,' Abtey noted, darkly.[60]

As Josephine breezed into the airport building, the sea of humanity seemed momentarily to part before her, before the crowds came rushing back in again. She moved through them 'with the casualness of a star among her girls'.[61] But finally, three figures with dark caps – airport immigration officials – stepped forward to bar their way. This time, the scrutiny seemed altogether more rigorous. Passports were studied closely, as the officials kept checking their names against a list they had close at hand. As the seconds ticked by, Abtey began to wonder if by any devilish chance his new identity had been blown. Though his passport gave his year of birth as 1899, Jacques Hébert, tour manager, was in truth but a few weeks old. Surely, M. Hébert could not already have made it onto the *Fahndungsbuch*, the Gestapo register of wanted persons?

But with Josephine, it was quite different. She'd been Josephine Baker since the mid-1920s, after her marriage to Willie Baker, and that was the name by which she was universally known. If her true role had been discovered – her service as an Honourable Correspondent – she was done for. In fact, *they* were done for – as Abtey was inextricably linked to her, not to mention the secret contents of her tour trunks. All it would have taken was for one file to have fallen into the Gestapo's hands, or for one captive to have talked . . . At any moment they were half expecting to hear the demand to open their luggage. Finally, the three officials glanced up . . . smiling. Were these knowing smiles? Predatory ones? It seemed not. The passports were handed back and the travellers were waved through.

Their flight was called. The two special agents – fugitives – stepped towards the waiting DC3, as the figures in dark trench coats ranged around the apron turned, stood and stared. They made it inside without being challenged, the precious luggage was loaded aboard, and the DC3's starter-motors whined. Moments later the propellers were spinning up to speed. Shortly, the airliner trundled across the rough grass, turned onto the runway, nose into the breeze and clawed its way into the skies.

No sooner were they airborne, than a fighter aircraft rolled into position, close by the DC3's fuselage. What did this airborne intruder intend, Josephine wondered, as she nosed deeper into her furs. Was it an escort? A guardian angel? Or a predator? No way of telling.

For a good forty kilometres the warplane kept pace with the DC3, putting Abtey's nerves on edge. As for agent Josephine, she'd snuggled deep and was soon dead to the world; exhausted and utterly drained by day after day of highwire subterfuge. A dry 'lunar landscape' unrolled before Abtey's eyes, as the airliner pushed west. After a short while the fighter pilot accelerated past the DC3, executed a dramatic roll and disappeared from view.

They were on their own at last, their precious luggage safely stowed in the hold, and speeding through the burning blue.

Left: Josephine Baker – 'The most sensational woman anybody ever saw. Or ever will' according to Ernest Hemingway – pictured in 1940, at the height of the so-called Phoney War.

Below: Recruited as an 'Honourable Correspondent' – a voluntary secret agent – for the French intelligence services prior to the war, she used the cover of her celebrity to rub shoulders with those in the know, securing vital intelligence for the French, and for the British Secret Intelligence Service (SIS, also known as MI6).

At the time women were frowned upon in secret intelligence circles, and especially high-profile celebrities like Josephine Baker. Commander Paul Paillole (*left, above*) and Captain Jacques Abtey (*right, above*), her French recruiters, feared that Josephine was one of 'those shallow showbiz personalities who would shatter like glass if exposed to danger.'

Above: Josephine proved to be a born-natural at the spying game. Using her voluminous tour luggage and her musical score sheets daubed with invisible ink, she smuggled vital intelligence to London (sometimes even secreted in her underwear). It included details of Operation Sealion, the planned German invasion of Britain, of key Luftwaffe air bases, and of the spies recruited by Nazi Germany to be sent to Britain on sabotage missions.

Despite her superstar status, there was a down-to-earth, hands-on side to Josephine – here seen watering her garden in 1937 – which made her an ideal special agent when the going got tough.

As the world prepared for war, Josephine teamed up with showbiz star Maurice Chevalier (*on stage*), to perform a special show, entitled *Paris-London*, to boost the morale of French and British troops. Even so, France and most of western Europe was set to fall.

Above: Adolf Hitler and his entourage at the Eiffel Tower, in Paris, following the lightning seizure of France by German forces. Josephine had retreated to her Dordogne château shortly before the city fell, intent on finding a way to strike back.

Left: A Nazi propaganda poster issued by the SS and entitled 'Der Untermensch' – the subhuman. Josephine found herself the target of such attacks orchestrated by Joseph Goebbels, Germany's *Reichsminister* of Propaganda. It only served to stiffen her spirit of resistance.

Above: Suffering defeat on all fronts, Britain's wartime leader, Winston Churchill, vowed to fight on. He was joined in London by General Charles de Gaulle, leader of the Free French forces. As both knew, crucial to any fight-back would be accurate and timely intelligence.

Above and right: Commander Wilfred 'Biffy' Dunderdale, a close friend of Ian Fleming and reputedly the role model for James Bond, was ordered by Churchill to get intelligence flowing from France. Pictured are some of his many wartime identity cards and memorabilia. A daring spymaster of the Secret Intelligence Service, Dunderdale urged Josephine, plus her French intelligence partner, Jacques Abtey, to re-establish an espionage network across France. Their partnership, though not without its dramas, would prove ground-breaking.

Left: Christened Josephine Freda Macdonald at birth, Josephine had been born into poverty in the city of St Louis, in the USA. From her earliest years she saw her natural-born skill as a dancer and singer as her ticket to a new life. At age nineteen she emigrated to France, taking Paris and all of Europe by storm. By her early twenties she was one of the most high-profile and photographed women in the world; a global superstar.

Right: The icon: Josephine Baker, singer, dancer and movie star, being offered a bouquet of flowers by her pet cheetah, Chiquita, in a promotional poster for her 1930 debut at the exclusive Casino de Paris.

Josephine in a similar, real-life pose. She nurtured a life-long love of animals and her exotic stage menagerie became a signature of her stage shows, later providing the perfect cover for her most daring espionage missions.

A woman of action, Josephine had earned a pilot's license and flew clandestine mercy and spying missions in her light aircraft, at the risk of being shot down. But all of that came to a sudden end when the forces of Nazi Germany invaded France.

Left: In the summer of 1940, Josephine mustered her resistance crew at the Château des Milandes, in the Dordogne, secreting a clandestine radio set in one of the towers and grenades and guns in the cellars. Refugees, former soldiers and disaffected intelligence agents – all were drawn to her, as word of her resistance spread. But so too were the enemy.

Albert Guerville – here shown in a page from his wartime file – founded the *Résistance-Fer* (Iron Resistance) network, recruiting French railway workers. Hailed as a 'Brilliant network chief', Guerville and others would make common cause with Josephine in the autumn of 1940.

Jesuit priest, war hero and outspoken anti-Nazi, Father Victor Dillard would endeavour to get the first wartime intelligence dossier into Josephine's hands. For his efforts to combat the rise of the Third Reich, Father Dillard would be murdered at Dachau concentration camp.

CHAPTER TEN

The Black Angel

In Portugal, Josephine finally felt able to breathe again. The sun was shining. There were smiles on many of the faces. Lisbon seemed a world away from the grim realities of the war.[1] She had breezed through Lisbon's Portela Airport, with Hébert – Abtey – and the luggage in tow, after which she'd made a beeline for the Hotel Aviz, one of the city's finest. Due to the mass influx of refugees, Lisbon's hostelries were crammed, but no one was about to turn away Madame Baker, and for all the obvious reasons. Abtey found a room a short stroll away, at the Avenida. Nowhere near as exclusive as the Aviz, but then again, he *was* the grey man.

The Aviz lay just off the Avenida da Liberdade, Lisbon's equivalent of the Champs-Élysées in Paris or The Strand in London. A kilometre and a half long, the grand, sweeping avenue hosted two theatres, four cinemas and some of the city's finest hotels. The Aviz vied with the Tivoli to be the best, and according to British-Armenian businessman Calouste Gulbenkian, reputedly then the richest man in the world, the Aviz had the edge. The man known as 'Mr Five Percent' due to the oil deals he'd brokered across the Middle East, Gulbenkian would make the Aviz his home for the duration of the war, running his business from his suite, with his secretary and valet close at hand.[2]

With outbreak of war, Lisbon had truly become the espionage capital of the world. It was awash with impoverished refugees, affluent Jewish families in flight from the Nazis, European aristocrats and the continent's wealthy seeking to escape wartime privations, plus assorted smugglers, forgers, pirates and adventurers. It was a city of bruising contrasts: of vile, bloated wealth and obscene poverty; of wild partying and brutal suffering; of sex and death; of the world's glitziest casinos overlooking a sun-kissed coastline, and of despairing families fighting to board overcrowded ships bound for anywhere but war-ravaged Europe, and seemingly at any price. For the truly desperate, life hung in the balance and everything and anything was for sale.[3]

At every corner, all of the dark and the light shades of life seemed to collide, cheek-by-jowl, chaotic and jarring. And everywhere, there were the secret police and the spies of all nations, watching, noting, following. The press were there too, nosing around, asking questions, seeking stories. The Aviz was a favourite haunt of reporters, and the instant that Josephine Baker's arrival was known she became the story of the moment. What was she doing in Lisbon, the journalists demanded? Was she staying long? What had brought her there, in the midst of war?

'I come to dance, to sing,' she told them, simply. 'I am stopping in Lisbon, before going to Rio, where I have further engagements.' In other words, there's no story here. Move on.[4]

Of course, there were those among the Lisbon press pack who knew of her anti-Nazi sentiments and the questions came thick and fast. The last thing that she and Abtey needed right now was to attract any hostile attention, especially as there were Axis agents thronging the city. After all, her room at the Aviz, and Abtey's at the Avenida, were piled high with her tour luggage along with its top-secret contents. It was vital that they remained above suspicion and everything undetected.

But for matters of the heart and the soul, Josephine was not about to lie. 'Yes,' she admitted, her face a shroud of wistful smiles, 'yes, I have sung for the soldiers at the front. Yes, I saw many sad things. No, I have not returned to Paris since the defeat. No, I don't like the Germans.'[5] The Germans who had invaded her country and others, at least. The next day her photo, plus the story of her arrival at the

Aviz and her sentiments, was headline news. Josephine cursed the journalists who had broken the story of her arrival in Lisbon and possibly also her cover.[6]

But sometimes in life and in espionage, you have to make a virtue out of necessity. Surely, there was an upside to all the media interest. Surely, they could put the press to work, for the good of their mission. Surely, they could use it to boost their cover. If Josephine the superstar kept spinning different versions of the same story – Lisbon was the springboard for a grand Brazilian tour, first-stop sunny Rio – it would bolster their cover. It would leave her tour manager, Abtey – Hébert – free to quarter Lisbon to his heart's content. Indeed, he could do so laden with her tour trunks, claiming the need to make eleventh-hour alterations to Josephine's outfits. It made perfect sense, especially when handling such a superstar client, with whom there always tended to be a slew of last-minute tour demands. In fact, Josephine had been famous – some would say notorious – across Paris theatre-land for her repeated changes of plan, for her terrible time-keeping, for her unpredictability and, as some would claim, her volcanic temper (especially when things didn't go as she intended).

Of course, the Lisbon press coverage led to the usual round of invitations. There was one from the Belgian embassy, for a glitzy gathering (Belgium, though 'neutral', was under German occupation). Another came from the French representative in Lisbon – Vichy in name, but not necessarily in nature. Somewhat inconveniently, there was an invite from the British embassy to grace the British diplomatic mission with her presence.[7] It was an obvious call. She was a spirited opponent of the Nazi regime. But of course, accepting such an invitation right now could prove problematic.

Josephine was supposed to keep well away from anything to do with the handover of the Paillole dossier. Abtey – Hébert – was to deal with all of that, in the hope that he might slip through – the grey man unnoticed. Those diplomats at the British embassy who had issued the invitation to Josephine could be forgiven for not knowing any better. Her role in Paillole's dossier was only ever to be known to the chosen few. She was best off hunkering down at the Aviz, teasing out the press, keeping a close eye on her tour baggage, while she let Abtey hit the streets and make the running.

But even at the Aviz she would be watched. Lisbon's hotels mirrored the great game of espionage playing out right across the city. The Allied and Axis powers looked upon certain hostelries as being 'their turf'. The aptly named Hotel Inglaterra was a known haunt of the British, while the Hotel Atlantico was favoured by the Germans. The guest books reflected this, but by no means exclusively. Taking breakfast with the enemy seated at the next-door table was an all-too-common occurrence. Often, hotel bars were graced by German spies rubbing shoulder with British agents, plus a swell of refugees from across the nations of Europe. 'It was a classic case of watching you, watching us,' historian Neill Lochery wrote of Second World War-era Lisbon.[8]

Invariably, the hotel staff were on the books of one intelligence outfit or another, and often all of them. Keeping watch over everyone – noting the 'rumour, counter-rumour and fantasy' – were the ubiquitous Polícia de Vigilância e Defesa do Estado (PVDE), the Portuguese secret police.[9] An impoverished nation desperate to stay neutral, Portugal was torn. A long-standing British ally, the country was ruled by a dictator with a distinctly fascist bent. At war's outbreak, António de Oliveira Salazar had reaffirmed the 550-year-old Anglo-Portuguese Alliance, but at the same time he was a firm supporter of General Franco of Spain. As his loyalties were split, so was the nation, and the PVDE were charged to keep a lid on everything, to prevent war from reaching these shores.

There was one driving reason why Portugal might be dragged into the conflict, whether it liked it or not: wolfram (tungsten). Mined in the centre and north-east of the country, the mineral was in scarce supply across Europe and in huge demand. Since the outbreak of war its price had spiralled. The reasons were simple. One of the hardest and heaviest metals known, wolfram is used to toughen armour, to tip armour-piercing shells and to make ball-bearings, among many other uses in the armaments industry. Germany was desperate for wolfram, and the fight to secure Portugal's supplies would become known as the 'wolfram wars'.[10]

Portugal was the world's largest exporter of wolfram, for which Lisbon would only accept payment in gold. War tends to destroy the value of paper money and to do the reverse to precious metals. The forces of Germany were even then looting the conquered nations of Europe, and staggering amounts of plundered gold would be dispatched to Portugal. At the start of the war, the nation possessed 63.4 tonnes of gold reserves; by its end, that figure had swollen to 365.5 tonnes, the vast majority of which had originated in payments from Berlin for wolfram.[11]

As Britain was well aware, most of that gold was stolen. As the wolfram wars heated-up, SIS quietly boosted its presence in Portugal, while London raised merry hell with Lisbon. Berlin's answer was smuggling. At its most basic, gold was strapped onto pack donkeys and trekked into Portugal along remote mountain trails. Brown paper bags stuffed with cash were passed to Portuguese guides – past-masters in the clandestine trade. At its most sophisticated, gold was packed aboard German 'ghost trains' that ran from France, through Spain and into Portugal – often taking the same route that Josephine and Abtey had used – but which appeared on no rail timetable or schedule.[12]

Among all of this intrigue, smuggling and racketeering, one figure in Lisbon had felt absolutely at home: knife-bladed face, steel-grey eyes, Hans Müssig. Two weeks after he and Abtey had parted company in France, the latter had received a postcard at the Château des Milandes. It had read simply: 'Come, everything is fine – there's good sunshine here.' Of course that phrase 'good sunshine' was the codeword they had agreed between them, if Müssig's Lisbon mission had gone well.[13]

The postcard had been signed 'Your Father Ubu'. As Abtey well knew, Müssig was a fan of the French writer Alfred Jarry, whose play, *King Ubu*, delivers a vicious satire on power, wealth and greed and the evils they tend to spawn. There was also a return address: 'Stanislas Müssig, c/o Antonio's, 14 Rua Canaris, Lisbon.' The false papers that Abtey had helped procure for Müssig, to speed him on his way to Portugal, had given his first name as Stanislas, a Polish national. It was definitely Müssig's sign-off.

Müssig had been their covert Lisbon advance party, and they sought him out now. The rendezvous he suggested turned out to be a bar in a 'cut-throat environment, where a dirty and raggedy crowd swarmed'.[14] When Müssig breezed in, typically he was attired in a dark grey suit, with white shirt and black tie, plus matching hat and ornate black cane in hand. Even so, it was unusually sober dress for a man of his dash and style.

'Where did you come from? A funeral?' Abtey demanded, mockingly.

'Look around you,' Müssig countered, phlegmatically. 'They all look like undertakers.' After which he proceeded to tear apart Abtey over his own appearance – the Jacques Hébert, tour manager, downbeat grey-man look. 'No wonder you went unnoticed,' he remarked, of Abtey's journey.[15] Mercilessly, Müssig harangued him. He should shave off his horrible moustache and trade in his 'dirty little mackintosh for a well-cut suit, black of course'. Then, in Lisbon he would be sure to fit in. By contrast, Müssig had only praise for Josephine. He had long been one of her foremost fans, and for her present clandestine role he held her in the very highest esteem.[16]

Of course, there was a serious purpose to their meeting. Müssig was supposed to have reached out to the British embassy, and to have made contact with SIS. This Müssig had done, but in the interim he'd also become ensnared in a passport-faking scam, which had ended with him spending a month locked in a Lisbon gaol, but typically talking his way out again. Revelling in his tale, Müssig explained how the consul of a 'certain Latin American country' had understood how 'some political refugees aspire to visit his country', and were thus in need of passports. For 50,000 francs a pop – the equivalent of $1,000, to be split fifty-fifty with Müssig – the consul had offered to provide those papers. Trouble was, there were only three blank passports in the consulate's safe.[17]

Müssig's answer was to commission a Lisbon printer to knock up a job lot. Unfortunately, when he'd gone to collect those freshly minted passports, the PVDE were waiting. Müssig's response was to claim that he had simply been printing spare papers for the consulate, his place of work. When the consul was approached, he could not deny Müssig's story, for 'he needed me as much as I needed him.' Müssig was set free, although not before the consul had pocketed the profits from their illicit scheme. 'But as you can see, you have to be careful,' he concluded of his glorious tale.[18]

Müssig talked Abtey into moving into the suite next to his own, at the Hotel Palácio, in Estoril, the city's glitzy riviera district. How he afforded to stay there, Abtey could not imagine, but Müssig had 'always shown a great contempt for money. Money was only of value to him in so far as it enabled him to live life to the hilt. He earned fortunes and never hoarded it.'[19] This was the hotel that would become renowned as 'the international Allied spy HQ in WWII'.[20] It was there that Ian Fleming would stay, for he was shortly to visit Lisbon on cloak and dagger business of his own.

The world's spies and adventurers gathered at the roulette tables of the adjacent Casino Estoril – the basis for 'Casino Royale' in Fleming's Bond books. Lodging at the Hotel Palácio would put them at the very heart of things, Müssig argued. As proof, he presented Abtey with a list of all the Abwehr's agents that he had identified in Lisbon. It was 'small but precise, as to the names and pseudonyms and function of each one'.[21] They could track all of them from the casino's gambling tables, Müssig boasted. But it tended to be a two-way process. The enemy would of course be tracking them.

For sure, in Lisbon there were spies to hunt aplenty. None other than Dr Kurt Haller, the Abwehr's Irish section chief, was about to fly into Portela airport, intent on nefarious business. Tracking Haller's movements during the war, MI5 would record this Lisbon visit as being by a 'Sonderführer [special commander] . . . of the German sabotage

141

H.Q. in Berlin, who from time to time visits Spanish and Portuguese territory'.[22] There was a strong anti-British faction in Portugal, and it was Haller's speciality to recruit such elements. Allied shipping had been targeted in Lisbon harbour, and an Abwehr operation to use port-side brothels as honey-traps for British sailors – a crafty and devious 'waterfront organisation' – had been uncovered.[23]

But before Abtey and Müssig could start tracking down spies, there was an important rendezvous afoot. One of Wilfred Dunderdale's deputies, a certain 'Major Bacon', was expecting contact to be made. Bacon was a cover name; his real identity is lost to time. Officially, he worked as the British embassy's Financial Attaché, or the Air Attaché; contemporary accounts remain unclear. Either served as fairly standard cover for an SIS officer, their man in Lisbon right then.[24] With Dunderdale holding the fort in London, he'd primed Major Bacon to receive his 'personal friend', Captain Jacques Abtey, formerly of the Deuxième Bureau, at the Lisbon embassy.[25]

Of course, it was their long-lived relations – the Paris years – that had paved the way for the final steps in Abtey and Josephine's epic journey. That vital partnership – SIS to Deuxième Bureau – served as the imprimatur. While Abtey, Josephine and Müssig could not know it for sure, London was very much hoping that their approach would herald what all hungered for: reforging the 'valuable link to Commandant PAILLOLE, that Commander Dunderdale was very anxious to re-establish at that time'.[26]

For months, Paillole and Dunderdale unwittingly had been of the same mind. Ever since the fall of France, the two spy chiefs had hankered after the same thing. Abtey and Josephine were about to deliver it, as long as the last stage of the great deception went undetected. But for these two very special agents, there would be a sting in the tail. By rights, agent Josephine's role, that of the cloak and the cover, should have been almost done by now. All being well, she and Abtey should be heading to London for their rendezvous with Biffy Dunderdale, General de Gaulle and other key players.

In truth, London was not so very far from Lisbon, at least in terms of travel time. For the select few, BOAC (British Overseas Airways Corporation, the forerunner of British Airways) ran regular flights from Portela to Whitchurch Airport, on the outskirts of Bristol. That was the chief means by which diplomats, political figures, businessmen and spies flitted between the two cities. The lightly camouflaged but ostensibly civilian DC3 airliners had to run the Luftwaffe gauntlet for the 1500-kilometre journey, and the BOAC pilots had developed a standard procedure to avoid detection – flying as low as possible. If spotted, they would make for the nearest clouds in an effort to hide.[27] Even so, during the course of the war some BOAC flights would be shot down.

In the citation for Josephine Baker's post-war Légion d'Honneur – the highest French order of merit, civilian or military – her role in the present mission attracted particular mention: 'In order to facilitate the departure of intelligence . . . for England, an artistic troupe is formed, consisting only of people wishing to join the F.F.L. [Forces Françaises Libres, de Gaulle's Free French]; passes through Spain supposedly bound for Brazil . . .'[28] In fact, the two special agents were bound for London, or so they believed. By rights she and Abtey should have earned a stay in Britain, to bask in the glory of all they had achieved.

But it was not to be. Josephine would be heading straight back into the fray. Her Légion d'Honneur citation goes on to record: 'In Lisbon, receives a telegram from LONDON asking her to organise a new intelligence service in France.'[29] Out of the blue, wholly unexpectedly, that is more or less exactly what happened.

Furtively, Abtey ensured that Josephine's precious musical scores with their hidden writing, plus the reams of original documents and photos, were passed across to Major Bacon. Their rendezvous was the British embassy, located at the palace of the Viscounts of Porto Covo de Bandeira, a name of such stateliness that it does much to conjure up the building's opulence, its pomp and splendour. Some forty weighty files were delivered safely to its door.[30] From there the prized trove was rushed to Britain's capital, post-haste and under maximum security. (Thanks to the BOAC flights, there was a regular route to transport such urgent and precious material.)

Four days later a telegram arrived in Lisbon, direct from Dunderdale. Abtey dashed to the embassy to receive it. 'I went there alone,' he would write, 'for under no circumstances were Josephine's contacts with the British to be spotted by the Axis . . .'[31] Needless to say, London was 'delighted' to have received such a rich haul of intelligence, from those who, despite everything, had remained 'loyal to the Allied cause'. Abtey himself had been 'fully endorsed . . . by the Chiefs of this organisation'. In other words, by the heads of SIS.[32] In the telegram, Dunderdale spoke for all when he wrote: 'You can deal with Abtey, who . . . has all our confidence.'

'You are much loved in London,' Major Bacon told his visitor, underlining to him all that they had achieved, while stressing that there was a great deal more to be done. 'Tell your friends at the Deuxième Bureau that we are thrilled with their offer.'[33]

By 'their offer' he meant the proposal to reforge the close working relationship: in effect, what would be a Secret Intelligence Service–Deuxième Bureau – or whatever Paillole was now calling his agency – pipeline. It would need to flow both ways, taking intelligence out of France, and filtering instructions, requests and analysis back in again. Ideally, it would also be able to carry agents. But all in good time. As Bacon stressed, this was to be Abtey's sole focus, for it was a top priority as far as London was concerned.[34]

'When will Josephine and I leave for England?' Abtey ventured. That part Bacon hadn't touched upon.

The SIS officer coughed, in an effort to conceal his discomfort. 'I fear it will not be soon. London attaches great importance to your returning to France with Miss Baker.'[35]

Surprised, Abtey asked how that was supposed to work. He wasn't certain, Bacon admitted. Abtey would need to remain in Lisbon, to await further instructions, which were even then being drawn up by Dunderdale. They might take a week to formalise, but the key priority was to let Paillole know that London had received his message – not to mention the dynamite dossier – and that all was being organised, so to stand by.

That of course begged the question: how was Abtey supposed to remain in Lisbon, awaiting instruction from London, and also let Paillole know the success of their mission, and that the deal was on? He left Bacon with that seemingly insoluble question, as he headed back through the city streets, making a beeline for the Aviz. As he could not be in two places at once, there was only one possible solution that Abtey could foresee. He put it to Josephine right away.

Since she had demonstrated her remarkable ability to slip through closely guarded borders undetected, it made sense for her to return to France. Abtey would remain in Lisbon, awaiting further instructions. This would be Josephine's first international mission executed on her own – flying solo, as a lone agent among the enemy. Though it was not at all what she was expecting, Josephine accepted her new mission. In a time of war, sacrifices would need to be made.

Maybe Abtey would manage to get to London, even as Josephine returned to France. Maybe he would get to rendezvous with Dunderdale and to meet with de Gaulle. Maybe, in due course, they both would. Either way, they were buoyed by that hope. Yet in truth, neither was about to get to Britain any time soon. And very possibly, by not bringing them over, Dunderdale was trying to protect them both. Paradoxically, by keeping them away from London he might be shielding them from the very worst.

Dunderdale had been in Lisbon recently, seeking just such a breakthrough as Abtey had now gifted to him. A few weeks earlier he'd flown out with a radio set and high hopes. Where else in all of Europe was such a liaison to be made? Spain, under General Franco, was borderline hostile. Switzerland, neutral in name but heavily menaced by Berlin, was at best ambivalent to the Allied cause. Over all the rest of Western Europe the veil of Nazism – and of fascism – had fallen like the executioner's axe.

On 5 September 1940, Dunderdale had set off for Portugal, travelling on a passport reportedly in the name of 'John Green'.[36] He flew into Lisbon for a rendezvous at the former monastery of the Order of Saint Jerome, a vast and ornate Gothic edifice set on the banks of Lisbon's Tagus River. His contact was a man known only by his codename 'Victor' – then, and to this day. Victor claimed to speak for Colonel Louis Rivet, since 1936 the Director of the Deuxième Bureau but, since the fall of France, chief of the Vichyite Bureau of Anti-National Activities (the BMA).[37]

Even as Dunderdale and 'Victor' whispered in the shadows of the former monastery, there was growing disquiet in London. As Claude Dansey, the deputy chief of SIS, warned his boss, Stuart Menzies, forging links with Vichy was likely to provoke de Gaulle. Menzies accepted there was a risk, but he felt the ends justified the means. In London, de Gaulle had founded a Free French intelligence service, what would become known as the Bureau Central de Renseignements et d'Action (BCRA). Its chief was Major André Dewavrin, better known by his cover name 'Colonel Passy'. SIS duly appointed the redoubtable Kenneth Cohen to the role of liaising with de Gaulle's intelligence service apparatus.[38]

But trouble was brewing. De Gaulle's fledgling security service repudiated all contact with anyone associated with the Vichy regime. While this was perhaps understandable, it resulted in the tragic situation of 'Frenchmen working in an independent and often hostile way' wherein politics 'divided [those] whose principal object was necessarily the same.'[39] In other words, it was a recipe for confusion, infighting and intrigue. Just as soon as de Gaulle's security service realised that its London partner, the Secret Intelligence Service, was recruiting Frenchmen and women to its ranks, it was not best pleased. SIS was 'poaching' agents that rightly belonged to Free France. This was a turf war, and it was destined to become poisonous.[40]

Quietly, SIS decided to adopt a more pragmatic approach. They gambled that if they could keep the two factions apart – de Gaulle's security service on the one side, and the Vichy-based agents on the other – they could avoid the worst of the conflict. But of course, no such firewall was ever going to prove unbreachable. In time, Dunderdale would get accused of 'purloining Frenchmen before they had a chance to declare themselves for de Gaulle'. He would complain in turn about a glaring lack of cooperation. Finally, Menzies himself would have to step in, suggesting that if potential French recruits could be 'persuaded' to join de Gaulle's security services, 'less bother will occur'. Dunderdale would find himself doubly in the firing line, for he was overseeing the operations of the Polish intelligence service in exile, and their extensive missions in France were also seen as trespassing on de Gaulle's turf.[41]

By keeping Abtey and Josephine away from Britain, SIS was insulating them from all of that. It was in keeping with the policy of the firewall, one in which Dunderdale would play a foremost role. Yet even while preventing Abtey and Josephine from visiting London, Dunderdale was to 'agree' that they would henceforth serve as agents of the Free French. In truth, of course, he had no right to do any such thing. When Colonel Passy found out, as inevitably he would, he was incensed.

He would write to SIS demanding an explanation. How was it that 'MR. BACON . . . sent Captain ABTEY back to France . . . and that further he was guaranteed a commission in the service of La France Combattante [the Free French forces].'[42] As the truth could not be told, the oversight was put down to the fast-moving and confused situation of the war at the time, plus the incompetence of a certain Major Bacon, who by then – conveniently – was 'no longer available', in other words, making him the perfect fall guy.

'Captain ABTEY evidently was anxious to go where he was to be of most service to the common cause, but asked BACON . . . to see to it that he should be commissioned in La France Combattante,' SIS would explain, in an effort to mollify Colonel Passy. 'Mr. BACON, whose French . . . is not of the highest order, probably said he would do his best to see to it, and that is where the confusion took place . . .'[43]

As Abtey killed time in Lisbon, awaiting Dunderdale's orders and chasing spies with Müssig at the Casino Estoril, he was oblivious to the trouble that was brewing. In any case, he had far weightier things on his mind. Whenever he and Müssig stepped out of their rooms at the Palácio, the enemy was all around: brash, blatant, basking in their victory. This was a conflict that would engulf the entire world. It was a total war, and it would need to be fought with every weapon at their disposal, and with every essence of their souls. Those pursuing such petty infighting and turf wars in London could go hang.

Each morning on the fine beaches of Estoril, Abtey would encounter Heinz Reinert, head of the Abwehr in Lisbon, 'long giraffe neck . . . tanned head with an eagle profile . . . blond hair receding . . . eyes a glaucous blue'. Bizarrely, the two of them would play ball together, while refraining from exchanging a single word; 'if we meet on the street, our eyes avoid each other.'[44] Reinert's wife would be stretched out on the sand, 'a bronze statue with golden hair, wearing dark glasses and a fake cardboard nose against the sun . . .' Müssig would be keeping a careful eye, German watching German.[45]

Later, it would be Karl Glump, 'stocky, bald, with a ruddy face and a nose that looks like a ripe strawberry', cigar permanently jammed between his teeth, monocle in his eye socket. A foremost banker to the Gestapo – a man who was running gold, dollars and papers from Paris to Lisbon to Berlin and back again – for his efforts Glump would end up with 'a bullet in his skin'.[46] Later still, at the casino after dinner, Abtey would make sure to tell the concierge that his departure for Rio was imminent, as Josephine's tour group was about to set sail – just in case anyone was listening.

One evening, he felt a hand on his shoulder at the Casino Estoril's bar. He turned to discover a former Deuxième Bureau colleague, one with whom he had lost all contact. They spoke briefly about the collapse of France, but this was not the place to talk. They agreed to meet at Abtey's hotel the following morning. The agent never showed. Abtey would later learn that he had shot himself in the head, so shattering had the events of the last few months proved.

Another evening, as he and Müssig cruised the Casino's card tables, he noticed his friend being accosted by a familiar figure – one of Heinz Reinert's Abwehr comrades. The man leaned close to Müssig, whispering in his ear: 'We would like you to come back to Germany, Mr H.F.M. We need people like you. Don't worry about your past. The Führer's leniency is immeasurable . . .'[47] Germany had won the war, the man added, and Müssig as a 'true Aryan' could be of great service to his country. 'The Führer knows how to forgive those who have made mistakes.'[48]

As Müssig had warned, *you have to be careful.*

It was high time to get out of Lisbon – Abtey could feel it in his bones. There was fighting to be done; espionage to be orchestrated, battles to be won. Lisbon was awash with rumour that the attempted invasion of England had gone ahead but been foiled. In 'appalling conditions', German troops and landing craft had 'fallen prey to a burning sea'.[49] Maybe, just maybe, the fates were turning; the darkness lifting imperceptibly. Either way, he needed to get back to France.

Josephine was already gone, and in determining the means of her departure Abtey had very possibly saved her life; the first of many such occasions to come. She had wanted to take the Rapido, the fast sleeper train. Abtey had persuaded her otherwise. The flight would be less prone to checks, he'd argued. As chance would have it, the express train would be involved in a cataclysmic crash, as two locomotives collided. It was 3 December 1940, and two hundred of those riding in the sleeping cars were reported killed.[50]

Thankfully, Josephine had agreed to fly from Lisbon to Barcelona, and from there to take the train to Marseilles, the seat of Paillole's clandestine headquarters. Before heading to Lisbon airport, she had agreed to one last media interview, this with the director of the Lisbon National Radio. On a previous tour of the country, her first, in March 1939, she had performed to rapturous audiences, earning the accolade in the press of being 'the Black Angel.'[51]

She was well known to many of Lisbon's top reporters, as were her views. 'So, we will see you again, Josephine,' the radio host signed off the interview. 'If you see Hitler, tell him that we are impatiently waiting for him here . . . to send him to St. Helena!'[52]

St Helena, in the south Atlantic, is one of the world's remotest islands. Uninhabited when first discovered in 1502, it was made a British crown colony, and it was where French ruler Napoleon Bonaparte was sent into exile, after his defeat in 1815. Of course, the radio broadcaster's inference regarding St Helena being a fitting destination for the Führer was not lost on agent Josephine.

Though it lay only seven kilometres from the city centre, Lisbon's Portela Airport still felt isolated, remote, lawless even. Used by both the Allied and Axis powers, it was a smuggling hub – inevitably – and it drew spies to it, as a honeypot does flies. At night, sea mists tended to drift in, tendrils snaking up from the Tagus River estuary or rolling down from the nearby Sintra hills, enveloping all. Agents of all the warring nations watched the airport closely, recording comings and goings, and bribing customs officials to get copies of cargo manifests.

Fortunately, Josephine was leaving with not the slightest shred of incriminating evidence on her person. All of that – every last scrap of usable intelligence – had been spirited to London. The December sky above the airport frightened her somewhat, thick clouds glowering, promising thunder and rain.

She took to the skies anyway, for there wasn't a second to lose.

CHAPTER ELEVEN

Invisible Ink And Secret Steamships

Commander Paillole was adamant: Josephine Baker had to break her self-imposed purdah; *she must perform*. The reasons why were compelling. Though she might have vowed never to sing or dance again, not until the last Nazi had left France, her very principles were in danger of being her undoing. Her stardom was her cloak, and it was proving to be the cover for so much more. It had enabled the success of the Lisbon mission, the passing across of that mass of intelligence, and as Paillole had just learned, the re-establishing of the pipeline to London and the SIS.

Just as he'd hoped, Wilfred Dunderdale – their old friend, the Paris spymaster – had stepped out of the shadows to deliver. Against all odds, via Abtey's good offices and Josephine's brilliant cover, the setting up of this clandestine intelligence pipeline had been 'done and done well'. Josephine's role had been critical, and no one could afford for her to falter.[1]

Timely and accurate intelligence was the key to winning wars. The British were desperate for such information, but with the fall of France they had no means of gathering it 'other than eavesdropping and observation by plane', Paillole would remark. 'The only one with the means to inform them – it was us! During this crucial period . . . it was our service that gave them the critical information.'[2]

Once they'd linked up in Marseilles and Josephine had told him all that had transpired, he urged her: 'Return to the stage. It's necessary. There's no better cover for you.'[3] When still she resisted, he chided her gently: 'Perhaps if you sing, you will make them leave sooner.'[4] The enemy might be forced out of France by her presence on the stage.

Behind the gentle humour there was a hard core of truth. She needed to perform to keep up appearances; stardom required the star to shine. Equally, Josephine was all out of funds. There was a heap of precious jewellery stashed at Château des Milandes, much of it the fruit of her celebrity, priceless gifts showered upon her by her super-wealthy admirers. But she was reluctant to risk returning there right now. And the Deuxième Bureau's slush fund was not inexhaustible.[5]

As Paillole argued, Josephine needed to glitter and shine, and she needed to earn. On that last point, she was in full agreement. She certainly didn't expect to get paid when she was working for France and the Allies. That decided, the key question remained: what exactly should she perform in Marseilles, in the bleak and dark mid-winter of 1940? The answer would come from the most unexpected of quarters.

Frédéric 'Fred' Rey was a long-time dance partner, sometime lover and close friend of Josephine's from the Paris years. Having every reason to fear the Nazis, he had fled as far south as he could, before the Mediterranean had barred his way. He was hiding out in Marseilles, when the two bumped into each other quite by accident. It was an emotional reunion. Fred Rey wasn't just another Hans Müssig-type Aryan lookalike with an equally burning hatred of the Nazis, he was also an Austrian national. More to the point, he was – mostly – gay.

When he'd first left Austria for France he'd done so secretly, smuggled into the country in a basket-full of feathers – theatre costumes – fleeing the rising tide of vitriol emanating from Berlin. As a result he had no papers, and with the sea before him and Vichy France at his back there was nowhere left to run. Under the terms of the Armistice, any vessel wishing to sail from a French port needed clearance from the Armistice Commission, and all ships were under surveillance, which meant the seaborne means of escape was all-but closed to a fugitive like Rey.[6]

Under the Nazi's credo, homosexuality had been criminalised.

Thousands of gay men would be hounded remorselessly and sent to the concentration camps, where they were forced to wear a pink triangle under the Nazi classification system.[7] As a dancer and a singer, Josephine had many friends within the gay showbiz community. She very possibly herself had a tendency towards bisexuality. There was talk of the comfort young and lonely chorus girls gave to each other, when forced to share cheap rundown digs in New York, as they sought to find from each other the love that abusive and predatory male theatre managers failed to provide.[8]

There was also talk of how top female stars in Paris were expected to double as very high-class call girls. It was de rigueur to sleep with a select clique of clients – super-rich individuals who would shower them with gifts in return.[9] Josephine had very possibly done all of that, none of which made her any the less capable, or hungry, or worthy to fight this war, and to serve as a warrior in the shadows. Arguably, it made her more able. By default she'd had to learn a chameleon-like ability to adjust and adapt, to evolve and improvise to survive. She could be all things to all people, while remaining unbreakable and unyielding in adversity. She would embrace what was right – liberty, equality, fraternity – and damn the consequences.

Of course, she related to the predicament of Fred Rey most personally. At the start of the war he had volunteered to serve in the French Foreign Legion, which made him all the more of a target now. He was holed up in a Marseilles brothel, he explained, which he figured was the last place the enemy would ever think to look. But one way or the other, he simply had to get out of France.[10] She could help, Josephine promised. She understood exactly why he was so desperate. '*Il faut!*' – it's necessary – she declared, fist punching the air in her signature gesture of defiance. She would get him out, she promised. But first, they needed to put on a show.

'Why not a revival of *La Créole*?' Rey suggested. Nothing was showing at the Marseilles opera house just then, and the management were desperate for any kind of performance that might draw in the war-weary crowds.[11]

Josephine's eyes flashed with excitement. Now that would be something. In 1685 the city of Marseilles was only the second in France ever to have an opera house built. Though it burned down in 1919, they had rebuilt the Opéra de Marseilles bigger, better and more grandiose, featuring an urn-shaped auditorium, three rings of boxes, two balconies and a gallery. Together, Fred Rey and Josephine convinced the managers of the Opéra de Marseilles that they could get *La Créole* ready for a Christmas opening, though that was barely two weeks away.

'You don't know Josephine!' Rey enthused, when the managers aired their doubts. 'She can do anything.'[12]

La Créole – it was so fitting. If Josephine were to break out and perform, even as the enemy seemed universally triumphant, there was no better show with which to do so. Josephine had first performed Jacques Offenbach's *La Créole* in Paris, in 1934, thirteen years after she had taken the city by storm, in the wild, provocative, semi-naked, supercharged *La Revue Nègre,* in which she had appeared at times clad only in a girdle of feathers. Superficially, that show had been all about appearing as half-human half-beast, about wild instinct versus staid, stolid civilisation, but subliminally the show was imbued with a mocking undercurrent, a hidden message of rebellion and subversion.[13]

How things had changed in the interim. *La Créole* had been Josephine's coming of age as a serious performer, and in opera, no less.[14] The French composer Henri Sauguet declared of her performance that is was 'dazzling', and that no one else displayed 'such radiance, spontaneity and unique charm'.[15] More to the point, in many ways the story behind the opera echoed her own. It told of a young woman's daring travels from the Caribbean island of Guadeloupe to France, in tandem with her sweetheart, and how love conquers all. To Josephine's way of thinking it mirrored her journey from the slums of St Louis to Paris, the City of Light.[16]

That personal resonance made it all the more special. Josephine had put all of her heart and all of her soul into *La Créole*. Indeed, she tended to make a point of echoing the different stages of her life's journey in her performances. For Josephine, all the shows she performed and all the songs she sang had to have spirit and soul. That was what she strove to inject into each, giving each a special value and meaning.[17]

Returning to the stage now, at what felt like the Allies' darkest hour, she would have to breathe life and soul into *La Créole* as never before. But it would prove a phenomenal challenge. In less than two-weeks she had to scour the city like a whirlwind, begging, borrowing and purloining costumes; she had to select a cast, coach them in their parts, and she had to relearn the score of an opera she hadn't performed in years. To make matters worse, a freezing, biting wind tore through the city, driving everyone inside. Across France, a thick blanket of snow lay like a shroud, hampering everything. It was the coldest it had been for an age, and Josephine felt it deep in her bones.

In an effort to ease the load, she called in a favour from one of her foremost Milandes Resistance crew. At her request, Emmanuel Bayonne, former French Navy officer and Deuxième Bureau man, now TR agent under Paillole, agreed to play the role of her Marseilles impresario. She dispatched him to Milandes laden with gifts for her Resistance crew, and with her warmest greetings – 'I would have liked to have spent Christmas with them all' – after which he returned laden with her costumes, scores and other stage paraphernalia.[18] And sure enough, bang on schedule, Emmanuel Bayonne, Fred Rey and Josephine Baker had got *La Créole* ready to roll.

The opening night was to be Christmas Eve 1940, the very day that Jacques Abtey was to arrive from Lisbon.

Abtey had been travelling for forty-eight hours, first on a Junkers transport aircraft crammed full of Germans – seated next to a 'behemoth with a scarred face' – and gazing out at a Swastika twisted in black shadows across the plane's tail.[19] Conscious that he was carrying a thick wad of British – SIS – cash, for several hours he'd tried to keep a mask on his fear. His enemies had been watching him in Lisbon just as closely as he'd been watching them. They could easily have lured him aboard a flight which would end in a Gestapo cell. If that were the case, would he really be able to hold out? Or would he be forced to reveal all: the SIS connection, Paillole's role, that of agent Josephine?

It was only when the Junkers had emerged from thick cloud above Barcelona, the unmistakable white-walled city hugging the Spanish coastline, that he finally felt he could breathe a little more easily. Thankfully, the journey onwards from there to Marseilles by train had proved to be a great deal less fraught.[20] Upon arrival, he'd headed for a rendezvous with Josephine, through streets plastered with posters announcing her debut that very evening in *La Créole*.

Her place of lodgings was the Grand Hôtel Noailles-Métropole, which for decades had played host to the world's leading celebrities, artists and performers. Boasting six floors and over three hundred rooms, the Noailles was graced with several fine restaurants, the most remarkable of which glittered and beguiled, with 'everywhere gilding, rich fabrics, tapestries with shimmering reflections, artistic floor lamps, metal and gold, giving off an extraordinary impression of luxury'.[21]

Josephine ushered Abtey into her suite, one that was cluttered with costumes, musical scores and trunks, as she prepared for the big opening. No sooner had she shut the door than she declared: 'Jacques! How happy I am to see you again! Tell me quickly, what did you do in Lisbon? First, tell me if everything is all right? Tell me, tell me!'[22]

'Of course, Jo! Do you think I would have come back otherwise?' he reassured her. 'We have everything we need.'[23]

Even so, he came as the bearer of surprising news.

He related how he'd had a series of meetings with Major Bacon, as they'd put flesh on the bones of the plans being drawn up in London by Dunderdale. The route of the pipeline had been the subject of fierce debate, but eventually a plan had been set. From Marseilles – Paillole's TR headquarters – the intelligence dossiers would be dispatched to Casablanca, the city lying on Morocco's Atlantic coast. As Morocco was a French North African colony – so formally under Vichy French rule – that route was thought to be 'safer than transit through Spain', with all the checks that would entail.[24]

From Casablanca, the dossiers would be dispatched by sea to Lisbon, and from there flown BOAC to Britain. To facilitate the pipeline's smooth running, London had 'decided to buy a small commercial ship, which will sail under the Portuguese flag,' Bacon had explained.[25] That ship would serve as the Deuxième Bureau–SIS courier vessel. It would operate under the cover of being a steamship of the Louis Dreyfus Company, ferrying phosphates to Portugal – phosphates then being in high demand as a raw material to manufacture explosives. With every reason to stop and load at various ports, intelligence dossiers could be slipped aboard, or off again, seemingly at will.

Founded in 1851 in France by the Jewish Dreyfus family, the Louis Dreyfus Company was by then one of the world's largest shipping, agriculture and oil concerns. But as Vichy's anti-Jewish laws began to bite, the company would see its assets confiscated and family members forced to flee. Sensing the way the wind was blowing, the Dreyfus family threw their weight behind the Allies, and most notably in a court case concerning the SS *Lichtenfels*, the world's first ever heavy-lift ship, which employed groundbreaking technology to enable the hull to be semi-submerged, so that extremely heavy cargoes – other ships; locomotives; oil rigs – could be loaded aboard.

In 1941 a German vessel, the SS *Lichtenfels* had been scuttled, as a blockship. With that had come a bizarre series of court cases emanating from occupied Holland, in which the British Government was sued under the 'Netherlands War Risks Insurance Scheme' for the loss of various vessels, including the SS *Lichtenfels*. Acting on behalf of the British Government, the Dreyfus family had helped shoot down those claims in flames.[26] In short, the Louis Dreyfus Company was firmly on the side of the Allies.

At the Casablanca end of operations, a Captain Lanz, the director of the Compagnie Chérifienne d'Armaments – a French weapons manufacturer based in North Africa – would act as SIS's contact in Morocco. He would furnish apparent legitimacy for the Casablanca side of things. With all of that in place, the operations of the Louis Dreyfus-SIS-Paillole steamship should appear as if part of a bona fide armaments business, which was a booming sector in a world convulsed by war.[27]

It was a somewhat circuitous route and would be slower than using air travel. But London had determined it was the safest, and security was the key priority bearing in mind 'the importance of the information that was going to be conveyed'.[28] In any case, the volume of traffic was going to be significant, and only so much could go via air; even less, by radio. In fact, encoded radio transmissions were largely useless, save for sending the shortest kind of messages, and especially when transmitting from hostile territory. Any time spent on air risked the transmitter being detected by the enemy and its operators captured.

Abtey and Bacon's final rendezvous had been a somewhat shady affair, as they walked the dark Lisbon streets, making for his car. They'd ducked inside, after which Bacon had introduced Abtey to his pretty secretary, Jane, who was poised at the wheel. Once under way, Bacon passed Abtey an envelope stuffed with £1,000 - the equivalent of around £60,000 today – cash for those serving 'on the orders of the IS [SIS]'.[29] Abtey checked that de Gaulle would be acquainted with his and Josephine's role, and that they woud be signed up as agents of Free France. 'Major Bacon had given me the most formal assurances in this respect,' Abtey would later record, in his French governmental files.[30]

In truth, de Gaulle and his security services had not been told a thing. Abtey and Josephine had been sold a lie. While this was arguably done for the greater good, it would come back to haunt them. Of course, Bacon had to maintain the intrigue, the illusion. He told Abtey that as they were volunteers working for de Gaulle, the SIS cash was for expenses only.[31] Abtey should expect to receive the pay due to a man of his rank – a captain – from the Free French. But as Josephine had made clear that 'she did not want to hear about money,' she would not be on anyone's payroll.[32]

They had agreed that if the worst came to the worst, and either

Abtey or Josephine became trapped in North Africa, SIS would do all in its power to get them to Britain. With that, their final business was done. The car came to a halt, so Abtey could alight. In a world fraught with danger and plagued by uncertainties, the moment was heavy with emotion. Major Bacon was of an older generation, a veteran of the First World War, and Abtey had developed a certain respect for him. They feared that they wouldn't see each other again for some time.

'Cigarette?' offered Bacon.

Abtey struck a match, lit his own, did the same for Jane, before turning to Bacon, as if to light his. But as the older man went to take the light, he blew it out instead.

'Never three,' he counselled, somewhat ominously. 'Never three. If I'd taken it, the youngest would die, and I care for young Jane.'[33]

This superstition had arisen – or at least taken hold – during the Great War. It was based upon the fear that upon first striking a match, an enemy soldier would spy the flame; the second light would enable him to take aim; as the third cigarette was lit, the enemy soldier would fire. In Bacon's version it was the youngest who would die, so a slight variation on the theme. For some reason, Bacon's words had struck Abtey most powerfully. Three years later, in North Africa, he would momentarily forget about the older man's warning, with what would seem to be tragic consequences.

But that was way in the future. Right now, as Abtey finished briefing Josephine on his final days in Lisbon, they contemplated all that lay before them; their new mission. In Abtey's wartime records the deal cut with SIS in Lisbon would be recorded simply as: 'Liaison established . . . sent back on mission into France by I.S. to ensure liaison with the SR Vichy (Group PAILLOLE) and to set-up a particular NETWORK.'[34] Abtey had left Hans Müssig in the relative safety of Lisbon, though neither he nor Josephine figured this would be the last they would see of him. For now, Abtey was keen to catch up with Paillole and the other TRs, and to share the grand plan.

'How are our friends?' he asked Josephine.

'I saw Commander Paillole.' She smiled. 'What did he tell me? That I need a good cover!'

'He's right. Was he the one who encouraged you to stage *La Créole*?'

He was, she confirmed. 'At first I didn't want to. "As long as there is a German in France," I said, "Josephine cannot sing." But he insisted. And then, of course, I had no more money!'

Her face grew serious for a moment. She eyed Abtey, unease etched in her gaze. 'But how I regret that you didn't make it all the way to London, to see General de Gaulle . . .' Josephine felt a towering respect for de Gaulle, one of the few Frenchmen to stand firm when all had seemed lost. The hunger she and Abtey felt to get to London was very real, but typically they had sacrificed that for the cause.

'We'll see about that later,' Abtey told her. 'For now, we must fight. Where is our friend, Paillole?'[35]

They would meet the Marseilles spymaster shortly, Josephine explained. First, it was showtime.

La Créole opened that evening, with Josephine resplendent on stage and Jacques Abtey sitting awestruck in the audience. The opera, a fantastic tale of ship's captains and swashbuckling swordsmen in which love triumphs over all, was perfect for wartime Marseilles. Almost fairytale-like, it carried the audience away from the trials and tribulations of life under the Vichy regime. Josephine portrayed Dora, a beautiful young woman from the Caribbean island of Guadeloupe, who falls in love with René, a young and daring musketeer. René and Dora's love survives parental meddling, sham marriages and adventures on the high-seas, with much hilarity and drama along the way.

Josephine appeared in a pleated costume, with long trains and leg-of-mutton sleeves – a voluminous puff of fabric ballooning at the upper arm, tapering to a skin-tight fit from elbow to wrist. She played her part to perfection. When Dora and René's love seemed lost, she 'screamed to the rafters in a voice that sent chills through the audience'.[36] But more often the auditorium rocked with laughter, as the opera's delicious humour hit home. Abtey was truly amazed that Josephine had managed to pull all this together in such difficult circumstances. Incredibly, she seemed to have put all the stress, the tension, the worry and the fear about the war, and her own clandestine role within it, to one side. But as he was increasingly realising, she possessed 'an extraordinary will that nothing seemed able to weaken'. She had a steely ability to discipline her effort to the service of that will. Now, more than ever, on the opening night of *La Créole*, he was struck by her 'intelligent and courageous dynamism'.[37] This would be a recurring theme of their war.

On Christmas Day 1940 they met Paillole. He didn't seem at all surprised at the Casablanca development. In fact, North Africa – 'miraculously spared by the German occupation' – had long been on his radar. Running the SIS pipeline through there made sense, especially as Morocco, with its vast stretches of Mediterranean and Atlantic coastline, was prime terrain from which to launch the liberation of southern Europe. Paillole had long believed that North Africa would prove pivotal 'when the day came to resume combat and our official security and intelligence functions.'[38]

In hankering after a Moroccan base, Paillole was of a mind with Britain's prime minister. Incredibly, in the final days of June 1940, just weeks after Dunkirk and suffering overwhelming defeat in Europe, Churchill had demanded the drawing up of plans to seize Morocco. Codenamed Operation Susan, the mission aimed to take Casablanca – 'a modern port with suitable facilities for disembarking troops' – as a base for Allied operations, and as a headquarters for the Free French. It was all part of Churchill's aim of keeping the French in the fight, but it got short shrift from his senior commanders.[39]

With no British troops available to support Operation Susan – none could be spared from the defence of the British Isles – the proposed forces were some 4,000 French Foreign Legion, Alpine and assorted colonial troops, along with some 20,000 Polish soldiers, all of whom were woefully ill-equipped. If the Vichy forces garrisoning Casablanca put up only token resistance, the landings might be feasible, 'but we do not feel that we should be justified in expecting a welcome of this kind,' the Chiefs of Staff warned, especially as there was little reliable intelligence to hand.[40]

There was also little in the way of air defences or warships that could be spared. 'We cannot recommend that we should divert, at this crucial moment, forces essential to the defence of the United Kingdom, in order to keep alive a French Resistance which we know must very soon collapse,' the Chiefs of Staff warned. The number one priority had to be 'making the United Kingdom and Eire secure against attack. They are by no means secure. We cannot therefore undertake unprofitable commitments which would prejudice their security.'[41] Operation Susan was never to get the green light, but the germ of an idea – of an Allied landing in North Africa – had been planted.

Very probably an adventure doomed to fail, Operation Susan nevertheless revealed much about the mindset of Britain's wartime leader in the summer of 1940. Just days after suffering cataclysmic defeat, he was all for offensive action. Churchill believed absolutely that the best form of defence was attack. The harder and deeper and more unexpected the thrust, the more likely it was to take the enemy by surprise. When all feared invasion and defeat, Churchill had hungered to go on the offensive, to take risks, to dare all – as Op Susan had amply demonstrated.

In that sense he shared a certain steely spirit and pugnacity with Josephine Baker. During the Phoney War, she had complained bitterly about why Britain and France didn't simply march on Berlin. Why wait for Hitler to make the first move? Why not strike first and strike hard?[42] Maybe she had had a point. In fact the two figures – this black female superstar and sometime special agent, and this ageing, stubborn, bulldog-spirited Caucasian male – had more than a little in common. Josephine would later write of how she and Churchill had exchanged telegrams during the war and how he would invite her to London to perform. Certainly, in Churchill's unbreakable spirit – as with de Gaulle's – she found a source of deep inspiration.[43]

Despite the Operation Susan knockback, North Africa remained firmly on Churchill's radar.[44] Likewise, North Africa was most definitely on Paillole's. Indeed, he'd tried to get the surviving Deuxième Bureau archives shipped to North Africa, but Vichy had blocked such efforts. Paillole's agents had been busy cataloguing what they called their top 'bastards ... characters that the TR stations reported ... as having contact with the enemy, who, sooner or later, will have to be called to account.'[45]

At the same time, Paillole had been warned by his bosses – those at the helm of the Vichy intelligence apparatus – that he should have no further 'direct contact with London'.[46] The Germans were accusing the French of playing a double game, and were threatening dire consequences. The vulnerability of the archives proved intensely worrying for Paillole, especially since the Abwehr were busy scouring the vast quantity of French documents that they had already seized.

At their Hotel Lutetia headquarters in Paris, two hundred Abwehr agents were eviscerating the archives of the *Sûreté Nationale* – the French equivalent of Britain's Scotland Yard or America's FBI. As well as 'harvesting' those records, teams under the SS beavered away at the Ministry of Foreign Affairs, on the grand Quai d'Orsay, plus they were gutting the files of the French military High Command that had been seized aboard the train at La Charité-sur-Loire and taken to Paris in triumph.[47]

That in itself gave 'an idea of the extent of the knowledge the Germans had acquired' about the once-secret French state. In Paris, the Abwehr had opened various 'apparently commercial enterprises' that were in truth fronts for the recruitment of yet more agents. Added to that the Abwehr commandos – the Brandenburg units – and the Wehrmacht had freed scores of shadowy characters who had been serving time in French gaols. 'The worst French, Arabic and foreign recruits will be used to infiltrate intelligence and resistance organisations,' Paillole warned.[48]

If caught, Paillole's people would face either the concentration camps or execution, and it was debatable which was worse, for both were basically a death sentence. Worryingly, there were rumours that the Germans were poised to occupy the entire Free Zone of France.

Tensions were at fever pitch between the Vichy regime and that in Berlin. 'If the weather were not so bad, Fritz would have invaded the Free Zone by now,' Paillole warned. 'We shall see more of them.'[49] He feared it was only a matter of time before the Free Zone was overrun, which made it all the more important for his two special agents to head for Morocco, as the SIS had determined.

Josephine was under contract to the Opéra de Marseilles for a multi-week run, which meant the show had to go on. She needed the cover, she needed the money, plus there would be financial penalties if she tried to end *La Créole* early. As her profile in Marseilles mushroomed, so other desperate individuals were drawn to her, seeking help. One was Daniel Marouani, the Tunisian-born theatre manager who'd first introduced her to Abtey. Another was the film producer Rodolphe Solmsen, who had fled Germany with his family. He'd already sent his wife and daughter to Peru, but he was finding it impossible to get the papers to follow.

Solmsen frequented the Noailles Hotel, buying drinks for Peruvian, Spanish and Portuguese diplomats – basically anyone who might conceivably help. It was there that he ran into Josephine Baker, whom he knew from Paris. As with Fred Rey, Josephine had vowed with Solmsen, *Il faut!* Somehow, she'd see to it that he would also be spirited to safety.[50] Having enlisted Abtey's help, one morning a passport and papers were delivered to Solmsen at his hotel. Somehow, they'd also managed to get his name added to those permitted to leave the port of Marseilles by ship.

During recent weeks Solmsen, a German Jew, had grown increasingly despondent of ever getting out of Europe alive. 'Josephine and Jacques had kept their word,' he would remark. 'When I almost did not believe in it any more, they had opened the door to liberty . . . For me, it was Josephine and Jacques who saved my life.'[51] For Josephine, too, that life-saving journey across the water was about to become so much more urgent.

She was about to learn how closely she was being hunted.

CHAPTER TWELVE

On The Gestapo Hitlist

As the new year dawned Paillole came to visit. He was the bearer of grim news. 'You must leave as soon as possible, for I have heard that "Miss Baker" is on the German blacklist,' he warned. 'The boat that departs for Algiers the day after tomorrow will perhaps be the last to leave Marseilles.'[1] Josephine and Abtey needed to be on it, he stressed. Having made his point, Paillole handed over a thick dossier – the latest intelligence that needed to be spirited out of France. 'I'd prefer you to take the information to Lisbon yourselves,' he advised, underlining its crucial import.[2]

Things became a frenetic whirl, as they prepared for their sudden departure. Josephine still had two shows to perform, and it was Abtey who paid a visit to the opera house, to make the argument that she should be released from her contract. Obviously, he couldn't breathe a word about her ultra-secret role with the SIS, so he used the excuse that she was known to the Germans, due to 'the eminent services she had rendered to France in 1939–1940, as a volunteer agent for the Deuxième Bureau'. Taking the opera managers partially into his confidences, he explained how crucial it was that she 'put herself out of reach of the invader'.[3]

The managers of the Opéra de Marseilles said they understood completely and that they applauded 'Miss Baker's patriotism.' All they asked for was a medical certificate, stating that she was too ill to continue performing, which should be easy-enough to procure in Marseilles in January 1941. That way, the contract could be cancelled with good cause, and all could do their duty to help liberate France.[4]

Getting that certificate proved to be less of a challenge than even they had imagined. When Josephine was duly examined by a medical doctor, it turned out that she *was* genuinely sick. An X-ray revealed a shadow on her lungs. Due to the days and days of biting cold, combined with the long months of stress and her relentless schedule, she had developed a nasty chest infection. The doctor's advice was that she should leave the country without delay for rest and recuperation in sunnier climes.[5]

With all of that squared away, the trunks began to pile up in Josephine's hotel suite. Around five o'clock that evening, with the boat due to sail the following day, things became a whole lot more hectic. Emmanuel Bayonne arrived at the Noailles Hotel, bringing with him Josephine's menagerie of animals from Château des Milandes – those that had survived the retreat from Paris and the long weeks that she had been away. Josephine had refused to be parted from them any longer: they were going with her to Morocco, come what may.

As a bonus, sailing with such a colourful and exotic menagerie, which was so synonymous with her career as an entertainer, should furnish even better cover. After all, what kind of spy laden with top-secret intelligence travelled with Bonzo the Great Dane, Glouglou the monkey, Mica the golden lion tamarin, Gugusse the moustachioed marmoset, plus Bigoudi and Point d'Interrogation, the two white mice? It just wasn't done. That wasn't the way spies tended to operate.

Or at least, not normally. But there was little that would be normal or conventional about agent Josephine's war.

Once set free in the hotel room, Mica – convinced he was the man of the house – took possession of the bed; the hot-headed Gugusse raced to the top of the wardrobe and refused to come down; Glouglou vaulted onto the curtain rail, from where he rained a torrent of abuse onto Bonzo; as for the Great Dane, he would permit no one but Josephine to lay a hand upon him. He flopped down, immovable, with one white mouse perched on the end of his nose and washing itself.[6]

Despite the pandemonium, Josephine was adamant: her furry friends were travelling with her. 'I can't understand abandoning animals,' she would declare. 'They would never do it to us!'

When those around her tried to object, she turned the argument on them. She was convinced that America would soon join the fight, which would turn the war rapidly in the Allies' favour. In light of which, how could she possibly leave her animals behind?[7]

Somehow, Josephine seemed happier, more content – more complete – when surrounded by her menagerie. In her 1927 memoir she'd written of how animals captured her interest and her love, for they were both simple and complex, being a lot like small children. But it went deeper than that. She actually believed that the fates would smile upon her when blessed by such company.[8]

In a sense, it all went back to an event in her teenage years, in New York. Having joined the jobbing dancing troupe in her teens, she'd managed to get out of St Louis, but touring third-rate venues wasn't really her thing. Desperate to win a part on Broadway, one evening an odd-looking figure turned up at her door, with bright red hair, bulging eyes and a misshaped shoulder, as Josephine described him. Oddly, he claimed to have come direct from her family, bearing the gift of a good luck charm. A rabbit's foot. It was one that he warned her to treasure for life and never to misplace.[9]

Superstitious by nature, Josephine placed it reverentially in her make-up box and that night she slept with it under her pillow. The very next day she was approached by another individual – a tall, skinny man – who turned out to be a theatre manager. He proceeded to offer her a part in the New Plantation Cabaret . . . on Broadway. She was so happy she laughed and danced with joy and embraced her rabbit's foot. After that, she and her lucky charm had been through thick and thin together.[10]

Likewise, in the bleak winter of 1940–41 she would rely on her animals and their spirits of good fortune to see her through. She dashed about, trying to get the right animals back into the right cages, as she readied them for the great adventure that lay ahead. Whatever might transpire, she was determined that they would be in it together to the last.[11]

Moored in the city harbour was a grand-looking passenger ship with a cabin booked in her name. The *Gouverneur-Général Gueydon* was a French liner serving the North Africa line since 1922, and operating out of the port of Marseilles. In eighteen months' time the vessel would be seized by the Germans and turned over to troop transport duties.[12] But for now, she was crammed full to bursting with those desperate to flee France, and who had somehow managed to beg, borrow, bribe or steal the requisite papers.

Massive, slab-sided, iron-clad, the *Gouverneur-Général Gueydon*'s dark flanks rose from the harbour waters, below a tiered white superstructure like a wedding cake, topped off by two tall funnels etched in smoke. She was a graceful and beautiful thing, despite the war, and Josephine would be in good company for the coming voyage. Abtey had travelled this way before, spending some of his military service in North Africa. He knew the region well and spoke half-decent Arabic.[13] Paillole had vowed to join them, for he sensed the key to the liberation of Europe lay on North African shores. Plus Josephine had come good on her pledges: Fred Rey, Rodolphe Solmsen and Daniel Marouani were also joining her aboard.[14]

Once her exotic menagerie hit Josephine's cabin all was chaos once more. 'It was indescribable hustle and bustle, as well as the funniest show I ever saw,' Abtey remarked.[15] Of course, even now the party aboard the *Gouverneur-Général Gueydon* would be closely monitored and watched. But if anyone had anything to hide – if anyone was trying to slip through unnoticed – the last people to give off any such appearances were Josephine and her troupe. As long as Paillole's precious documents didn't get eaten by an animal by mistake, this was perfect cover for hiding top-secret intelligence.

Some sixteen years earlier, as a mere nineteen-year-old, Josephine had boarded another imposing ocean liner, the RMS *Berengaria*. Originally a German passenger ship, the SS *Imperator*, she had been part of the reparations made by Germany to the Allies at the end of the First World War, being used to ship some 25,000 US troops home to America. Transferred to the British as the flagship for the Cunard fleet and renamed the *Berengaria*, Josephine had sailed from New York to France aboard her, with a heart full of excitement, anxiety and hope, caught between her troubled past and the uncertainty of what might lie ahead.[16]

In the 1920s, America was a country still plagued by segregation. Across much of the nation – public transport, hotels, schools, universities, night-clubs, theatres – the 'whites-only' diktat was enforced rigorously. It was that which had compelled Josephine to strike out for European shores, where she had been told that such prejudices were all but unknown. As the Statue of Liberty faded into the distance, she had stood on the deck of the RMS *Berengaria* realising what that signified: from somewhere, she would need to find the strength and the courage to start afresh, plus the ambition to succeed. But at least she hoped that she was sailing towards freedom, sweet freedom.[17]

Now, in January 1941, she was doing something similar, but very much in reverse. She was leaving France on another sea-going liner, but this time fleeing the darkness and evil that had engulfed Western Europe, in the process of which she had herself become the hunted. Of course, she risked drawing the enemy to her, as she embarked upon a new journey on behalf of the Allies' foremost intelligence services, with only her stardom – and her animals – as her cover. Facing the unknown on such a daring mission, once again she would have to find the strength and the courage to endure.

Even as the *Gouverneur-Général Gueydon* pulled away from that Marseilles dock, so another secretive delegation was bound for North Africa, this one emanating from the United States. As Churchill had surmised, Morocco held great promise: some 2,000 kilometres of Atlantic and Mediterranean coastline; excellent ports modernised and improved under French colonial rule; military-grade airbases; plus the vast sweep of the Atlas Mountains stretching east into Algeria and Tunisia. 'Great battles had been fought here to control the fertile plains and access to the sea . . .' wrote American author Hal Vaughan, 'and great battles lay in the near future.'[18]

At its closest point, just a few dozen kilometres of water separated Morocco from Gibraltar, that choke point – the Strait of Gibraltar – being the key route through which German U-boats sallied forth to wreak havoc among Allied convoys. In Washington, President Roosevelt was well aware of North Africa's strategic significance. There was no way he couldn't be. Churchill was forever bending his ear about an Allied landing in North Africa – in the spirit of the late lamented Operation Susan – and why it was the first such counter-strike that they should ever consider.

Not that the USA was anywhere near declaring war on the Axis powers: the Japanese attack on Pearl Harbor was still many months away. But as with Josephine, Churchill shared a conviction that America *would* join the Allies in the war, and that once that happened the tide would finally start to turn. Indeed, so much of Churchill's early speeches, policies and strategies – his burning desire to show that Britain retained the will and the wherewithal to fight – was directed at Washington, and at convincing Roosevelt that the USA should join the struggle against Nazi tyranny, which, if left unchecked, was sure to reach American shores.

With North Africa in mind, on 4 November 1940 Roosevelt (often referred to by his initials FDR) had called American diplomat Robert Daniel Murphy to a meeting in Washington. Murphy had served as a key figure at the Paris embassy, even as the French capital had fallen to the German enemy, and he had no idea why he was being summoned. Though Murphy couldn't know it, his dispatches from a beleaguered France had impressed the US president greatly. Murphy had written of 'a monstrous exploitation' being inflicted upon the French people; of disaster facing the twenty million crammed into the Vichy zone, including the millions of refugees. But that wasn't what had caught the president's eye: it was Murphy's reports on French North Africa, with all of its strategic and military potential.[19]

In French North Africa there were some 300,000 French troops, who had reportedly not lost their fighting spirit. As Murphy concluded, 'if France was going to fight again anywhere . . . North Africa will be the place.' FDR had taken note, even as the Axis powers seemed to be victorious everywhere. Germany had invaded Romania; Italy was moving on East Africa, Egypt and Greece; across the length and breadth of the Atlantic German U-boats stalked Allied shipping. Even so, before a large map displaying the extent of the French North African colonies, FDR proceeded to outline to Murphy his ultra-secret mission.[20]

Murphy was to head to North Africa, to work 'unostentatiously' on a report for the president's eyes only, detailing the economic and military potential of the region. So secret was their meeting that FDR had decreed that no records should be kept. Should news of their dealings leak to the press it would be a disaster, for the US president had promised the American people that he had no intention of taking them to the war. But as Murphy left Washington he was convinced otherwise: 'FDR meant to lead the United States into war against the Axis powers,' with North Africa being key to those intentions.[21]

Murphy's whirlwind tour began by seaplane as he landed at Algiers, the capital of Algeria, which had been a French colony since 1830. From there he headed direct to a meeting with General Maxime Weygand, the French military's commander-in-chief. Weygand, a determined anti-Nazi, was clinging precariously to power within the increasingly collaborationist Vichy system, fearful that Berlin would soon do away with him. The enemy's reach, even within French colonial Africa, was long. As proof of this, Murphy's every move would be tracked by Gestapo agents embedded within the Armistice Commission, plus the Italian equivalent, the OVRA (the Organisation for Vigilance and Repression of Anti-Fascism), Mussolini's secret police.[22]

From Weygand, Murphy received quiet assurances that the 300,000 troops under his command would fight, should Germany attempt to invade French North Africa. Sensing an alliance of sorts – *the enemy of my enemy is my friend* – the two men drew up what became known as the Murphy–Weygand Agreement. In this, the US Government would ship non-military essentials to French Africa, to help keep Weygand's troops, and the local populations, from starvation. Berlin was demanding ever greater payments in money and kind from France, and her colonies were being bled dry. The Murphy–Weygand mercy shipments would help relieve such suffering. But there was a quid pro quo. In return, Murphy demanded that a dozen so-called US diplomats be allowed unfettered access to French Africa, ostensibly to monitor those mercy shipments, ensuring that no military use was made of America's aid.[23]

In truth, those twelve men – who would become known as Murphy's '12 Apostles' – were to be Washington's first overseas spies in the Second World War, the pioneers of what would become America's fledgling foreign intelligence and special actions agency, the Office of Strategic Services (OSS), itself the forerunner of the CIA. To round off his North African tour, Murphy flew ito Tunisia and to Casablanca, whose Atlantic harbour – one of the largest man-made ports in the world – was the jewel in the crown as far as Washington was concerned.[24]

Murphy arrived in Casablanca, Morocco's largest city, on 3 January 1941. Within hours of checking into his hotel, he received a phone-call from Theodor Auer, who oversaw both the Armistice Commission's work in the city, plus Abwehr operations. Auer reminded Murphy of their shared time together as diplomats in Paris – Auer had served as First Secretary of the German embassy – before demanding that they meet. Murphy wasn't keen to have Auer 'poking into my affairs', but eventually, under the urging of the city's Vichy officials, they rendezvoused at Casablanca's luxurious Hotel Transatlantique.[25]

Having demanded of Murphy exactly what he was doing in Morocco, and got suitable fudge and prevarication by way of a response, Auer gave it to the American straight. As far as he was concerned, 'that prize ass in Berlin' – Hitler – was missing a trick in not seizing all of French North Africa. Auer's mission was to open the Führer's eyes to the 'importance of the Mediterranean [in general] and of Morocco in particular'.[26] Murphy felt his spirits sink. From a port like Casablanca, the German U-boat packs could tear into American shipping, for it would offer the perfect point of departure for the East Coast of the United States.

In short, the race to win North Africa was on.

Murphy flew back to Washington, carrying that very message to President Roosevelt. With the Murphy–Weygand agreement in place, he now faced the daunting task of recruiting twelve would-be spies for overseas operations – something that just wasn't being done by the US right then. At the same time, Roosevelt had somehow to offer quiet assurances that those mercy shipments would in no way jeopardise the Allied war effort. Even as Murphy was cutting his deal with Weygand, FDR had penned a letter to Admiral Leahy, the American ambassador to France. In it, he made the US Government's allegiances crystal clear: 'only by defeat of the powers now controlling the destiny of Germany and Italy can the world live in liberty, peace and prosperity.'[27]

The letter stopped short of an outright declaration of war against the Axis, but only just. Roosevelt wrote that, '[T]he policy of this administration is to support in every way practicable those countries which are defending themselves against aggression,' pledging to 'continue to afford to the Government of Great Britain all possible assistance . . .' Roosevelt intended his message to be conveyed to the heart of the Vichy regime, and he stressed that 'the primary interest of the American people . . . is to see a British victory.'

At the same time, he wrote that '[T]he hearts of the American people go out to the people of France in their distress,' and that America would do all to aid the 'unoccupied regions'. Tellingly, Roosevelt signed off by stating that he had 'noticed with sympathetic interest the efforts of France to maintain its authority in its north African possessions and to improve their economic status'. To that end the US was 'prepared to assist . . . in any appropriate way'.[28] The mercy shipments were to be that means of assistance, setting the stage for Murphy's 12 Apostles to hit North African shores.

*

Just days after Murphy had flown out of North Africa, Josephine Baker would arrive there. She and her retinue had endured a horribly rough passage across the Mediterranean, but otherwise it had been largely uneventful. Bonzo, her Great Dane, had been struck by a terrible bout of seasickness, made all the worse when one of her trunks had come loose as they were tossed around in the storms, tumbling onto his head. Fortunately, nothing had fallen onto any of her monkeys, or else they would all be in mourning.[29]

With no funeral attire being called for, the stately liner had docked at Algiers. After that long trip ploughing through gale-force seas, Josephine would describe their North African landfall in glowing, evocative terms.[30] Being in part a descendant of slaves, there was African blood that coursed through her veins, African rhythm in her soul. For Josephine, this arrival felt like something of a homecoming.[31]

In her Légion d'Honneur citation, Josephine Baker is described as having left French soil bound for North Africa, 'rather than be captured'.[32] But it was actually upon arrival at Algiers that she would face something of a similar fate. She'd barely set foot ashore when she was arrested by the Vichy police. For a moment she feared the worst – betrayal. In truth, she had been betrayed, but on matters far more prosaic than high-stakes espionage work. It turned out that the managers of the Opéra de Marseilles were not quite as patriotic as they had suggested. They were trying to sue Josephine for breach of her performing contract, to the tune of 400,000 francs.

It would take eight days and the intervention of Paul Paillole himself, from Marseilles, to straighten things out. It was mid-January 1941 by the time Josephine was able to set out for Casablanca, after which she would begin the journey to Lisbon, or so she and Abtey presumed.[33] Abtey had argued that she should place her menagerie in 'kennels' – if such a thing could even be found for such an exotic assortment of beasts – but she had determined otherwise. Josephine Baker the superstar needed to be seen travelling with her animals – it was the perfect cover.[34]

The train ride from Algiers west to Casablanca crosses 1,200 kilometres of North African coastline. For most of that journey Josephine's menagerie were running amok. Forty-eight hours of 'a constant battle with Bonzo, Glouglou and Mica' had pushed even Josephine's 'natural fighting spirit to the limit', especially as Gugusse had been lost while taking a toilet break, and Bigoudi and Point d'Interrogation had somehow disappeared, although it wasn't quite so difficult to mislay two white mice. Still, Josephine had taken all this as a bad omen. It did not bode well.[35]

Consequently, when Abtey's application for a Portuguese visa was summarily refused, Josephine was in no mood to parley. She stormed into the Portuguese consulate in Casablanca, demanding action. She didn't get it. 'I don't know what's the matter,' she told Abtey, of the Portuguese consul, 'he doesn't want to know. I got my own visa . . . even free of charge. For you, nothing . . . I begged him, saying I couldn't organise my show without you. He just shook his head. I don't know what to do.'[36]

Nothing she tried made the blindest bit of difference, and no matter what strings she tried to pull. At the Portuguese end, Major Bacon was likewise doing all in his power, buttering up his Lisbon contacts, but all was in vain. None of it made any sense. Abtey was blocked from travelling and no one could offer the slightest explanation as to why.[37]

Desperate to reach Lisbon and the end of the Paillole–SIS pipeline, Abtey suggested he stow away aboard the Louis Dreyfus vessel, making 'a clandestine departure from Morocco onboard the phosphate steamship', so as to get to Portugal that way. Bacon, perhaps wisely, told him that any such suggestion 'was premature', not to mention hazardous in the extreme.[38]

'I cannot guarantee that your landing on the Portuguese coast would be under good conditions,' he wrote. Moreover, it risked blowing the entire Louis Dreyfus shipping-line cover. 'The smooth running of that link must not be compromised at any cost,' he cautioned. 'Take it easy!'[39]

Abtey countered by asking Bacon if he could be 'taken in the open sea by an English boat' to Portugal. The very few in the know were aware that some kind of secret 'fishing fleet' was operating out of Gibraltar, plying the strait on murky business. Covert landings by night were being executed on remote Moroccan beaches; agents were being dropped and collected. There were even rumours that 'toys' – code for weapons – were being unloaded. Hence Abtey's request. But as Bacon made clear, such a voyage to Portugal was beyond the reach or scope of any such operations.[40]

'Do you think they may have blown your cover, Jacques?' Josephine ventured. What else could explain why Abtey was being refused permission to travel?

'I doubt it,' he answered. 'But we've got to keep going no matter what.'

Realising that he was right, Josephine declared frustratedly that she would have to go it alone. 'I cannot wait any longer! . . . I'll go and see Bacon and arrange everything . . .'[41]

It was the end of January 1941 when Abtey found himself doing something he had never once imagined: seeing his fellow agent – his understudy – off on a solo mission, one on which she was not only acting as the cloak and the cover, but as the lone courier for their newest, and highly sensitive intelligence dossier. Having settled Josephine into the eight o'clock couchette – sleeper – train to Tangier, he hurried along the platform as the train pulled away, Josephine giving a squeeze of his hand through the carriage's open window, while in the other she grasped a suitcase carrying 'Paillole's synthesis, transcribed in invisible ink . . . on a musical score.'[42]

In a Casablanca hotel room she had watched Abtey write 'with water', which had amused her greatly. But that was before either of them had realised that she would be forced to continue alone. As the locomotive gathered speed, her eyes cried out to him, shot through with 'a deep emotion'.[43] But what could Abtey do? The experienced Deuxième Bureau veteran and now sometime SIS agent was powerless to help.

'I can feel Captain Abtey's anxiety, when he puts me on the train . . .' Josephine would write of their parting. 'This is the first mission I'm going to do left to myself, without his protection.'[44]

Finally, puffing and wheezing, the locomotive outran Abtey's legs and he lost his grip of her hand. 'God bless you, Josephine,' he cried after her. 'And good luck.'[45]

Rooted to the platform, Abtey watched the carriages dwindle into the distance, as he mouthed a silent prayer: *May God save you, great daughter . . . and bring you to the aid of a world that is crumbling. May he guide your steps and bless them!*[46]

How they had come to this juncture Abtey could not even begin to comprehend, and especially since the dossier was so important that he and Paillole had decided that Abtey should personally ensure it made it into Bacon's hands.[47] But with no visa and no means to travel he had been stymied. So it was that Josephine had boarded that train steaming north to Tangier, from where Portugal was but a short hop away, either by sea or by air – and with little inkling of the mortal danger that she was heading into. Alone, unsupported, this time she would be running the gauntlet as never before.

Ostensibly, she was traveling to Portugal to perform, and in truth, a handful of concerts had been arranged. Posters displaying the iconic image of Josephine the singer and dancer were pasted on every street corner in Lisbon.[48] She'd used all of that to underscore the arguments as to why she absolutely needed her impresario, Jacques Hébert, to travel with her, for he was crucial to the smooth running of her tour. But all such appeals had been rejected. Hence her departing alone, and laden down with her musical score-sheets thick with invisible scribbles, noting down the positions of the enemy's defences in south-western France, among many other things.[49]

Unbeknown to them both – and to any of those on whose behalf they served: Paillole, Bacon, Dunderdale, SIS – the Louis Dreyfus steamship cover was in grave danger of being bust wide open. The trouble had arisen at the Portuguese end of operations. In an effort to secure Abtey's visa, Major Bacon had leaned upon a 'Mr Oulmann', the Lisbon manager of the Louis Dreyfus company, who was secretly one of SIS's Portuguese agents. Oulmann in turn had piled pressure on his contacts, but his efforts had backfired. With the wolfram wars reaching boiling point, the PVDE – Portuguese secret police – were hyper-vigilant. Somehow, they had worked out that Oulmann doubled as an agent for the British. Due to his efforts on Abtey's behalf, they concluded that Abtey must also be a British agent. If he tried to travel, the PVDE had decreed that Abtey would 'be arrested in Portugal as an agent of the I.S.'.[50]

That much was known to the PVDE, even as Josephine set out on her present mission. If the PVDE knew about Oulmann and Abtey – Hébert – and that Hébert served as Josephine Baker's tour manager, then surely they must also know about her own secret role. And from there it wasn't a great leap of detective work to realise that Mr Oulmann's steamship line would make the perfect conduit for the covert carriage of documents, reports, photographs, or even for agents serving on behalf of the SIS.

Josephine had had her suspicions that Abtey's cover may have been blown, but it was no more than that.

So she had set out anyway, sailing into the teeth of the storm.

CHAPTER THIRTEEN

Abandon All Hope

Several days after he had bade farewell to Josephine at the Casablanca train station, Jacques Abtey received a letter from Major Bacon. As their mail was carried on the Louis Dreyfus steamship, they were able to exchange communications with each other in a matter of days. Bacon's coded note announced the successful arrival of Paillole's newest dossier, which meant that Josephine must have made it through.

But Bacon added, ominously: 'Abandon all hope of obtaining a visa.' While they had successfully 'inaugurated the maritime link' – the final leg of the Paillole–SIS pipeline – there was still no way that Abtey could play a part in it. It was hugely frustrating. All he had to grasp onto was Bacon's promise that fresh instructions 'would follow by next mail'.[1]

Abtey was left frustrated, angry and vexed: he was also worried sick that Josephine was out there, running the gauntlet, while he was safely ensconced in Casablanca. But Bacon made sure to send him a series of coded reassurances: 'It was of the greatest importance that [Abtey] remain in Morocco ... They absolutely wanted to keep [him] in North Africa.'[2] His inability to travel should not trouble him greatly. He was ordered to consolidate their base in Casablanca. In Morocco, things were about to get very busy, and Abtey – plus Josephine – were going to be at the forefront of it all.

If Abtey was going to be marooned anywhere, there were worse places in which to kill time. Casablanca – *Dar al-Beida* in Arabic (The White

House), or *Maison Blanche* in French – was the glittering jewel of Morocco, sun-washed and dazzling, but bathed in cooling Atlantic breezes. Early Portuguese, or possibly Spanish traders had christened the city 'Casa Blanca', due to its whitewashed streets and sweeping ocean-side facades. Steeped in history, romance and intrigue – a haunt of international fortune-hunters and adventurers – it also had a modern side that fused French flair and urban planning with traditional Arabic architecture and style.

In the colonial *ville nouvelle* – the new town – the French had constructed a Paris-like quarter, complete with hotels, offices, street cafés and shopping complexes, grouped around a central square, the Place de France. In the newly refurbished harbour, complete with its two massive breakwaters, sleek French warships lay at berth, and modern wharves and jetties loaded phosphates – one of Morocco's chief exports – onto waiting vessels.[3] Lying just beyond the Pillars of Hercules – the rocky massifs that flank the Strait of Gibraltar – Casablanca's timeless spirit seemed to have weathered the storm of war, at least in the early months of 1941.

Shortly, Casablanca would be the chief destination to receive the first of the mercy shipments – the aid being carried across the Atlantic by American convoys, under the Murphy–Weygand agreement. That alone would make it a chief stalking ground for Murphy's 12 Apostles. Still being recruited in America – Murphy was furtively scouring military bases in search of anyone with even the remotest credentials – the Apostles would not arrive for another two months. Before that, the first blasts of real, gut-wrenching fear – swingeing wartime dread – would tear through the streets of *Dar al-Beida* like a whirlwind.

With America still officially neutral, rumours and reports swirled around the wide boulevards, the medinas and the souks, and into the dark underbelly of brothels and bars that made up the city's Bousbir red-light district: Hitler's legions were preparing to invade. They would advance through Spain, set sail across the Mediterranean, slip past Gibraltar and hit Morocco like a dark storm of steel. If this were true, no one – least of all Jacques Abtey – doubted that Casablanca and its port would be their number one target.

With Axis forces scoring victory after victory, the evil was spreading. In Paris, the first round-ups of Jews had begun; they would be shipped by their thousands east to the concentration camps. Facing the iron march of the Wehrmacht, Greece, Bulgaria and Yugoslavia looked set to fall. On 10 April 1941, an American destroyer, the USS *Niblack*, fired upon a marauding German U-boat that had violated American waters. It was the first hostile action between those two nations, demonstrating just how close the war had come to US shores. Some 16 million Americans signed up to the draft, but Hitler remained undeterred. He was pushing for Spain to march on Gibraltar and for France to ally its powerful naval fleet, and its extensive African Empire, to Berlin's cause. To many, the stage looked set for the foundation of a Eurafrican Reich.[4]

In Spain, the pro-Franco press warned Lisbon to 'play ball' with Hitler, and in the USA, *Time* magazine ran a banner headline: VICHY CHOOSES. *Time* reported: 'Unless the whole world was deceived, the Vichy government last week squarely and publicly placed its bet on Germany to win WWII.' Wild rumour beset Whitehall and Washington concerning Morocco: there was talk of German agents having seized all the aviation fuel in the country; talk of the French ceding dozens of ships to the Wehrmacht, by which they would speed their troops to Moroccan shores.[5]

The fears were intensified by what was happening within the country. Just as Nazi Germany had in France, so in Morocco there was a bitter underground war being waged – one of subversion, propaganda, of disappearances and murder most foul. Morocco had been flooded with Axis agents and spies. If Paillole's people could be found, they were to be snatched from the streets, spirited to Germany and dealt with, but not before they had been forced to reveal all. The Abwehr's mission, as Paillole well realised, was to search out 'arms depots', 'English or Gaullist networks', 'the "officers of the 2nd Bureau"' and to 'infiltrate Muslim nationalist movements'.[6]

Any invasion by Axis forces was to be combined with a collapse of morale and insurrection from within. In November 1940, Berlin had published a 'manifesto', promoting the throwing-off of the colonial yoke in the name of Arab independence. The Grand Mufti of Jerusalem, arguably the highest Muslim leader in the Holy Land, was ensconced in Berlin, from where he orchestrated a well-financed propaganda campaign. Arab leaders preached revolt over Berlin radio, while hundreds of thousands of leaflets flooded Morocco, fomenting unrest. Indeed, the Nazi-financed campaign had embraced all of North Africa, from Cairo in the east to Casablanca in the west.[7]

Once again, *Sonderführer* Dr Kurt Haller – the Abwehr's Irish operations chief and its Lisbon fixer – had been busy, 'stirring up disaffection among the Arabs under French rule'.[8] While there was every reason for the native peoples of North Africa to hunger to throw off the colonial yoke, forging an alliance with Germany was not the means to do so. If Hitler did win dominion over North Africa, his Eurafrican Reich was hardly likely to be any more benign than that of the colonial powers. Quite the reverse. But in a region hungering for change, the Nazi propaganda hit home.[9]

Paillole feared that such efforts might scupper 'Allied action in Africa' completely. In an attempt to hit back he established a TR sub-station in Casablanca, codenamed TR 120. Abtey would serve under it, as would several other key agents. One of TR 120's first priorities was to shut down the operations of the Italian Armistice Commission (*Commissione Italiana d'Armistizio*, or the CIA). The means alighted upon were of the Big Louie/Little Pierre kind – a Marseilles mafia-type operation exported to North Africa. One evening, senior figures in the CIA were 'assaulted by "strangers" swinging batons' on the city beachfront. Only the 'slow arrival' of two Vichy policemen saved them. After that, the Italian officers were advised not to leave their offices, or their 'protection' could not be guaranteed.[10]

In a deft counter-strike, the German Armistice Commission ousted its Italian counterparts. In their place came foremost Abwehr agents, including none other than Navy Captain Fritz Gibhardt, the man who had recruited Henri Aubert, the French traitor caught by Paillole and Abtey, in 1939. Via his lover, Aubert had been persuaded to turn traitor, but with his unmasking the Deuxième Bureau had turned his treachery back on the Abwehr. Yet now, under Gibhardt and Co., there was an onslaught of 'intrigues and propaganda ... sabotage and intelligence', which put Morocco at the centre of the Abwehr's operations.[11]

This was the kind of dangerous milieu that Josephine stepped into, upon returning from her February 1941 mission to Portugal. There is uncertainty about how exactly she had endured; how she made it through to Lisbon. She rarely spoke about it, or if she did it was in elliptical, almost coded terms. She described train journeys to Lisbon, during which her luggage was stuffed with tour papers, but upon which there were secrets inscribed in a certain liquid. She wrote of adopting a deliberately eye-catching appearance during those trips, wherein she used her celebrity to mask her true purpose; wherein she took on the mask of starry-eyed innocence, to hide the fears and worries that she was really experiencing.[12] (For an explanation as to why this reticence may have endured long after the war, see the Author's Note and Preface at the start of this book.)

If, as seems likely, the Lisbon PVDE knew about her clandestine role, then they opted to play their cards close to their chest. Of course, they had any number of reasons to do so. Lisbon's number one priority was to keep the nation neutral: to keep the bloodshed from washing onto their shores. If they lost that battle, Portugal would become a war zone, as the rival powers fought it out over territorial gain and seizing the Atlantic naval bases, but chiefly over wolfram. Indeed, London had secret plans in place in case of just such an eventuality – in case Portugal was invaded by the Axis powers.

Even before the outbreak of war the SIS had formed a secret arm within a secret organisation. Codenamed 'Section D' – allegedly D for 'Destruction' – its remit was to 'plan, prepare and ... carry out sabotage and other clandestine operations.'[13] Founded in 1938,

Section D identified a slew of potential objectives in Germany, including sabotaging the power and telephone networks and railways, the 'adulteration of food supplies' and 'the introduction of pests to crops or diseases to animals'. By 1939, plans were being hatched for blowing up the lock gates on the Kiel Canal – a vital waterway for Germany, linking the North Sea to the Baltic – and for the 'placing of mustard gas on the seats of the [Berlin] Opera House before a major Nazi rally'.[14]

SIS chief Stuart Menzies was certain that both propaganda and terrorism would need to be used against Germany, just as Berlin was planning to use them against France and Britain.[15] With the fall of Western Europe, Section D was hived off into a wholly new agency – the Special Operations Executive (SOE), what would become known as 'The Ministry for Ungentlemanly Warfare'. Backed to the hilt by Churchill, SOE's remit was to carry out the kind of operations which were just not the done thing, and which were distinctly – avowedly – ungentlemanly. But this was total war, and in total war all things were necessary.

As SOE was a child of SIS, and because sabotage and subversion – firmly SOE's remit – could often disrupt the quiet, careful, painstaking gathering of intelligence, SIS demanded that all of SOE's coded communications be run through their headquarters, as would all intelligence gleaned by SOE, and that SIS would get to vet all their recruits.[16] Despite the commonly-held view that 'sabotage and espionage were never easy bedfellows,' and that SIS and SOE were often at each other's throats, this would actually prove to be the start of a largely fruitful wartime relationship.[17]

In the spirit of total war Churchill had charged SOE to 'set Europe ablaze'. He argued that covert action had been forced on Britain, under the age-old rationale: 'If the enemy do it, so must we.'[18] Due to the wolfram wars, Portugal had been made one of SOE's top priorities. It was this that would bring Ian Fleming to Lisbon, in February and May 1941, when he would lodge at the Palácio Hotel and play the card tables at the Casino Estoril. Fleming was very likely there even as Josephine sang and danced in the city's theatres, acting as if she had not a care in the world, as cover for her own high-stakes espionage work.

Fleming had flown to Lisbon to organise Operation Goldeneye, under which SOE agents would lead bands of guerrilla fighters, should German forces invade Spain and Portugal, the one being the route to the other. (Goldeneye would be the name Fleming would give to his Jamaican home, from where he would write the James Bond novels.) As for the Germans, their covert operations capabilities were equally sophisticated. They had 'brought the development of sabotage and kindred subterranean services to a high pitch of efficiency', concluded a senior SIS figure, as their efforts to sink Allied shipping in Lisbon's ports had already shown.[19]

In short, Portugal was a powder keg waiting to blow. The PVDE knew this. They knew the Allied and Axis powers had flooded Lisbon with agents and saboteurs and had guerrilla armies-in-waiting. Each was awaiting the provocation that would set a match to the fuse. The PVDE's mission was to prevent that from happening. Their security police were everywhere, all-pervading, all-knowing. They kept a close watch, an iron grip of control. Very possibly agent Josephine's first solo intelligence run – inaugurating the final leg of the SIS pipeline – was facilitated by all that. It made sense for the PVDE to watch very closely, while also choosing to turn a blind eye.

There were conflicting accounts as to how exactly Josephine had evaded the PVDE's scrutiny, and that of her other adversaries: talk of a mystery stowaway aboard the Louis Dreyfus steamship; of a 'clandestine landing on the Portuguese coast . . . such a risky thing'; of mystery flights across the Mediterranean organised by Josephine's influential North African contacts; of Josephine pulling strings at the highest levels, to ease her way.[20]

There were even reports that after Lisbon, Josephine had paid a fleeting visit to Château des Milandes, where she had pulled out a suitcase cram-full of money – 'bills of all different currencies' – and demanded of her workers: 'What do I owe you? Pay yourselves, and keep the accounts straight.'[21] Of course, her workers doubled as the Milandes Resistance crew, and they were busy with their underground business, with Malaury the blacksmith's clandestine radio set firmly ensconced in the château's tower.

Certainly, due to the time Josephine had spent filming the movie *Princesse Tam Tam* in North Africa in 1934, she had powerful contacts in Morocco and across the region. There were strings that she could pull. She was known to be a friend of the Sultan of Morocco, Sidi Mohammed Ben Youssef – Mohammed V. He ruled the country in an uneasy alliance with the French colonial powers. Morocco was a French Protectorate, leaving the Sultan some leeway to officiate over his subjects, while the French colonial administrators kept a grip on commerce, defence, finance and overseas relations.[22]

The Sultan was one of Josephine's numerous high-born fans. Prior to the war, her shows had drawn widespread royal acclaim: the King of Sweden, the former King of Spain, the Danish royal family and assorted British royals were all fans. The King of Siam – modern-day Thailand – was so taken with her performances that he'd offered her the gift of an elephant, which, unusually, considering it was an animal, Josephine had politely declined. In 1937, the Sultan of Morocco and his retinue had spent fourteen nights in a row watching Josephine perform, when she had starred in *En Super Folies*.

Having departed Casablanca for her solo Lisbon mission, she had stopped off with some of the Sultan's closest relatives, including a prominent member of the royal court.[23] Josephine had friends in the very highest echelons of Moroccan society, and she worked such contacts remorselessly. They in turn sought to guide, safeguard and nurture her.[24] Indeed, Josephine's connections with the Moroccan elite – and the trust she enjoyed among them – would become one of her greatest assets in support of the Allied cause.[25]

Tangier and Tetouan, the cities lying at Morocco's northernmost tip, had been the jumping off points for Josephine's departure to Lisbon. There, sumptuous dinners had been thrown in her honour.

Prominent Spanish diplomats and senior military officers had been invited, and Josephine the superstar was 'showered with gifts of all kinds'. But by the far the most valuable was a permanent transit visa for Spain. That opened up another potential route for getting her, and her secret dossiers, to Lisbon. It was gold dust.[26]

By the time she was reunited with Jacques Abtey, back in Casablanca, Josephine was exhausted; she felt drained, utterly spent. After the long months spent operating in the shadows, and of living a double life and surviving on her wits, it was hardly surprising. It was late February 1941 and she had been serving variously as an HC or as an SIS/TR special agent, with little or no back-up if captured, for approaching two years.

'It's crazy how tired I am,' she confessed. She felt like she was running a temperature, and she was worried whether she could take it any more.[27]

It was the warnings of the impending German landings in Morocco that served to galvanise her. She would need to dig deep to do more; to find the spirit of resistance and the energy to endure. She regaled Abtey with stories of her Lisbon adventures. Not without difficulties had she managed to meet Major Bacon and pass across their precious dossier. Mr Oulmann, their Louis Dreyfus man in Portugal, had behaved most strangely, at first pretending to have no idea who Bacon was. Of course, the fact that Oulmann's cover had been blown was the root cause of much of his bizarre behaviour.

In order to explain away her presence in Lisbon, Josephine had given several sell-out performances, in the process of which she'd 'made some good friends who will be very valuable to us'. But still, nothing could be done about Abtey's visa. She'd even tried appealing to 'the best support possible, notably that of the Swiss ambassador, M. Henri Martin', but with no joy.[28] 'They don't want you in Lisbon,' she told Abtey, bluntly.[29]

This would set the tone for what was to follow: Abtey had been cut out and she was on her own. Rising to the challenge, in the coming weeks she would truly take flight. As an agent she would grow wings. Several times she would make that journey from Casablanca, personally carrying Paillole's newest dossiers to Lisbon, from where they were spirited to London.[30] There, SIS chief Menzies was on permanent call to Churchill, for Britain's wartime leader kept a famously unpredictable schedule. Menzies 'rarely left his desk' in case of a summons, which could come at any time, day or night.[31]

As Dunderdale was passing choice snippets of intelligence via Menzies direct to Churchill, Paillole's dossiers would be hitting the prime minister's desk. Did Churchill know of their source? Normally, intelligence briefs would never be pinned to named individuals, for obvious reasons: doing so would risk compromising his or her security. But either way, Josephine's Lisbon deliveries were going to the very top.

During her Lisbon missions she continued to perform; she needed the cover for her espionage work, but likewise she needed every seat filled, the theatres packed out. Josephine's earnings from the box office were becoming ever more crucial, as the swingeing financial and travel restrictions imposed upon France made it all but impossible to access funds or valuables. It had become as much of a problem to move money, gems or gold out of France as it was human beings, and Josephine still needed cash for the cause. Between shows, she glittered and beguiled at embassy functions and society parties, hoovering up snippets of intelligence from star-struck diplomats, Axis officials and military leaders alike, whose tongues were loosened by her company, by high-spirits and alcohol.[32]

While apparently quaffing flutes of champagne and twirling with abandon on the dance floor, Josephine remained all-ears. At key moments she would retire to the ladies' room, scribbling snippets of information along her arms and even on the palms of her hands. This was a habit she'd first developed during her earliest Paris assignments, when Abtey had charged her to wheedle out of the Italians and Japanese their true intentions. He'd scolded her then for the slapdash nature of such measures, warning his rookie agent how dangerous it was and how it risked discovery.

'Oh, nobody would think I'm a spy,' she'd retorted with a laugh.[33] It was a habit she was yet to break.

Despite such amateurish methods, her Lisbon espionage apparently went undetected, as it had across Paris, Marseilles, Tetouan and further afield. Acting as if enraptured as high-ranking Axis officers chatted away, in truth she missed nothing, gambling that no one would ever suspect a glittering star of such subterfuge. In Lisbon the PVDE were doubtless watching, but whether they would take any action remained to be seen.[34]

Yet it was at this very juncture – just as agent Josephine was truly coming of age, and the Paillole–SIS pipeline was flowing thick and fast – that she would be forced to call a halt. Out of the blue, both she and Abtey would be stopped in their tracks.

Whether by design or by accident, a messenger arrived in Casablanca purporting to hail from Paillole and ordering them both to 'stand down'. Identified only as 'B', a lieutenant who served as one of Paillole's deputies, the individual's real identity will likely never be known. But the message he carried, which he claimed came direct from their French intelligence chief, was a real shocker. Paillole had supposedly ordered Jacques Abtey and Josephine Baker to 'immediately cease all relations with the I.S.'.[35]

The mysterious Lieutenant B was known to Abtey. TR 120 was Paillole's Casablanca office, and on more than one occasion Lieutenant B – a fellow TR agent – had acted as a conduit for Paillole's dossiers, passing them into Abtey and Josephine's hands. If the 'stand down' order had come from any other source, they would have challenged it most rigorously, it was so inopportune and unexpected.

Even with Lieutenant B acting as the message's courier, Abtey remained disquieted. He raised his objections, but was told again to cease all dealings with the SIS, while being warned, ominously, not to 'make any fuss'.[36] Lieutenant B went on to justify the directive by arguing that it was all for their own good. As the British were so clearly losing the war, to continue to have any dealing with them would be suicidal. The Allies faced defeat on all fronts, including in North Africa. Under *Unternehmen Sonnenblume* – Operation Sunflower – General Erwin Rommel's Afrika Corps had driven the British back across the Egyptian border and had laid siege to the fortress port of Tobruk. There were reports of British diplomats burning sensitive documents in Cairo, and a snowstorm of ashes descending over the city, as it had in Paris in June 1940.[37]

Lieutenant B's explanation left Abtey appalled and dismayed. He talked it over with Josephine, who was likewise shaken and mortified. 'The pro-Germans were jubilant,' she remarked of this dark moment, 'the rest of us heart-sick.'[38] Yet typically, she remained defiant, scornful even. She would continue with her espionage duties regardless, she declared. She was confident she could 'easily reach Lisbon' no matter what roadblocks were put in her way, although what intelligence she would actually have to carry was in doubt, if Paillole's end of the pipeline had suddenly run dry.

Yet she and Abtey felt torn between two sets of conflicting spymasters right now: on the one hand, de Gaulle's Free French and the SIS in London; on the other, Paillole and his TR/Vichy network in France. Somehow, they needed to check whether Lieutenant B's stand down order was genuine. Josephine figured Abtey should write to Bacon, querying the shock directive with London – with Dunderdale himself, if necessary. While he was at it, Abtey should ask Bacon for his Free French pay, as his coffers were running dry. Certainly, the £1,000 of SIS money was all-but exhausted.

Abtey did just that, stressing to Bacon how it was 'essential we consult each other', and of the urgent need to meet.[39] If necessary, he was prepared to stow away aboard the Louis Dreyfus steamship, after which he would get himself arrested on the high seas by the Portuguese authorities, even if Bacon then had to bail him out of a Lisbon gaol. But the reply that came back proved deeply disheartening.

It was 'too complicated' to allow Abtey to be 'caught on the high seas'. In any case, a meeting was so risky that Bacon ruled it out completely. He also made it clear that there would be no further funds for Abtey, even though he was supposedly serving as an 'officer of the Free French'. Abtey was starting to feel as if he had been cut loose and left to fend for himself. He could not believe that Dunderdale had approved of 'Bacon's way of doing things'. It was 'inexcusable', and it filled Abtey with 'immense disgust'.[40] But try as he might, he had no way of reaching the London spymaster himself.

In truth, Dunderdale was completely in the dark. Increasingly, the SIS Lisbon station had been 'bedevilled by staffing problems', and was plagued by a lack of the kind of vision and decisive action that was required in the cut and thrust of war. Some in the Lisbon office were accused of losing their nerve; their focus; their edge. Eventually, Menzies himself was forced to intervene, warning Lisbon that 'the war is at [a] stage at which risks must be taken, and the question of being compromised must take a back seat.'[41]

Dunderdale would be 'incensed' when he learned of Abtey's attempts to make contact with him, which had gone uncommunicated to London.[42] He realised, all too late, that he should have spirited this French agent – his personal friend – to Britain, when he had first had the opportunity, in the utmost secrecy of course. Bearing in mind the 'importance of the information' Abtey and Josephine were passing across, getting them to Britain should have been a priority, and despite the risks involved. But Dunderdale had been misled by Lisbon. 'Unfortunately, it was too late.'[43]

Shortly, Dunderdale would fly out to Lisbon. Arriving there in March 1941, in part his mission was to set up a liaison with an ultra-secret Polish team – codenamed CADIX – secreted in Vichy France, who were using Polish Enigma machines to break enemy signals. Dunderdale carried with him a radio, crystals and codebooks, to enable the most vital CADIX intelligence to be communicated to London.[44] The CADIX group would also become a hub for wireless signals emanating from North Africa, which would be relayed to London, where Dunderdale – 'Wilski', as the Poles knew him – oversaw the operations of the Polish intelligence service in exile.[45]

But Dunderdale was also in Lisbon to put a rocket under the SIS office, which was dogged by poor staffing, security and morale.[46] All seemed convinced that Portugal was about to be invaded.[47] Dunderdale must have succeeded in his mission, for the Lisbon station was transformed. By the end of 1941 the amount of signals sent from there would be greater than any other SIS station worldwide. The Lisbon office would play a key role in the 'body-lines' – the routes via which escaped Allied POWs were smuggled through Spain into Portugal and from there to Britain. By the end of the war Lisbon had scored many notable successes, including exposing British traitors, identifying over two thousand known or suspected enemy agents, plus outing scores of businesses in Portugal that were actually covers for Abwehr operations.[48]

But all of that would come too late for Josephine and Abtey and for the Paillole–SIS pipeline.

CHAPTER FOURTEEN

Unbreakable

Facing what seemed like rejection from both France and Great Britain, Josephine and Abtey had few options left open to them. They would have to fall back upon influential local contacts. Utterly spent from the relentless pace of operations, and with this dark uncertainty and intrigue hanging over them like a sword of Damocles, Josephine was exhausted and felt desperate for a break. She needed to rest and recuperate. Accordingly, she left Casablanca and headed south the 250-odd kilometres to Marrakesh, where she intended to link up with powerful friends.[1]

Morocco's fourth-largest city, Marrakesh lies at the foothills of the dramatic, snow-clad Atlas Mountains. Josephine had high-level contacts in the city, and it was a place with which she and Abtey would fall deeply in love. But for now, he had chosen to remain in Casablanca, desperate to receive some kind of concrete news. In light of the 'information of huge importance' they had sent, how could the pipeline simply be shut down? Nothing made any sense. Twice the Louis Dreyfus steamship docked at Casablanca, and twice Abtey sought an update, but each time the captain emerged looking furtive and hounded and, Abtey lamented, 'without bringing me any mail'.[2]

Two weeks became four and still not a word from Lisbon or London. Weary to the bone from it all, and of the war, Abtey resolved that he would follow in Josephine's footsteps. He would head to Marrakesh, hoping to find the same kind of solace and respite with her as he had eight months earlier, when he had sought her out at Château des Milandes.

If Casablanca was the nation's commercial heart, Marrakesh – known as the Red City, due to its ancient ochre-hued walls and sandstone buildings – was its cultural and spiritual one. The Red City had been founded in 1070 by the Berber people, who made up around half the population of Morocco and were renowned as being a fiercely independent warrior race speaking their own Berber languages. Securing their allegiances was key to winning the nation militarily, and to any wider North African conquest, Berbers also being found across neighbouring Algeria, Tunisia and Libya.

The hub of Marrakesh is the famous Djemaa el-Fna square, into which pour Berbers from the Atlas Mountains, nomads from the southern deserts and Arab farmers from the rich agricultural hinterland. There they swap news and gossip over glasses of sweet mint tea, have their heads shaved by open-air barbers, marvel at the acrobats and jugglers and haggle over street-side deals. Off the square lie labyrinthine streets, interspersed with rich tropical gardens perfumed with orange and pomegranate groves, irrigated by the city's canals and lakes, which are fed by meltwaters running off the Atlas.

A famed place of rest and recuperation, Churchill had found respite and inspiration here, hailing Marrakesh as 'the most lovely spot in the world'.[3] The city hosted some of the nation's grandest palaces, one of which was to welcome Josephine. Via the good offices of her Moroccan friend Moulay Larbi El Alaoui, the Sultan of Morocco's cousin, she was introduced to a man who was arguably the second most powerful figure in the entire country – the Berber chief Si Thami El Glaoui, the autocratic Pasha – Governor – of Marrakesh. ('Moulay' is the Moroccan term denoting a royal prince; 'Si' the nearest equivalent to 'Sir'.) Crucially, El Glaoui commanded the allegiances of the Berber tribes across the Atlas, hence his English title, the 'Lord of the Atlas'.

Due to his reach and power, El Glaoui was being courted by Berlin and likewise by Allied leaders. In the winter of 1935–6, Churchill had spent several months in the Red City on a painting holiday, falling in love with 'the Paris of the Sahara'.[4] While there he had met with the Lord of the Atlas and the two had become firm friends.[5] Now, a fierce tug of war was in train for the loyalty of the Berber chief. In this, Josephine Baker was set to play a leading role, along with Jacques Abtey. It was April 1941 when she arrived at the Pasha's glorious palace, the fantastic luxuries of which were concealed behind a dull, reddish-brown facade, the better to obscure what lay within.

As with most Moroccans, El Glaoui was a Muslim, and his beliefs decreed that earthly wealth and luxury should remain hidden, so as not to incite the envy of his fellows.[6] Consequently, the glittering fountains, luxuriant gardens, richly embroidered pavilions and magnificent rooms of his palaces were seen by only the select few. The Pasha proved to be shrewd, worldly-wise, cultured and highly educated – he had studied widely in Paris. Lean, hawk-faced, dark-eyed, he was reputed to keep a harem of 365 women. While his manners could be impeccable, and he could prove fabulously generous and attentive, he was in effect a medieval lord whose home was served by scores of slaves.[7]

With the absolute feudal power that he wielded, the Lord of the Atlas was an anachronism to many in Morocco who hungered for change, and to throw off the French colonial yoke. But to the Allies and the Axis powers, winning his allegiance was going to prove critical. As Josephine Baker sat down to a feast in his palace, she little realised the key role this figure would come to play in her own fortunes. Fellow warriors, charismatic visionaries, charmers and survivors, the Berber chief and Josephine-the-superstar would hit it off, and via their shared strength of character would forge a special bond.

In time El Glaoui would 'adopt' Josephine, and her mission, wholeheartedly. But while he was very taken with her, he could not have her staying as a guest at his palace. He had uneasy alliances to maintain – principally with Morocco's French colonial rulers, who answered directly to Pétain's Vichy government. Hosting such an outspoken opponent of all things Nazi would infuriate Morocco's Vichyite elite. Giving refuge to such a high-profile and spirited partisan of Free France was not a smart move, and El Glaoui was anything if not smart. He might have his beliefs and his allegiances, but in the spring of 1941 it was all about survival.[8]

Instead, Josephine – this special agent that the Allies had seemingly cast aside – was offered sanctuary in a relatively modest villa in the city's medina, a maze-like warren of narrow, twisting streets, wherein Westerners rarely tended to tread. The house came courtesy of the Pasha's brother-in-law, Si Mohamed Menebhi, who was a powerful figure in his own right, being the son of the former Grand Vizier of Morocco, in effect the Sultan's head of state.[9] In time, Si Mohamed would become her most dedicated supporter in all Morocco; a loyal friend through good and bad times alike.[10]

The villa lay barely a stone's throw from the centuries-old Kutubiyya Mosque, Marrakesh's largest. It was a 'residence worthy of *One Thousand and One Nights*', or the *Arabian Nights* as it is more commonly known – the collection of Arabic folk tales which include *Ali Baba and the Forty Thieves*, *Aladdin's Wonderful Lamp*, and the *Seven Voyages of Sinbad The Sailor.*[11] The unassuming entranceway lay at the end of a narrow passage, snaking between two high mud walls. An old man with eyes as blue as the sky above the Atlas Mountains and a long beard as white as their snow, ushered Josephine inside. He welcomed her with the traditional Moroccan greeting, placing his palm to his heart, his hand 'gnarled like a vine'. Despite the villa's humble-seeming exterior, through three doors and across cool blue mosaic floors lay a wonderful central courtyard. It sheltered 'an enchanted garden', the centrepiece of which was 'a fountain whose murmur mingled with the chirping of the birds', which flitted between trees laden with oranges.[12]

There was something immensely restful about the place. It struck Josephine as being a house shaped by God, wherein 'the spirit of the Creator still seems to blow.' Her view of religion was as unorthodox as so much else about her. Much that she believed, she did not think that God necessarily rested in one place, or that any one religion had an exclusive claim to holiness. For Josephine, God was as likely to be found in a synagogue, a mosque, a cathedral or a warehouse, as a mud-walled house in the Marrakesh medina.[13] While the world was 'cracking on all sides in its old carcass', and millions were 'fighting each other, killing each other', here in the Red City she had found a place of spiritual calm and peace.[14]

Josephine was a complex, multifaceted character. To some, the many sides of her appeared to be in conflict. To others, there was a magical fusion; a harmony. She was fond of wandering her homes dressed in very little, or even naked, believing that was how we all came into the world. But at the same time, most nights she would kneel at her bedside to pray. Often, she would do so from a tiny Jewish prayer book, rendered in both Hebrew and French. She'd developed the habit when married to Jean Lion, finding a universal truth in those verses. Even when so many were doing all they could to deny that very heritage – Jewishness – she kept that book with her all through the war. Thousands would go to the gas chambers for far less, but Josephine would not be dissuaded.[15]

Becoming almost an adopted child of Si Mohamed's family, she allowed his three daughters, Fela, Rafet and Hagdousch, to cloak her in a thick djellaba, a traditional, hooded Berber robe.[16] Dressed like that, she would wander the streets of the magical city come dusk, being almost unrecognisable. It conferred a delicious anonymity on this foreigner and superstar, one that she thrilled to. At first she ventured out in the company of the girls, but then she took to wandering out alone to experience the wonders of Djemaa el-Fna at night.

She was entranced by the snake-charmers and their dancing cobras; she mingled with the crowds, listening to the storytellers' timeless tales; she paused at stalls selling baby falcons, live snails, intricately patterned rugs and glossy leather goods; she let her senses be assailed by the heady scents of lemons, spices and mint. She marvelled at this magical city with its age-old defensive walls and its stout gates, with its tombs of foremost Berber leaders, with its traders strolling barefoot next to their beasts of burden. At times she fought with the street vendors because they were too tough on their animals, but they too had been raised in a hard school of life. She immersed herself in the poverty, the beggars, the disabled and infirm, giving generously, and letting it all wash over her.[17]

From Si Mohamed Menebhi's daughters she earned the nickname 'Tata Joe' – Auntie Joe. She had always wanted children and she doted on those girls. From Fela, Rafet and Hagdousch she learned to sing the songs traditional to these ancient mountain people, like the one that greets the dawn, a very special time of day in Marrakesh.[18] With sunrise over the Red City came the magical sight of snow-covered peaks – the distant Atlas – while closer at hand small streams were channelled between majestic groves of palm trees.[19] It was here in the Red City that Josephine would take refuge, whenever she was exhausted; too finished to continue; desperate for rest and recuperation. She did so now, in the spring of 1941, as the war raged on all sides, distant but closing in, and as the fortunes of the Allies darkened.[20]

After weeks of frustration in Casablanca waiting for something – anything – from Bacon, Abtey had finally given up. The Louis Dreyfus steamship seemed to have ceased all operations, meaning that their means of communication with Bacon, with London, was terminated. It felt like the final death knell. It was almost as if Lieutenant B's warnings had come to pass: Britain was finished. The dream had died. He made his way to Marrakesh, and to Josephine in the villa, discovering there a place of refuge. For a short while this became their family home – their redoubt – and it was one for which they would develop a close affection.

'Days followed days,' wrote Abtey of this interlude, 'renewing our souls.'[21]

Gradually, Josephine got her menagerie settled in. Her animals loved the cooling shade of the courtyard, plus the orange trees that clustered around the central fountain. In this 'private world, remote from prying eyes', she would have been content, save for the war.[22]

The two special agents had been removed from the fight, due to circumstances they could neither fathom nor control, but they were still not completely separate from it. There was always a part of them that remained alert, watchful for something, some small event that might propel them 'back into the infernal circle' of a world at war.[23]

Their friend Rodolphe Solmsen joined them in Marrakesh. The Jewish film producer was seeking a means to travel to Peru, to be reunited with his family. Via his contacts, Abtey managed to get him the proper papers. One morning Solmsen set off to work his passage on a cargo boat bound for the USA, and onwards to Peru. His departure was a reminder of the countless families torn apart by the war.

Josephine and Jacques were paid a visit in their medina home by Moulay Larbi El Alaoui. Cousin of the Sultan of Morocco, he served as his mentor, overseeing his education. A powerful figure, Moulay Larbi brought news that would shake his hosts to the core – for if he was right, the war would soon be on their very doorstep. He shared with them the news that Spanish and German troops were already in the Tetouan area, undergoing joint operations, and were poised to sweep south to take all of Morocco. Tetouan was the location of the nation's second port. If their friend's warnings were true, this was tantamount to disaster, and especially if Spain were poised to join the war on the Axis side. But what could they do about it? Paillole had not had a single operational agent in Spain, which was a closed book to his networks, as it was to Abtey and Josephine.[24]

The British had a little more insight, but what their agencies were picking up seemed equally worrying. In mid-May 1941 a note had been sent from 'A/DB' to 'H', A/DB being Lieutenant Hugh Quennell, the chief of SOE's Iberia Section, covering Spain, Portugal, Gibraltar and North-west Africa, and H being Charles Hilary Scott, one of Quennell's most capable operators.[25] Quennell was in civilian life a lawyer with leading London law firm Slaughter and May, and he was reputed to have a brilliant mind, but to be prickly and to not suffer fools. His 'highly confidential' role was to coordinate SOE activities across the region.[26]

In his note to Scott, Quennell lamented how the infiltration of Axis agents into 'Spanish Morroco and also into North Africa has been giving me a good deal of trouble. The Germans,' he wrote, '. . . travel as Poles, Czechs, and any other nationality they can think of and the Spaniards are undoubtedly afraid to interfere.' As neither the Spanish nor the Germans were playing it by the book, something had to be done. Quennell's proposal was to 'cause an accident on the ferry', which was the chief connection between Spain and Morocco, the idea being to sever the conduit, to stem the flow.[27]

But that flow was about to become a flood, if reports from British diplomats were to be believed. There were warnings of 60,000 German troops converging on Spain, in preparation for the Morocco landings. Britain's ambassador to Spain, Sir Samuel Hoare, warned of streets thronged with aggressive German agents, and a 'feeling of impending catastrophe in the air'.[28] German troops had also been sighted in Spanish Morocco, a narrow strip of land to the north of Morocco proper, controlled by colonial Spain. No SOE sabotage by Quennell and Co. could hope to halt the onslaught.

The Spanish–German 'expeditionary force' that Moulay Larbi had warned about, was very likely the advance party for tens of thousands that would follow, Tetouan port making the perfect bridgehead.[29] The day after Moulay Larbi's visit, Josephine announced that she intended to travel to Spain, 'to give some performances'. This came from out of the blue, and Abtey didn't doubt for one moment what she really intended: 'her redskin blood was leading her back to the warpath.' Possessing no Spanish, nor even a Portuguese visa, Abtey had no way of accompanying her. This dichotomy – his apparent impotence in light of her potency and spirit – rankled. Right now, it would lead to the first major falling-out between these two special agents . . . and lovers.[30]

As Mica, Josephine's golden lion tamarin, swung from the orange branches in the villa gardens, Abtey tried to get Josephine to listen to his concerns. Spain was no Portugal, he argued. The entire country was virtually under Nazi occupation. Ever since General Franco had called on Berlin's military aid in the Spanish Civil War, Spain's allegiance to Germany was set in stone. The Gestapo's detention centres in Spain were rumoured to be some of the very worst, their means of torture utterly brutal and echoing the horrors of the Spanish Inquisition, with its infamous torments.

'A short stay in their cellars would doubtless have a salutary effect on you . . .' Abtey warned, angrily, 'because it would cool you down a little. But go ahead! Go ahead . . . Nobody cares. Bacon doesn't care. I don't care, but you go ahead . . .'

As he fumed, Abtey felt a sudden stab of pain in his shoulder. Josephine with glaring eyes, 'flaring nostrils and her hair standing on end' had just pinched him with all her strength.

'Enough, Jacques, enough!' she cried. 'You wimp! Is that all you've got in your belly! I'll shake you all up, you lazy bastards! You'll see . . .'[31]

This was not the first turn of rage that Abtey had witnessed from agent Josephine. She could be famously fiery. In an effort to calm her, he attempted to offer reassurances. He had only been trying to help. He was trying to check that she had prepared for every eventuality, 'given the surprises that this trip . . . might have in store'. In that spirit, he offered to 'examine with her seriously' whatever plans for Spain she may have made, just to be doubly sure.[32]

She rounded on him, her eyes flaming. 'Checking? Examining . . . What do you take me for? An innocent . . . I know how to refine what I do and I think I'm strong enough to do it. Let that be a lesson to you.' With that she turned her back on him. Her plans were set. She didn't need his help.

Abtey was left with the one overriding impression: *What a panther!*[33]

They did not let the spat fester. The day was spent packing Josephine's trunks. As she pointed out, with no invisible ink written on her scores, what in truth was she risking? What did she really have to lose? Of course, what most worried Abtey was that once again, his trainee agent was striking out solo, bereft of her seasoned handler.

In truth, what he was witnessing here was the student gradually becoming the master. Still, he didn't underestimate for one moment the risks embodied in what she was about to attempt.

Not only would Josephine be travelling solo on this mission, but blind. She had no intelligence agency to guide her, or provide any up-to-date briefs, let alone any top-cover. At the same time they had few illusions as to Spain's importance to Berlin. As Paillole knew well, 'German policy was orientated towards Spain, where Canaris had maintained many relations . . . It was a real battlefield,' especially where the spying game was concerned. 'There were death sentences, both on one side and the other . . . it was bloody repression that reached a crescendo.'[34]

Josephine's mission was a shot in the dark by an agent who was desperate to return to the fight and strike a blow in freedom's cause. What a panther indeed.

Despite Abtey's concerns, Josephine did not delay. A day later she was in Casablanca; the day after that in Tangier, her jumping-off point for Spain. Her first stop in General Franco's supposedly neutral country was to be Barcelona, where she was scheduled to perform her opening shows. Across war-ravaged Europe, theatres were crying out for artists who could lift a nation's spirits, and with her incredible stage presence and her gifts, Josephine Baker fitted the bill. In many ways she would feel very much at home in Spain, despite the sinister Gestapo and SS types who lurked on every street corner, for she was returning to a country that she adored.

When first she'd visited Spain, in April 1930, she'd discovered a magical country, with its exotic, but captivating music, its ancient cities, each a seeming fortress, with its lush gardens thick with heady scents, and its cool, shadowed churches lit by dancing candlelight. With Barcelona lying in Catalonia, a semi-autonomous region, she'd learned to sing in Catalan, gaining inspiration from the city's gypsies, whose wild flamenco dances transformed the women into spirits of pure rhythm, passion and love, capturing the very essence of Spain in Josephine's eyes.[35]

In Huesca, a city that lies not so far from where she and Abtey had crossed the Spanish border on their first mission to Lisbon, her shows had been greeted with a veritable storm; a deluge. The audience had unleashed a barrage of cries and yelps, inundating the stage with a fusillade of hats, jackets, handkerchiefs, ties, braces and even shoes. At first Josephine was mortified and close to tears. But when she realised this was the ultimate accolade – a wild and heartfelt show of ebullient Spanish appreciation – she was overjoyed.[36]

At the end of her 1930 tour she'd concluded that while she had sung and danced in all these places, in truth she'd made a pilgrimage of love across the Spanish nation.[37] That had been her experience a decade or so earlier; but now she was heading into a country and to a people overshadowed by war. Touring first Barcelona, then the southern city of Seville and on to Madrid, the fact that she was Josephine Baker the superstar had major advantages, especially when trying to conceal her real purpose. Wherever she went, she never declined an invitation 'to embassies, consulates' or the homes of 'notables' – anywhere at which she might glean information. Fortunately, the diplomatic parties she attended proved full of people only too ready to talk to such a celebrity as her.[38]

As ever, her presence made headline news. Not all the stories were accurate. In Madrid, she was reported to have been received by General Franco himself, and even that they had discussed the future role of Spain in the war. The truth was somewhat more prosaic, if just as fruitful. She'd actually met the *Generalisimo*'s brother, Nicolás Franco, who served as Spain's ambassador to Portugal. More to the point, Nicolás Franco was the chief architect of the Iberian Pact, the March 1939 non-aggression agreement between Spain and Portugal. He had signed on behalf of Spain, with Portugal's President Salazar as the other signatory. With Portugal having its age-old treaty with Britain, the Iberian Pact represented a Spanish–British alliance by the back door.

The Iberian Pact had played a fundamental role in keeping Spain and Portugal out of the grasp of the Axis powers, in which process

Nicolás Franco's close relations with Salazar were pivotal. After the fall of France, the agreement had actually been strengthened, with additional clauses being added to help ensure both nations retained their neutrality. Much of General Franco's quiet reluctance to sign up to Hitler's game-plan could be explained away by this pact. In meeting with its instigator and champion, Josephine had access to intelligence from the very uppermost echelons.

In Nicolás Franco she'd discovered an exemplary diplomat; a man of dignity and honour who was truly exceptional. As was her wont she'd drawn him into her confidences, but with her secret, ulterior motives very much to the fore. After each rendezvous, she returned to her hotel and made careful note of all that she had learned. Of course, those notes would prove the end of her, should they be discovered. So it was that she set upon a new means to conceal them, one predicated on the daring assumption – 'Who would dare search Josephine Baker to the skin?'[39]

Inventive, maverick, free-spirited, Josephine decided to conceal the intelligence that she was gathering where no one would ever deem to look. No longer content with snippets of information scribbled on hands and arms, she ended her Spanish tour with her very body and her clothes cram-full of little slips of paper, what she would describe as her hidden butterflies. Just as the Abwehr had developed secret ink to be inscribed on women's underwear – assuming that no self-respecting official would ever deem to search it – so Josephine concealed her notes transcribed in tiny lettering on scraps of paper which were pinned in her underclothes.[40]

Josephine had an innate instinct to adapt herself to any situation as the need arose. She was always herself, but never quite the same. She moulded her character as the individual seemed to demand, whether that be the highest-ranking general or diplomat; the lowliest combatant or refugee. Adaptability; flexibility; thinking on the fly – these were the secrets to her success as a spy, and to drawing people into her confidences. And of course she had to master the ability to conceal her deepest, heartfelt emotions and feelings, wherever and whenever necessary.

In Madrid, she was taken to a cinema and forced to sit through a Nazi propaganda film. In it, scenes of a vanquished France – of smashed bunkers and armour; of defeated troops; of cities and towns bombed into shattered ruins – were juxtaposed with images of victorious columns of Wehrmacht troops, accompanied by martial music and with a crowing, gloating commentary. Swallowing her anger and disgust, Josephine forced herself to smile and to nod politely, as the defeat and debasement of the country she had come to love was paraded across the big screen.

In such situations, no one could know her real feelings. She could not let them show. Instead, a steely resolve – an iron-mask – had to slam down. Yet how she hungered for all of this to change. For a reversal in the Allies' dark fortunes. For the tables finally to turn in the favour of all that was good and right and just in the world. Of course, she longed to play her part in all of that, but how? With the Paillole–SIS pipeline terminated, where and how was she to transmit the information that she had gathered, even if she could spirit it back to Morocco? Great Britain was the only dog in the fight right now, and all their conduits to London had reached a dead end.

As luck would have it, Jacques Abtey was about to stumble upon the answer. With Josephine absent and risking all for the cause, he was determined to be busy; to find a role in this war or to make one. There was little point in agent Josephine daring all in Spain – or anywhere for that matter – if they had no means of communicating her findings to those who could act upon them. Nothing else mattered.

Out of the blue, their big breakthrough was about to hit Moroccan shores.

CHAPTER FIFTEEN

The Twelve Apostles

In the spring of 1941, the first of Robert Murphy's 12 Apostles reached North Africa. Mostly, he had selected well-spoken, blue-blooded, monied types, but with a certain roguish bent and a hunger for adventure. All had studied overseas, five had fought in the First World War and two were French Foreign Legion veterans. Most had been living and working in France when that nation had fallen, and they had been shocked at the speed of her demise. While they loved the French food, culture and wine, and the tendency to live life to the full, all were red-blooded Americans who couldn't wait to get busy in the war, seeking 'glory, romance, escape' on the road to defeating the Nazis.[1]

Murphy had been forced to recruit from a broad church, and in the world of espionage the twelve were mostly amateurs. They included a high-born Cartier jeweller, an eccentric Harvard anthropologist, assorted lawyers and bankers, an Annapolis – United States Naval Academy – graduate, plus a foreign adventurer and hardened First World War veteran. That man, David Wooster King, still bore the scars from 1914, when he'd served initially as a volunteer for the French Foreign Legion. Tough-talking, wiry, rough around the edges – with a body still peppered with shrapnel – he referred to the Germans as *les Boches*, a disparaging term he'd picked up in the trenches.[2]

Of the Apostles May 1941 arrival in Casablanca the Abwehr and Gestapo were well aware, and quick to disparage them. In a cable to Berlin, they reported that Murphy's men – formally 'vice-consuls', to maintain their diplomatic cover – were 'a perfect picture of the mixture of races and characteristics in that wild conglomeration called the United States of America. We can only congratulate ourselves on the selection of this group of enemy agents who will give us no trouble. In view of the fact that they are totally lacking in method, organisation and discipline, the danger presented by their arrival in North Africa may be considered nil.'[3]

The real mission of the Apostles was to gather military, diplomatic and economic intelligence. Incredibly, bearing in mind that the United States was still several months away from declaring war, they'd been ordered to prepare the way for the landing of American troops. Prior to leaving home soil, they'd been briefed by the Military Intelligence Services (MIS) – the Army, Navy and Air Force intelligence apparatus, the only such US agency at the time – to scrutinise key points of interest. MIS needed photos, maps and sketches of the main ports and airfields, plus detailed documentation on roads, bridges, railways, locomotives, plus any bunkers and other defences. And while doing all of that they were to keep a close eye on the operations of the – future – enemy.[4]

From the very first the Apostles made no bones about being somewhat out of their depth; Murphy, their chief, admitted that they 'winged it'. There were only one or two among them who, 'with luck, might be able to distinguish a battleship from a submarine . . .'[5] More to the point, Morocco – all of North Africa – was a world away from the USA, or even France for that matter. Dropped into *Dar al-Beida* – Casablanca – these American pioneers were on a very steep learning curve.

At first, it all felt utterly alien. 'Our whole diplomatic drama . . . was played out against this exotic and little-known background,' wrote Kenneth Pendar, one of the vice-consuls, describing the 'sultry, intriguing' atmosphere, 'which made personalities seem over-important, which produced fantastic plots, and led to petty personal bickering of all kinds'. It was a milieu they were 'ill-prepared to deal with . . . because of our general American ignorance of this strange part of the world'.[6]

That being said, and despite the withering Abwehr/Gestapo assessment of their capabilities, David King – plus his chief cohort, W. Stafford Reid, or 'Staff' to his friends – would score a notable early victory. With his classic good looks, impeccable dress sense and cultured persona, Reid - a Yale graduate and another Great War veteran – was the civilised foil to King's cut-throat, piratical ways. In Casablanca, they would make a dynamic pairing. Shortly after their arrival, they heard that a villa was up for rent in the city's plush Anfa district, but that the Gestapo were after it too. Acting swiftly, they got a foot through the door, moving in overnight. When the German officers came to look over the place, Abdullah, the houseboy, gave them the bad news.

'Sorry, big Americans move in now,' he told the visitors.[7]

Despite the Gestapo's withering assessment of their capabilities, two of the vice-consuls had somehow outwitted their detractors. It was score one to Murphy's boys.

King was cut from the right cloth for covert action and guerrilla warfare – he had 'killing Germans in his soul' – and he was Murphy's man on the ground for dirty tricks and black operations.[8] Reid would be the brains for such assignments – what they termed the 'underground rough stuff'.[9] Noting that Abdullah cut around Casablanca by bicycle, King decided they would do the same. The Gestapo had taken to tailing the vice-consuls' official cars, which stood out a mile with their diplomatic plates. They weren't expecting to have to go dashing after bicycling Apostles, speeding through the souks and darting down alleyways.

Across Algeria and Tunisia, but first and foremost Morocco – the 12 Apostles' chief area of operations – they were in dire need of intelligence sources, if they were to seize their 'chance to get into the game'.[10] They favoured the big cities – Tunis, Algiers and above all Casablanca – in which to recruit. Few fancied Marrakesh or the surrounding deserts and the foothills of the Atlas Mountains – Berber territory; backcountry – as their base of operations. But when the last Apostle reached Casablanca, arriving late after many mishaps, by tramp steamer, Murphy was to get his backcountry volunteers.

Kenneth Pendar was one of the most widely travelled, having quartered the length and breadth of the Middle East and Europe before the war. A Harvard graduate, he'd gone on to study the history of the ancients at the Library of the Byzantine, a prestigious seat of learning in Paris. A hunter of antiquities and of historical secrets, he would fall in love with Morocco, making it his home for many years. Before being recruited by Murphy, he had been working at Harvard's Houghton Library, a depository of rare and ancient books and manuscripts.[11] It was some kind of move from there to the spycraft that Murphy sought. Regardless, Pendar volunteered for one of the most challenging of roles, heading deep into Morocco's interior, to cultivate sources in a land with which he was totally unfamiliar.[12]

'I knew exactly what I wanted to do . . .' Pendar would write in his memoir of the war years, *Adventure in Diplomacy*. He was 'fascinated by the drifting, shifting Arab world . . . an eternal human tide flowing endlessly around the precise little island of French civilisation, and seemingly totally indifferent to it.' He spoke to Murphy and they cut a deal in which Pendar would find out 'how much the Axis had infiltrated and corrupted the Arab world, and how receptive that world would be,' when and if the US decided to take action in North Africa.[13]

'I've been waiting for someone to offer to do that particular job,' Murphy told Pendar. 'If you can persuade one of the other control officers to go with you, go ahead.'[14]

Formally, the Apostles were known as 'Control Officers', as their official mission was to control the American mercy shipments, ensuring that none of the aid found its way into enemy hands. This was a real worry for London, bearing in mind the goods being shipped, which included sugar, condensed milk, sacking, rope, coal, petrol and oil. With Allied fortunes in North Africa hanging by a thread, the leaking of such supplies to the enemy could well tip the balance. But Murphy and his Apostles believed the risks were worth it: if the Allies could seize control of French North Africa, it would prove that American forces could deliver and punch above their weight.[15]

Suave, charming, well-travelled and urbane – both an intellectual and a physical adventurer – Pendar set about convincing fellow Apostle Franklin Canfield to join him on this foray into the unknown. With Canfield, Pendar had something of an edge, for both had attended the elite St Paul's boarding school, in New Hampshire, on America's north-east coast. Working as an ambitious and talented lawyer before being recruited by Murphy, Canfield was also an obsessive card-player and gambler, and as gambles went this foray into the unknown just had to appeal.[16]

Sure enough, Canfield signed up to Pendar's mission. It would turn into 'the most fascinating assignment I have ever known,' Pendar would write, as he and Canfield 'drove through nearly every village in Morocco, chatted in souks with all sorts and kinds of Arabs and Berbers, visited the medieval mountain castles . . . and drank endless cups of mint tea with Arab princes . . . as we crossed and recrossed the path of the German Armistice Commission, and tried to elude the watchful eye of the Vichy secret services.' They knew 'almost nothing' when they set forth. How that was about to change.[17]

Perhaps inevitably, the two intrepid Apostles' wanderings would lead them to Josephine Baker and Jacques Abtey's door. Or rather, just to Abtey's door, for agent Josephine was away, running the gauntlet in Spain. It was through the offices of one Robert Tenoudji that the vital link was made. Abtey had first run into Tenoudji, a Moroccan, in Casablanca, where he'd been recommended as a safe and reliable source with certain useful contacts across the region. Tenoudji sought Abtey out now, in May 1941, for very good reasons.[18]

When Abtey had been at his lowest ebb – Bacon going deathly silent; the intelligence pipeline imploding; the Louis Dreyfus steamship vanishing, seemingly without trace – he had confided in Tenoudji. When Tenoudji looked him up now, it was because he believed he had found the answer to all Abtey and Josephine Baker's problems: the 12 Apostles, and more specifically Pendar and Canfield, the aficionado of the ancients partnered up with the city lawyer-cum-gambler.

There was something of *Indiana Jones* meets the *Pirates of The Caribbean* about Pendar and Canfield. Drawn to adventure and foreign climes, they were compelled to Marrakesh like moths to the flame. There, far from being the grey men – the 'quiet Americans' – they moved into one of the city's most prestigious addresses, the Villa Taylor, a luxurious 1920s 'Moorish extravaganza' owned by the millionaire Taylor family of New York.[19] Hugging the old city's walls, it lay in Marrakesh's upmarket Ville Nouvelle district, where the French colonists held sway. A standout residence within the plushest and wealthiest of enclaves, this was no modest home tucked away in the medina.

At Villa Taylor, Canfield and Pendar declared they were very much open for business. From the outset, they made it clear they would work with anyone and everyone, no matter how shady or disreputable. Needs-must, as far as they were concerned. Curious – 'romantic, often given to indiscretions' – Pendar was nevertheless steered by the right motives. 'I wanted to do something useful for my country, for the anti-Nazi cause.' Canfield was equally driven, but his penchant for gambling 'huge stakes' with anyone who was willing to play made him a marked man.[20]

Canfield would not last long as an Apostle; he would spectacularly crash and burn. But Pendar would stay the course. There was a certain core of steel to him, which belied his debonair exterior, his bookish, 'preppy' look. In one of his first encounters with the SOE, he had been approached by a British agent, who asked if the amiable-seeming American might deliver a parcel to a chum in Casablanca.[21] The package was quite innocuous, he explained. Suspicious, Pendar opened it, only to discover it contained a bomb. A note detailed how it was to be used to sabotage a stock of rubber in Casablanca harbour. Realising how this could endanger the entire mission of the Apostles if it were discovered, Pendar had dumped the device into the sea.[22]

But from the start, Pendar and Canfield were beset by troubles. The Villa Taylor's owners complained that their 'winter palace' had been occupied by the two vice-consuls who had no right to be there.

Then there were the cocktail parties thrown for the local Berber and Arab dignitaries, complete with alcohol. That had gone down like a lead balloon, for their guests were, of course, Muslim. And despite Murphy's exhortations to be discreet, the Germans and the Vichy French quickly realised exactly what Pendar and Canfield were up to. In short, they seemed to have come to the adverse attention of just about everyone – their American hosts at Villa Taylor, key local leaders and power brokers, the Vichyite authorities, plus their soon-to-be enemies.[23]

Yet in espionage as in life, sometimes you have to shake the tree, to see what falls from the branches. Canfield and Pendar had done their fair share of shaking, and in due course they were to 'gather a great deal of highly secret military information'.[24] In the process, they would forge a remarkable link with Britain's Secret Intelligence Service. This was the start of such a close working relationship, that Washington's espionage and special operations would be run in tandem with those emanating from London. Headquartered in Morocco, this US–British joint initiative would have one aim only: to wrestle this territory into Allied hands, with all that would follow.[25]

After making contact, Canfield, Pendar and Jacques Abtey would form an alliance reminiscent of the Three Musketeers – at least, until Canfield's indiscretions became so blatant that he was evicted from North Africa. Superficially at least, it was a marriage made in heaven. To Abtey – who was still posing under the dubious cover of 'Jacques Hébert' – the two vice-consuls offered a golden road back into the spying game. For Canfield and Pendar, Abtey – and Josephine Baker in particular – offered the intelligence windfall of a lifetime, not to mention a direct route to the very highest-level contacts in Morocco, which would be vital for all that was to come.

Abtey's first suggestion to the Villa Taylor adventurers, one born of frustration with all the setbacks he had suffered, was that they help spirit him to London. In Britain lay his erstwhile controller and friend, Wilfred Dunderdale, plus the inspirational leader that he believed he and agent Josephine were still somehow serving under, General de Gaulle. It made perfect sense to try to get to Britain, in an effort to clarify all that had transpired and to forge a route ahead. He was sure the Apostles would have the means to get him there. But he was to be disappointed.[26]

'I'd much rather keep you here with me, Mr Hébert,' Canfield, the lawyer and the gambler, told him. 'You'd be doing as much service to the Allies here as anywhere.'

When Abtey queried how that was so, he was told that he would understand everything in good time. Abtey remained sceptical. 'I would first like to seek the agreement of an English friend I have in London,' he suggested, guardedly.

'May I ask his name?'

Abtey had to place his trust in someone, and as the Apostles emanated direct from Washington they were about as good as it got. 'Major Dunderdale,' he ventured.

'Dunderdale? I know him. I met him several times in Paris before the war. I'll send him a radio message.'

As Abtey had put his trust in Canfield and Pendar, so they were doing the same with him. The mention of that radio link to London was the clincher. Murphy's boys did indeed possess a highly secretive radio set-up, which was able to reach Britain. But in Morocco, the hue and cry was up for such clandestine sets and the hunt was very much on. Mobile direction-finding (D/F) vans of the Funkabwehr – Germany's Radio Defence Corps – cruised the streets, seeking to intercept and seize hidden radios and their operators. With the Funkabwehr teams embedded within the Armistice Commission, this was a dark and dangerous game, as each side strove to outwit the other.

As all phonelines were tapped, the Apostles had been in dire need of a secure means of communications. It had required some wonderfully Heath Robinson-esque tradecraft to get a wireless set up and running, yet so beautifully hidden that it was almost undetectable. Formally, the Morocco-based Apostles operated out of the US consulate, in Casablanca. Murphy had tasked Staff Reid – King's partner in the underground rough stuff – to set up a radio at the consulate, but to keep its existence a strict secret from all bar the Apostles.

Courtesy of the SOE, Reid got his hands on a Paraset, a small, portable radio whose name denotes its purpose: it was designed to be parachuted behind the lines for clandestine operations. With a range of just over 800 kilometres, messages from the Paraset could be relayed to Gibraltar, for onward transmission to London. When Reid approached the US Consul, General H. Earle Russell, for permission to set up the Paraset, he was less than keen. If it were discovered, US diplomats would be kicked out of Morocco and possibly all of French North Africa, he warned. While giving his reluctant consent, he cautioned Murphy: 'I hope you know what you are doing . . . I should like to make it clear that I disapprove of espionage.'[27]

In the consulate's basement Reid discovered a disused lavatory. It was the perfect hiding-place for their ultra-secret radio, and it would become known to the chosen few as 'Staff's outhouse'. With the equipment bricked in, the toilet could remain in place, unless the set was required, at which point the lavatory would be slid aside. Because the signal was still prone to interception, Reid alighted upon a wily means to fox the Funkabwehr. He purchased a bulky commercial wireless and carried it into the consulate, telling all within hearing – porters, watchmen, receptionists – that it was going to the basement, so they could listen to the news from the BBC.[28]

Tongues were sure to wag, and reports would filter back to the enemy, thus explaining away any wireless signals emanating from the consulate. As the Vichy authorities came under increasing pressure from the Germans to crack down on such clandestine wireless sets, so they banned the sale of car batteries, and kept a record of all those brought in for charging (they were the chief means to power such sets). Reid's response was to beg a pedal-powered foot-charger from the British, and later to develop a motorised charging system operated via a car's engine.

As the 12 Apostles were officially diplomats, they enjoyed all the privileges that came with that, including the use of 'diplomatic bags' or 'pouches'. A relatively slow, but secure means of communication, these were perfect for lengthier, more bulky items of intelligence.

All such material was to be funnelled via the SIS in London. Finally, there was a means to communicate spoken about only in whispers – the ghost ships.

From Gibraltar, SOE was known to be running a deniable, shadow fleet, one that did not exist as any kind of British government operation. It consisted of a handful of piratical-looking 'fishing vessels', which were in truth crewed mostly by genuine pirates, although very much of the Big Louie and Little Pierre kind; bad guys somehow now serving in the Allies' cause. Overseen by Hugh Quennell, chief of SOE's Iberia Section – the Slaughter and May lawyer, who did not suffer fools gladly – this was the apex of the underground rough stuff. Apostle King would help spirit escaped Allied servicemen onto those ghost ships, and, at a stretch, they could also be used to courier intelligence.[29]

This then was the network that Abtey had been invited to sign up to. What did he bring to the table, other than local knowledge and raw intelligence? The answer, of course, was Josephine Baker and her high-level connections. Josephine had access to and influence over priceless human assets across Morocco and neighbouring nations. As an indication as to just how rare a thing that was at the time, after the fall of Paris and the rise of Vichy France, SIS had been left with no reliable assets in Morocco at all. *None.* That made Josephine Baker a world-beating special agent, especially as the Allies geared up for action.

A few days after Pendar and Canfield had sent their radio check to Dunderdale in London, a response came in. It confirmed that Abtey – and Josephine – should remain in Morocco and strike up a partnership with the Apostles, passing all intelligence through them. But oddly, it was signed with a mysterious single name only, that of a female – 'June'. Actually, this was vintage Dunderdale, and fortunately Abtey had a good idea what it might signify. From their time together in Paris he was well aware that Dunderdale's wife's name was 'June'; it had to be a coded means for him to sign off the message.

In 1931, June Woodbridge Ament, a striking-looking blonde woman hailing from the USA, had got married to Dunderdale, after which they'd set up home in a luxurious flat a short stroll from the Eiffel Tower. The granddaughter of the inventor of Morse Code – the system of dots and dashes used for transmitting coded messages by radio – June was also known by her nickname, 'Morse'. She would go on to fulfil what appears to be a spying role, serving in New York under the British Security Coordination, a deep-cover SIS offshoot based on American soil. But in the summer of 1941 she was in Britain and presumably serving in some capacity – if only as a cover name – at her husband's side.[30]

Either way, via 'June's' sign-off Abtey had got the go-ahead from London. With their diplomatic status, their immunity, and their pouches and their radio, the 12 Apostles offered an inviolable means to speed intelligence to London, and onwards to Washington thereafter. So much was clear to Abtey, after his first meetings with the Villa Taylor adventurers. Even as the Paillole–SIS pipeline had ruptured and died, so a new conduit had opened in its place. They were back in the game.

The new partnership having been forged – Jacques Abtey and Josephine Baker with the 12 Apostles – Canfield would be their initial handler. The nature of their mission was made clear. It was one that Abtey summed up in his official French government file thus: 'The I.S., through the intermediary of the American Vice-Consul Canfield, who was working in liaison with the English, was not long in orientating my activity towards a new objective, the preparation of the landing in North Africa.'[31] As Abtey appreciated, he and Josephine would now be able to serve as agents of de Gaulle's Free French (or so they believed), and of the British, but also in America's cause. In short, they were truly at the heart of it all.

They were back in business – but only if agent Josephine could make it out of Spain with her hidden, secret notes undetected.

CHAPTER SIXTEEN

Dances With Death

They met at a restaurant in Ain Diab, Casablanca's fashionable district that fringes the Corniche, the city's dramatic Atlantic coastline. The dining terrace faced the Lalla Meryem beach, an expanse of glistening sand washed by rolling Atlantic breakers, overlooking the ancient walls of the Ribat of Sidi Abderrahman, an island fortress whose origins are lost in the mists of time. It was just the three of them: seasoned agent Jacques Abtey, absolute beginner Franklin Canfield, and American-born French superstar turned doyenne of espionage, Josephine.

It was late June 1941, and sure enough Josephine had slipped through the series of border crossings and checkpoints lying between Spain and Morocco with her secrets intact. Bowled over by her celebrity, her panache and her sheer star quality, when assorted customs officials had demanded of Josephine her papers, more often than not they were seeking 'autographs', she would explain, making light of it all. Her high-risk gamble had paid off, for the very idea of strip-searching her had proved anathema. All of the intelligence she had gathered stayed 'snugly in place, secured by a safety pin'.[1] In short, with her front and her attitude she had confounded all who might have thought to stop her.

Josephine's Légion d'Honneur citation states simply of her 1941 Spanish mission: 'Invited to the Embassies and Consulates during a "tour of Spain", she collects precious information.'[2] Those few short words do little to convey the risks she had run. Now, here in the form of Franklin Canfield was a conduit to spirit that 'precious information' to those who needed it most. Her ability to get that intelligence into the right hands was all thanks to Abtey, of course, and he welcomed her back with heartfelt relief. It was good to have her home again, although 'home' right now lay in a modest villa tucked away deep in the Red City – Marrakesh. They intended to head there shortly, but first there was important business to discuss.

Josephine tended to make decisions about people on the spur of the moment. She warmed to Canfield right away and she sensed in his presence the hand of fate, in terms of America joining the war.[3] In addition to passing over her intelligence garnered in Spain, she had another priority right now. Ever since arriving in Morocco, she had been regaling all who would listen about the prodigious economic power and military potential of the USA, and how America was certain to join the war on the side of the Allies. But if the key players could hear such sentiments from a vice-consul, a bona fide – if somewhat shadowy – representative of America, surely that would make all the difference. First of all she wanted to introduce Canfield to Moulay Larbi El Alaoui, the Sultan's cousin, for in him they had a direct line to Morocco's head of state, Mohammed V.

In time-honoured fashion, Berlin's propagandists had raised groups of agitators to launch pro-Nazi protests – rioting, breaking windows, even throwing the odd bomb into souks. Most Moroccans realised what was going on and were not convinced. But at the same time they admired Germany's martial prowess, especially as General Rommel's forces continued their remorseless advance across North Africa. In this part of the world, strong and powerful leaders tended to impress.[4] Josephine's aim was to convince the Moroccan high-ups that America was a mighty warrior nation without equal, and soon to be a foremost champion in freedom's cause.

In driving home her message, the actions of the Abwehr chief in Morocco, Herr Theodor Auer, would play an unwitting part. In a report written for Berlin, Herr Auer had painted the locals as a 'degenerate people, unworthy of consideration by the *Herrenvolk*' – the master-race. The report had been leaked and it was passed widely from souk to souk. Auer had cast the French as little better. They were 'degenerates' who were overseeing the 'Africanisation of the French'.[5] Those documents were being used against Auer and his ilk, in a propaganda war that raged far and wide. Yet Auer boasted two hundred agents in Morocco, compared to the few dozen the Americans and British could muster.

It wasn't only the Moroccan high-ups that Germany's 'insidious propaganda' was targeting, as Abtey pointed out over their Ain Diab meal. Berlin's agents had another, more devious means than purely lobbying the Arab and Berber chiefs. They were targeting the Vichy French notables in Morocco, those who answered to Pétain's collaborationist regime. As Abtey lamented, many of those individuals were still 'betting on a German victory' and 'were ready to fly Swastika flags . . . and become perfect Nazis'.[6]

After decades of colonial rule, those French notables held significant influence. For Canfield's benefit, Abtey listed the key offenders, those who were keen to become 'hobgoblins' in Hitler's cause. Together, they shared a moment of high spirits, as they vowed that those hobgoblins would be put to the sword.[7] That decided, they set upon a plan of action. Once Canfield had got Josephine's Spanish intelligence spirited to London and from there to Washington, their programme with Moulay Larbi, and other key Moroccan figures, would begin in earnest, starting first in Marrakesh.

Somehow, during the weeks that she had been away Josephine had found time to meet up with her key contacts in the north of Morocco, at Tangier and Tetouan. In part, she had been on a clandestine mission of mercy. Ever since arriving in North Africa she had worked her charms at the highest levels, wangling Spanish Moroccan passports for what were supposedly 'Moroccan Jews'. In truth, most were refugees from Europe fleeing the death camps. Once they had those precious papers, she helped secure their onwards passage to South America, just as she had done with Rodolphe Solmsen.

*

On reaching Casablanca, Josephine had also paused for another reason entirely – her health. She'd wanted to check if the shadow on her lung, first detected in Marseilles that winter past, had lifted. A series of X-rays proved that it had. The sun, sea breezes and fresh mountain air of Morocco seemed to have worked wonders. But she'd also sought out the clinic for another reason entirely – her hunger for a child. Wherever Josephine went she impressed with her spirit of resistance, and the way in which she lifted the morale of all. But deep within her there burned the desire to be a mother. Josephine believed it was her purpose in life to have children. She was obsessed by this, as she had declared most powerfully in her 1927 memoir.[8]

Josephine had long feared that she would be unable to conceive. Mostly she kept this private, but it had come to a head rather publicly in the early 1930s, when she had staged a charity concert at a Bordeaux orphanage, and had helped raise funds for a new wing of l'Hôpital Saint-André. Afterwards, she had gone out partying with the staff, and in high spirits she'd sung for them most of her repertoire. The next morning they invited her on a tour of the hospital's maternity ward. As she cooed at and kissed the babies lying in their cradles, she'd turned to one of the nursing staff and confessed, tearfully, that she feared she was unable to have a child of her own.

She'd consulted any number of Paris doctors over the years, and she had been warned she would have difficulty conceiving (there are many conflicting accounts of why this may have been so). Drawn to children, she'd become the patron of the Saint-Charles Orphanage, which was located near her Paris home, and where they mostly cared for the orphans of those killed in war. They organised a yearly trip to the seaside, known as *Les Gosses à la Mer* – Kids at the Sea – and Josephine donated furs and jewellery to help fund it. She had a playground built at her Le Vésinet home, allowing the orphans to come and play, and to cavort with the animals she kept there.[9]

By June 1941, Josephine and Abtey had been lovers for approaching two years, and in a sense in their Marrakesh villa they had found their home together. Theirs had been a somewhat fluid relationship. She had taken other lovers, as had he. But this was war, and any day could end in capture, torture or death, so each took what pleasure and escape they could whenever they could. Still, they were anxious for Josephine to conceive. During her visit to the Casablanca clinic to check on the health of her lungs, she also requested a second X-ray, to see if she was able to conceive.

'I want a baby more than anything in the world!' she'd confided to the doctor.

His reaction was one of shock. 'A child? Don't you know there's a war on, madame?'

With the world convulsed by conflict, death and destruction, how could she want to create a new life, the doctor demanded? Perhaps that was the chief reason, Josephine countered, as an antidote to the horror. Hope in the midst of darkness. Surely, the world needed children to build a brighter, better future, especially as America was poised to enter the war, after which victory would be swift and sure.[10]

The doctor remained sceptical. Regardless of his downbeat attitude, Josephine had come away from that clinic 'happy as a lark', for the results of the X-rays had been positive.[11] The doctor had confirmed that she could have all the children she wanted. She'd left Casablanca for Marrakesh riding on a 'pink cloud'.[12]

The road south to the Red City offered a rough, boneshaker of a journey. The day after their return, Abtey went to Djemaa el-Fna square, to have his head shaved in the traditional fashion, which often denoted those Muslims who had completed the Hajj, the pilgrimage to Islam's holiest shrines, in Saudi Arabia. Of course, Abtey had not travelled as far as Mecca, but regardless he was determined to adopt the 'local' look. Josephine was off bargaining for something or other, and when they met up again at first she didn't recognise him. Finally realising who this shaven apparition was, she dissolved into fits of laughter.

'I have never seen such an egg in all my life,' she giggled. 'If you were trying to make yourself unrecognisable, you succeeded. As for discretion, judge for yourself!'

She gestured to the bread vendors squatting in the nearby shade, their veiled faces revealing only their eyes. The volleys of shrill laughter they let fly in Abtey's direction left little to the imagination. Josephine suggested they retire to a place of refuge, where he might hide his glistening dome. Pulling him by the hand, she hurried towards the series of narrow passageways at the end of which lay their villa. There was one final gauntlet to run, the crowds of beggars that lined the exit to the square: 'emaciated ghosts, supporting each other, holding out begging bowls . . . turning their blind eyes towards us, chanting their . . . monotonous lament.'[13]

With so many of them being unable to see, Abtey's shaven-headed look went largely unnoticed, but only until they reached the villa. There, they had a visitor. It was Emmanuel Bayonne, their former Deuxième Bureau colleague, Château des Milandes resister, TR agent and sometime theatrical impresario. Unsurprisingly, Bayonne found Abtey's new appearance utterly hilarious, especially when Abtey tried to convince Bayonne to switch to the 'lawnmower' look himself. All three were in high spirits. With Bayonne's reappearance, they could re-establish their links to Paillole. Canfield and Pendar were keen to reconnect the French end of the intelligence pipeline, and here was the perfect means to do so.

But before they could celebrate, or discuss and plan much, Josephine began to complain of feeling sick. She had a dull ache in her stomach. Famously reluctant to succumb to any ailment, Abtey and Bayonne managed to persuade her to lie down and rest. As the pain worsened, they administered some camphorated tincture of opium, or Paregoric, an opiate-based medicine then available over the counter. But even that brought little respite, and around one o'clock in the morning Abtey called a doctor. Having examined the patient, he emerged from the bedroom looking decidedly concerned.

'What is it?' Abtey demanded.

'I can't say yet,' the doctor replied. He hadn't been able to reach a clear diagnosis. But whatever was the matter, it didn't look good. He promised to return in the morning, and in the meantime they should ice the most painful area. That was the best they could do for now. As Bayonne hurried off to fetch some ice from the marketplace, Abtey took Josephine's hand in his. She was moaning and clutching her stomach and her limbs were burning hot with fever.

'What's happening to me?' she murmured, weakly. 'It's awful . . .'[14]

He did his best to calm her. 'It can't be anything serious, my dear Josephine.' He told her a small lie, offering reassurances that the doctor wasn't concerned. 'Bayonne has gone to get some ice . . . You'll see how it will help.'[15]

After Bayonne returned they sat up all night, alternating tasks. While one held the ice pack to a feverish Josephine, the other took a hammer and crushed ice out on the villa's patio. It was a long night, and when the doctor returned the situation looked dire. He diagnosed the onset of peritonitis, an infection of the silk-like membrane that lines the inner wall of the abdomen, cushioning many of the body's organs. Most likely, it had been caused by an infected needle being used to administer the contrast fluid, prior to Josephine's X-rays at the Casablanca clinic.[16]

Left untreated, it would very likely spread to the blood, causing sepsis and widespread organ failure. At that time, prior to the widespread advent of antibiotics, most people did not survive peritonitis. Certainly, there was nowhere in the Red City fit to treat Josephine, the doctor warned. They needed to get her to Casablanca as quickly as possible. The road between the two cities was atrocious, so they'd have to find an ambulance to carry her.

With Josephine racked by crippling stomach cramps, Abtey took the first train to Casablanca to find both a clinic and a suitable conveyance. He returned frustrated and beside himself with worry. No ambulance was available for such a long drive over such an appalling route. The best he'd been able to do was to get his hands on a large inflatable inner-tube, to at least cushion the ride. He'd also managed to borrow a car, but he couldn't get it anywhere near the villa's entrance, due to the narrow alleyways, which were even too constricting to allow for the passage of a stretcher.

Abtey and Bayonne decided they should leave in the cool of the evening, in an effort to make things a little more tolerable. They dressed a feverish Josephine in warm clothes, wrapped her in a blanket and carried her to the vehicle. Upon reaching it they were forced to lay their burden 'in the dust of the street', before trying to make Josephine as comfortable as possible on the inner-tube, which they slid into the rear.[17] Thus began their journey north through the darkening desert, jolting over potholed roads and dirt tracks, weaving through jumbled, rocky gorges, and slipping between mighty shadowed dune seas, which seemed to whisper beguilingly in the moonlit silence.

'The night was beautiful and the sky was full of stars,' Abtey would write. But from the back of the car Josephine was saying not a word. Her silence lay heavy upon them, as they stared into the darkened terrain, nosing ahead at a snail's pace and trying to shield their patient from the worst jolts and pain. Typically Josephine would make light of the situation: 'They were a sight to behold, my brave companions! I could see a greater concern than mine in their smiles.'[18]

Abtey and Bayonne had every reason to be worried. The doctor had warned them not to breathe a word to Josephine about what was wrong, which had a 'terrible effect' on the both of them.[19] There was good reason to keep the truth from her. Back in 1927 the very same ailment – peritonitis – had killed Josephine's stage rival-cum-co-star, Florence Mills. Eleven years her senior, when a teenage Josephine had first won her breakthrough part on Broadway Florence Mills had been the headline attraction of the show. Years later, after a gruelling but sell-out 1926 London season, Mills had returned to New York for a routine operation. She'd contracted peritonitis and died from the resulting complications – chiefly tuberculosis – aged just thirty-one.[20]

Josephine had followed Mills' glittering career, describing her as a 'pixyish' dancer with 'a light, high voice'.[21] In many ways her London triumphs had echoed Josephine's success in Paris. Likewise a descendant of former slaves, Mills had been billed as 'the Queen of Happiness'. Her premature death had robbed the world of one of the most talented black female performers. Partly, her tragic demise was put down to exhaustion. She'd completed three hundred shows in Britain with barely a break. In similar vein, being two years into the stress and strain of the war, the cumulative effect had taken a heavy toll on Josephine. As Abtey realised, if she died of this illness it would be the war that had killed her, just as certainly as if she had taken an enemy bullet.

The drive to Casablanca lasted the entire night. On reaching the city they made straight for the clinic at which Abtey had reserved a bed. It lay adjacent to the city's cathedral, the Church of the Sacred Heart, and just a short drive from the beach front. They arrived to find the clinic's director waiting for them, an austere-looking woman dressed in a crisp uniform.

'Would you tell Miss Baker to come up?' she suggested, gesturing at the several flights of stairs leading into the hospital.

By way of answer, Abtey explained that Josephine was too sick to move, and he asked the director to come and check on her. Bizarrely, she refused, arguing that surely Miss Baker was capable of making her own way into the building.

For once, Abtey was lost for something to say. He stared at 'this curious human specimen', this 'dragon', unable to think of a suitable riposte. Instead, he turned and without another word hurried back to the car.

'Let's get out of here,' he exclaimed to Bayonne.[22]

Back on the road, Abtey asked the first policeman they came across to direct them to the best clinic the city had to offer. The Mers Sultan was the place, he advised. It was run by a 'surgeon with an excellent reputation', and was but a short drive away.[23] As a bonus, the clinic lay on the north side of the city's Parc Murdoch, a lush, palm-shaded green space known as Casablanca's second lung.

Thanking him profusely, they headed there right away. Upon first impressions the Mers Sultan – better known as the 'Comte Clinic', after its chief surgeon, Dr Henri Comte – looked full of promise. Abtey rang the doorbell, noticing the smart, whitewashed walls clad with bougainvillea – vigorous, ornamental vines – and hoping to God that they had space. A lady answered with a ready smile, and in short order a room was made ready for Josephine.

Abtey asked for a cot to be made-up. Unless his work compelled him to be away, he was determined to remain at Josephine's side and to see her through the worst. Little did he appreciate how long or dark the road ahead would prove. So 'began our struggle with death', he would write, in which the 'rage with which we said no to death', married to 'our unshakeable will and faith' was about all that might save her. Ahead lay months of suffering, during which Abtey would fear that Josephine would 'collapse under blows that were impossible to parry'.[24]

Shortly, Dr Henri Comte came to examine his new and unexpected – and famous – patient. He emerged from Josephine's room looking troubled. 'Not brilliant. Not brilliant,' he remarked to Abtey, who was pacing the corridor outside. Just as the Marrakesh medic had surmised, Josephine had contracted peritonitis. They would need to work a miracle 'to stop the evil', Dr Comte warned. They would know the worst in three to four days, but for now he needed to get busy preparing his treatment.[25]

Alone again, Abtey crept back into the room. The shutters were closed and Josephine looked dead to the world. He slipped off his shoes and retreated to his cot. There, he was assailed by the most terrible thoughts. The doctor's words kept swirling around his head. The fact that Josephine might die was beyond his comprehension. She had more spirit and life-force than just about anyone he knew. *She could not die.* Every way he looked at it, she simply could not perish like this: 'It was neither the place nor the time.'[26]

Josephine herself had said that the human body only ever lets go of life when the mind decides it is ready to. There was so much left to do. Just at the point when they had forged their new partnership, brokered via the Apostles, surely they were not to witness the tragic end of Josephine's war. He glanced at the sunlight streaming in through the shutters. No one died on a day of such splendour, Abtey told himself, as he tried to buoy up his spirits. Momentarily, he caught his reflection in the mirror on the wall. He cursed his crass stupidity in getting his head shaved; cursed the 'clown face' that stared back at him; and he cursed his impotence in not being able to help.[27]

For two days and nights he kept his lonely vigil. All that second night Josephine was delirious, crying out in her dreams about her menagerie; about Mica and Gugusse, plus a small African sparrow that she'd adopted and named Gigolo. Abtey lay awake, eyes open, throat tight, listening out for any coherent, sentient sentence that she might utter. Then, very early on the morning of the third day, she finally spoke.

'Jack, I feel so strange,' she murmured. 'I don't know what's the matter. This ice pack seems so heavy to me . . .'

He hurried to her bedside. If anything, she looked even less well. He called for Dr Comte, and shortly Josephine was wheeled away to the operating theatre. An hour later she was back. Deeply anaesthetised, her face seemed peaceful, her pulse regular, her fever less severe. The attendant nurse smiled. Nature had run its course, she explained. The infection had peaked, and Dr Comte had managed to isolate it with a simple incision and drain it out.

By the time Dr. Comte himself came to see his patient, Josephine had opened her eyes. Gradually, over the coming hours, her strength returned and she seemed finally on the road to recovery. That day would be the first in many when Abtey would find his appetite again. While Josephine's life had hung in the balance, he'd been too worried to eat.

Abtey was determined to remain by her side until she was fully well. Not all would welcome his presence at the clinic. With his shaven blond hair, piercing blue eyes and his 'nose shaped like a sabre's blade', Abtey was distrusted by Dr Bolot, Dr Comte's assistant. He disliked Abtey's 'Aryan' look and distrusted him. He was forever wondering if Abtey was a Gestapo plant, or an agent of the Vichy French police.[28]

Regardless, Abtey wasn't going anywhere.

*

Since their dinner in Ain Diab several days earlier, neither he nor Josephine had seen Canfield, or any of the Apostles. But thanks to Josephine's good offices, Canfield had got to meet with Moulay Larbi El Alaoui. Shortly, he made a beeline for the Comte Clinic. The reason for his visit was two-fold. First, he'd come to check on the health of the Apostle's newest, and most potent special agent. Secondly, he wanted to report how well things had gone at his recent meeting. Hot on Canfield's heels, Moulay Larbi himself paid a visit. Both figures – Moroccan notable and American Apostle – were of the same mind: Canfield's depiction of the 'colossal war output of American industry' had convinced the Moroccan that when America joined the war, the Allies were sure to triumph.[29]

Even as Josephine seemed to turn the corner towards recovery, her doctors warned that many days of bed-rest lay ahead. When finally she was told she could get up and move about, her 'joy was like that of a child'. She confided in Abtey how happy she was, just at the simple pleasure of being able to take a few steps.

'It seems to me that I am coming back to life,' she told him, 'and that everything was just a terrible nightmare. You'll see, I'm going to make myself beautiful for my first outing. I'll put on my pretty yellow dress that I've always found a little too long, and my small brown felt hat that is "so lovable". With that dress we won't be able to see my legs, which are so thin . . .' she added, laughing at her own dark humour.[30]

Her first outing in the clinic became an event in itself. She realised she'd forgotten how to walk. She had become a dancer whose legs were unable to carry her anymore, she lamented.[31] Supported by two nurses, she managed to execute a short lap of the corridor, carefully placing one foot in front of the next. Still she insisted on going to visit her fellow patients, especially the young ones. Look children, look at me, she told them. If I can recover after such a terrible sickness, you've got nothing to worry about.[32]

But those first few, faltering steps, and her hope and heartfelt optimism, proved premature. Two days later her fever spiked again. The infection had returned and it was attacking the very same organs as before. Overnight, Josephine's abdomen became 'hardened like a drumhead'. Icing, surgery and a whole range of measures – including dosing her with sulphonamides, the nearest to an antibiotic then available – were employed, as the battle against death was resumed with a vengeance.

Josephine's gaze was filled with 'an immense desolation', even as she tried to remain strong. Relapses happen, Abtey tried to reassure her, but 'you never die from them'.[33] Yet having spoken to the doctors, he knew otherwise. There was still a chance she might pull through. If this peak of infection passed without killing her, she might live. But if not . . .

For three weeks her life hung in the balance. Josephine lay there, haunted by shadows, feeling as if the very Devil and all his hellhounds were hot on her trail. Eventually, she sensed that the darkness was receding. Once more, inch by inch, she seemed on the uncertain road to recovery.[34]

Even as Josephine wrestled with death, Canfield came to visit, explaining that he had been called back to Washington. Neither Abtey nor Josephine should worry, he reassured them, for his replacement would be fully briefed. In the meantime, Pendar would work with them closely – not that they would be capable of a great deal, at least not until Josephine was fully recovered. For their part, they told Canfield how much they regretted seeing him leave.

In truth, Canfield's departure had come about due to an unforgiveable diplomatic faux pas, as far as Murphy, his boss, saw it. Brigadier Antoine Béthouart, a senior commander in French North Africa, had made it known to King – the master of the underground rough stuff – that he wanted to meet. Béthouart was known as being a man the Allies could do business with, and Murphy was keen to bring him onside. But his message to King authorising a meeting happened to fall into Canfield's hands, at which point Canfield had decided to take the bull by the horns. He'd driven direct to Béthouart's headquarters in a car displaying US diplomatic plates, for all to see, including the German and French agents who were sure to be watching.

Brigadier Béthouart was so concerned that he point blank refused to meet. He broke off all contact and put a plane on standby to speed him to Gibraltar, should the German or Vichy French security services make moves to arrest him. King and Murphy had been stymied, and Canfield had to go. At first Murphy was determined to dispatch Canfield to Dakar, in French West Africa, to get him firmly out of the way. But Canfield baulked at that, so was sent home to the United States.[35]

Even so, through Canfield's visits to the Comte Clinic, and those of Moulay Larbi and others, Josephine and Abtey had started to realise something rather startling: perhaps there was a way to turn her illness, terrible though it was, to their benefit. Abtey, in particular, had noticed how the clinic offered the perfect clandestine rendezvous point. After all, what could be more natural than assorted American officials paying a call on this American-born star of stage and screen? It was the same for any visiting Moroccans, or nationals of any nation for that matter. Josephine Baker's celebrity was global, which meant that practically anyone might want to pay a visit.

Equally, the intensely private, inviolable confines of a clinic provided the perfect setting in which to talk, no matter how sensitive the subject matter might be. There were few guards or cooks or secretaries within earshot. As for the medical staff, they were respectful and discreet, announcing their arrival long before they might barge in. As an intelligence clearing house – a hub – the clinic was perfect. It could double as a dead-letter drop, a place at which Abtey might leave a dossier in the custody of a bedridden Josephine, for a certain visitor – Pendar for example – to collect. In short, everyone had a reason to visit and discretion was the letter of the law.

Misfortune could also prove providential, Josephine would realise, as she resolved to make a virtue out of necessity. Her sickbay became 'an information centre, a quiet meeting place for men who had to talk quietly about the future'.[36] The clinic would become all of that and more, as Josephine's Légion d'Honneur citation intimated: she

'Carried out a large intelligence and propaganda mission ... after a serious illness that had not interrupted such activity.'[37] 'Sick, exhausted by fatigue, stays for ... months in a clinic in CASABLANCA, her room serving as a meeting place for the Allies' agents.'[38]

With Josephine on the long road to recovery, Abtey felt as if his vigil might be coming to an end. He began to head out on espionage business once more. After each outing, he would return to brief Josephine on the outcome, which served to boost her morale no end. It also put her at the very centre of things. As Abtey would write of Josephine's role at this time: 'This tragic situation was to serve as an exceptional cover for my intelligence work by allowing me, under the pretext of visits to the patient, to give her most of my secret appointments ...'[39]

At the Comte Clinic – the espionage hub – Josephine would serve as the spymaster, while Abtey was out there at the coalface, mining the intelligence. There was one other invaluable benefit to having Josephine ensconced in her 'sickbay': *safety*. World-famous, instantly recognisable, there was simply no way in which she could adopt any kind of cover, other than to be herself and to hide her espionage in plain sight. But in Morocco and further afield, her sympathies, her passions and her clandestine role were becoming more and more evident; she had been noticed.

From the Comte Clinic she'd sent Marcel Sauvage, her friend who had published her life story, in 1927, a telegram. It had alerted him to her predicament – that she was in a Casablanca hospital, had undergone operations but was fighting through. She'd signed off, never once having moaned about her own plight, wishing him luck and sending warm embraces. In due course Sauvage would be attacked by the Vichy press, simply for having served as Josephine Baker's biographer and historian. Her enemies were circling. They knew what Josephine was about. Her outspoken stance coupled with her clandestine work had earned her powerful foes.[40]

*

All across France the Abwehr, working hand-in-glove with the Gestapo, had been rounding up Honourable Correspondents. One of those seized was a key Paillole deputy, Colonel Paul Gérar-Dubot, a man with extensive connections in the Paris Resistance and a long-standing HC. Gérar-Dubot proved such a thorn in the side of the Nazis that he would be reccomended for an OBE, for rendering 'particular assistance to the British Security Services in the common task of liquidating German subversive organisation.'[41] Deported to Germany in the spring of 1942, Gérar-Dubot was just one of many HCs who faced a dark and uncertain fate. These were men – and women – whom Paillole feared he had pushed too hard, asked too much of, and driven too remorselessly, until the worst had happened.[42]

In Casablanca, the German and Vichy French agents had uncovered the true role of Josephine's clinic room. They would trail, follow and keep close watch. Yet clandestine meetings held behind her shuttered windows still 'escaped the enemy's vigilance'.[43] Who could target an ailing star on her sickbed? To raid the clinic and drag Josephine Baker from her sanctuary – it was unthinkable. It would make headline news around the world, as indeed would her illness itself, once word reached the press. If Josephine was seized, the backlash in Morocco, and the wider world, would be terrible.[44]

She should be safe to weave her vital intrigue, if only she could keep the Grim Reaper at bay.[45]

CHAPTER SEVENTEEN

Operation Josephine B

Even as Josephine fell desperately ill, so her legacy seemingly cut deep. From England, the SOE had executed its first successful raid into occupied France, codenamed Operation Josephine B. Backed to the hilt by de Gaulle, and with Churchill's express blessing, it involved a party of French SOE agents carrying the spirit of resistance back into their homeland. Had it been named Operation Josephine B to inspire them? To put her spirit and example to the fore? The plans and correspondence detailing the mission are unclear, but either way the resonance was surely there.[1]

After training at SOE's Station XVII – its school for industrial sabotage, set at the stately Brickendonbury Manor, in leafy Hertfordshire, just to the north of London – the four-man team was parachuted into France, armed with pistols, fighting-knives and laden with explosives. Their target was a major electrical transformer station, which powered a U-boat base in Bordeaux, on France's south-west coast. On the night of 7/8 June 1941 they scaled the perimeter fence, planted their charges, before pedalling away on bicycles, even as explosions erupted at their backs and flames seared the sky. Shortly, searchlights lanced the heavens, probing for a fleet of British bombers, which those guarding the facility presumed must have carried out the attack.[2]

All four of the saboteurs made it safely back to England, escaping via Spain and then Portugal, but not without significant dramas along the way. The aftermath of the attack in France was equally dramatic. For weeks, the Bordeaux submarine base was hamstrung, scores of electric trains servicing the region being put out of action, and local factories shut down. But the German occupiers took severe reprisals, once they realised the true genesis of the attack. Some 250 locals were arrested and imprisoned. Twelve German soldiers were also executed for failing to safeguard the facility from saboteurs.[3]

In London, SOE was ecstatic: the mission had proven how such raids could pay real dividends. Those who had carried out this audacious attack were duly decorated, including Lieutenant Forman – the mission's commander – receiving a Military Cross (MC) and Lieutenant Letac and Sergeant Varnier receiving a Military Medal (MM). While these were British honours duly approved by the King, equally they had been endorsed by de Gaulle, who had 'lent' the saboteurs 'to SOE for the purpose' of the raid. As a note to Hugh Dalton, the minister in charge of SOE, made clear, 'the French put a high value on such honours being awarded to Members of the French Military Forces.' The raiders had also gathered 'a very large quantity of extremely valuable information', and laid the foundations for a resistance network that would rise in the area, in their name.[4]

Operation Josephine B was a mission of which Josephine Baker herself would have been proud. By the time the saboteurs' decorations were being signed off by the King in the autumn of 1941, she was several months into her stay at the Comte Clinic. There had been other, signal changes in the war, even as she'd languished on her sickbed. On the 22 June Germany had launched Operation Barbarossa, the invasion of the Soviet Union. Much that the Allies had tried to warn Stalin what was coming, including furnishing him with copies of battle plans, signals intercepts and detailed breakdowns of the forces massing on Germany's eastern border, he had refused to pay heed.[5]

Aimed at seizing *Lebensraum* – living space – and the vast agricultural and fuel reserves that lay to the east, the final objective of Barbarossa was the enslavement, extermination and/or Germanisation of all Slavic peoples, who made up the majority of the then Soviet Union. Directly behind the front-line troops – in the wake of the blitzkrieg – Hitler sent his *Einsatzgruppen*, his mobile death squads. Millions would be starved to death, and murdered in mass shootings and gassings.[6] As the Soviet Red Army collapsed in the face of the Wehrmacht's onslaught, London would predict the 'defeat of Russia by 1 January 1943', after which Berlin would turn all of its attention back to the invasion of Britain.[7]

In short, the situation for the Allies looked unbelievably bleak, and nowhere more so that in North Africa, where General Rommel appeared unstoppable. In an effort to counter the spread of Axis propaganda, which painted the war as all but won, the American and British powers joined forces to publish the Atlantic Charter, a joint proclamation on what a new world order would look like, should the Allies triumph. It enshrined such values as self-determination for all peoples, self-government, global cooperation to ensure prosperity and liberty for all, and freedom from armed aggression. In North Africa, it was seen as being a nod from London and Washington that, come the end of the war, the age of colonialisation would also be at an end.

The Atlantic Charter had really hit home in Morocco and across the wider region, as the 12 Apostles soon realised. Acutely aware of Germany's virulent antisemitism, the locals understood that the average Nazi held Arabs and Berbers in equal contempt as Jews. By contrast, the Atlantic Charter struck a 'chord of idealism in the Arab mind', wrote Pendar, whose mission to bring the locals onside was at fever pitch. 'It made a truly profound impression upon them . . . The effect it had on the Arabs, the way it helped win them to our cause, cannot be too highly emphasized.'[8]

Of course, Josephine and Abtey were aware of the Atlantic Charter's impact; everyone was talking about it. But it seemed a relatively small and insignificant victory, when set against the otherwise dark and dismal pattern of global setbacks. It was inconceivable, yet somehow in a little over a year Nazi Germany's empire – Hitler's much-vaunted Third Reich – looked set to extend from Moscow in the east to Bordeaux in the west, encompassing all points in-between, with North

Africa increasingly threatened. That made it all the more urgent that they return to the cut and thrust of battle.

For now at least Josephine would have to remain at the Comte Clinic, but Abtey was determined to get out and mix it. In order to do so, he was in dire need of a fresh cover. Jacques Hébert had long outlived his usefulness and would be far better off dead and buried. Accordingly, London furnished him with a new identity. Upon first recruiting agent Josephine, Abtey had been the Briton, Mr Fox. He would return to his roots now. Once again, he would be British, this time being a certain James Bradford, better known to his friends as 'Jim'.

Back in contact with London via the Apostles, Abtey got SIS to procure for him new cover and papers. Jim Bradford came with a fully fledged backstory that should stand the test of capture, or at least until his captors managed to break him. The thirty-eight-year-old Bradford hailed from Wick, a small town in the far north-east of Scotland. With a father serving in the judiciary, Bradford had spent several years in the diplomatic service in the Middle East, becoming an expert in 'Muslim affairs'. In London during the early months of the war, Bradford had become exhausted and shellshocked from the blitz. He'd been sent to Morocco to convalesce, and to indulge in his passion for all things Arabic – especially the culture, language and history.[9]

As SIS warned Abtey – Bradford – the next stage of his mission would pit him against German agents directly, in a country 'where daggers are very sharp and killers are sold cheap'.[10] The key focus, that late summer and autumn of 1941, was to investigate the reach of 'the Huns', and whether the locals could be counted on to rise up against them, in tandem with the Allied landing. Raising and arming guerrilla armies, bringing key chiefs onside, plus rubbing out enemy agents – all of that lay within Abtey's remit, as did providing the kind of intelligence that London and Washington hungered for.[11]

Meanwhile, Josephine held the keys to the espionage hub and the vital, top-level contacts. She would ease Abtey's passage to those in positions of influence, while passing on the intelligence he gleaned and handling essential liaisons.

That, at least, was the plan.

Abtey returned to what had been his and Josephine's home in the Red City, his intended base of operations. One night, he awoke to a violent hammering on the door. Grabbing his Luger P08, a German pistol he had acquired, he crept towards the entranceway. But as he approached, all fell silent once more. He slipped aside the iron bar that held the doors in place and settled down to wait. Something told him the intruder would be back. Thirty minutes later, the smashing began again, the third blow forcing open the doors.

No sooner had a head appeared, than Abtey brought the bar down in a savage blow, felling the figure at his feet. Upon closer inspection, he turned out to have the features of a local, but by his 'glassy-eyed' look Abtey figured the man was dead. Alarm pulsed through him as he struggled to comprehend what on earth this might signify. Was this simply a common burglary? Or was it something more sinister? Had he targeted the villa on the orders of others? If so, was it somehow connected to a 'shadowy acquaintance' who had been dogging Abtey's every step? He feared as much.

That 'shadowy acquaintance' called himself Charlie Hosby. They'd met at the bar of the Mamounia Hotel, Marrakesh's finest. Hosby claimed to work for an American oil company, and to be in Morroco carrying out survey work. The problem was, he clearly knew as much about the petrochemicals world as did Abtey, which was just about zero. He also had that girlfriend, a stunning blonde called 'Ingrid', who was supposedly Swedish, but whom Abtey suspected was German. He'd asked London to run a check on Hosby and was awaiting the results. Was tonight's intruder somehow Hosby's man?

Shortly, word came back from SIS headquarters: 'Charlie Hosby' was believed to be Major Peter Randegg, a crack agent of the Abwehr. London had provided Abtey with a copy of Randegg's 'trace card,' summarising what they knew of the enemy agent so far:

Peter Randegg

Pseudonyms: Johann Heinzel, Charles Hosby.

Born 13 May 1905 in Brandenburg.

German nationality.

Doctorate in law from the University of Heidelberg.

The card outlined how Randegg had left Germany in 1932, emigrated to the USA, and became an American citizen in 1937, returning to Germany two years later. By 1940 he was on active service with the Abwehr. 'According to A1 sources, he is considered to be one of the best counter-espionage agents ... Speaks literary Arabic, Spanish, French and English ... Currently holds the rank of major.'

Randegg's appearance was summarised as follows: 'Oval face, high forehead, medium straight nose, medium mouth with strongly defined lips, grey-blue eyes, brown eyebrows, ash-blond hair, slender hands with long flat nails. Distinctive features: slight scar at the base of the thumb in the hollow between the thumb and index finger. He has an unhurried walk, although drags his leg slightly. Generally handsome appearance.'[12]

If Abtey had any lingering doubts that Hosby was in fact Randegg, the photo attached to the card dispelled them. Though taken in 1932, the figure had not aged much, the only significant change being that he had shaved off his moustache. In light of this discovery Abtey decided to make himself scarce, and to leave not a trace that Hosby – Major Randegg – could hope to follow. He hurried north to Casablanca, bade a temporary farewell to Josephine, and flitted onwards from there to Tangier – a riotous hotbed of intrigue and mischief where one could truly lose oneself, or so he presumed.

In Tangier Abtey made for the famous El Minzah hotel, which lies just back from the city's seafront and overlooks the Strait of Gibraltar. Built under the direction of John Crichton-Stuart, the Fourth Marquess of Bute – a wealthy British aristocrat, who was also a Knight of the Most Ancient and Most Noble Order of the Thistle, a Scottish chivalric order – the hotel blended traditional Moroccan

Moorish architecture with all the luxuries of a top London gentleman's club. At the El Minzah Abtey hoped to find the privacy and peace in which to make some plans. It was not to be.

He was hit by two shocks within twenty-four hours. The first was a note delivered anonymously, warning him to 'leave Morocco and especially Marrakesh. Your skin is at stake.' It was signed simply: 'Muslim Brother'. Abtey had no idea who it might be from, unless Major Randegg had somehow tracked him to Tangier. If anything, the second was far more disconcerting. He awoke after a heavy night's drinking – an effort to calm his frayed nerves – to find a figure standing in his hotel room. Massive, covered in body hair, the man had a distinctly menacing air. Abtey 'felt suddenly puny' by comparison.[13]

Calling himself 'Bill' – he was clearly American – the mystery caller made it clear that they needed to talk. He was the enforcer for a man named Sydney, he explained, and unfortunately Sydney was not very happy. Abtey's arrival in Tangier had upset him. Bill proposed three solutions to improve Sydney's temper. The first was that Abtey should catch the next flight to the US, and never darken Morocco's shores again. The second, they take him out to the 'deep sea' and feed him to the fish. 'In my opinion, that's the best,' Bill mused. The third was that Abtey and Sydney cut some kind of a deal, to allow Abtey to live.

'It wouldn't be the first time we had come to a deal with a guy from the F.B.I.,' the man known as Bill growled.[14]

The entire thing was like a 'scene from a gangster movie', as 'Bill' lounged on Abtey's bed, quaffed his whisky, smoked his cigars and issued dire threats, and Abtey struggled to grasp what on earth he was on about. Bill claimed they knew all about Abtey. He'd been 'sent to Morocco to investigate cigarette and dope smuggling', which in turn had led him to Sydney's Tangier-based operations. Clearly, Bill and Sydney had to be some kind of gangster types, and someone – Major Randegg was Abtey's chief suspect – had set Abtey up.[15]

Pleading his innocence, not to mention his ignorance, Abtey agreed to meet with Bill again the next day. It didn't seem as if he had much choice. Once the menacing figure was gone, he decided to head for the hotel bar. Upon arrival, he was about to order something to calm the nerves, when a familiar voice rang out.

'Hello! What a surprise.' It was Ingrid, Major Randegg's 'girlfriend'.

Having no alternative but to play along, Abtey joined her for a drink. She claimed to be travelling alone and to be on her way to Spain – Andalusia, Grenada, Seville – on vacation. 'Charlie Hosby' had remained in Marrakesh, she claimed, 'an American daddy's boy', propping up the Hotel Mamounia bar.[16] Abtey suggested he drive her to the airport. At least that way, he would have some reassurance that she was gone.

With Ingrid duly dispatched, Abtey returned to face his rendezvous with Bill, whereupon he demanded to meet Syndey, if they were to talk turkey. Just as he'd envisaged, Sydney turned out to be something of the Beauty to Bill's Beast. Tall, slim, snappily dressed and strikingly good looking, he had a refined, debonair look. He was everything the 'Hollywood studios' would want of a glamorous gangster boss, Abtey figured.

Having apologised for sending in the 'shock troops', Sydney got down to business. From sources he could not reveal he knew that Abtey had been dispatched by the FBI to run surveillance on Sydney's operations. Washington had sent previous agents, Sydney explained. It hadn't ended well for any of them. It wouldn't end well for Abtey, unless they reached an understanding. For an 'allowance' of $1,000 per month – around $17,000 at today's values – Abtey would come onto Sydney's payroll, he suggested.

Sensing an opportunity Abtey countered: 'To safeguard the millions you collect? Let's be serious, shall we?'

Sydney agreed to stretch to $1,200 – over $20,000 at today's values – 'take it or leave it, okay?'

Abtey said he would think about it, but it was now that he decided to make his real play. 'Do you think the Germans are going to let you make your money in Tangier for long? As an American, you're safe for now, but if the United States decides to go to war—'

'We'll try to hold out for as long as possible,' Sydney parried.[17]

Piling on the pressure, Abtey outlined a scenario. America declared war, which it certainly would, at which moment any US citizen seen as aiding and abetting the enemy was in deep trouble. Smuggling was one thing, but doing so to supply the Germans would be a death sentence. With Sydney's dubious contacts, he might even be suspected of using his criminal networks to provide intelligence to the enemy.

Sydney looked worried. He denied vehemently that they were 'spying for the Jerries', insisting: 'We're merchants, nothing more.'[18]

They parted company, agreeing to think about what kind of a mutually beneficial partnership might be forged. Abtey had let Sydney persist in the misapprehension that he was FBI, and for very good reasons. A plan was forming in his mind about how he might turn all of this to his advantage, and ultimately to the wider benefit of the Allies. But first he needed to know exactly who he was dealing with here: he needed the lowdown from London.

The challenge was how exactly to get that right now. Randegg's people were bound to be watching him, and very likely Sydney's too. But via the Apostles, he figured he could get a coded radio message to London. He did just that, and the reply that came back proved dynamite. Abtey had truly hit the jackpot.

Sydney's real name was Ralph Parker, a US citizen operating in Morocco on behalf of the Chicago-based Costello gang, named after its boss, Frank Costello. Born Francesco Castiglia, his family had emigrated from Italy to America when he was just a boy. Shortly, his brother had introduced him to crime, his big break coming when he teamed up with Charlie 'Lucky' Luciano, the foremost Mafia figure of the time. Together, Costello and Luciano had forged a criminal empire built upon gambling, extortion, narcotics and bootlegging, one that became known as the 'National Crime Syndicate'.[19]

In 1936, Luciano had been tried and convicted of racketeering and sentenced to gaol. He appointed Costello as acting boss, with Jewish-American crime mastermind Meyer Lansky in a supporting role. Via the British Security Coordination (BSC) – the New York based deep-cover outstation of the British secret services – London had forged a close partnership with the FBI, a wartime collaboration that reached 'far beyond the confines of officialdom', while remaining 'entirely unofficial'.[20] In truth, the BSC with its hundreds-strong staff was the British base for covert operations on American soil, and it knew most of what was happening there, including in the underworld.

Working on the basis that the enemy of my enemy is my friend, the US Mafia had been recruited to the Allies' cause. Their anti-Nazi stance was well known, as were their Jewish sympathies, especially with figures like Lansky – known to all as the 'Mob's Accountant' – to the fore. Across the US, Mafia gangs had fought running battles with the German-American Bund, a pro-Nazi federation of American citizens of German descent. In a deal brokered with Luciano in prison, he was offered certain leniency, if he brought the Mafia onside. The initiative, codenamed Operation Underworld, was conceived by Lieutenant-Commander Charles Haffenden of US Naval Intelligence, and the Mafia's first 'mission' was to clear the New York docks of pro-Nazi spies or agents (the Mafia controlled the dock workers). They were also to keep watch for German U-boats lurking off the American coast and dropping any saboteurs.[21]

Crucially, 'Sydney's' boss, Costello, was acting as the lynchpin – you could almost say, mastermind – of Operation Underworld. Costello figured that the Mafia could insert undercover FBI agents into existing smuggling networks, which were perfect conduits for gathering intelligence. Equally, such networks could move drugs, alcohol and cigarettes in one direction, and weaponry in the other, so covertly arming bands of guerrilla fighters. It was the US Military Intelligence Services (MIS) that cut the deal with Luciano and Costello, the same agency as had quietly orchestrated the deployment of the 12 Apostles.[22] In short, there was a beautiful deal to be done here in Tangier, and Abtey had a hunch as to how to go about cutting it.

The SIS briefing informed Abtey that Sydney's main business was cigarette trafficking – running shipments from the USA to Morocco, Spain and even into Vichy France. A yacht named the *Sunflower* collected shipments off the coast, and smuggled them far and wide. With wartime shortages, embargoes and blockades, cigarettes were in desperately short supply, but via Costello's deal with the US Government they had access to a copper-bottomed source. Sydney had the reputation of being 'skilful and courageous', yet at the same time he and his gang were known to be supplying the Spanish and German security services.

And that, of course, was their Achilles heel.[23]

Just as Abtey was getting into serious negotiations – playing hard-ball – with Sydney, he had an unexpected stroke of good fortune, as he saw it: Japanese forces unleashed hell on the US naval base at Pearl Harbor. It was 7 December 1941 when the surprise attacked unfolded over the dawn skies of Hawaii, a date that President Roosevelt declared would 'live in infamy'. Over the course of the airborne attack, nineteen US warships were sunk or damaged, over 300 warplanes hit or destroyed and there were over 3,400 casualties. On the Japanese side, no more than sixty-five men had been killed or captured.[24] The following day America and Britain declared war on Japan, and three days later Germany and Italy declared war on the USA, which reciprocated.

Abtey decided to head for Casablanca, for these were momentous events and he needed to confer with Josephine. The train journey took him south along the Atlantic coast – a few short hours and he was there. He may well have been followed. He didn't know for sure. But once again, if he was found to be paying a visit to an ailing French-American superstar, what of it? No one was about to follow him inside the clinic, so they could scheme and plan to their heart's content. This being a seminal moment – the world felt as if it had shifted on its axis; this was truly a world at war now – he'd asked for an Apostle to be there to meet him. Fittingly, they were getting Staff Reid, King's partner in the underground rough stuff, for Abtey felt sure that if Sydney were to join the fray, things were going to get decidedly rough indeed.[25]

Upon reaching Casablanca Abtey met up with Reid, and together they set off through the streets of the dark and wintry city, December having brought rain and dull grey skies. As they walked, the American gave full vent to his fury at all that had transpired over the past forty-eight hours. The two men had met before, and Abtey had always found Reid to be 'calm, level-headed and quiet'. But on the evening of 8 December, in Casablanca, he discovered a very different person. Reid was adamant that Japan's perfidy – there had been no declaration of war – needed to be avenged and the Axis vanquished once and for all.

They were all in this together now - Free French, Americans, all freedom-loving peoples of the world. Of course, for the Apostles their mission had just become darker and more sinister by far. A day or so ago, they were citizens of a neutral nation and diplomats overseeing mercy shipments – at least in theory. Now, their country was at war and here in Morocco they had the agents of the enemy dogging their heels. Even now, Reid and Abtey were very likely being tailed. Either way, upon reaching their destination any unwelcome shadows would be left at the gates.

Arriving at the Comte Clinic they hurried inside, eager to share their newfound spirit of resolve with the convalescing patient, and never imagining that no one had seen fit to tell her about what had happened. By bursting in and announcing the 'happy event' – the entry of America into the war – they provoked the most unexpected of reactions. At once Josephine's pulse spiked, as she was overcome with breathless excitement, and moments later she was suffering from an episode of tachycardia 'that frightened us to death'.[26]

According to Dr Comte, Josephine was on the mend. The infection was receding, and no further surgery looked necessary. But what the patient didn't need were sudden shocks of the kind that Abtey and Reid had just delivered, especially since all the sulphonamides that she had been taking made tachycardia – a dangerous condition where the heart rate spikes uncontrollably – a recurring issue. Cautioned, chastened, Abtey and Reid settled in with Josephine for a calmer, more measured talk.

Josephine declared herself overjoyed at America's entry into the war. Somehow, she had always known this would happen. All those who had mocked her for her certainty – they could eat their words. The news went down a storm with Morocco's leaders. In addition to Moulay Larbi being a regular visitor to the Comte Clinic, Si Thami El Glaoui, the Pasha of Marrakesh, was also a regular, passing on choice nuggets of intelligence.[27] Josephine in turn had organised several meetings between him and the Apostles.

With America finally in the war, the Berber chief reiterated his firm 'belief in the Allied cause'.[28] He also offered the Apostles sanctuary in any of his many homes, should the enemy come hunting. They were likewise on offer as covert radio bases for Allied agents. In time, El Glaoui would set up a network of radios secreted in his various palaces, and scattered across remote homesteads in the Atlas Mountains, primed to transmit radio traffic across the nation and onwards via Gibraltar to Britain.[29]

Josephine was convinced that the war was won, for America would lend the military and economic clout to ensure victory. In this conviction, she was of a mind with Winston Churchill, of course. Britain's prime minister had overseen seventeen months of stubborn, dogged resistance, but he was certain that the USA would grind the Axis into submission. As he would write in his memoirs, 'now at this very moment I knew the United States was in the war, up to the neck and in to the death . . .' It was now all about 'the proper application of overwhelming force'.[30]

Churchill had already begun lobbying Roosevelt about the key target against which to apply that American-led force of arms: French North Africa. Shortly, the two leaders would meet in Washington to decide upon a joint strategy, which would clear the way for the North African landings. So would be born the operation that was to be codenamed Torch. It would be the first ever large-scale amphibious operation by Allied forces, and if successful would mark a turning point in the war. The Allies would have seized the offensive, and North Africa would become the springboard for the liberation of Europe.

But before then lay many difficult months, and there remained a majority of senior Allied commanders who believed the whole idea behind Operation Torch was misplaced and misguided in the extreme. It was up to those few agents on the ground in North Africa to convince the naysayers otherwise. If Abtey and Josephine – plus the 12 Apostles – could pull in Sydney and the Costello gang, they would have a long-established, wide-reaching, smuggling and information-gathering network at their disposal, just at the crucial moment. It was a golden opportunity.

With Christmas just over two weeks away, the clinic staff had thought to install a tree in one corner of Josephine's room, complete with red, yellow and green candles. This was Josephine's favourite time of the year. It was a time when she'd remember her own childhood, and of sweeping the snow from the steps of rich folks' homes, to earn a little money. With her pennies she'd buy a few small decorations for the Christmas tree at home. It was a time for giving, and she loved to give.[31]

During Christmas 1926, as her fame had mushroomed, a Josephine Baker doll had become the must-have present for girls in Paris, New York and London. It had shared prominent space in the windows of top apartment stores along with Santa, the Virgin Mary and Nativity scenes of baby Jesus in a manger. Ironically, as a young girl Josephine herself had rooted in the bins in the affluent neighbourhoods of St Louis, searching out a headless doll that she managed to fix up as a gift for her younger sisters.[32]

Though the family couldn't afford any 'proper' presents, still the magic of Christmas had endured. The year that the Josephine Baker doll had taken the world by storm, so the real Josephine had thrown a festive party in aid of the children of the Paris police. She'd hosted it at none other than the Folies-Bergère, the iconic Paris music hall venue, filling the theatre with a giant Christmas tree, hundreds of candles, glistening glass eggs, plus cakes and toys for all. She figured she had found as much joy at that party as the children did.

In her festive room at the Comte Clinic, Josephine had taken the trouble to make herself look beautiful for Abtey and Reid's visit. Once the Apostle had left – their discussions done, their plans sorted – the atmosphere in the room softened. Abtey could read the zest for life returning to Josephine's gaze, accompanied by 'a childlike joy'. Partly it was the Christmas spirit. Partly it was due to her recovery. Partly, it was because he was there. But mostly, it was due to America's entry into the war.

'Do you remember, Jacques, the Christmas the first year of the war,' she ventured, 'how beautiful it was?'[33]

Of course he did. She'd invited him to Le Beau Chêne on Christmas Eve, though he hadn't been able to make it. He had come the following day, and found Josephine surrounded by 'a mountain of toys'. They were for the children whose parents were away manning the trenches. He teased her about what good that would do on the Maginot Line, and she'd reproached him in a similar, easy-going spirit. Pointing to the donkey with the huge ears, curling eyelashes and cardboard tail, and the duck with its head dibbling on the floor, she'd talked about the deep happiness giving bequeathed to the giver.

That had been the magic of Christmas 1939, and how they had both longed for those times. But before anything remotely like that might be possible again, there was a war to be fought. For Abtey, that meant decidedly unseasonable cheer. It meant an uncertain rendezvous to cut a shadowy deal with a gangster. For Josephine, it meant concentrating on her recovery, and on overseeing the intel hub and everything that now entailed. With America's entry into the arena, war was coming to North Africa with a vengeance. They had better be ready.

Abtey returned to Tangier and met with Sydney (Ralph Parker), Costello's man in Morocco. The deal he had in mind was one he believed Sydney could simply not refuse. 'You're a shoo-in for the electric chair,' he warned, especially in the wake of Pearl Harbor. 'Suppose we prosecute you for sharing intelligence with the enemy?'[34]

Sydney protested his innocence. He would take out any of his people, he vowed, if Abtey could prove they had dealings with the Germans.

Better still, he promised to put his entire organisation at Abtey's disposal, if Washington would simply leave him alone to run his business. Abtey countered that he could do much better than that. If Sydney lent his network to Abtey's – to the Allies' – cause, he would guarantee him a supply of English cigarettes beyond his wildest dreams.

'Are you serious?' Sydney demanded, incredulously.

'We're all out of jokes,' Abtey confirmed.[35]

The deal they cut went like this. Sydney agreed to shield Abtey from the likes of Major Randegg and his ilk, while acting as an 'unbeatable asset' in Abtey's 'search for information'. In return, Abtey promised to supply English cigarettes, which were the most sought-after, being preferable even to the American brands. They shook on the deal. Now all Abtey had to do was organise a first delivery 'in the vicinity of the Tangier waters', as long as he could convince London and Washington to play ball.[36]

In fact, as far as Washington was concerned, he was pushing on an open door. Lieutenant-Commander Haffenden – the Naval Intelligence officer who had brokered the Operation Underworld deal with Lucky Luciano's New York Mafia – was actively seeking North African recruits. What had worked so well in the USA should be expanded into North Africa, Haffenden reasoned, and long before 'the landing of US forces'. Those North African recruits would come to Haffenden 'through the instigation of Luciano', he reasoned, and of course Syndey was Luciano's man in North Africa.[37]

Abtey would be assessed by his bosses in the world of French intelligence thus: 'Intelligent, definite energy for such work . . . Great adaptability and extremely flexible character. Vigorous, with more of a taste for the active life and individual action . . .'[38] For what was coming he would need all of those qualities and more.

His great deception – his great gamble – was about to be put into play, and the stakes would be life and death itself.

CHAPTER EIGHTEEN

Operation Underworld

It wasn't just the French security services – Paillole, with Big Louie and Little Pierre – or the Americans with Luciano's Mafia, who were turning bad guys into good guys in freedom's cause. In fact, you could argue that the British were the past-masters at such 'deals with the devil'; the lords of the racketeers. In Gibraltar, they had founded the foremost such operation, one that had been built into a daring and audacious money-making operation combined with an intelligence-gathering network. It was named 'Musson's Smuggling Fleet', after its leading light, Englishman Peter Musson.[1]

In the aftermath of the fall of Paris, Biffy Dunderdale – along with his opposite number, Kenneth Cohen – was charged with finding ways to get SIS agents back into France. At the northern (British) end of operations they founded what became known as the Helford Flotilla, a mixed bag of trawlers and motor torpedo boats based out of the Helford River estuary, in Cornwall, to execute clandestine dashes to and from the French coast.[2] The operation run from the southern (Gibraltar) end was a different ballgame. A joint venture between SIS and SOE, Musson's Smuggling Fleet would take government-sanctioned gangsterism to a whole new level.

Ever since its seizure in 1704 by a British naval fleet, Gibraltar had had a long history of military action, mixed with smuggling and piracy. In time, the Rock became a byword for illicit trade, as well as drunkenness and disease. As William Thackeray, the English novelist writing in the 1800s put it: 'Gibraltar is the great British depot for smuggling goods into the Peninsula.'³ In essence, Musson's Smuggling Fleet was simply a continuation of that time-honoured tradition.

Its skipper, Peter Runciman Musson, would win a Military Cross and an OBE for his wartime exploits, during which time he would have quartered the globe. The Musson family home was Neasham Abbey, near Darlington, in the north-east of England, a sprawling red-brick, ivy-clad mansion, but Peter Musson's parents lived mostly overseas, running an agricultural estate in Argentina. By the time he was sent to the top British boarding school of Rugby, in Warwickshire, Peter was fluent in Spanish, which would prove most useful. After Rugby, Musson went on to study at Oxford and Cambridge, a perfect schooling for piratical adventures, it seems.⁴

Recruited into SOE at age twenty-five, Musson was sent for guerrilla instruction at Special Training Station 21 (STS 21), based at the grand Arisaig House, in Lochaber, on the west coast of Scotland. There he was assessed as being 'a very good, tough type who is capable and experienced in looking after himself . . . Can make the best of any circumstances . . .'⁵ Speaking fluent Spanish and decent French, Musson was an ideal choice for the Gibraltar smuggling operations. Hence in February 1941, 'BOX London' – codename for SOE headquarters – dispatched Musson to 'BOX Spanish Section'. There he would serve as 'Commander of the Smuggling Fleet' with such distinction that he would be proposed for honours for 'his exceptional work in Gibraltar.'⁶

The question of what exactly to smuggle didn't really trouble BOX London. With the Royal Navy maintaining a blockade of hostile nations, bona fide smugglers were being intercepted and their illicit cargoes impounded. This included significant quantities of tobacco, which was in very short supply in those countries targeted by the Royal Navy. If some of those smugglers could be co-opted to work on behalf of the Allies, the tobacco confiscated from the 'bad' smugglers could be passed to the 'good' smugglers, who would be given carte blanche to run the blockades. The beauty was that the contraband would be cost-free, but the customers would pay for it at the delivery end, making the venture potentially highly profitable, which in turn would make it a self-financing intelligence gathering and agent-running operation.

Musson was the architect of the cunning scheme, initially entitled CONTRABAND TO IBERIA PLAN, in which he proposed using 'one or more boats of the "Maidstone" pool' – HMS *Maidstone* being a submarine depot ship then based in Gibraltar. Assisting HMS *Maidstone* were several smaller vessels, which Musson proposed should be able to 'change their appearance during the night', for which a 'selection of flags and of different coloured paints' should be carried. The fleet would be shape-shifters, and Musson envisaged a rapid 'change over from contraband to more dangerous articles'. To that end, an arms and explosives depot was established in Gibraltar, some of which was earmarked for Morocco, for distribution to the Berber tribes.[7]

In Musson's view, war, capitalism and criminality made for fine bedfellows: 'The idea of all activities being for profit must be firmly rooted.' Recognising the somewhat controversial nature of his proposals, he stressed that 'the only people who shall know the scheme in its entirety in Gibraltar shall be H.E. the Governor and ADB. NO ONE ELSE.' His Excellency the Governor of Gibraltar at the time was Field Marshal John Standish Surtees Prendergast Vereker, 6th Viscount Gort, who'd won a Victoria Cross, Britain's highest decoration for valour, in the First World War, among numerous other martial exploits. 'ADB' was the former Slaughter and May lawyer, Hugh Quennell, chief of SOE's Iberia Section.

From the outset, Musson's fleet blurred the boundaries between private criminal enterprise and public service in the most extraordinary of ways. Indeed, this would be a standout feature of SOE operations throughout the war: the most-secretive projects involved contraband, gold and currency trafficking, all oiled by a good dose of bribery and corruption. SOE was bankrolled from secret funds which were subjected to no parliamentary scrutiny whatsoever. So profitable were its nefarious activities, and especially its world-wide money-laundering operations, that by 1944 it was turning such a significant profit it was ordered to tone down these clandestine money-spinning schemes. Such licentious profitability was inexplicable and it was becoming somewhat embarassing.[8]

Fittingly, Musson's fleet 'would have no connection with any existing organisation – civil, military *or secret service*,' and all smuggled goods 'would be paid for in cash, thus strengthening the "smuggling for its own sake" aspect'. In the first instance the crew – the smugglers, or 'the Thieves' as Musson termed them – would be recruited among the refugees, adventurers, pirates, assorted combatants and others then gathered at Gibraltar. Via this 'racket' SOE in Gibraltar would 'turn ourselves into legitimate smugglers, and lines of communication would thus be opened for more serious purposes . . .'. In time Musson would discover that the most 'speedy and unobtrusive' smuggling craft turned out to be those traditionally used by the locals. Thus Major Musson – the rank had been conferred upon him by SOE - would end up commanding a fleet of feluccas, traditional wooden-hulled sailing boats used widely across the region, with names like 'Lottie', 'Dofah' and the 'Niño de la Torre', among an assortment of vessels.[9]

From London, Dunderdale orchestrated it all, dispatching a team of Poles to help pioneer the Gibraltar operations. Leading them would be a thirty-one-year-old Polish Navy lieutenant named Marian Kadulski. Kadulski would prove himself to be an outstanding captain of the Gibraltar fleet, and would win a Distinguished Service Order (DSO) for his daring voyages across the Strait of Gibraltar to Morocco, mostly on 'body-lines' work – rescuing Allied escapees.

Apart from the assorted Poles and Brits, the majority of Musson's crew would be Spanish, Portuguese and Moroccan – long-standing smugglers. Of these, Musson's kingpin was José Herrera Saavedra, the former mayor of San Roque, a town in southern Spain overlooked by the Rock of Gibraltar. Even before the war, Saavedra was known as the 'King of All Smugglers'. Serving in SOE's fleet since the autumn of 1941, he would transport over a hundred 'bodies' – agents and escapees – during the course of such operations. On average, Saavedra would make two trips per week, on any of which his capture would likely result in his being 'shot or put into prison for life'.[10]

Saavedra's righthand man was identified only by his fabulously evocative codename, 'Subhumanity'. Both individuals had become notorious among the Gibraltar police and customs for being smugglers who were somehow above the law, 'free from arrest' and apparently untouchable.[11] That alone made them powerful enemies. Without SOE and SIS's top-cover, they didn't stand a chance, and that was the glue that bound the one to the other – smugglers to security service, and vice versa.

Perhaps the existence of Musson's fleet should not be so surprising. After all, Churchill had founded SOE to do the unthinkable: to wage ungentlemanly warfare and to break all the rules. Even so, Quennell, when writing of what he termed the 'Contrabandista Fleet', acknowledged that the aims and objectives were 'slightly inflammatory', adding, 'I prefer not to put them on paper.' Which was bizarre, for that was exactly what he had done in penning his note. Either way, the fact they were operating on the very edge of legitimacy was clear to all.[12]

As operations expanded, profits became 'enormous', but the tobacco seized from genuine smugglers simply wasn't sufficient. While the 'racket' might be proving 'very successful financially', stocks seized 'from less fortunate smugglers' simply would not last. Accordingly, London was asked to source supplies of raw tobacco from the Dominican Republic, Brazil and Cuba, which could be shipped to Gibraltar, where cigarettes could be manufactured specifically to supply Musson's Fleet. In London, Alfred Dunhill Ltd, a well-known tobacconists, was contracted to ship 200,000 cigarette papers to the Rock, so as to speed up the manufacturing process.[13]

Tobacco was the 'fuel for the underground', and the beauty of such a genuine smuggling business was that everyone profited – it 'had not cost us [SOE] a penny' – while it provided the perfect cover. If anyone was caught on the high seas, they were genuine smugglers involved in genuine smuggling, just with a certain sideline in intelligence-gathering, arms-running and people-trafficking. The smugglers had little motive to betray who exactly they worked for, for then their supplies of tobacco would vanish. In short, everyone had too much to lose from talking out of turn.

By 1942, Musson's feluccas were running dozens of such shipments every month. Vessels would set forth 'under cover of darkness', commanded by 'one or two British officers', and with a local crew, all dressed in civilian clothing, and keeping 'as close inshore as possible in order to avoid naval or air patrols'.[14] On average, his vessels would smuggle 109 bales of tobacco per month, which equated to as much as 40,000 kilograms. Of course, they were also carrying weapons, explosives, radio sets, radio operators, SOE and SIS agents, and bringing out escaped POWs and downed Allied airmen. They were running regular trips to and from southern Spain, the Vichy French coast, and across the Strait of Gibraltar to Tangier, and even as far as Casablanca.

In time, Musson would propose expanding such operations to embrace the smuggling of wolfram, other rare minerals, diamonds and gold. Eventually, objections would be raised from on high that 'SOE is not allowed to run a private navy'. But for now, in the spring of 1942, that is exactly what SOE was doing and the operations of Musson's Smuggling Fleet were positively booming.[15]

When Abtey had run from Major Randegg and murder most foul in Marrakesh, he'd ended up in Tangier, which just happened to play host to one of Musson's smuggling franchises. In fact, via Musson's fleet, SOE was busy establishing safe houses, arms caches, clandestine radio stations and agents across Tangier, a city which also happened to be the North African base of operations for Sydney and the Costello gang.[16] So when Abtey asked London for a bulk delivery of English cigarettes, Musson's Smuggling Fleet was ideally placed to deliver. They knew the run well from Gibraltar to Tangier waters. All any passengers and crew had to put up with was '48 hours' misery of sea-sickness', which wasn't much 'if it means a safe journey'.[17]

They were also used to dropping shadowy cargoes and agents to seaborne rendezvous just off the coast. Most recently, in January 1942, a 312-pound explosive charge made up by SOE in Gibraltar had been delivered to Tangier. On the 11th of that month it was detonated at a clifftop villa on the city outskirts, so destroying a German infrared surveillance device, codenamed *Bodden*, which the Abwehr had been busy installing. From signals intercepts and other intelligence, SIS had deduced what it was, and that there was a sister station positioned directly across the strait, on the Spanish coast.

If it hadn't been sabotaged, the *Bodden* system would have deployed infrared beams to detect any shipping passing through the strait at night – potentially a disaster if the Allied landings, under Operation Torch, were to go ahead. In a bloody reprisal, the Abwehr blew up a diplomatic bag aboard the Tangier–Gibraltar ferry, killing twenty-nine people in the process. But the sabotage had done its work, and the *Bodden* system never became operational.[18]

By comparison, running cigarette shipments to Sydney's crew, and a midnight rendezvous with the *Sunflower*, should prove child's play.

It was early 1942 when Abtey received a message from SIS, confirming the first cigarette run was on. He was ordered to make every possible use of Sydney and his network, 'both in terms of intelligence and counter-intelligence'. Sydney and Bill had checked out: 'nothing unfavourable' was recorded in their files. London also alerted Abtey to Sydney's powerful Moroccan sponsor, a certain Sherif (noble or highborn chief) Moulay Hassan El Hadj Omar ben Messaoud, more commonly known as 'El Hadj'. If Sydney could engineer Abtey an introduction with El Hadj, that would prove invaluable.[19]

Abtey briefed Sydney. He would need to navigate the *Sunflower* to a specific point of longitude and latitude off the Tangier coast, to a rendezvous under the cloak of darkness. To safeguard Abtey's cover – that he was an agent of the FBI – London had promised that a British warship flying the American flag would execute the drop. In the Gibraltar 'pirate flotilla' there were several suitable vessels, including HMS *Fidelity*, a ship engineered for disguise and deception.

Formerly the cargo ship the SS *Rhin*, in summer 1940 the

2,450 tonne vessel had been refitted in Britain as a clandestine armed merchant cruiser, sometimes called a Q-ship. Renamed HMS *Fidelity*, she operated out of Gibraltar as a shape-shifter, able to adopt different Spanish and Portuguese disguises, allowing her to repeatedly pass muster when being buzzed by German warplanes. *Fidelity* had executed body-line, weapons-drop and sabotage operations, and she could appear either as an unremarkable merchant vessel or a sizeable warship bristling with weaponry.[20]

Having briefed Sydney on the coming rendezvous, Abtey made clear that getting a meeting with El Hadj was crucial if their relationship was to prosper. More cigarette-drops would follow, but only if Abtey got to meet the great and powerful Sherif, a man whose influence extended across the Rif Tribes – Berber clans who inhabited the Rif Mountains, the strip of rugged coast where Morocco meets the Mediterranean, and the Atlantic coastline of North Africa. Commanding their allegiances was key, for obvious reasons: control of the coast was vital to any successful landings, whether by Axis or Allied forces.

Sydney's response was to warn Abtey that the Sherif was 'a man who can be very dangerous.' It was risky enough just to know him, let alone to know what his business entailed. If Sydney introduced them, if would be at Abtey's own risk. When Abtey confirmed he was happy with that, Sydney agreed to sort a rendezvous, but only after the first cigarette shipment was landed – in other words, when Abtey had proven he could deliver.[21] Each had given the other their word. Even so, Sydney was taking no chances.

On the night of the drop he drove Abtey to his home, situated in the exclusive Marshan district of the city, which sits on a plateau offering a glorious view of the Strait of Gibraltar and the Spanish coastline, some twenty kilometres away. Sydney's place was a sumptuous Spanish-style villa, with a sweeping staircase leading to a raised winter-garden-type room, expanses of glass gazing out over the Mediterranean. Sydney left Abtey in Bill's company. For tonight's pick-up the Mafia boss himself would be captaining the *Sunflower*, just in case Abtey had set them up. As Bill served drinks, the sun set and a blanket of darkness settled over the scene. Bill appeared uncharacteristically on edge, while Abtey did his best to enjoy his drink and the view. He had every confidence that London – the Gibraltar fleet – would deliver.

Even so, when Sydney returned at four in the morning, Abtey was more than a little apprehensive. It was the Mafia boss' outstretched hand and broad smile that reassured him. Even though the sea had been rough, the transfer had gone like clockwork, Sydney explained. Twenty minutes, and all the cigarettes had been cross-decked from one vessel to the other.

'Do you know who brought us the crates?' Sydney exclaimed, with amazement. 'A US Navy ship. I am your man.'[22]

Sydney went on to explain how his boss, Frank Costello, had 'strong connections in the FBI,' and that Costello had warned him to be wary of Abtey. He could work for anyone. They just didn't know. But to have such a warship at his beck and call, Abtey had to be 'special services', Sydney enthused – 'special services' being a catch-all phrase for those who served with special operations. With America in the war, the FBI were dispatching their people abroad, and here in North Africa, American and British special operations ran side-by-side. Brits, Americans, Free French – all were in this together now, as, it seemed, were the Mafia.[23]

Having proved he could deliver, Abtey repeated his demand to meet with El Hadj. Sydney agreed to make it happen, but he warned: 'If someone gets in his way, he is eliminated. Too bad for those who are not his friends. And he doesn't have many friends.'[24]

Even as he went about setting up that rendezvous with the mysterious El Hadj, Sydney used his network to fence the English cigarettes, cutting Abtey a percentage of the profits. Just as Musson's Smuggling Fleet was doing in Gibraltar, so here in Morocco Abtey had found a way to establish a freewheeling, self-financing intelligence operation. It suited him admirably, for by his own admission he was a maverick. 'I don't like to be ordered around and I hate giving orders.'[25]

Likewise, when he needed an unofficial, untraceable meeting point, or to drop off a red-hot intelligence dossier, he had Josephine and her clinic to fall back on.

And sure enough, at the Comte Clinic Josephine had been busy.

In among countless visits from assorted Apostles and Moroccan notables, Josephine had formed a number of vital liaisons, one of which was with the top Polish spymaster, Major General Mieczysław Słowikowski. After the fall of Poland, Słowikowski was one of the many Poles who'd made their way to Britain. There, he'd played a key role in setting up the Polish intelligence service in exile, under Dunderdale's watch. Then, in the summer of 1941, Słowikowski had been dispatched to North Africa, to help prepare the ground for the Allied landings.

Słowikowski had made his base in Algiers, the capital of Algeria, Morocco's eastern neighbour. Setting himself up as a supposed entrepreneur, he'd built a hugely profitable business manufacturing cereals, within which he'd embedded a network of agents. Adopting the war name 'Rygor'– Polish for rigour, and by which he would become universally known – his network was codenamed 'Agency Africa'. Its output had been prolific, and with the arrival of the 12 Apostles he'd struck a deal to use their diplomatic pouches to spirit his intelligence dossiers to London. Josephine and her operations had come to Rygor's attention and they had made common cause.

In October 1941, a few months before the first cigarette drop to the *Sunflower*, Rygor had come visiting. He brought with him Marcel Dubois, a massive, powerfully built Frenchman who 'hated the Nazis and was a good friend to the Poles'. Dubois served in a senior position in the Vichy French security services, which had done nothing to dampen down his abhorrence of the Nazis. He had joined forces with Słowikowski to unmask a German spy posing as an escaped Polish officer, after which the impostor was 'speedily liquidated'. Driven to a patch of forest lying on a steep stretch of coastline, the unsuspecting agent was shot and his body thrown over the cliff.[26]

Dubois had invited Josephine to be the godmother of his new-born son, Philippe, and for Rygor Słowikowski to be the godfather, reflecting the police chief's true loyalties. In Słowikowski's eyes, the atmosphere across French North Africa was 'becoming very unpleasant', as pro-German propaganda and Vichy crackdowns intensified. The secret police 'tightened their grip; listening to the BBC was forbidden . . . and an officially inspired anti-Semitic campaign was stepped up in the press.' In light of all of that, having a senior – secret – sponsor such as Dubois could prove invaluable.

Josephine might have need of Dubois, particularly as she had made her anti-Nazi, anti-Vichy stance so public. 'Unlike some of her contemporaries, she had refused to perform in occupied France . . .' Słowikoswki would write of Josephine, in his memoir, *In The Secret Service*. 'A staunch French patriot, Josephine was one of the sweetest and most beautiful women imaginable.' As for Dubois, as well as being 'a well-seasoned spy-catcher', he could be 'completely ruthless when it came to German and Italian agents'. During their rendezvous at Josephine's clinic they forged a natural alliance, especially as Josephine and Rygor shared the same spymaster in London, Wilfred Dunderdale.[27]

Dunderdale had put the Gibraltar smuggling fleet at Rygor's disposal, dispatching the *Dogfish,* a battered-looking felucca, to deliver Polish agents to join his Agency Africa network. Operating under the noses of the enemy, this was a dark and deadly game. 'The danger in espionage is always present . . . the possibility of losing one's life lurks around every corner,' Rygor remarked. 'The danger is invisible, and this constitutes its greatest threat.'[28] There were very real risks in maintaining their links to the Apostles. The US consulate was under constant surveillance. Anyone dropping by was at risk of interception. If just one of Rygor's agents, or those linked to Josephine and Abtey, were unmasked, entire networks could quickly unravel.

Despite the dangers, the Comte Clinic had clear advantages in terms of plausibility, deniability and sanctity for all. Some would claim that Josephine was only ever quiet – truly at rest – when she was unconscious, so busy was she on clandestine business.

Others would suggest that her illness was in part a 'guise' – a cover under which she could report to London 'about airfields, harbors [sic] and German troop concentrations'.[29] Some even claimed that she needed to be sedated by the medical staff, so as to distract her from her mission; to keep her bed-bound and resting, as opposed to up and about and fighting the enemy.[30]

No matter how sick she might be, Josephine tried to look her best for her visitors – and she retained her irrepressible good humour. At one time, the husband from whom she was separated, Jean Lion, came to visit, pleading for help in getting his Jewish family to safety. Lion himself had signed up to fight and would earn a Croix de Guerre during combat. For his visit, Josephine put on one of her finest outfits and made herself look beautiful. On another occasion a priest was called, supposedly to administer the last rites. But when he placed his crucifix against Josephine's chest, she came around, laughed and exclaimed: 'Not yet, Father.'[31]

During that autumn of 1941, one of her visitors – who, like Rygor and Dubois, would become a clinic regular – was Victor Guillaume, a former agent of the Deuxième Bureau and a stalwart of the Free French resistance in Morocco. A man of rare courage, Guillaume would twice be landed by submarine on the French coast, on missions of great daring. Josephine entertained Guillaume with tales of her iron-willed nurse, who kept a rigorous watch, refusing even to let her eat her favourite foods.

Josephine had strong links with the Red Cross, and the organisation's Casablanca director had volunteered a nurse to tend to her care day and night. The daughter of a French Army officer, Marie Rochas took her mission – that of saving Josephine Baker's life – very seriously indeed. She had few doubts as to how sick Josephine really was, much that she might try to hide it from her visitors. 'My grandmother used to talk about her, raving about her beauty and her vitality,' she would remark, 'but in that bed I saw a woman who was bone thin. Her arms were scrawny. Her skin was spotty and wrinkled. She had fits of crying that were pitiful.'[32]

Marie Rochas kept an eagle eye for any forbidden foods that visitors might try to smuggle in. Guillaume's answer was to bring Josephine 'a monumental bouquet of flowers', which passed the nurse's scrutiny admirably. Once inside her room, he undid the bouquet, to reveal half a roast chicken secreted inside. 'Our hungry star devours half of it in a few minutes,' Guillaume would write, in his wartime memoir, *Mes Missions Face à l'Abwehr* – My Missions Against the Abwehr. It was a trick that he would repeat several times over.[33]

Putting on a brave face, Josephine joked with Guillaume that if the Germans had only thought to place bugs in her room, they would secure priceless intelligence for very little effort. But in truth all of this activity – the high-wire tension and the pace of operations; holding the centre together, the 'Coordination Office' as some would describe it – was certainly not what Dr Comte had ordered.[34] Undaunted, Josephine did not let up until the seemingly inevitable happened.

In early 1942 Josephine suffered another relapse, only this time Dr Comte detected the onset of sepsis – 'blood poisoning'. Sepsis causes the body to attack its own tissue and organs, with potentially devastating consequences. The doctor muttered dark warnings that unless she concentrated on getting well, the odds against her pulling through were no better than one in five. At times like these Josephine needed Jacques Abtey – who she saw as her protective angel during these, her toughest, darkest days – as never before.[35] But even as she was struck down in Casablanca, so too was he in Tangier.

Abtey would be put irretrievably beyond her reach, just when she was in need of him most.

CHAPTER NINETEEN

Captured, Imprisoned

He had been expecting to visit a magnificent palace of the type that Si Thami El Glaoui, the Berber chief of Marrakesh, boasted. Instead, Sydney had led him to a run-down property situated in one of the most impoverished parts of Tangier, overlooking a scruffy souk. Inside, El Hadj's house was reminiscent of Abtey and Josephine's erstwhile home, in the Marrakesh medina: a courtyard with four pillars enclosing a rose garden, arranged around a fountain. El Hadj had an extensive harem, Sydney explained, but all of that was housed in his palace at Fez, a city to the south of Tangier.

In one corner of the courtyard Abtey noticed a group of Berber men, barefoot, with long curved daggers at their sides. As if by unspoken command they vanished. Moment later El Hadj himself appeared – tall, straight-backed, with a thin face, a aquiline nose and a 'dark and penetrating look'. He wore a black silk robe, overlaid with one in a lighter fabric, and he moved with a swift and sure vigour. *An eagle*, Abtey told himself; *a golden eagle*.

Shaking Abtey's hand, El Hadj bade his visitor make himself at home. For a while they chatted about banalities – family, health, business, the price of sheep – before El Hadj suddenly asked: 'Don't you miss America?'[1]

Replying with care, Abtey countered that he'd learned to leave what he loved if it was necessary. They fenced verbally. El Hadj was curious to know how Abtey spoke such fine Arabic; where he had learned it; where exactly he had visited in North Africa. When Abtey seemed to answer everything to his satisfaction, El Hadj clapped his hands, mint tea was served, and they relaxed and drank to their heart's content.

They parted warmly, and once out of earshot Sydney asked Abtey what he thought. El Hadj didn't strike Abtey as being any kind of a terror, he replied. Sydney told him that was because the Berber chief had liked him. But still, he warned Abtey to be careful. He had an intimation, a sixth sense, of impending danger. Abtey needed to take great care.

Back at his hotel, Abtey was enjoying a drink at the bar when one of the staff alerted him that he had a visitor. A young lady with the name of Juanita was waiting at the entrance. With the cash that he was making from Sydney's underground business, Abtey had been able to buy a two-seater Chevrolet convertible, and he and Juanita – a Spaniard, 'tall and slim' with 'long hair, black and shiny' – had become romantically involved. They'd taken to driving out on the coast road, on intimate liaisons. They'd had a small falling out in recent days, and Abtey hurried out, as he was keen to see her again.[2]

No sooner had he exited the hotel than he was pounced upon by unseen assailants and bundled into a nearby car. His last conscious sense was of the sickly-sweet smell of ether (a powerful anaesthetic) filling his nostrils. When finally he opened his eyes again he felt like death. He was lying upon a hard wooden board, in a narrow, dirty cell. He heard voices speaking in German, before a figure ordered him to undress and take a shower. Abtey felt his 'blood run cold'. The Gestapo had a certain predilection for a particularly brutal form of water torture, and he feared that was what awaited.[3]

In fact, he was made to shower, before being taken before an unidentified German officer. As soon as he laid eyes upon the man – stiff, ageing, a certain Prussian formality about him – Abtey recognised Colonel Harthammer, whom he'd spied at the El Minzah bar. Harthammer was a senior Wehrmacht commander, a prominent figure in the Armistice Commission, and, Abtey suspected, in the Abwehr. Harthammer was also one of the individuals that London had identified as being a customer of Sydney's cigarette smuggling racket, which conjured up dark images of just who might have betrayed him: Sydney, Bill, Juanita, or maybe even El Hadj.

Harthammer announced that he hoped Abtey had not been mistreated, only he had been keen to meet, hence the need to snatch him off the streets. Having offered him a glass of whisky, Harthammer got down to business. They'd searched Abtey thoroughly, finding his passport, which matched the name embroidered on his shirt – that of one 'Percy Hughes'. As he was supposedly an American working for the FBI, Abtey had been obliged to adopt yet another cover identity, that of a US academic who'd studied oriental languages at a top American university. As with James Bradford, his new cover had been intensively researched by SIS, and a real Percy Hughes did indeed exist.

But as Harthammer made clear, he did not believe for one moment that Abtey was an American called 'Hughes'. After a lengthy grilling, he sent Abtey back to his cell, to enjoy a little reading material the colonel had provided. It was a copy of *Seven Pillars of Wisdom*, the First World War memoir written by the British Army officer T. E. Lawrence, better known as 'Lawrence of Arabia'. Abtey had already noticed that the toothbrush and toothpaste provided to him were British made, as was the packet of Player's cigarettes. The colonel clearly suspected that he was British, or worse still possibly even French: a copy of *La Vie Parisienne*, the French weekly magazine, had also been placed in his cell.

Layer by layer, his cover seemed to be unravelling.

While he had little idea where his captors might have taken him, he could tell that it was some kind of a cliff-side fortress, his narrow slit window looking out over a deep ravine. He dropped a water glass from the aperture. It took five seconds to fall and to shatter below. At night, he heard cats mewing on the roof above, so he was clearly incarcerated on one of the highest levels. While Abtey couldn't know it, he had been placed in *Zelle Null* – Cell Zero – one from which no prisoner was ever supposed to get out alive. It was the local manifestation of Hitler's *Nacht und Nebel* order – his December 1941 decree that all captured political prisoners, enemy agents and Resistance fighters should be snuffed out, disappearing into the Night and Fog without trace.[4]

As he pondered who might have sold him out, Abtey figured it could only be Major Randegg – Charlie Hosby – and Ingrid. It made little sense for Sydney to have done so, as their partnership was flourishing. When he was next dragged out of his cell, it was to face an altogether different kind of inquisitor, a SS–*Hauptsturmführer* – captain – Stutz. Stutz made it clear that he knew Abtey was 'a British subject'. He would force him to talk, after which he would be dispatched to a concentration camp. At one stage he demanded to know what Abtey, a supposed American academic, thought of National Socialism (the Nazi party). Abtey told him it was a wonderful machine, in that it created 'supermen, by throwing the rest in the crematoria'.[5]

In response to Abtey's bare-faced defiance, Stutz slammed a whip onto his desk, threatening to dispose of Abtey in the very 'crematoria you seem so upset about!' He launched into a long and bitter tirade against 'the Jewish peril, the black peril, the yellow peril ... democracies, the decadence of capitalist Europe', while lauding the mission of the Third Reich, which would bring order and salvation to all.[6] In the midst of Stutz's rant, Colonel Harthammer's disapproving face appeared at the door. The SS–*Hauptsturmführer* was called away and Abtey was returned to his prison cell.

He tried to take stock. There was clearly no love lost between *Hauptsturmführer* Stutz and Colonel Harthammer, who outranked him. He figured Stutz had to be bluffing about dispatching him to a concentration camp. As with any British agent, which was clearly what they suspected him to be, he would not be working alone. He would be part of a larger group. They needed to keep him here and break him, if they were to bust open his network. If they did that, it would lead them to agent Josephine in Casablanca, of course. She was a sitting duck at the Comte Clinic, and there was no way on earth of getting a warning to her.

Over the coming days Stutz dragged him back for repeated inter-rogations, seeking to know all about his 'relations with the Arabs, especially those in Marrakesh'.[7] Abtey sensed an opportunity to coun-ter-attack. He told Stutz that his Arab connections were all down to Charlie Hosby and the beautiful Ingrid, but Stutz didn't bite. Clearly, those individuals were off-limits, which confirmed in Abtey's mind just who they were and what role they'd played in his capture. He was grilled about Sydney, and their 'curious relationship', not to mention Sydney's 'peculiar business'.[8] Abtey claimed they'd struck up a friend-ship as fellow Americans, no more.

Abtey endeavoured to keep a track of time by scratching a mark on his cell wall for each day that passed. In an effort to boost his spirits he kept reminding himself that the game wasn't over. He reckoned they had to be holding him somewhere in the Rif Mountains. He could sense their cooling breezes through the cell's narrow window. If he could just get out, he could lose himself in their remote wilds. But how to break free? Tales had done the rounds about how the Apostles had used Arab dress to disguise their most valuable local contacts – dressing Berber leaders as women, in full robes and veils.[9] Maybe he could sneak out of the prison that way? But how on earth was he to get hold of such a disguise, locked away in this heavily guarded cliff-side fortress?

Having scratched his thirty-fifth day of captivity, Abtey was lying awake when the door to his cell opened without a sound. Ghost-like, Abderrahman, his local Berber gaoler, crept inside carrying a shapeless bundle. They'd spoken barely a word before now, though Abderrahman had been in daily attendance, delivering Abtey's food and the like. He threw the bundle at Abtey, urging him to get dressed.

'Put this on quickly and follow me. Your friend is waiting for us.'

The bundle turned out to contain a traditional woman's Berber robe and face veil, and his gaoler had even included a pair of ladies' slippers. But was this a set-up by Stutz, Abtey wondered? If he was caught trying to escape, the SS man would have every reason to have him shot, or whisked off to a dark fate in Germany. Abderrahman kept urging him to hurry. Finally, throwing caution to the wind Abtey dragged on the garments, and together the two figures slipped out of the cell. The gaoler led him down a steep staircase and across a courtyard, which ended at a stout wooden door.

'It's Abderrahman and Saadia,' he cried, hammering on it. 'Open up.'[10]

Saadia was one of the cooks who worked at the prison. The door swung open, the German sentry offered a cursory glance, before waving them through. But then the sentry grabbed the gaoler's arm, making it clear he wanted a word. Abderrahman told Abtey – Saadia – to hurry ahead. He'd catch up once he and the guard were done. Abtey felt his pulse pounding with the fear of discovery, but it turned out that the guard was simply after some sour milk, a local delicacy that he wanted Abderrahman to fetch for him.

Abderrahman rejoined Abtey and the two fugitives slipped along a darkened hedge, and from there into a forest of evergreen oaks. There two mules were tethered, decked out in full riding gear. Having ordered Abtey to change into the dress of a Berber male, Abderrahman handed him a slender, curved dagger of the exact type that he had spied in El Hadj's Tangier home. Abtey glanced at his Berber guide-cum-rescuer in surprise. Did this signify what he thought it did?

'A gift from your friend, the Sherif,' Abderrahman confirmed.[11]

Moments later they mounted the mules and headed into the dark trees, Abtey's beast of burden seeming to naturally follow that in the lead. They climbed quickly, emerging from the woodland onto a wide, moonlit plateau. There, they paused briefly while Abderrahman removed some roast sheep from a basket slung from his mule. Abtey was 'as hungry as a cannibal' and he ate ravenously. Before hurrying on again, he asked when Abderrahman had last seen the Sherif, and why El Hadj was helping him. The Berber replied that El Hadj had described Abtey as having a good heart, and as being a friend of Morocco, hence they must ensure his rescue.

Before pushing on Abtey asked where exactly he had been held and where they were headed now. The prison was at Souk el-Arma, not far from the city of Tetouan, in the midst of the Rif, Abderrahman explained. They were making for a remote mountain farmstead owned by a trusted friend of El Hadj.

Abtey posed a final question. 'What do you think of the Germans?'

'They are lions.'

'Do you think they will win this war?'

Yes, said Abderrahman, he believed they would.[12]

Back at the Souk el-Arma prison, Abtey's absence was discovered at around one o'clock in the morning, when a junior officer made his rounds. Pandemonium ensued. As no one had left the prison save some local staff, at first Stutz figured that Abtey had to be hiding inside. Frantic searches proved abortive, and Stutz concluded that 'native scum' had to be behind the escape.[13] His men searched the locality and questioned every Arab, but all to no avail. Finally, an enraged Stutz worked out that Saadia, the kitchen assistant, had seemingly left the prison twice, but during different guard shifts, hence no one noticing.

Dawn was breaking over the mountains when Saadia was brought in for questioning, as a result of which the deception wrought by Abderrahman and Abtey was uncovered. Stutz was incandescent. More to the point, all were terrified of Berlin's reaction, from the lowest guard to Stutz himself. People had been sentenced to death for far less than letting a British spy break out of an escape-proof prison, which this supposedly was. Stutz ordered every available man to join the search. Abtey had to be recaptured before sunset, or they would bear the consequences.

For Stutz the situation was made all the worse as a result of a letter he had just received, from Berlin. It identified the individual shown in Abtey's passport photo as also being known as James Bradford, a British spy. Stutz had been ordered to dispatch Abtey – 'Bradford' – to Berlin, for he was too big a fish to leave languishing in Souk el-Arma. He had just started arranging for his travel when the bird had flown. In addition to sending forth search parties, Stutz posted a sizeable reward for any information leading to Abtey's recapture. He also ensured that word was spread far and wide that the escapee was really a SIS agent, and that hunting him down was imperative.

Finally, he sought to deflect any punishment from himself, should Abtey not be found. If he could saddle Colonel Harthammer with the blame, that would be perfect. They hated each other, as Harthammer was no fan of either the Führer or the Nazi party. Stutz would be overjoyed to see the Wehrmacht colonel take the fall.

Long before sunset, Abderrahman guided Abtey into his place of refuge, a mud-walled farmstead set high in the Rif surrounded by olive trees. Inside, Abtey discovered none other than the Sherif, El Hadj, seated at a low table. Getting to his feet, he bade Abtey make himself at home. He gestured at the simple spread – roast pigeon, flat bread, butter and a wonderfully scented honey, plus a pot of steaming mint tea.

'You are surely hungry? Sit down and eat.'

'You saved my life,' Abtey announced, as he took a seat. 'Without you I would have ended up in Germany.'[14]

El Hadj demurred. It was a small favour. Abtey had the *baraka* – a beneficial force that flows from God to the individual – and it was his *baraka* which had saved him. He urged Abtey to remain at the farmstead for a few days, until the hue and cry had died down. No Rif Berber would ever dare go against El Hadj. Abtey was safe here. Once the dust had settled, Abtey could go about making contact with his people, to get a new identity sorted. After which, El Hadj would like Abtey to be a guest at his palace. They had much to discuss.

In the meantime, there was a small trout stream that cascaded down the nearby hillside. The Sherif put some basic fishing tackle at Abtey's disposal. After resting, he headed to the river, letting all thoughts of Stutz, Harthammer, Randegg and Ingrid slip from his mind. As he cast the line and reeled in a few small trout, his thoughts drifted to fond memories of the Dordogne, of the Château des Milandes and of Josephine. Abtey was seized by a sudden urge to reach out to her, to check if she was safe and well. But he could not, of course, and certainly not before he had re-established a usable cover identity.

Over the coming days Abtey made his way to the Sherif's Tangier home, travelling on mule trails that criss-cross the Rif. El Hadj had reminded Abtey that another English cigarette delivery would always be appreciated. Abtey didn't doubt that the Sherif had a hand in Sydney's trade, as he would do in all underground activity in his fiefdom. For the journey into Tangier, Abtey adopted local Berber dress, and in that way he made it to the Sherif's modest villa in safety. In similar local guise, the following day he headed to the British consulate in Tangier, to arrange for a new passport and identity.

He also had a visit from Sydney. From the gangster boss he learned all about how he had come to be captured. Juanita, Abtey's Spanish lover, had alerted Sydney to his disappearance, after which Sydney had alerted El Hadj, who had used his Berber networks to find him. In essence, he had been saved by his Spanish girlfriend, his Mafia brother and the Berber chieftain. But since then Juanita had disappeared and no one doubted that the Germans were responsible. In the hunt for Abtey, there were other seeming victims. Sydney vowed that he would find her. They would ensure she was safe.

Shortly, Abtey linked up with El Hadj who had cheering news. Rather than face the wrath of Berlin, *SS-Hauptsturmführer* Stutz had shot himself dead. The Sherif proceeded to introduce Abtey to his foremost Berber friends, all of whom it seemed were in the Istiqlal – the Independence Party – a group of powerful Moroccans who believed the country was ripe for throwing off the French colonial yoke. Believing Abtey to be an American, and in view of the Atlantic Charter issued by Roosevelt and Churchill and its promised freedoms for all, they shared their views with him freely.

Abtey's capture and escape had truly brought him to the heart of things. As El Hadj made clear, Abtey was no longer just his friend. He had 'become his brother'.[15]

As soon as he was able, Abtey made a beeline for the Coordination

Centre – Josephine's Casablanca clinic. It was an emotional reunion, for while Abtey had been locked up and facing torture and death, Josephine had herself been at death's door. But with the return of the spring weather she had rallied, spending hours sunning herself on the terrace. She was on the road to recovery, Dr Comte assured Abtey. During his visit they received an unexpected guest, the French General Augustin Xavier Richert. General Richert – a Saint-Cyr graduate, a decorated commander of the French Foreign Legion, and a Croix de Guerre recipient from the First World War – had heard reports about how sick Josephine was and had come to investigate.

As the esteemed French war hero settled in to talk with Abtey and Josephine, General Richert made plain his hatred of Nazi Germany and all that it stood for, while outlining his efforts at covert cooperation with various Allied intelligence outfits, including the 12 Apostles. It was a meeting of minds, and the three pledged to unify their actions. Fired up with energy and enthusiasm, General Richert went to fetch Sidney Lanier Bartlett, the Apostle who had taken Canfield's place, when the latter was returned to Washington. Bartlett turned out to be a tall, craggy, tough-talking Californian who had the easy gait of a cowboy. He was also something of an all-action adventurer. Working in Paris as an executive for Shell Oil when war broke out, Bartlett had volunteered as an ambulance driver for the American Field Services, a front-line medical corps staffed wholly by volunteers.

After Canfield's precipitate departure from Morocco, Staff Reid had stepped in as Josephine and Abtey's chief handler, but the garrulous Bartlett was more than keen to take over his role. 'I'll make a deal with Stafford Reid,' he proposed, 'and we'll do some good business together. Your clinic is a great place to meet, Miss Josephine.' As she was American-born, no one would find it remotely surprising if Bartlett were a regular visitor. 'And don't worry,' he reassured them all, 'we won't be bored.'

Bartlett asked if they would re-establish contact with Paul Paillole, in Marseilles. It would be fantastic if the French intelligence chief could plug the Apostles into his French intelligence networks.

'Tell them you've been contacted by me,' Bartlett urged, 'and that I would be very interested in working with them . . .'[16] Abtey did just that, getting a message through to Paillole. In response the French spymaster confirmed that building an intelligence conduit via Bartlett through to London and Washington would have his full backing.

For Paillole, nothing was more important than the flow of accurate and timely information. 'Intelligence is like the air we breathe,' he would declare. 'We realise that it is indispensable when we lack it.' From his base in Vichy France, he'd been increasingly hunted, as had all his TR agents, with the result that they'd suffered 'hundreds of dead comrades, deported and mutilated families'. Regardless, he knew that their efforts 'had to be amplified', even though the enemy's response would be 'increasingly savage measures of repression'. Via Bartlett, Paillole would have a direct route to get his intelligence to those who mattered most.[17]

The divorced Bartlett, thirty-six, was possessed of a certain 'suavity and courtesy that is exaggerated almost to the extent of eccentricity', according to the American consul in Casablanca, H. Earle Russell. Murphy's assessment was a little kinder: Bartlett was 'conscientious, dependable and industrious,' and would learn 'discretion and judgement'.[18] In time, Bartlett would crash and burn, and even more spectacularly than Canfield had before him. But for now, his up-front enthusiasm and candour won them all over at the Comte Clinic.

In his French government file, Abtey would record the forging of this alliance with Bartlett, plus General Richert and Paillole, as being a signal moment on the long road of resistance. 'In the months preceding the landings, a Committee of . . . Fighting France ['*France Combattante*' – another term for the Free French forces] was constituted in Casablanca under General Richert . . . and a General Staff was formed, in which I was entrusted with the Deuxième Bureau.'[19]

In mid-April 1942 the second offshore cigarette drop was made, courtesy of Gibraltar's ghost fleet, after which Abtey decided to up the ante. He promised to guarantee two such deliveries per month – double the present rate – if El Hadj and Sydney, plus Frank Costello in New York, agreed to back him. He planned a tour of Morocco's main cities, taking in Rabat, Fez, Agadir, Safi, Marrakesh and Casablanca. At each, El Hadj and Sydney would introduce Abtey to their contacts, including the Rif chieftains, so he could test the waters about whether they would welcome the Allied landings. Securing that intelligence was critical. If the Berbers resisted, it could spell disaster.

Sydney and El Hadj endorsed Abtey's plan and the tour got under way. As well as sounding out the local Berber chiefs, Abtey secured crucial extra support. The Rif chieftains offered to use their networks of cigarette smugglers to track, identify and keep watch on the Armistice Commission agents. They would use their dock workers to report on the movement of warships. They'd tap their contacts among senior Moroccan officers serving in the French military, to gather intelligence on the strength of French garrisons. The sponsorship of El Hadj, combined with the backing of the US Mafia, had certainly opened doors.

All of this information Abtey worked into the hands of the Apostles. They sought more and more detail: the depths of the main ports; the composition of the stretches of beaches upon which landings were being planned; the state of the tides; the ferocity of the waves, especially along the Atlantic coastline; the breadth of any roads running inland, their composition and state of repair, and the weight-bearing load of any bridges. Clearly, the planners were envisaging landing heavy armour, hence the nature of the queries. Nothing like this had been tried by the Allies, and if successful, it would pave the way for what was to come in Europe. The stakes were huge.

But during their stopover at the coastal city of Agadir, to the south of Casablanca, Abtey ran into two old acquaintances who were most unwelcome. In the bar of the city's Marhaba Hotel, Major Randegg and Ingrid were waiting. Beautifully tanned, dressed in matching white outfits, it struck Abtey that they looked like 'two Nordic deities'.[20] In a seemingly light-hearted manner they questioned him about how and why he had dropped off the radar and for so long.

After a sustained bout of verbal fencing, Abtey made his excuses. Places to go, people to see.

Major Randegg was also on the trail of El Hadj. Realising his crucial role as a power broker, Randegg was doing all he could to woo the Berber chief, including using Ingrid as bait. Abtey confided in Sydney that 'the most dreaded of his German enemies' was courting El Hadj.[21] When Abtey explained exactly who Randegg was, and that he was closely aligned to the Gestapo, Sydney spat disgustedly. He revealed that he was actually Jewish himself, and he would gladly take Randegg out. All Abtey had to do was give the word and Randegg was a dead man. For now, Abtey asked Sydney to keep a close watch. It was better to track, trace and roll up Randegg's network.

In among his frenetic schedule Abtey found a moment to flit across to Spain, travelling on a false Costa Rican passport, in part to check that Juanita was all right. Through Sydney's contacts, they'd managed to track her down. She'd been hunted and hounded by the enemy, but through it all she had remained loyal and true. She was being watched closely by German agents, and for now at least would have to remain in hiding.

In Casablanca, Josephine was just emerging from her long months of sickness. She began to take gentle strolls in the Parc Murdoch, adjacent to the clinic, lingering in the dappled shade cast by the olive groves. As she strengthened, she and Abtey decided that she was ready for a first proper outing – lunch at the Coup de Roulis, one of the finer restaurants that lined the Corniche.

They took a table before the fireplace, where logs crackled merrily, dispelling the last of the spring chill, chatting away and enjoying their first taste of normality for what felt like an age. In truth, it actually was. Abtey and Bayonne had rushed Josephine from Marrakesh to the clinic back in June the previous year, making it ten months or so that she had been confined there. It was long past the due date when Josephine should spread her wings again and soar.

At one moment during that celebratory lunch, she paused and stared at the fire, her face growing serious. The sight of the flames brought images to her mind of homes and families burning in torment across the battlefields of Europe and further afield. In a world consumed by 'monstrous hatreds', if only a purifying fire could take hold, she told Abtey, vanquishing 'human beasts of their criminal ambitions'.[22] World dominion by a so-called master-race under Nazism – under Hitler – still needed to be fought and defeated. There was much to be done.

Of course, she was right. Although their work in Morocco was bearing fruit, on the wider canvas the war was not going well. Across the Atlantic, over which they enjoyed such a spectacular view from the Coup de Roulis, a battle was raging, a bitter and bloody fight to the death. The U-boat packs were hunting, and the losses suffered by the Allies were proving crippling. In the first ten months of 1942 over 500 ships would be sunk, as the wolf packs operating off this coast plundered America's eastern seaboard.

The battle for the Atlantic would peak in May and June 1942, with over two hundred ships lost in just two months. This included a Norwegian tanker and a US destroyer steaming just off the New York and New Jersey State coastline. A complete blackout was imposed on the dock areas in New York City, as President Roosevelt was forced to admit that all was not going well, via a broadcast to the nation. 'We have most certainly suffered losses,' he acknowledged, 'from Hitler's U-boats in the Atlantic as well as from the Japanese in the Pacific – and we shall suffer more of them . . .'[23]

Today in Casablanca they might well toast Josephine's recovery, but not the turning of the tide in this war. As matters transpired, even those limited celebrations would prove premature. The day had seemed to tire Josephine out of all proportion. By the evening she was running a terrible fever. She murmured to herself words of encourage-ment, but shortly she lapsed back into unconsciousness.[24] By dawn of the following day, she was seriously unwell. Bedding down on the cot in her room, Abtey resumed his vigil, but as Dr Comte warned him, the patient appeared to be suffering a relapse. A bad one.

The infection was back with a vengeance. Within hours, Josephine's condition was deemed critical. 'Extremely serious . . .' The good doctor's words reached Josephine only faintly, 'through a blur of pain'. [25] If anything, 'the evil was getting worse', as Abtey described it. 'Once again, death lurked around the room . . .' Tortured, anguished, he was consumed by fear: 'everything seemed to be coming together, this time, to reduce us to nothing.'[26]

In response to Apostle Bartlett's request to reforge their links with Paillole, Abtey was already in the midst of planning a trip to Marseilles. He intended to travel under the cover of being a Red Cross official, supposedly inspecting the conditions in the camps holding French prisoners-of-war. But he put the trip on hold indefinitely, due to Josephine's parlous state, and in spite of her spirited remonstrations.

'Where would we be,' she objected, her voice weakened by fever, 'if, in the midst of combat, the soldier gave up the fight to go to the bedside of a wounded comrade?' He should go regardless, she urged. Abtey refused. He knew how his presence 'could help her to get through the battle'. And he knew how crucial it was that she rallied, for the 'very particular services she could . . . render' to France and the wider Allies.[27]

It wasn't until Dr Comte reassured him that Josephine was past the worst, that Abtey relented. As spring 1942 rolled towards summer, he caught a boat to Marseilles, to meet with Paillole, but he carried his worries about Josephine everywhere he went. He travelled in the company of Big Bill, Sydney's enforcer, for he also sought to fire up their gangster network across France, to extend the dragnet of underground intelligence-gathering still further. In Marseilles, he would recruit the Andreani brothers, Antoine and Simon, Sydney's close associates and kingpins of the French crime scene.[28] Their underworld network reached as far as Paris, and Abtey had Abwehr and Gestapo agents in his sights, plus their gold- and currency-smuggling rackets.

Much of the wealth stolen from Jewish families, and other victims of the Nazis, was being laundered via those supposedly policing that process, so they could line their own pockets. Of course, they were hedging their bets, in case the Allies actually won the war. While in Marseilles, Abtey kick-started the Paillole pipeline, with immediate results. He secured intelligence on the departure from the port of Bordeaux of a fleet of U-boats, plus other warships; details of the Atlantic defences erected by the German military along the French coastline, plus a list of Abwehr agents working across France. The information was red-hot, and Abtey would spirit it into the hands of a delighted Bartlett.

It was early summer 1942 when he telephoned the Casablanca clinic, to check in on Josephine. Her nurse, Marie Rochas, took the call, for Josephine was unable to talk. During the long months that she had spent with her patient, Marie Rochas' devotion had become 'a passion' and she hovered over Josephine protectively, like an 'angel'.[29] Abtey had huge respect for her, so when she told him how bad things had got, he made a dash for the clinic to be at Josephine's bedside.

He arrived, only to find the long-suffering patient tortured with pain, 'her body folded in two, her legs up to her head'.[30] Abtey was distraught. 'What I saw made a deep impression on me: her face was taught, her skin had taken on the colour of wax, her eyes were extinguished.' Josephine smiled weakly but seemed unable to speak. He took her hand, and was struck by how thin she had become. She was being fed intravenously, for the repeated bouts of infection had led to an intestinal obstruction. Dr Comte was contemplating surgery, but feared his patient was too weak to survive it.

The first night that Abtey spent with her proved one of the most difficult of his entire life. Marie Rochas had just given Josephine her medicines, and he believed she'd fallen asleep, but then she started to speak to him in whispers. She moved her arm in his direction, her voice barely audible. 'Jack, take my hand,' she murmured. 'Jack, I would like to pray. Jack, I would like to pray.'[31]

In the midst of their prayers, Josephine drifted into a fevered sleep.

CHAPTER TWENTY

The Grim Reaper Calls

Time passed and from somewhere deep in her soul Josephine found the strength to rally. It was not yet her time. As she strengthened, Dr Comte decided to risk surgery. Without it, he doubted if she would ever truly be well. As the good doctor waited for just the right moment, June drifted towards July 1942, and Abtey was rarely absent from Josephine's side. His network was self-supporting, the deliveries of 'English cigarettes' to Sydney's Mafia proving regular as clockwork – the fuel that kept it running. He could remain at the centre, and all intelligence would be reported in, and from the Comte Clinic to Bartlett.

How did Josephine react to Abtey's underworld connections and his espionage-driven smuggling operations? She was no stranger to that milieu, certainly. In her early teens, before breaking into Broadway, she'd toured the illegal drinking dens of Chicago to perform. It was the era of prohibition, when alcohol was banned in the USA, and the only places to get a drink were the illicit gin halls. With the Mob controlling the streets, as they did in Chicago in the 1920s, the police were paid off, to ensure they turned a blind eye.[1]

Then, during her early Paris years, Josephine had taken to frequenting the notorious nightclub Le Rat Mort – The Dead Rat – after her theatre performances, giving a second, private show. She worked tirelessly and she was perfectly at ease mixing with a crowd many of whom were Mafia-types. In fact, Le Rat Mort was actually owned by Corsican gangsters. It was a rough place, but Josephine was quite at home there. At two o'clock in the morning she'd twirl and laugh and spin, letting her most ardent – and wealthy – fans get an up-close taste of the superstar.[2] She had never had so much fun, and among her clientele were the wealthy, the famous and more than a few Paris gangsters.

If, in the spring and summer of 1942, cutting a deal with the Moroccan/New York Mafia would help win the war, so be it. After all, the New York Mafia were good enough for the American Government to partner with, in Operation Underworld, and the British had their highly profitable, piratical smuggling fleets plying the seas, which Josephine and Abtey had to thank for their cigarette deliveries. They were simply following that lead.

During that early summer of 1942, Bartlett, the Californian cowboy, proved to be in an unusually ebullient mood. He'd received warm congratulations from Washington for the intelligence that he was providing via his Comte Clinic sources had proved to be absolute dynamite. An upbeat Bartlett railed against those senior French fig-ures in Morocco who were still blindly dancing to Hitler's tune. Why couldn't they see the writing on the wall? He instructed Abtey to investigate each of them. If they only knew what was coming, he warned, they would think twice about retaining their Nazi sympa-thies.

Her strength returning, Josephine begged Dr Comte to operate, to put an end to her suffering. 'We have to end it, Doctor, one way or another . . .' she told him, bravely, 'going backwards will not help . . .'[3]

On the morning of 28 June 1942 she finally got her way. As Josephine was wheeled into the clinic's operating theatre, Abtey decided to head out, preferring to kill time in the Parc Murdoch. From the shade of the palm trees he kept watch on the window where he knew Josephine was going under the knife. When they lowered the blinds, it would signal the surgery was done. He'd been warned it would last two hours at least. Even so, his 'nerves were stretched to breaking point', as the life or death struggle unfolded.[4] With the minutes ticking by, he was unable to keep still. As he wandered through the trees, images from his and Josephine's shared past crowded into his head: of Château des Milandes, of kayaking on the Dordogne, of Lisbon, Marseilles, Marrakesh and so much more.

Abtey was pulled out of his reverie by a worried Dr Comte. He had had to halt the surgery prematurely. 'If I had continued, I would have killed her,' he confessed. 'Maybe it will work itself out. I have done everything that is . . . possible, but the result is not so brilliant . . .'[5]

Short of Josephine not surviving the surgery, this was the news that Abtey had dreaded most. They were in limbo again . . . That night the patient was restless. The nurses could tell Abtey very little. They remained silent, tense, troubled. But early the following morning Josephine seemed to rally. She was conscious again. She started to chatter 'like a magpie'.[6] She picked up a radio and began to tune it to the music that she liked. It seemed impossible to think that she had just undergone surgery, even less that she was in mortal danger.

She demanded real, solid food. It was out of the question, of course, but they were amazed at such a spirited recovery. Later, Dr Comte passed by. He seemed astounded at the vitality of someone who had just been under the knife. Even so, he counselled caution. 'We have to wait four days. Impossible to say anything before then.'[7]

On the 6 July 1942, eight days after her surgery, the doctor gave the magical pronouncement: Josephine would live. An analysis of her blood showed an unusually healthy number of red blood cells. She had deep, hidden strengths. They would have to wait two or three months, but as long as there were no further complications all should be fine. For Abtey, it felt like resurrection; a miracle.

Three weeks after the surgery, Josephine was out of bed. They were expecting a visitor. During his recent voyage to Marseilles, Abtey had by chance shared a cabin with one Ferdinand Zimmer. Zimmer, a Frenchman, had served as a submariner at the start of the war, which was odd, considering his physique – he stood over six feet tall and had an imposing build. They'd hit it off during the voyage, and Abtey had recruited Zimmer to the cause. He came to the clinic now, bearing news. A man of great daring, he was just back from Paris where he'd rendezvoused with a French agent working for the Gestapo.

That man was keen to get Zimmer to Berlin, to recruit him as a spy for Germany. Zimmer had told him they should meet in Casablanca, to flesh out their plans. He was due to arrive shortly, and Zimmer wanted to discuss exactly what they should do with such a traitor. Abtey argued that the first priority was to get him to talk. To pump him for information. Zimmer should engineer a meeting at which all could be present and they'd also warn Bartlett. Together, they'd ensure their visitor received just the right kind of a welcome. As with Sydney, Big Bill, El Hadj, General Richert and so many more, Zimmer was to become an indispensable part of their team; the Comte Clinic Resistance.

With the arrival of the warm summer weather, a thick cloud of locusts descended over the city. They whirled into Josephine's room, crashing into the screens and piling up on the floor like leaves blown from the trees, their shiny wings reflecting the sunlight, which danced off the walls. Josephine thrilled to these exotic visitors – the glistening swarm. She tried to tame them, but to no avail. One of the nurses bustled in and began to stamp the insects underfoot. Josephine was furious.[8]

Abtey was buoyed by her reaction to the surprise airborne invasion, as Josephine played 'like a schoolgirl' amongst the locusts.[9] At her request, he brought her books: her second biography of the Sun King – Louis XIV, Europe's longest-serving monarch; a memoir of Napoleon's exile on the island of St Helena. She had another welcome distraction, as she chafed at the bit to be free; welcome at least to her, but not so much with the clinic staff. She'd heard mewing at the window – a tiny stray cat, his voice sounding so far away.[10]

His legs were so weak, he kept collapsing into a ball. But not a ball of fluff. He had almost no hair, he was so riddled with pests. She demanded the cat be given refuge in her room. The clinic staff named him Fleabag. Josephine called him Saki. No bigger than a rat, she was sure she could nurse him back to health. All animals needed were some small acts of kindness, just as did people. Likewise, surrounded by tenderness herself – from Abtey, from Marie Rochas, from Dr Comte, and from her visitors – Josephine went from strength to strength.[11]

Across Europe other figures rallied to the call, the fight. In London, General de Gaulle – the leader whose June 1940 broadcast had first shown Josephine and her Château des Milandes crew the way of resistance – issued an appeal to arms. It was 24 June 1942, and his powerful words were published by underground newspapers across France and beyond.

'The outcome of this war has become clear to all Frenchmen: it will be a choice between independence or slavery. The sacred duty of all must be to contribute to the . . . total annihilation of the invader. There is no hope for the future except in victory.' Striking a distinctly Churchillian tone, de Gaulle signed off by appealing to all his compatriots to fight in the spirit of the country's time-honoured motto, 'of Liberty, Equality and Fraternity . . . Such a victory is worth all possible effort and all possible sacrifice . . .'[12]

De Gaulle was a figure not without controversy. The Americans remained reluctant to back him, despite London's reassurances that this was the man to lead the French resurgence. But like it or not, by the summer of 1942 he was fast becoming the standout figurehead of the French Resistance. As the widely respected *Economist* news magazine declared of de Gaulle, he was 'the unheeded and unrecognised prophet, the "voice in the wilderness",' which lent him an enduring appeal. 'To the mass of Frenchmen, General de Gaulle remains the symbol of French resistance,' the *Economist* concluded.[13]

In Washington, Roosevelt and Churchill gathered for their second wartime conference. In the midst of cementing their plans for Operation Torch – the first major joint US–British (Allied) counter-strike – there was calamitous news. A telegram arrived at the White House. Roosevelt read it first, before handing it to Churchill: 'Tobruk has surrendered, with twenty-five thousand men taken prisoners.'[14] (In fact, some 33,000 Allied troops had been captured at Tobruk).

At first, Churchill refused to believe it. If Rommel had taken Tobruk, he could use that strategically placed port to bolster his forces and complete his drive into Egypt. The Suez Canal would fall, severing a vital British lifeline for wartime supplies. Churchill demanded a call be put through to London, to check. It was, of course, all true. 'I did not attempt to hide from the President the shock I had received,' Churchill would write. 'It was a bitter moment. Defeat was one thing; disgrace is another.'[15]

At the same time, the fighting on the Eastern Front had descended into horrific bloodshed and carnage. While Moscow was holding out, Leningrad lay under a brutal and bitter siege, and foremost in Churchill and Roosevelt's minds was the need to relieve the pressure on the Russians. They'd pledged that America and Britain would open a second front, and by no later than the end of 1942. They were gunning for the French North Africa landings – Operation Torch – as the means to do so.

But many senior commanders demurred. As they were at pains to point out, such an operation would involve dispatching a vast fleet of warships from the USA, packed with men and machines, across 4,000 miles of an Atlantic ocean plagued by U-boats. The convoys would need air-cover, and how was that to be maintained over such distances? By contrast, Northern Europe – specifically France – lay just a few dozen kilometres from British shores, allowing British ports to be used as a staging post for any such invasion. But Churchill remained set on French North Africa, convinced as he was that seizing that territory would allow the Mediterranean to be won, enabling thrusts into the 'soft underbelly' of southern Europe.

The Combined Chiefs of Staff – the top American and British generals – presented a united front: North Africa was logistically impossible, they argued. The Allies should land in north-western

France. They were overruled. In part, it was the fall of Tobruk that won Roosevelt and Churchill the day. It served to underline just how precarious was the Allies' foothold in North Africa. Much that the Combined Chiefs objected – it went against everything they had been intending; one or two even stormed out of the meetings – Churchill and Roosevelt were immovable. The North African landings – Operation Torch – were on.

Shortly after his visit to Washington, Churchill flew to Moscow, to sell the plan to Stalin. He bore something of a poisoned chalice. The Soviet leader had pushed for a second front in Europe. Operation Torch wasn't quite that, and Churchill felt as if he was 'carrying a large lump of ice to the North Pole'.[16] But equally, he believed he owed it to Stalin to let him know in person. In fact, when he began to outline the plans for the landings, Stalin became animated, as he imagined how such a venture might boost their fortunes on the Eastern Front. Having heard from Churchill that Torch was planned for no later than October of that year, he vowed: 'May God prosper this undertaking.'[17]

As Torch gathered pace, Murphy, the chief of the Apostles, was called to Washington to brief FDR. During their discussions, Roosevelt stressed the absolute need for secrecy about the timings and thrust of the landings. Barring the 12 Apostles, US diplomatic staff in North Africa were to be kept absolutely in the dark regarding what was coming. They were to wake to the sound of gunfire, as Allied forces hit the beaches.

From Washington, Murphy flew to the UK, under a false name, his visit shrouded in intense secrecy, to meet with US General Dwight Eisenhower, the Supreme Allied Commander in the Mediterranean Theatre, and the man charged with making the Torch landings a reality. Above all, Eisenhower stressed the need to strike by surprise. If they could maintain that, Torch was doable. If not, things could end up decidedly messy.[18]

In Casablanca, things had turned distinctly messy, and all due to an unexpected arrival at the Comte Clinic. Out of the blue, Maurice

Chevalier had turned up. While he and Josephine had shared the stage together, when performing to the French and British troops, theirs had been an uneasy alliance. Some two years later, Chevalier's presence was far from welcome. Upon Germany's seizure of Paris, Chevalier had become one of the cheerleaders for a rapprochement with Hitler and his ilk, at least in Josephine's eyes. He had taken to singing the song 'Ça sent si bon, Paris' – How good Paris smells – on German-controlled Radio Paris.[19]

Paris was a city under occupation in which all restaurants, cafés, theatres and other public spaces were banned to Jews. Some 77,000 would be deported from across France and sent to their deaths, mainly at Auschwitz, together with tens of thousands of Resistance members and their families, all of whom were sucked into the *Nacht und Nebel*.[20] If that smelled good to Chevalier, it certainly didn't to Josephine. In 1941, Chevalier had agreed to perform at the Altengrabow prison camp. Formally known as Stalag XI-A, and located in central Germany, it held some 60,000 Allied POWs, including French, British, American, Russian and Polish nationals. His appearance was at the request of the Vichy regime, but it was widely reported in the pro-Nazi press.

When Josephine heard that Chevalier was at the clinic, intending to see her, she unleashed a barrage of invective: 'Traitor! Coward!' No one was allowed to let him in. Rebuffed, Chevalier gave an interview to the press as if the visit had gone ahead. The sad Miss Baker was 'dying in a small room of a Casablanca hospital', he declared. She had 'taken his hands, in the manner of the little black girls of the Carolinas', and begged him, tearfully, 'Maurice, don't leave me; I'm so unhappy.'[21] When Josephine read that news article, she countered, icily, to a reporter: 'His type of propaganda, trying to put Nazism over to the French people, is worse than a speech by Hitler.'[22]

Chevalier attempted to hit back, remarking superciliously: 'Poor thing. She's dying penniless.' Josephine had the perfect rejoinder: 'He's a great artist but a very small man.'[23] In her world-view, one's achievements on the stage paled into insignificance before one's moral and ethical stance, what one was truly willing to fight and to die for. That reflected how greatly she had matured and been transformed by her experiences of the war.

Chevalier's abortive visit seemed to bolster Josephine's spirits. Somehow, it reinforced in her mind that she was fighting for entirely the right cause. He was one of those individuals that she most despised – French citizens of standing who, believing that the enemy was all-triumphant, sought to accommodate the Nazi occupiers in any way they saw fit.[24] In her eyes he was one of those trying to get the French people to accept the path of collaboration, hence her refusal to see him.

On one level Chevalier's cruel propaganda hit home. The Vichy press took up the hue and cry. They duly reported that the once-vibrant star, Josephine Baker, was 'dying in the blackest misery in a Moroccan hospital'.[25] In the US, the black American writer and poet Langston Hughes, an old friend of Josephine's, picked up the story. Writing in the *Chicago Defender*, he described Josephine as being 'as much a victim of Hitler as the soldiers who fall today in Africa fighting his armies. The Aryans drove Josephine away from her beloved Paris. At her death she was again just a little coloured girl from St. Louis who didn't rate in fascist Europe.'[26]

When Josephine's mother, Carrie, was shown the newspaper article, she shook her head slowly and with a deep certainty, she remarked, 'Tumpy ain't dead.'[27] Ever since sailing for Paris, Josephine had sent letters and money home to her family, at one time enabling them to buy a fine St Louis townhouse.[28] She may have moved thousands of miles from her nearest and dearest, but she had not forgotten them, nor they her.

There are conflicting accounts of Maurice Chevalier's role during the war, and some debate about whether the taint of collaboration is warranted.[29] However, one thing is absolutely certain: in early 1945, the British government would refuse Chevalier entry into the UK, because 'it would not be in the national interests.' Paris echoed those sentiments, stressing how it would not be helpful to Anglo-French relations. Chevalier was widely criticised in the British press, especially since he had not scheduled to perform any shows for the benefit of 'the British war effort'.[30]

BAN ON MAURICE CHEVALIER. NO BRITISH PERMIT, ran the 13 March 1945 headline in the *Telegraph*. The *Star* newspaper declared that the London public was in no mood 'for Chevalier or for other entertainers who . . . found themselves in the unfortunate position of having to entertain Nazi audiences.' In a delicious irony, the *Daily Express* ran two headlines on the same page, the first reporting the ban on Chevalier, while that directly below it trumpeted: 'Josephine Baker may dance here.' The story continued: 'Miss Josephine Baker, coloured dancer from the old Folies-Bergère, may entertain at Army Camps in Britain.' For the Allies, she was the standout star.[31]

After the long years of bitter conflict, feeling ran high in Britain. The public penned letters, expressing their indignation and anger that Chevalier might be considered for such a visit. 'As mothers of sons fighting for this country, we object strongly,' wrote one. He would not be welcomed by 'people who have paid so hardly [sic] and so dearly to get freedom', declared another. One member of the public even wrote that 'keeping Chevalier out of this country is the best thing it has done so far.'[32]

Still, in the summer of 1942 the 'news' of Josephine's 'death', planted by Chevalier, had spread like wildfire. In Casablanca, mourners flocked to the Comte Clinic. When they learned that the star was actually very much alive, they became well-wishers, returning laden with flowers, fruit, home-cooked meals; anything, to help her fight through. The abundance of rich food was vetoed by Dr Comte, of course, but the sentiments were sincere, and for Josephine they proved deeply heartening.[33]

With zero hour approaching, the momentum towards Operation Torch kept building. Josephine's recovery was timely, for the Comte Clinic was busy as never before. Among her visitors, Pendar came often; he was keenly interested in Abtey's work with El Hadj and the Berber chiefs, whose support would prove critical. As with all the Apostles, Pendar was elated that the landings were on and that all were standing by.[34] In the privacy of the clinic room, he briefed Josephine and Abtey on what exactly they should expect.

Likewise, Bartlett – the Californian Cowboy – could not keep away. He kept pumping Abtey for intelligence, and especially from Paillole. 'Soon, you will see, we will be in Morocco,' he promised, 'and the war will take a new turn.'[35]

As the Casablanca summer turned towards autumn, Josephine knitted Saki a jumper. The weight made the little cat sway on his legs and tumble over. It was like a metaphor for the Allied war effort, which was likewise still struggling to find its feet. But all the signs were that the fightback was coming. That realisation – that the war might be balanced on its fulcrum, the initiative about to turn – brought unexpected visitors. One day, it was M. Poussier, the Vichy French Prefect of Police – its commander – in Casablanca. He knew Abtey well enough, for Abtey had been trying to get to London and he'd been badgering Poussier for the necessary visas.

In hushed tones, the Casablanca Prefect explained exactly why Abtey's Portuguese visa had remained blocked for so long (a flight via Portugal was the only realistic means to get to London). Since early 1941 the Portuguese authorities had identified Abtey as an 'agent of the Intelligence Service'.[36] The SIS. Finally, Abtey understood some of the failures they had suffered, when the SIS–Paillole pipeline had imploded, and he and Josephine appeared to have been abandoned. Either way, it didn't particularly matter now. Thanks to the Apostles, Sydney and El Hadj, their network had risen phoenix-like from the ashes, and in a far more potent form.

On 15 October 1942, Abtey received urgent orders from London. As an absolute priority, he was to check on the strength and locations of the French troops manning the coastal defences of Safi, Port Lyautey (present day Kenitra) and Casablanca. Port Lyautey, lying 150 kilometres to the north-east of Casablanca, was a key Atlantic harbour, but it also boasted one of North Africa's finest military air-fields, being the only concrete strip across the region.[37] Safi, lying to the south of Casablanca, was another key port, which played host to the nation's fishing fleet. Unwittingly, Abtey had just been made privy to the three key targets of Operation Torch in Morocco. While neither he nor Josephine could know the exact timing, it was clear that 'the big shot was approaching.'[38]

Five days later, seemingly from out of the blue, Bartlett was recalled to the USA. He came to bid farewell at the clinic. Josephine and Abtey were saddened to see the departure of a man whose gutsy cowboy spirit, eccentricities and panache they had come to admire.

'You'll see, it won't be long now, we're going to arrive with consid-erable strength,' Bartlett growled. Then he added, tellingly: 'America will never forget what you have done for her.'[39]

In truth, Bartlett's recall was mired in controversy. He'd fallen head over heels in love with a 'charming young French lady' then resident in Casablanca, one Mme. Escarment. Nothing so wrong with that for a thirty-six-year-old divorcee, except that Mme. Escarment was already married, and more to the point was known to be an enemy spy. Indeed, her Vichy/German codename was 'Nikki', and she had been trying to wheedle out the Apostles' secrets for an age. Murphy had informed Bartlett that he was being sent back to Washington due to 'personnel changes', so as to save him from the mortification of knowing that he had fallen victim to a honeytrap.[40]

Despite his indiscretions, Bartlett had worked tirelessly and coura-geously, and he'd provided a vital cog in the Comte Clinic machine. He left Josephine and Abtey in little doubt as to what was coming, or the crucial role they had played. Josephine sent a postcard to Marcel Sauvage, her biographer, bearing a single, triumphant word, indi-cating that salvation was very close at hand.[41]

In London, Dunderdale reported to Menzies, chief of the SIS, that he was receiving 'outstanding' information from his people in French North Africa, including photos of the key Atlantic beaches upon which the Torch landings were planned to take place, and of the major port defences, plus logs of shipping movements. There were worrying signs that the Vichy French forces 'had got a sniff of the impending Torch offensive'.[42] Dunderdale had warnings of French warships being recalled to their ports, and being held in readiness along the North African coastline. But by now, early November 1942, little could be done to halt Operation Torch.

The convoys had set sail from American shores. The last ships to have left, in the 102-strong Task Force 34, had done so from the port of Hampton Roads, Virginia, on 24 October. One of those vessels, the heavy cruiser USS *Augusta*, was carrying Major General George S. Patton, who would command the Allied landings at Casablanca, but only if the *Augusta* managed to brave the U-boat-infested seas. When it was assembled as one fleet in the middle of the North Atlantic, the Torch convoy included five aircraft carriers, packed with warplanes, plus a screen of submarines, and it covered an area twenty by thirty miles wide. To avoid detection, strict radio silence was enforced, with all communications delivered by the age-old system of signal flags.[43]

Patton's assessment of the probable outcome of Operation Torch was grim. In his view it was a desperate undertaking, and many of the 35,000 American troops under his command, forming what was known as the Western Task Force, might not be coming home. In his and Eisenhower's opinion, they faced a stark choice. It was either 'succeed, or die in the attempt. If the worst we can see occurs, it is an impossible show, but, with a little luck, it can be done at a high price . . .'[44] Also sailing for North Africa were a Central Task Force of 39,000 US troops, plus an Eastern Task Force of 33,000 mostly British forces.[45] But as all appreciated, the absolute key – Patton's responsibility – was seizing Casablanca.

Streaking through the thin blue above Casablanca that autumn of 1942, RAF reconnaissance planes came under Vichy French anti-aircraft fire. In the Second World War, no army ever moved without aerial photos, and the Allies were busy securing those vital images all along Morocco's Atlantic coastline. Josephine and Jacques watched from the clinic window, recognising the 'English fighters, Spitfires or Hurricanes. We cheer along.'[46]

Though impatient and chafing at the bit, Josephine was still convalescing. Dr Comte had left the incision from the surgery open, and would keep it like that until all risk of further infection was gone. If not for that, 'we would have been at the end of this long and terrible illness,' Abtey lamented.[47] Quietly, without fanfare, the good doctor Comte was a true supporter of the Allied cause. No matter how she might insist, he would not let Josephine pay a penny for all the months that she had spent in his care, during which few in the clinic had doubted the real nature of the work being orchestrated from her sickbed, or what fate might befall them if it were discovered.

As zero hour for Torch crept closer, Abtey ran into Major Randegg and Ingrid once more. He didn't particularly let it worry him. The landing fleet was coming, and there was little they could do to him, or Josephine, or their network any more. In any case, El Hadj had vowed to hunt Randegg down, just as soon as Abtey had alerted the Sherif to the man's true identity. Recently, one of Abtey and El Hadj's close associates had been found with his throat cut on a piece of waste ground. Things were getting vicious across the region, as the coming landings ratcheted up the pressure.

El Hadj had vowed to ensure that Major Randegg would not survive to see the US troops land on Moroccan shores.[48]

The vast convoy of vessels now converging off the North African coast was the largest yet assembled by the Allies. Come hell or high water, no one was about to order that fleet back to port. Its assembly, departure and arrival would be accompanied by one of the greatest deception operations of the entire war. As Churchill would so famously state: 'In wartime, truth is so precious she should always be attended to by a bodyguard of lies.'[49] Testament to the success of those early wartime lies, would be the approach of this gigantic Allied war fleet seemingly undetected.

There were two main planks to that deception. The first, orchestrated by the loose coalition of Apostles, SIS, SOE and OSS agents, Mafia-types, Berber chiefs, and more, in North Africa, was designed to convince the enemy that an Allied landing was indeed coming, but that it would target Dakar, in Senegal, some 3,000 kilometres to the south of Casablanca. The second, orchestrated from London, was a brilliant disinformation campaign aimed at convincing Berlin that the convoy apparently steaming towards the Mediterranean was doing so with the aim of relieving Britain's besieged island fortress of Malta, and to launch amphibious landings in Sicily.

Utilising fake documents, plans, letters and messages, half-a-dozen double agents controlled from London managed to convince the Axis that those were indeed the convoy's intended destinations. Simultaneously, teams of codebreakers at Bletchley Park scrutinised the enemy's radio traffic, so as to ensure that the lies being cranked out from London were hitting home. Sure enough, Rome Radio was heard to interrupt normal programming to broadcast warnings to listeners to be on the lookout for Allied landings in Sicily and neighbouring Calabria, the toe of Italy.[50]

'The movement of the gigantic armada couldn't go unnoticed,' Paillole would write of the Torch convoys, and 'the enemy had to be deceived as to its destination.' His TR network would also play a key role in engineering the extraordinary deception.[51] Pulitzer-prize-winning author and historian Rick Atkinson would echo those sentiments, in his seminal book *An Army At Dawn: The War in Africa, 1942–43*. 'No other operation in World War Two surpassed the invasion of North Africa in terms of complexity, daring or risk, or – "the degree of strategic surprise achieved".'[52]

In fact, the deception and the surprise would prove to be almost too complete, too perfect, too all-consuming. President Roosevelt had penned a letter, outlining how the Torch landings were aimed at liberating French North Africa from the scourge of Nazism. Apostle Pendar was supposed to deliver Roosevelt's letters to General Charles Noguès, the French Resident General in Morocco – basically, the colonial ruler of the nation – and to the Sultan of Morocco. But he was only cleared to do so on the morning of 8 November, the very moment when the Allied troops were scheduled to hit the beaches.

Even as the Allied landing fleet approached, none of those Frenchmen or North African leaders in positions of power or influence knew what was coming. Vichy French forces outnumbered the troops packed aboard the invasion fleet, and General Noguès, certainly, had vowed that any such landings would be met in kind – the Vichy French Navy and Army would look to blow the invaders out of the water. Total surprise would either deliver North Africa to the Allies, or it would usher in a bloodbath.

As the clock ticked down, at US consulates and at their private residences across North Africa the Apostles were busy destroying sensitive documents, using metal trash cans transformed into makeshift incinerators. Not one incriminating document could be left for the Vichy agents or the Germans to find, should the landings not go as planned.[53] Gathering at the Casablanca consulate, David King and Staff Reid manned the secret radio – 'Staff's outhouse' – as they prepared for the underground rough stuff to bite hard; for the Free French and Berber resistance forces they had helped organise to rise up. They vowed to each other to defend the consulate, do or die, should all go badly. The enemy would not get their hands on the radio, or the safe in which lay the most sensitive secrets.

At four o'clock on the morning of 8 November, with the landing craft scheduled to hit the beaches in less than two hours' time, they took to the consulate roof and gazed out over the silent, darkened city. Earle Russell, the US consul, joined them. He'd just been let in on the secret. Rallying to the cause, Russell vowed to be of every possible assistance during the crucial hours to come. As no one had eaten – they'd been consumed by the frantic preparations – Russell returned to his villa and got his wife to ready sandwiches and flasks of coffee, to sustain them through whatever was coming.[54]

One of King and Reid's underground rough stuff operations had been to get a resistance cell embedded within the city's PTT (Postes, Télégraphes, et Téléphones), which would ensure that all power to Casablanca was cut, just prior to the assault. In the dim pre-dawn light, the city lay before the figures gathered on the consulate roof, the streets and avenues rolling out in rumpled tiers of faint, violet-hued shadow. As the minutes ticked by, fingers of mist crept in off the sea, enveloping all, killing what little light and detail had been reflected off the city's whitewashed walls.

It was as if all of Casablanca had been wrapped in a funeral shroud.

S. S. GOUVERNEUR GÉNÉRAL DE GUEYDON
Paquebot français de la Cie Générale Transatlantique.

Hounded out of France, Josephine sailed for Casablanca in January 1941 aboard the French steamship the *Gouverneur-Général Gueydon*, along with her menagerie of animals, and her partner in espionage, Jacques Abtey. There they would build a superlative intelligence network, to prepare for the Allied landings in North Africa, codenamed Operation Torch.

Josephine and Co. teamed up with Robert Murphy (*right of photo*), US President Franklin Roosevelt's secret envoy to North Africa, along with his '12 Apostles' – a dozen American diplomat-spies. Their mission was to secure details of landing beaches, enemy strongpoints, airbases and warships crucial to the success of the coming Operation Torch landings.

Fears of Nazi sabotage of the USS *Lafayette* in New York harbour led to Operation Underworld, an extraordinary alliance between the New York-based mafia and the Allied powers. In North Africa, mafia kingpin Frank Costello's men joined forces with Josephine and Jacques Abtey's intelligence operations, to help ensure the success of the Torch landings.

In November 1942, the Operation Torch forces hit the North African beaches, in what was then the largest and most complex amphibious landing by the Allies, one designed to secure the springboard into Europe. The role of Josephine and her partner-in-espionage, Jacques Abtey, proved vital. 'America will never forget what you have done for her,' they were told.

Foremost French Resistance hero 'Colonel Rémy' – Gilbert Renault – met Josephine in February 1943, at her come-back-to-life performance, in Casablanca, after the long months that she had spent battling death. They would become life-long friends, united in the cause.

Josephine followed in the wake of the Allied advance, sleeping in the desert, and performing at military camps, and hospitals crammed with the war-wounded. But even as she gave her all, at times coming under attack from enemy warplanes, she also had a secret espionage role to perform.

On the eve of the June 1944 Normandy landings, Josephine was tasked to fly into France, to boost the morale of the troops. She had been away for three-and-a-half years, and this was supposed to be a momentous return, but both engines on the French Air Force aircraft failed. Josephine – herself a pilot – faced ditching at sea.

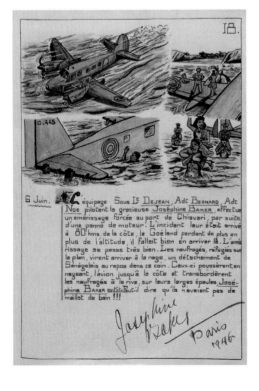

Left: The drama was recorded in the official war diary, signed by Josephine: 'The crew, under Lt. DeJean, Adt Bernard and Adt Noe, piloting the graceful Josephine Baker, made a forced landing . . . The incident happened 80 kms from the shore . . . The shipwrecked, who had taken refuge on the plane, saw a detachment of Senegalese [troops] who were resting nearby . . . They pushed the aircraft toward the coast and transferred the shipwrecked to the beach on their broad shoulders, Josephine Baker in the lead.'

Josephine had been appointed a 2nd Lieutenant in the French Women's Air Force Corps, under the command of war hero Alla Dumesnil-Gillet (*centre*). Singing for Allied forces, Josephine accompanied the advance into Germany itself. Performing on the frontline, she came under attack, but shrugged off the risks, arguing: 'I'm a soldier too.'

In spring 1945, Winston Churchill invited Josephine to London, for a victory tour, during which time she visited RAF Elvington, in Yorkshire, to perform to the 25,000 airmen based there. The photo dedication reads: 'To Colonel Venot, with all my sympathy and thanks.'

In the dying days of the war, Josephine witnessed hundreds of looted church bells, heaped up in German ports, supposedly to be melted down for the Nazi war effort. Symbolic of the dark horrors that had engulfed occupied Europe, she was to see much worse.

At war's end Josephine was asked to visit Buchenwald concentration camp, to sing for the survivors and the dying. The terrible horrors to which she bore witness proved a chilling indictment both of the evils of Nazism and of the need for good to prevail.

Left: In 1975, Josephine performed her final show at the Bobino theatre, Paris, celebrating fifty-years as a star – here shown with her young dance partner, Jean-Pierre Reggiori. She appeared in a vehicle with the numberplate 'JOSIE JEEP', recreating the scene in 1943 when British troops rescued her, christening the jeep in her name. When asked by the press what was the highlight of her career, she replied: 'The war years.'

Almost five decades after Josephine's death, she was interred in the crypt of the Pantheon, a Paris monument which serves as a resting place for those considered as foremost National Heroes. Fewer than one hundred individuals – and only five women – have been awarded such a high distinction.

Today, Château des Milandes is a living memorial to Josephine Baker's life and enduring legacy. World War Two takes centre stage, being memorialised in the château's French Resistance Room, which showcases Josephine's war years, her decorations and memorabilia from her espionage duties. There is also displayed a copy of Jacques Abtey's rare 1947 book, *La Guerre Secrète de Joséphine Baker*, telling of his and Josephine's daring wartime story.

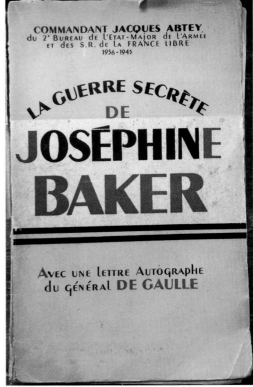

COMMANDANT JACQUES ABTEY
du 2ᵉ Bureau de l'Etat-Major de l'Armée
et des S.R. de la France Libre
1936-1945

LA GUERRE SECRÈTE
DE
JOSÉPHINE
BAKER

Avec une lettre Autographe
du Général DE GAULLE

CHAPTER TWENTY-ONE

Lighting The Torch

At 6.30 in the morning on 8 November 1942 Casablanca awoke to the deafening roar of aeroengines cutting through the skies. At the Comte Clinic, Abtey tore himself from his cot and darted to the window. Above, he saw what looked like a snowstorm descending from the heavens. Across the city the air was awash with leaflets, drifting earthwards. Dropped by a squadron of US warplanes, each displayed President Roosevelt's photo alongside the American flag, and bore a message from General Eisenhower, informing the city's residents that American forces were about to land, and that they came as friends to liberate all from the tyranny of Nazi and fascist rule.[1]

For the last few hours, Eisenhower and Roosevelt's words had been broadcast repeatedly over the BBC, urging French forces to lay down their arms. In his best French – tweaked by the BBC engineers to sound more statesmanlike – the US president had announced: 'We come amongst you solely to destroy your enemies and not to harm you.'[2] To signal their intentions not to fight, shore batteries were told to orientate their searchlights vertically, shining directly into the heavens. But in the spa town of Vichy, seat of the French government, Marshal Pétain's regime had been alerted to the invasion. Pétain, expressing outrage, exhorted the French forces to resist to the last.

As those were their orders, the shore-based garrisons opened fire, Roosevelt and Eisenhower's sentiments being met with thunderous blasts. The batteries in Casablanca harbour belched flame, peppering both the American aircraft overhead and the warships out at sea with heavy explosives and shrapnel. Moments later, the American commanders issued the order they had least wanted to give – to meet fire with fire. As rounds from the 15-inch guns of the *Jean Bart*, the formidable French warship anchored in Casablanca harbour, tore up the sea to either side of the USS *Massachusetts*, so Admiral Robert C. Giffen, task force commander, gave the command: 'Play ball!' The first salvo from the battleship's 16-inch guns hurtled towards the *Jean Bart*, leaving a pall of smoke enveloping the *Massachusetts*, and shattering the windows on the bridge.

At the Comte Clinic a leaflet had landed on the terrace directly outside Josephine's room. Abtey scanned the text hurriedly, noting the iconic images and Eisenhower's signature. Beside him, Josephine was going wild with excitement. At the first rattle of gunfire, she had bolted out of bed. Now she stood with her neck craned to the skies, a baggy-knit woollen jumper and pyjama trousers cloaking her emaciated frame. Barefoot, she shook a fist at the Casablanca gun batteries, whose blinding flashes lit up the portside derricks and cranes in stark, skeletal relief.

'What did I tell you!' she yelled at Abtey, above the roar of the guns. 'Europe doesn't know the strength of America! You don't know what we're capable of, across the water!'[3]

With one hand she clutched at her stomach, where the wound caused by Dr Comte's surgery was still open, as the other gripped the balcony's railing. Aware of the storm of red-hot shrapnel that was raining down – fragments from the exploding anti-aircraft shells – Abtey urged her to take shelter in the comparative safety of her room. He would be far happier with her tucked up in bed.

'Get back inside,' he urged.[4]

'Leave me be,' she fired back, her eyes blazing in the light thrown off by the gunfire. 'This hour is too beautiful for me to live it confined within four walls.'[5]

Unable and unwilling to hide, Josephine insisted they take to the streets, for this was the moment they had longed for: liberation day. Moving toward the beachfront and the docks, she and Abtey reached

Place de France (today's Place des Nations-Unies), a wide-open square at the heart of Casablanca's *ville nouvelle*, the 'new city'. It boasted such modern attractions as the Vox Cinema, the Galeries Layfayette de Paris – a plush department store – plus the grand Hotel Excelsior. But even as they entered the open space, a fighter dived from the heavens, unleashing a burst from its machineguns. The crowded square was thrown into panic, as figures stampeded for cover, and Abtey was only just able to prevent Josephine from being trampled by those driven wild with fear.[6]

They hurried back to the clinic, so that Josephine – still incredibly weak and vulnerable – could shelter from the storm. In the skies above, warplanes launched from the USS *Ranger*, one of the fleet's carriers, fought dogfights with French fighter aircraft scrambled from Cazes air-force base, on the outskirts of the city. As the powerful, snub-nosed Grumman F4F Wildcats held the French fighters at bay – shooting down eight and destroying another fourteen on the ground – Douglas SBD Dauntless dive-bombers tore into targets in and around the city's port. Both warplanes were excellent workhorses, and the air battle, at least, would prove a very one-sided affair. Targeting the submarine pens and warships at berth – all positions had been carefully mapped, from the intelligence provided – thirteen French vessels were sent to the bottom.

At Fedala Bay, twenty kilometres to the north-east of Casablanca, the first US troop-carrying vessels made landfall, crashing through the pre-dawn surf. One of a clutch of carefully chosen landing beaches, Fedala consisted of a three-kilometre stretch of gently shelving sand, and 19,870 troops, 1,701 vehicles, plus 15,000 tonnes of supplies were scheduled to be off-loaded there. From Fedala, Patton's forces would sweep south, moving in to occupy Casablanca itself. Or at least, that was the plan. But as soon as the skies lightened enough to see and to aim, the French shore batteries and machinegun posts opened fire. Just 3,500 US troops had made the beach, and in answer the big guns of the US warships offshore commenced their thunder.

An oil refinery was positioned in nearby Fedala town, and shortly, one of the tanks was hit, casting a thick pall of smoke over all. Appalled at the turn of events, Patton dispatched one of his deputies, Colonel William Hale Wilbur, to try to reach Casablanca, in an effort to make the French commanders see sense. Braving the fire, but with his jeep put out of action, Wilbur commandeered a civilian car, and flying both a white flag of truce and the American stars and stripes, he made it to the city's port area. There, the bodies of French marines lay in the grounds of the Admiralty building, victims of the barrage unleashed by the US warships, and Wilbur was told in no uncertain terms that the French were not about to surrender any time soon.[7]

Quite the reverse, in fact. General Noguès – the French colonial ruler of Morocco – ordered that the US consulate in Casablanca be stormed and the American diplomats, Apostles included, seized and arrested. An angry, pro-fascist mob had surrounded the building, leaving the consular staff and Apostles alike feeling like prisoners in their own domain. In due course they would be wrestled from the consulate, marched onto a bus and transported into the country's interior, to face a decidedly uncertain fate.[8]

Elsewhere, the Torch landings were faring far better. At the port city of Safi – one of the main locations to where Abtey had been dispatched by SIS in recent days, to secure intelligence – French resistance was quickly overcome and a surrender was negotiated by the early afternoon. During the next forty-eight hours, fifty-one American tanks would be unloaded at Safi port, which gave Patton a potent armoured force positioned south along the coast road from Casablanca. He would need those extra guns – and the threat they embodied – in the deadly game of brinkmanship that was to ensue.

At Algiers, the British-led Eastern Task Force, under the partial command of Major-General Charles Ryder, managed to link up with Robert Murphy – the chief of the Apostles – on the day of the landings. By mid-afternoon General Ryder had negotiated a ceasefire with the city's French authorities. Winston Churchill's son Randolph was one of the landing force officers, and Murphy was astounded to bump into him acting in a front-line role. The fighting at Algiers proved mercifully short. But come nightfall on that first day of Operation Torch, in and around Casablanca and Fedala the battle was raging.[9]

That evening, Josephine and Jacques took stock. The roof of the Comte Clinic afforded a bird's eye view. Watching the scenes of the fierce naval and air battle for the city's port and the land battle for the beaches at Fedala, the two observers were appalled. 'They arrived on the ground . . . as liberators,' Abtey would write of the American troops. 'They were greeted with cannons and machinegun fire.' They were horrified at the pointless waste of life: the 'hundreds and hundreds of white crosses' that would be erected in Casablanca's cemeteries, to mark the graves of those who had fallen in such a futile battle.[10]

Roosevelt had ordered the sparing of French combatants, wherever possible, for he wanted the 300,000 French troops in North Africa to join the Allied cause, helping spearhead the drive across North Africa. Instead, at Casablanca at least, this was the hell that had transpired. In theory, the bloodshed was all about abiding by the terms of the Armistice, signed between France and Germany. It was a sacrifice made in the hope that Hitler might reciprocate, by leaving the southern half of France under Vichy French rule. But with North Africa set to fall and to be transformed into an Allied springboard, it was inconceivable that Nazi Germany would abide by the terms of any such deal.

In Abtey's blunt and uncompromising view, the senseless fighting was no more than 'Fireworks, to prove to Hitler, who doesn't give a jot about what word he has given, that the Frenchman knows how to respect the word he has committed to . . .'[11] He shared his anger and frustration with Josephine, and overnight they hatched a 'daring plan,' as she would describe it. Together with General Richert, Lieutenant Victor Guillaume, Ferdinand Zimmer, the Apostles, El Hadj, plus Sydney and their underworld connections, they had formed the Comte Clinic resistance. If they could link up with Patton's HQ, they could offer to foment an uprising from within Casablanca itself, which might tip the balance in the Allies' favour. (Something similar had been orchestrated in Algiers, hastening that city's surrender.)

Trouble was, that would entail crossing the lines, for there was no means to make direct contact with those commanding the US landings. Josephine suggested a ruse. Taking full advantage of her medical condition, she'd ask to have the use of an ambulance. Abtey and a comrade would dress like Red Cross medics, and carry her out of the clinic 'on a stretcher'.[12] They'd load her aboard the ambulance and drive across the front line posing as a humanitarian medical convoy.

In deploying such a deception they had previous form. When Abtey had travelled from Casablanca to Marseilles, to rendezvous with Paillole, he'd done so posing as Mr George Robinson, a Costa Rican national. More to the point, his cover had been that he was a Red Cross official, heading to France to check if food parcels were reaching the POW camps.[13] It had worked admirably then, so why not now? The trouble was, Josephine's health. While her head said yes, her body said no. When Abtey pointed out that she just wasn't strong enough to risk it, reluctantly she had to agree.

But the basic plan still held good. Josephine used her contacts to secure an ambulance, after which Abtey, together with a Resistance colleague, donned white coats, driving out of the Comte Clinic posing as an ambulance crew. 'Protected by the Red Cross flag, it was relatively easy for us to move,' Abtey would write of their journey. The streets were littered with victims of the fighting, so granting free passage to an ambulance seemed only right. In this way they nosed through the 'no-man's-land', pressing ever north-east in the direction of the Fedala beachhead.[14]

They reached the front line on the French side – a squad of riflemen scattered across the bullet-scarred terrain. Towards one side a lone machinegun erupted, punching out a series of bursts. Appearing like genuine Red Cross medics, the pair of ambulance men were waved through. Beyond, they came across the corpses of the fallen – the first a French Senegalese soldier, face-down in the dirt. They paused to turn him to the light – it was just after dawn on day three of Torch – only to discover the look of surprise frozen on the dead man's features. A few dozen yards away lay a dead American soldier. He was on his back, his arms crossed as if in rest, but his youthful features – 'barely out of his teens' – expressed the same horrified astonishment at being killed, and worst of all 'by a bullet that was not intended for him'.[15]

Abtey cursed in frustration and anger. What a senseless waste of life, especially as the fallen should have been fighting side-by-side in order to defeat Hitler and his legions.[16]

'I turned my head away,' Abtey would write of this moment. 'I was ashamed to be French.'[17]

Up ahead, an American soldier lying prone in a ditch had them pinned in his rifle sights. They approached cautiously. Once within earshot, they asked to speak to his commander. Just as soon as they had explained why they had come, a jeep was made ready to speed them onwards to Patton's HQ. Though their aims and sentiments were laudable, as matters transpired they reached Patton's Fedala base too late to make any real difference.

The famously hard-charging American commander had lost patience with General Noguès and his senior officers. He'd issued an ultimatum: either they surrender, or he would use his naval guns and his armour – the tanks landed at Safi – to flatten Casablanca. 'Overwhelmed by the number of their dead . . .' Abtey noted, 'the Americans suddenly threatened to reduce the city to dust.'[18] Even as they sought to speak to Patton, so a staff car came speeding along the road from Casablanca, a distinctive flag flapping on the bonnet. Finally, senior French figures had come to negotiate.

As Abtey would record in his French Government file, they had successfully crossed the lines, even as the fighting was about to come to an end; 'the ceasefire came about while we were talking to an officer on General Patton's staff.'[19] Angered by the scenes of death and destruction they had witnessed, but also relieved it was all over, they made their way back into Casablanca, a peace of sorts having settled over the war-scarred city. There, the streets were thronged with jubilant crowds, who, upon hearing news of the ceasefire were 'waiting for the liberators'.[20]

*

On the morning of 11 November 1942, American and French troops finally got to march side-by-side through the war-torn city. Josephine watched them, standing to attention herself. The moment she had dreamed of, longed for, prayed for – kept herself alive for, kept the Grim Reaper at bay for – had finally come to pass. It proved hugely emotional. Josephine was tearful, regretting most of all that she was unable to embrace every one of them.[21] These were the soldiers of two armies who, just days before, had been locked in mortal combat. As Josephine appreciated, there was much work to be done in terms of reconciliation, so that all might unite against the true enemy.

At the same time she was swept up in a deeper, more residing sense of regret, making this such a bitter-sweet moment. While she saw herself very much as a soldier of the shadow war, she feared her secret mission was now finished, presuming that her spying days were done. Indeed, she felt so weak and infirm that she didn't know what role if any she could play. She still had her open wound. She was still far from healed. That sense of powerlessness infuriated her.[22]

Yet in believing that her secret war was over, she was sorely mistaken. In truth, her new role was only just beginning.

Operation Torch had succeeded, but the cost would prove considerable: some 526 American dead, plus double that number of British casualties, almost half of whom would perish when HMS *Avenger*, a merchant ship converted into an aircraft carrier (escort), was torpedoed by a U-boat in seas just to the west of Gibraltar. The French had suffered around 1,350 dead – soldiers killed following orders, even as they had endeavoured to repulse their liberators.

Yet the prize was glittering. Some 2,000 kilometres of North African coastline, with its strategic ports, now lay in Allied hands. In just three days the Torch armada had succeeded against a well-armed, well-trained military, in good defensive positions. Despite the losses suffered, they were far fewer than senior commanders had feared. Key to that success had been the loose network of Allied intelligence agents, Apostles, Mafia contacts and North African chiefs, who had kept the intelligence flowing and 'almost entirely eliminated resistance to the landing', as William J. Casey, then head of OSS European intelligence operations, and a future CIA chief, would conclude.[23]

Equally important, the largest amphibious armada the world had ever known had endured and overcome. The 850-odd warships of Operation Torch had delivered, across thousands of kilometres of ocean, in an operation that would rival the Normandy landings in terms of logistical challenges. And of course Torch set the tone for things to come. In London, Churchill was ebullient. At last, there was something truly to celebrate. Fittingly, he hailed the first major Allied victory over Nazi Germany by ordering the church bells to be rung across the length and breadth of Britain.[24]

On 10 November, in London, Churchill delivered his now famous speech, which included these immortal lines: 'Now this is not the end. It is not even the beginning of the end. But it is perhaps the end of the beginning.' He lauded how 'British and American affairs continue to prosper in the Mediterranean,' forging a 'new bond between the English-speaking peoples'. In the same speech he celebrated the victory secured by British forces, at El Alamein, in Egypt, where Rommel's advance had finally been halted in a 'remarkable and definite victory,' one that had been secured even as the last French forces in Casablanca had laid down their arms.[25]

No one doubted that months of fierce fighting lay ahead, in an effort to liberate all of North Africa. But this did feel like the first hints of spring, after the long and dark winter of Nazi domination. Across the vast swathe of territory seized under Torch, the priority now was shipping in war materiel and men-at-arms. At Casablanca harbour, the quays were still groaning under the off-load from the first armada, when a second convoy arrived – Task Force 38 – consisting of dozens of ships packed to the gunwales. Some 31,790 American service personnel disembarked, including thousands of engineers, signallers, quartermaster and transport troops, medical staff and more. The springboard was being established, ready for the big push across North Africa.[26]

In Casablanca, 'a city which combines Hollywood and the Bible,' as he described it, Patton held meetings with Noguès, the French Resident General, plus the Moroccan Sultan and his key deputies. With all, he stressed the need to bury the hatchet and to unite against the common enemy. At the same time he warned Eisenhower, his commander-in-chief: 'While I am convinced that Noguès is a crook, I believe that I can handle him.' For his part, Eisenhower was determined to do everything necessary to bring the French onside. After the fighting and bloodshed, there was much to be done to win their heart and minds.[27]

Those few in the know appreciated what an incredibly close-run thing Operation Torch had been. The absolute key had been the dual strands of intelligence and deception. In Morocco and Algeria, the Armistice Commission and the Abwehr had been warning Berlin about possible Allied landings since as early as July that year. But as the Abwehr in particular failed to come up with any definitive proof, and as the Allied disinformation campaign had proved so convincing, Hitler refused to be persuaded. Consequently, Operation Torch had taken the Führer by complete surprise.[28]

His counter-stroke was as swift as many had feared it would be. On 10 November, so even before the final French surrender in North Africa, German forces moved in to occupy all of Vichy France. General de Lattre de Tassigny, a die-hard anti-Nazi, led the French resistance, but while spirited, it proved short-lived. De Tassigny – a First World War hero who'd been wounded multiple times, earning both the Légion d'Honneur from France and a British Military Cross – was tracked down, arrested, and charged with 'abandonment of duty and attempted treason'.[29]

Across newly occupied former Free France, other enemies of the Nazi state were being hunted, first and foremost Paul Paillole. Helped by his underground contacts, he managed to get himself across the mountains into Spain, from where Dunderdale managed to secure his onward passage to Gibraltar and from there to London. On 19 December 1942 Paillole flew into Hendon Aerodrome, in north

London, where Dunderdale's deputy was on hand to receive him, whisking him direct to the British spymaster's office, where Paillole was received with 'many hugs and congratulations'.[30]

Feted in London by SIS, Paillole also linked up with de Gaulle and the Free French intelligence service, the BCRA. But there was precious little time to pause or to celebrate. The Torch initiative needed to be seized and capitalised upon. Shortly, Paillole would leave Britain by air, heading for those newly secured North African territories. There, he would establish his new headquarters and reforge his intelligence networks, as all Free French efforts were reorientated to this new and potent Allied springboard.

On 1 December 1942, Josephine was finally discharged from the Comte Clinic. She headed directly to Marrakesh, to rest and recuperate. She would spend such magical times in the Red City, but also ones that were full of pain. No matter where she might travel in Africa she would always come back to this place. She felt a deep and residing love for Marrakesh, and it was only natural that she would return here, when she was seeking to heal.[31]

As Christmas approached she found herself in the Mamounia Hotel – Churchill's favourite place to stay in Marrakesh, where he loved to paint the views over the gardens – as the staff prepared for the coming festivities. With Morocco's liberation they would have added poignancy. Abtey had remained in Casablanca, organising a cadre of Free French volunteers to fight in the Allied cause, and Josephine's focus was on regaining her strength, so she could rejoin the struggle.

But she started to feel sick and feverish. Finally she called a doctor, who diagnosed paratyphoid, a bacterial fever. While paratyphoid was eminently treatable, it would mean she would have to spend a second Christmas bed-bound. Abtey came to join her, as she endured her nineteenth month fighting to be well. Once more, she held out a fevered hand to him. 'Why do I have the despicable misfortune of being nailed once again to this damn bed, instead of being in the fight?' she lamented.[32]

He could offer no easy answers.

Instead, and for a second time, he found himself erecting Christmas garlands in her makeshift sickbay – 'a branch of a fir tree, which I decorated with stars, moons, suns and houses cut out of tinfoil, candles, oranges and lemons.'[33] Consumed by fever, Josephine was deaf to the noisy Christmas celebrations echoing up from the hotel bar. As she drifted into sleep, Abtey slipped away, drawn by the sounds of laughter and singing in English – American officers celebrating the festive season.

Barely had he made the bar, when a familiar yet sinister voice cried out a greeting. It was Major Randegg. Abtey could barely believe his eyes. The Abwehr agent was dressed in an American officer's uniform, and surrounded by similarly attired figures, which included several of the US military's top brass. Appalled, Abtey decided to blow Randegg's cover there and then.

Addressing a figure wearing the uniform of an American general, he declared: 'This man's name is Peter Randegg, General! He belongs to the Nazi secret service!'

Both the general and the accused burst into laughter. Over several glasses of whisky – 'on the rocks, of course!' – all was revealed. In truth, Randegg was a double agent. While masquerading as an Abwehr spy, he was actually working for the Americans and had never once 'wished for the victory of Nazism'. In fact, as they had pitted their wits against each other in Morocco, Randegg had come to believe that it was *Abtey* who was an agent of Berlin, and more specifically of the *Sicherheitsdienst* (SD), the intelligence service of the SS.[34]

Randegg had got his people in Washington to check on Abtey. As his passport and identity turned out to be false, and bearing in mind the shadowy nature of his work, what else was Randegg supposed to conclude? Sure enough, he'd reported Abtey to Colonel Harthammer and SS Captain Stutz, in an effort to neutralise him. It was only recently that he'd realised his mistake. As all of this was revealed at the bar of the Mamounia, Abtey realised how mistaken he had been about Randegg. They were natural allies, but neither had known it, and each had come so close to having the other rubbed out.

Other than Josephine's, there was another case of debilitating sickness in the Mamounia Hotel that December. Ollie Stewart, the black American war correspondent, had been stricken down with what seemed like food poisoning. In passing, a member of the hotel staff mentioned that 'the woman who sings, Madame Baker,' was also ill and confined to her room. Stewart immediately sensed a story. Hauling himself out of his sickbed, Stewart tracked her down. Josephine actually seemed pleased to see him. She'd lost track of her mother, Carrie, she explained. Amid all the chaos of war, her family must have moved, and she begged Stewart to find her 'through your newspaper'.[35]

Stewart vowed to do just that, while also breaking the news that Josephine Baker was very much alive. His story, syndicated via the Associated Press (AP), was published world-wide. It duly announced that 'Josephine Baker Is Safe,' as the headline ran in the *New York Times*.[36] Josephine was quoted as saying: 'There has been a slight error – I'm much too busy to die.'[37]

In truth, she was putting a brave face on things. The present sickness, coming as it did on the heels of her long struggle with death, was hard to bear. She was worried if she would ever truly be well. Her legs were stick-thin, her body emaciated. Would a time ever come when she could sing and dance and captivate, as she had before?

In fact, she was about to rise again, finer than ever – a phoenix from the ashes of war.

CHAPTER TWENTY-TWO

Die Another Day

With the story breaking that Josephine Baker was back from the dead, others came calling. One was Sidney Williams, the first black director of the American Red Cross. By the time he sought her out, Josephine was convalescing in the Marrakesh villa that she and Abtey had shared prior to her long illness. Williams, who had worked in St Louis prior to the war, was charged with establishing a Liberty Club in Morocco, a Red Cross café-cum-social-club where US servicemen could grab some quality downtime.[1]

The American armed forces were heavily segregated, and black soldiers were mostly barred from front-line roles. Many of those charged with setting up the Liberty Clubs saw them as an opportunity to highlight the nonsense and injustice of such blind discrimination. As George W. Goodman, the director of the American Red Cross in Britain, expressed it, his aim was to 'indicate as nearly as possible that color [sic] really does not run off and that human impetus comes out of the mind, not the complexion'.[2] Sidney Williams was cut from similar cloth. In Marrakesh, he was determined to open a club where black and white GIs could mix freely, one of the first of its kind.

Having learned that she was still very much alive, he was desperate for Josephine to headline the opening night. At first she was hesitant. She could barely stand. The very idea of staying on her feet for any length of time was daunting. If she tried, even for a short while, she saw dark spots swimming before her eyes. The wound from her surgery still carried stitches and was painful. She had not so much as sung a note or danced a step for two years. She was down to a fraction of her former weight, and she worried that no amount of makeup or costumes could disguise her gaunt, emaciated frame. Upon visiting her at the Comte Clinic, one high-society French portrait artist had lamented that there was nothing left of her to paint.[3]

Regardless, she agreed to Williams' request. In part, she did so out of a chill and brittle desperation. It was so incredibly sad and dispiriting to discover that even as the Allies were locked in a do-or-die struggle to vanquish Nazism – a system of beliefs based upon the mythical existence of an *Übermenschen*, an Aryan master-race, ruling over the *Untermenschen*, sub-humans – so those at the hard end of that war were likewise being segregated. It went against everything she had been fighting for, not to mention raising the ghosts of her past.

In 1917 Josephine had been caught up in the horrific race riots that had rocked her home town. In fact, it was one of the main reasons she had been so desperate to get out. Trouble flared in East St Louis, a grimy and smoke-enshrouded industrial quarter sliced through with railroad tracks and terraced slum housing, and where families lived in abandoned rail-cars. Tensions had been rising for months, and in July 1917 it had exploded – mobs torching districts and looting and lynching. It was the worst race riot in US history, a congressional report recording how at least thirty-nine black people and nine white people had been killed (though the numbers were very likely higher).

Josephine was aged just eleven at the time. She'd watched, aghast, as hundreds had fled – men, women and children running for their lives, with some of the youngest carrying their beloved pets. The horrors were so seared into her memory that she would speak of them again and again throughout her life. When interviewed for *Esquire* magazine in 1964, she would say of the riots: 'I was a little girl, and all I remember is the people. They ran across the bridge from East St Louis to escape the rednecks . . . I never forget my people screaming . . . I see them running to get to the bridge. I have been running ever since.'[4]

No wonder that coming face-to-face with a segregated US military had proved so unsettling. Josephine shared her feelings with Abtey. He had heard of how the Nazis had pasted posters across occupied France, banning entry to 'any black-skinned man' – no matter whether 'chocolate, cream and tanned, even slightly'. Frankly, Abtey hadn't been surprised to witness that from 'Hitler's men', but he had assumed those prejudices to be confined to the enemy. It was shocking to discover that skin colour was such a divisive issue in America. 'I had thought that these were practices very personal to those we were fighting against.'[5]

But Abtey was in two minds about whether Josephine should perform. Was she really even physically capable? Were the risks worth it? Her doctors were dead against it. They ruled it out completely, or at least they tried to. When they realised Josephine would not be dissuaded, they issued dire threats about the possible consequences.

'You're being extremely stubborn, madame,' one cautioned.

'If de Gaulle hadn't been stubborn, Doctor, you and I would be in concentration camps,' she retorted.[6]

Josephine was a firm believer that '[W]e die when we choose to . . . we abandon the fight and let go. That moment had not come . . . Too much remained to be done.'[7]

Even so, this first breaking of her Comte Clinic purdah would prove a desperate and gruelling trial. The Liberty Club lay on Rue Chevandier de Valdrôme, just a few blocks west of the clinic where she had spent her long months of sickness. Returning to Casablanca in February 1943, she sat before the club's make-up table, trying to do her best to disguise the ravages of almost two years spent knocking on death's door. But her face was hollowed out like a mask, her skin dull and lustreless, her arms and legs matchstick-thin.

She chose to wear a blue polka-dot dress, not because it was her favourite, but because it was voluminous and might hide her skeletal form. The sweat on her brow and the pain from the surgical incision warned her to take it easy, even as she stepped towards the curtain. The club was bursting, cram-full of black and white officers drawn to the pull of her celebrity and her reputation as a performer without compare. Troops had even clambered onto the roof, clustering around air vents and windows to try to catch a snippet of song or a glimpse of the famed magic - that was if she could still deliver, against all the odds.

The audience was studded with dignitaries, including US General Mark Clark, Eisenhower's deputy on Operation Torch. Offering her heart in her hands, Josephine stepped onto the stage. She opened with a 'Negro lullaby', a nod to the heritage she shared with many of those who formed her audience, before moving on to a song by George Gershwin, whose popular hits included 'An American in Paris' and 'Summertime' from his opera *Porgy and Bess*. The Gershwin number had been carefully chosen by Josephine, to showcase 'the poetry of the American soul'.

She closed her short repertoire, perhaps inevitably, with 'J'ai Deux Amours', the song that she had belted out in the trenches and bunkers of the Maginot Line. Her theme tune. As she descended a low staircase built upon the stage, she began to sing the opening lines: 'I have two loves/ My country and Paris./ By them always/ My heart is ravished . . .'[8] It appeared as if she had transformed the song into an anthem as she sank to her knees, hands clasped in prayer – a prayer for strength, for victory, for liberty.

As the last lines faded away, and the American Army band accompanying her fell silent, a hush settled over the auditorium. Many had been moved to silent tears. But this was the calm before the storm. Moments later, the cheers and whoops erupted, as the entire audience rose to its feet. Having sung those few songs, Josephine was desperate to dance. But her head was reeling, her stomach felt as if it were on fire, her sight was flickering and the air of the auditorium seemed as if it were thick with mist, or alive with insect swarms.[9]

The show had taken everything out of her. As the curtain closed to hoarse yells of delight, she all-but collapsed onto the stage. She had tears in her eyes. To truly perform and captivate, you had to allow yourself to be overtaken by the music, to be possessed by it, Josephine would declare. In the quiet between two beats, when silence rings out, when each member of the the audience feels as if they are holding their own breath, awaiting whatever is coming next – achieving that was a truly wonderful thing, one that it took a lifetime to perfect, while ensuring that it didn't kill the special magic. Tonight's show hadn't quite killed her. But she had to lie down right away.[10]

One of those present at the performance was the foremost French Resistance hero known by his *nom de guerre*, Colonel Rémy. His real name was Gilbert Renault, and he had founded the *Confrérie Notre-Dame* – the Notre-Dame Brotherhood – one of the most important Resistance networks in all of France. Rémy and his agents had played a key role in the February 1942 Bruneval Raid – Operation Biting – in which British paratroopers had seized a top-secret German radar from the Normandy cliff-tops, and in Operation Chariot shortly thereafter, the daring March 1942 raid on Saint-Nazaire.

Rémy had sat in the auditorium enraptured, as 'Josephine's appearance ... was greeted by thunderous applause. The make-up did not prevent her face from appearing emaciated, and her legs, once so admired, were as thin as a stork's ... The announcer thought he had to ask for the indulgence of the spectators, but his voice was drowned out by the shouts and the whistles, which, on the other side of the Atlantic, are evidence of supreme enthusiasm.' Rémy was suitably impressed, and this would be the start of a life-long friendship between the Resistance hero and the special agent.[11]

Once Josephine had recovered her strength, she was asked to join the soldiers for apple pie and coffee. The *Newsweek* reporter Ken Crawford was there. In among the gladhanding, she gave him an interview in which she stressed how, if she'd run from the war in France, it 'would have been like leaving a sinking ship. I am no rat. I have to be as good as I can for these American soldiers. I hope they'll like me.' If Crawford's view was anything to go by, they sure would. He would write of her performance that 'It was obvious after the first song that the old time magnetism was still there.'[12]

Her walkabout done, she was joined backstage by General Clark, who proffered his congratulations and extended a special invitation.

He had placed a personal plane at the disposal of Si Mohamed Menebhi and Moulay Larbi El Alaoui – the Sultan of Morocco's cousin – to fly them to tonight's performance. He wanted Josephine to bring herself and them to an after-show reception in one of Casablanca's glitziest hotels. All the top military and diplomatic leaders would be there.

Under Clark's persuasion, Josephine agreed to go. It was a showy gathering, the dinner jackets, sequined dresses and gaudy decorations reminding her of the countless high-society functions she had attended in the pre-illness days. So long had she been sick and locked away, she had to steel herself to do what she did best – to make 'an entrance', flanked by those two foremost Moroccan leaders, and with the imposing bulk of Ferdinand Zimmer on one side and Abtey on the other. With all the world's press there, few would be able to claim that Josephine Baker was 'half dead now'.[13]

She rubbed shoulders not only with senior French dignitaries, but also with the top Allied commanders in North Africa: Generals Clark and Patton were there, but so too were the British Generals Harold Alexander, Alan Cunningham and Kenneth Anderson, the last of whom had orchestrated the British end of Torch. 'That night, Josephine was reborn to life,' Abtey would remark of her remarkable comeback. 'Her life as a star.'[14] But the cumulative exhaustion had taken an inevitable toll. Upon being introduced to General Patton, she fainted into his arms.

That evening Josephine had been seen to perform what would increasingly become her role in the war, acting as the glue that held together the coalition of the willing in North Africa – Berber leaders, Rif chieftains, Arab dignitaries, American troops both black and white, (former) Vichyites, plus the Free French forces now mustering. She possessed an extraordinary ability to mix with and to charm all.[15]

Typically, the day after her performance she refused the offer of a flight back to the Red City, courtesy of the US military. 'I'd take it, if it were work,' she demurred. 'But I'm going to Marrakesh to rest . . . Besides, see: I already have my ticket for tonight's train.'[16]

Jacques Abtey and Ferdinand Zimmer escorted her to the railway station. They saw her off jammed into a crowded carriage, masking her extreme fatigue with a bright smile, on 'a journey that would last all night, standing, with her scar not yet closed'.[17] Josephine had an unquenchable spirit and fire, Zimmer commented to Abtey, as they watched her leave. 'I would like to work with her. I get the impression we would make sparks fly.'[18] They would, and Zimmer was about to get his chance.

General Clark had been so impressed by Josephine that he invited her to a gala dinner, at which she would be the guest of honour. Hosted by Clark, along with US President Roosevelt's personal representative in North Africa, Robert Murphy – the chief of the 12 Apostles – it would have particular resonance. While Josephine and Abtey's clandestine work remained top secret, it was an opportunity to offer quiet thanks for the role that Josephine had played, plus those key Moroccan dignitaries that she was closest to. The dinner was held at the sumptuous Villa Taylor, Apostles Canfield and Pendar's famed Marrakesh residence and the site of some of their most colourful adventures. After their arrest on General Noguès' orders, at the height of the battle for Casablanca, the Apostles had been locked up under harsh conditions and duress, but they were freed once peace was declared – just another chapter in their picaresque North African adventures.[19]

A few days after Josephine's Liberty Club triumph there was a gathering in Marrakesh. Major Donald Wyatt, who worked with the USO (United Services Overseas) – the US military's troop entertainment unit – came to visit Josephine Baker, plus Jacques Abtey and Ferdinand Zimmer. So close would that triumvirate grow – Abtey, Zimmer, Wyatt – they would become known as 'The Three Musketeers'. But for now Wyatt came bearing a particular proposition for Josephine, having witnessed 'the almost miraculous impact she'd made on the audience'.[20] Even if she didn't have the energy or the strength to dance and sing for long, the very fact of her rubbing shoulders with the troops had worked wonders.

Wyatt was himself black, and painfully aware of the growing anger and frustration among African-American GIs. They'd volunteered to fight fascism, in freedom's cause. They'd been trained as combatants in the US. But once they'd arrived in Morocco they'd realised they were being confined to logistical duties, or as drivers and the like. They were being denied a front-line role, which didn't make the slightest bit of sense, especially as they were the direct targets of Nazism due to the colour of their skin. The sentiments that Josephine had shared with the GIs as she'd mingled with them – let's win the war on racial segregation, but let's win the war against the Nazis first – had truly hit home. Wyatt wanted more – much more – of that.[21]

Donald Wyatt and Josephine Baker made a special connection. In time, their relationship would come to resemble that of brother and sister. Wyatt had first seen Josephine perform in 1935, during her short and bruising 'comeback tour' of America. She'd travelled over from Paris, the crucible of her stardom, with high hopes. In short order they had been shattered. Her performances had got panned, a *Time* magazine critic proclaiming, 'Josephine Baker is a St. Louis wash woman's daughter who stepped out of a Negro . . . show into a life of adulation and luxury in Paris . . . But to Manhattan theatre-goers . . . she was just a slightly buck-toothed young Negro woman whose figure might be matched in any night club show, whose dancing and singing could be topped practically anywhere outside France.'[22]

Her co-star was the American singer and actress Fanny Brice, and from the outset they really did not get along. One day in rehearsals Josephine made a remark in French. Brice turned on her: 'Ah, you n*****, why don't you talk the way your mouth was born.'[23] By contrast to Josephine, Brice's performances garnered widespread acclaim. That same *Time* reviewer declared: 'With Fanny Brice, on the other hand, there is practically never cause for complaint.'[24] According to the *Time* reviewer Brice's performance was a triumph, Wyatt for one had begged to differ, and he did so again in the early spring of 1943. In Casablanca, it had been very much Josephine Baker's evening, and it was going to be very much Josephine Baker's war.

Wyatt's proposal that she perform for the troops struck a powerful chord, but there would have to be conditions. First, while Josephine would accept transport and provisions from the military, she would absolutely not accept any form of fee. Just as she had done when serving as a special agent for French, British and American intelligence, she would only do so for free. Plus she would need to remain at liberty to sing and dance for all troops, not just Americans. In due course the US military would try to sign her up exclusively and for the remainder of the war. Despite the offer of a lucrative contract, she refused. She would sing for her brothers and sisters in arms, to lift their spirits, regardless of their nationality as long as they served in the Allied cause. For them, she would never ask for money.[25]

From Château des Milandes she had dispatched some of her choicest jewellery and gems. She intended to use the proceeds from their sale to bankroll her North African tour. Even so, her funds were far from inexhaustible, and when she joked about surviving on mouldy bread and rancid jam, it wasn't entirely in jest.

The deal with Wyatt agreed, she needed a tour manager and a supporting cast. Zimmer – an unusual and volatile character, but who was generous to a fault, and blessed with boundless energy and extraordinary courage – volunteered to serve as the former, while out of the shadows stepped her long-time dance partner, Fred Rey.[26] Rey's fortunes during these past months had been grim. Having made it to North Africa, the Vichy authorities had seen fit to arrest him and send him to one of their deep-desert internment camps. Abtey had managed to extricate him, and now here he was, volunteering to join her morale-boosting tour for the Allies.

With Eisenhower's blessing the coming venture was green-lit. Josephine was expected to hit the road in a fortnight's time: two weeks in which to muster her strength. It was a Herculean task. Thankfully, several dozen trunks of Josephine's costumes had survived the long months she had spent in the Comte Clinic, and all thanks to Si Mohamed Menebhi's protection and care. All through Josephine's sickness he had never wavered, keeping them safe in Marrakesh.

Now, his daughters – Josephine's 'sisters' – got to work under the star's skilful guidance. As her gowns were dragged from their trunks, it was clear how the moths had got to them. No matter: Fela, Rafet and Hagdousch 'wielded the needle', patching and darning wherever necessary.[27]

Fred Rey also tried to make himself useful, lending a hand to jazz up her tour costumes. The dancer had been appalled when first laying eyes upon Josephine, and spying her gaunt, strained appearance. How the war had cost her. When he queried if she was truly ready for such an undertaking as this, she told him: 'I'm made of iron.' Even so, he feared she was returning to the stage too soon. He knew it was pointless to argue. 'When Josephine got an idea she stuck to it! The war effort came first.'[28]

Before the tour group set out, Si Mohamed Menehbi and Moulay Larbi El Alaoui decided to throw a lavish farewell party, as only they could. It was the kind of evening that would never be forgotten, a night defined by oriental splendour, spectacle and panache. Berber warriors – 'straight from the mountains', each sporting a 'magnificent silver dagger' – guided guests to their tables, the seating plan chosen with infinite care.[29] With the great and the good in attendance, Josephine had insisted things needed to be done just right. This would need to be a celebration of American-Moroccan-French friendship, and of the values shared by all. Accordingly, they'd made sure that individuals from all nations and races were seated freely across the tables.

'The evening *has* to be a success,' Josephine insisted. 'I want to show that Arabs, blacks and whites can meet as brothers.'[30]

Josephine was painfully aware of how unsettled Moroccans were by the segregation they had witnessed in the US military. At every turn she was being challenged on how America could sponsor the Atlantic Charter and its supposed freedoms, yet not even manage to practise what it preached among its own armed forces. It was the cause of a huge amount of tension. Tonight, she intended to show them another way; to be the glue that melded all together, united against the one common enemy.

317

The setting was truly magical. Josephine would describe guests mingling beneath vines thick with ruby-red flowers, as Arabic music drifted evocatively around the gardens, which were bathed in a soft, velvety light. With Berbers from the Atlas mountains performing the Guedra – the blue dance, so called due to the distinctive, night-sky-blue robes the female dancers wear – fountains murmured, and streams of water tumbled onto the lilies below.'[31]

Apostle Pendar described it as 'the-party-to-end-all-parties'. Praise indeed, especially coming from the man who had presided over lavish cocktail gatherings at the Villa Taylor. Just about 'every American in North Africa, including most of the generals, received . . . gilt-edged invitations to dine and "to meet Miss Baker".' Indeed, Pendar had played a hands-on role, drawing up guest lists and seating plans, and guiding individuals to their tables. 'It would have done some American politicians a great deal of good to see how free . . . natural and simple an atmosphere was created amidst the fusion of races,' wrote Pendar of the gathering.[32]

Among the esteemed guests were Major Wyatt, Robert Murphy, prominent US war reporters, plus a host of senior Allied commanders, including the US president's third son, Lieutenant-Colonel Elliott Roosevelt, who served in the United States Army Air Forces (USAAF), commanding a reconnaissance squadron that had deployed as part of Torch.[33] At one point Josephine ushered Abtey to Elliott Roosevelt's side, announcing proudly: 'Colonel, please allow me to introduce you to my chief and brother-in-arms.' That done, she guided them to their table.[34] There was seating for eight and Abtey noted that as they tucked into the *mechaoui* – slow-roasted leg of lamb – the drink flowed freely.

As the night wore on a white officer remarked, drunkenly, that it was the first time he had ever 'eaten at the same table as n*****s'.[35] Seeming to think he'd cracked a fine joke, no sooner were the words out than he was grabbed by the collar and frogmarched away by an irate American diplomat, both individuals looking as 'white as shrouds'.[36] Even so, the words had been spoken and those Moroccan figures within hearing were aghast. The man who'd made the comment did not return. The diplomat did, arm-in-arm with one of those who had been most offended.

That diplomat was William Douglas Read, the newly installed US vice-consul in Morocco. He confided in Abtey that the man he'd ejected was a drunken 'moron'. Seated near by, Moulay Larbi El Alaoui - the Sultan of Morocco's cousin - had turned 'ashen grey'.[37] As Read pointed out, something needed to be done. Abtey hurried to fetch Josephine. It would take all of her charm to convince those present that the offending individual was an aberration and not the norm. Her efforts were boosted by the arrival of a fine jazz band, and the fact that the music and dancing lasted until dawn.

Partying done, the final, frenetic tour preparations were completed. Things kicked off on 30 April 1943 with a benefit show in Casablanca's Rialto Cinema, to raise funds for the Red Cross. It was a warm spring evening as Josephine stepped onto the stage, Fred Rey the dancer at her side, a curtain covering the cinema screen behind them. For the show – her official comeback – the stage was bedecked in greenery reminiscent of a jungle, dotted with a kaleidoscope of Allied flags. To either side ranged a phalanx of Spahis – local troops, resplendent in their ceremonial uniforms, swords flashing in the light. As she swayed and sang, Josephine transformed herself from Brazilian 'native' to traditional Asian dancer and finally to Breton villager. For her final number – 'J'ai Deux Amours' – she was cloaked in a red, white and blue crepe gown, reminiscent of the flag of France. The show was a sensation.[38]

Between the November 1942 Torch landings and the spring of 1943, the Allies had strengthened their positions in North Africa, before driving east and west, in an effort to encircle the enemy. Those campaigns had involved many months of brutal and hard-fought struggle, particularly as the American-led forces had pushed east across Morocco, consolidating their hold over that nation and neighbouring Algeria. Josephine's forthcoming tour was designed to follow in the wake of the advancing forces, stiffening their fighting spirit and their morale.

From Casablanca they would depart for Algeria, where she was scheduled to perform several times daily for the hundreds of thousands of Allied troops based there. She intended to use an army tent as her dressing room, and to dance and sing upon whatever makeshift stage might raise her up high enough so all could see. When performing after sundown, she'd get searchlights to illuminate the stage, in lieu of proper showbiz lighting. She intended to round off each show with a rendition of the national anthems of the three key Allied nations: 'La Marseillaise', 'God Save the King' and 'The Star-Spangled Banner'.

Josephine's repertoire was designed very deliberately to deliver a powerful show of unity. But this was not a journey that Jacques Abtey, Josephine's rock, was going to be able to share with her. Right now, in the spring of 1943, their union was about to be broken. In North Africa and London certain queries were being raised; dark aspersions cast. Just who was this Captain Jacques Abtey character, voices demanded? What was the true nature and allegiances of the man who had cast himself as Josephine the superstar's protector, and her partner in their secret wartime espionage missions?

The trigger had been a 17 April 1943 report, emanating from the office of the French Civil and Military Commander-in-Chief in Algiers. Just over a month earlier, the esteemed war hero General Henri Honoré Giraud had adopted that title, placing himself on a direct collision course with General de Gaulle. Giraud was the Americans' choice to lead Free France, once Torch had succeeded. Indeed, Giraud had played a leading role in the operation, though bizarrely, he had tried to argue that he should be the commander-in-chief of Torch, so usurping Eisenhower, and disregarding the fact that he had been brought onside only shortly before the landings. He had been denied, of course.

Despite de Gaulle having the backing of London, he – like so many – had been kept entirely in the dark about the Torch landings. In North Africa a fierce power struggle had ensued – Giraud versus de Gaulle – and many would be caught in the midst of the swirling conflict and intrigue, which at times would spill over into disinformation, back-stabbing and even murder.

That April 1943 report constituted a security assessment of: 'I: Josephine BAKER. II: ABTEY. III: ZIMMER.' Regarding the superstar, the report's conclusions were that 'BAKER's national sentiments are not at all in question. Her devotion is boundless, her selflessness is total. With a quick and dynamic mind, Josephine is capable of rendering us great services in the . . . circles of the great Moroccan chiefs, where she could not be better connected.'[39] All very true, of course.

But Josephine's two companions attracted very different sentiments. 'ABTEY AND ZIMMER also seem very devoted to our cause, but they are above all businessmen. They indulge in currency trafficking and take care to regularise the situation of certain Jews, whom they send to England, in return for large sums of money.'[40] In running self-financing intelligence operations, as Abtey had done, it had proven necessary to strike alliances with the Mafia and to tread the dark side of the law; likewise, in spiriting Jewish families to safety. Of course, while most of that activity had been sponsored by British and American intelligence, it might well appear borderline criminal to French investigators, especially if they knew nothing of those London and Washington connections.

Concerning Abtey, the conclusions of the report were especially damning. 'ABTEY would seem to regret his admission to de GAULLE and would be ready to take orders from General GIRAUD . . . he is no less dubious from a moral point of view.'[41] Caught between the two would-be leaders of the Free French, Abtey was in danger of becoming a 'victim of politics', even as he little understood just how and why. He would later write of this moment that 'for any Frenchman who answered General de Gaulle's call, an association with General Giraud constituted an act of treason.'[42]

That January, de Gaulle had flown into Casablanca to rendezvous with Churchill and Roosevelt, who had gathered for the Anfa Conference, named after the city's Anfa Hotel where it was held. Stalin had been invited, as the Allied leaders gathered to determine the future course of the war. But with the Battle for Stalingrad in full swing Stalin had declined, so between them Roosevelt and Churchill were left to determine a road map for victory. First off, the North Africa campaign had to be kickstarted, with a pincer movement to seize Tunisia. To that end, a major programme to rearm and refit the French military in North Africa was called for, to render those forces fully battle ready.

At Anfa, the Allied leaders issued a bullish ultimatum: they would only accept an unconditional surrender by the Axis powers.[43] In Roosevelt's view, this was not about punishing the German, Italian and Japanese nations, but more about wiping out 'the philosophies in those countries which are based upon conquest and the subjugation of other people'.[44] Churchill sought to reassure Roosevelt that Britain and her colonies were 'resolved to fight to the bitter end', standing shoulder-to-shoulder with America.[45] The meeting ended with a press conference at which Roosevelt and Churchill posed with a warring Giraud and de Gaulle, for one of the most awkward photo calls of the entire war.

Privately, Churchill and Roosevelt had aired their fears about the newly seized North African territories. Might those nations disintegrate into wars for independence, before the war to vanquish Nazi Germany could be won? Such in-fighting had to be avoided at all costs. Measures would have to be taken, and mostly this was going to be an intelligence and propaganda war. Sensing the Allies' weakness, the Abwehr were seeking to flood North Africa with agents, and to inundate the region with disinformation, fomenting insurrection. Over thirty Abwehr operatives would be dropped into the area that month alone.[46] Clearly, the last thing anyone could afford right now was protracted conflict between Giraud and de Gaulle – least of all Jacques Abtey.

Abtey's trouble revolved around the fact that de Gaulle's people knew nothing about his wartime activities, including that he believed his fealty lay firmly with them, for neither the British nor American intelligence agencies had let on. It all came to a head as Abtey tried to clarify his role with de Gaulle's intelligence apparatus, the BCRA. When he reached out to Colonel Passy, the BCRA's chief in London, the response he received was mystifying. His case was being looked into, Abtey was told. He needed to be 'patient'.[47]

The BCRA requested Abtey furnish them with his wartime career summary. Having complied, it triggered a veritable storm. Colonel Passy wrote to Claude Dansey, deputy chief of SIS, demanding how Abtey could have been led to believe that he was serving as an agent of de Gaulle's Free French, when they had no record of him whatsoever. How had 'Commander DUNDERDALE . . . believed himself authorised to ask Captain ABTEY to return to France and to have guaranteed him . . . the status of an officer of France Combattante [the Free French] . . . I would be grateful if you could give me all the information you have on Captain Abtey's activity during the last three years, to enable me to make a report to General DE GAULLE.'[48]

As if in afterthought, Colonel Passy crossed out Dansey's name and addressed the letter instead to Colonel Westmacott – Guy Randolph Westmacott being a First World War veteran who was then serving as a senior officer in SIS. In his reply to Passy, Westmacott admitted that the facts 'on the face of it . . . appear strange', but he argued that it was all down to the fog of war. 'November 1940 was early days,' and 'matters had not been regularised to the extent that we are accustomed to now.' The 'important thing', he continued, was that Abtey 'wished to join General de GAULLE in November 1940 . . . That assurance I think can be safely given to you from the British side . . .'[49]

De Gaulle's office wrote to their North Africa intelligence chief, informing him that Captain Abtey's story had been 'confirmed by the British'. But at the same time they pointed out that London had 'no right to promise Captain ABTEY that his F.F.L. [Forces Françaises Libres] officer status would be recognised by Carlton Gardens', 3–4 Carlton Gardens – set minutes from Buckingham Palace – being the headquarters of de Gaulle's Free French. The letter finished with this damning statement: 'Captain ABTEY's name was unknown to my department before now.'[50] *Unknown before now.* For two years Abtey had served as an agent at the very toughest end of operations, and often beyond the limits of the law, yet those he had believed he was working for knew nothing of him at all.

Where did all of this leave him, especially as de Gaulle seemed to be gaining the upper hand over Giraud? At the very best he was in limbo. At the very worst he was in deep trouble. Britain's security services had been wrestling with an unpalatable problem: it concerned the illegal detention and in some cases torture of individuals very similar in many respects to Captain Abtey. In the heart of London de Gaulle's intelligence services had established a secret detention facility. Many of those incarcerated there were French men and women who had had the temerity to serve as secret agents of Britain, and often, by extension, of the United States.

The scandal would reach the very highest levels due to a courageous Frenchman serving with the SIS, Lieutenant Maurice Dufour. Dufour had earned both a Croix de Guerre and was made a Chevalier (Knight) of the Légion d'Honneur, and had fought courageously in the 1940 battle for France. Severely wounded, he'd been captured by the Germans but released due to his injuries. Back in France and working at an internment camp, he had been recruited by the 'British Secret Services'.[51] But when his clandestine role had been uncovered by the enemy, he'd escaped to England, arriving in March 1942. In due course he'd reported for duty at de Gaulle's Free French headquarters.

A few days later Dufour had been invited to the BCRA's 10 Duke Street headquarters, an elegant-seeming townhouse just north of Oxford Street, in the heart of London. There, he was stripped to the waist, punched, and beaten with a steel rod bound with leather, while his interrogators sought to extract from him details of his 'activities with the British Secret Service'.[52] Imprisoned in a coal cellar beneath the building, Dufour was mistreated and held captive for days on end. On some levels MI5 was complicit in his incarceration, as it was in those of others so imprisoned.

At one stage Dufour's captors told him they had Andrée Borrel in their sights, a French agent of the Special Operations Executive with whom Dufour was having a love affair. Prior to Dufour fleeing France, he and Borrel had smuggled Allied POWs into Spain and Portugal, and from there to London. They had shared a villa near the Spanish border, from where they'd run their escape line. Dufour had engineered the rescue of at least fifteen RAF officers, and at one point had helped enable a massive breakout, in which fifty POWs were smuggled by sea to Gibraltar. Hunted by the Gestapo, he and Borrel had fled to Lisbon, from where they had caught flights bound for London.

In the 10 Duke Street basement, Dufour's captors threatened that they would seize Borrel and force her to talk, 'by whatever means are necessary'.[53] Dufour's case was sadly not the only one, but what would make it a cause célèbre was the fact that he decided to sue. In December 1942, Dufour began preparing a case to be heard in the High Court of Justice, seeking damages for 'assault and false imprisonment'.[54] A War Cabinet report concluded that Dufour's allegations were 'substantially true and that he will very likely win his case'.[55] Panic ensued in Whitehall. Once the case became public, it would be a scandal of monumental proportions. With 400,000 Free French troops spread across Africa and the UK, plus a 200,000-strong Resistance network within France, it could overshadow all that was intended in terms of liberating Europe.[56]

Senior government officials met with MI5, demanding they put an end to the Duke Street horrors. The secret cells were duly shut down, and a cover-up was sanctioned from the very top. The War Cabinet cleared a generous pay-off for Dufour, money that was massaged out of the 'Secret Service vote', a clandestine fund used to bankroll some of SIS and MI5's more clandestine activities. Dufour was provided with papers that would enable him to remain in Britain and that was to be the end of the matter.[57] How much de Gaulle knew of the Duke Street horrors is uncertain – possibly very little. It was a black, deniable facility, and no doubt what happened there was treated on a strict need-to-know basis. If you didn't need to know, you wouldn't be told. But some of his top deputies certainly knew and had overseen the worst.

The United States embassy in London had been closely watching the situation. In the spring of 1943 they had cabled a series of secret messages to Washington, outlining what they termed as 'the Duke Street atrocities'.[58] Their detailed report characterised the BCRA's attitude to counter-espionage operations thus: 'Better that nine innocents are killed than one who is guilty should escape.'[59] But as Guy Liddell, wartime head of MI5's counter-intelligence operations, pointed out about the Duke Street abuses, 'a confession obtained under duress is in 9 cases out of 10 perfectly useless . . . it is time Duke Street was closed down.'[60]

Shut down it was, and of course Dunderdale had made sure to keep Jacques Abtey and Josephine well away from Britain and any such possible predations. But all of this was coming back to haunt Abtey now. Trapped in Morocco, he was left kicking his heels, frustrated and confused by the bizarre – almost sinister – turn of events. Repeatedly he tried to catch a military flight from Morocco to London. It isn't hard to envisage why. Abtey felt wronged, misunderstood and slighted. He needed to clear his name. But he never managed to board an aircraft and take to the skies.[61]

Was agent Josephine, Abtey's partner in espionage, about to get ensnared in the same dark morass? Not yet it seemed. In the short term her stardom – not to mention her high-level connections across North Africa, and her new mission at the behest of the Americans – would render her immune. But as the weeks went by and her espionage role returned, she too would begin to reap the whirlwind.

For now, deprived of Abtey, her chief protector, it was Ferdinand Zimmer – big-hearted, devoted, irrepressible, prone to huge but short-lived fits of anger – who stepped into that role. He flitted ahead to Oran, their first Algerian showtime destination, organising make-shift stages at military bases formed out of wooden planks mounted on oil drums. While the setting might be rough and ready, and the star's costumes somewhat make-do-and-mend, the performances Josephine delivered would be five star and first class. More importantly they would come direct from the source of all her pain, and entirely from the heart.

Travelling in a small convoy – three cars with tour luggage strapped to the roofs, and everything caked in dust – the tour would take her and her entourage across four hundred kilometres of Algerian desert, from Oran to Algiers and east towards Tunisia and the front line.

It would also lead into the heart of battle, red in tooth and claw.

CHAPTER TWENTY-THREE

Into The Heat And Dust

An 'orchestra' cobbled together on the spot accompanied Josephine. It was made up of a handful of black troops – all volunteers, who just happened to be able to play magnificently.[1] Fred Rey doubled as Josephine's dance partner and stagehand, while 'backstage' consisted of a rough curtain behind which he changed the scenes as best he could.[2] Not a day went by when Josephine didn't appear several times in the open, at scattered camps, performing on a few planks laid across some oil drums. She didn't mind about the rough and ready nature of the shows – what mattered most was that the national anthems with which she rounded off were still met with deafening cheers.[3]

The soldiers sang along, belting out the words in unison, just as Josephine had intended. A week into her tour, she was scheduled to perform one of her most important shows. She was based at the city of Oran, which was surrounded by a vast sea of military encampments, stretching for thirty kilometres in all directions. Tens of thousands of GIs were expected to attend. It was set to open at nine o'clock in the evening, meaning it was after work hours and chow-time, to ensure maximum numbers could attend.

This being a night-time performance, the bulk of the lighting consisted of a phalanx of army trucks arranged so that their headlamps illuminated the makeshift stage. In the midst of singing and dancing her heart out, Josephine saw what she at first thought were fireworks erupting in the heavens above them.[4] In reality, this was anti-aircraft fire tearing apart the night. Moments later the truck's headlamps were doused, as the dark forms of enemy warplanes swooped out of skies laced with a latticework of fiery tracer.

The noise of the attack was deafening. Within seconds the entire audience had dived for cover. Realising what was happening, Josephine joined them face-down in the dirt.[5] After all that she had endured – surviving the long Comte Clinic battle with death – she felt she could not die here, not from an enemy bomb or bullet. Taking her life in her hands, she dashed across to the buffet, which had been made ready by the US Army in a nearby tent. Snatching a sandwich, she took a bite, in part to distract herself from the danger, but was forced to throw herself flat once more, as the attack grew in ferocity and violence.[6]

Later, she would laugh about being under fire. 'Me, belly down, amongst soldiers from Texas, Missouri and Ohio in my 1900 Paris dress, must have been an irresistibly funny sight. Mostly because I kept on eating . . .'[7] Among her audience were those who appeared to be equally brave and spirited; equally happy to laugh in the face of death. As she was finishing her sandwich, she heard a voice crying out her name in a broad Texas accent. It was a soldier carefully bringing her a bowl of dessert, while crawling on all fours.[8]

Fred Rey was struck most powerfully by how Josephine 'lay there calmly, eating the ice cream'. He yelled over: 'Watch out for your teeth, Josephine!' She clapped a hand over her mouth. She had joked with him that the only thing she really feared was if an enemy bullet fractured her famous, dazzling smile.[9]

Once the air raid sirens had fallen silent, Josephine clambered back onto the stage. The soldiers watched her brush herself down and resume her set, seemingly undaunted and undeterred. If anything, the GIs' enthusiasm was redoubled. Her example put steel in their souls, and the cries and cheers became increasingly wild and exuberant.

'To be in the midst of such a crowd,' Josephine would remark, 'to see those thousands and thousands of soldiers, to be the focus of so many eyes, is something incredible. I have never felt this way before.'[10]

Despite the privations, the dangers and the punishing schedule, paradoxically this tour truly brought Josephine alive again. She lived and breathed to perform, and she lived and breathed this war – to defeat the scourge of Nazism. After approaching two years of terrible sickness, this would be her coming-back-to-life-tour. 'Josephine needed to be with her audience; to connect with them,' Jean-Pierre Reggiori, one of her male dance partners, would point out. 'That was what drove her; what brought her truly alive.'[11] To do so in support of the war effort – it was doubly rewarding.

Josephine had stipulated one condition regarding the present tour: there would be no segregation at any of her shows. Black and white GIs would mix freely, or else she would not perform. In the spring of 1943 that simple request was still seen as controversial – anathema, almost – within US military circles. But Josephine was adamant. What was the point in waging war on Hitler, if segregation overshadowed the Allied war effort? Not all the senior US Army officers she encountered agreed with her, but her tour had the blessing from the very top, so few were about to voice their objections out loud.[12]

The day following the attack by the enemy's warplanes, Josephine was asked to perform in Mostaganem, Algeria's fourth largest city, which lies some eighty kilometres east of Oran. This time, she was presented with another singular challenge. The US military asked her to sing in the city square, as much for the benefit of the townsfolk as for the GIs. Mostaganem had a large Italian and Spanish population, and for obvious reasons they were not exactly extending the hand of welcome to the Allied troops. The top brass figured that a performance by Josephine Baker in such a setting might furnish a greater 'atmosphere of understanding', especially as US troops had also been told to 'mingle with the crowd'.[13]

Josephine had her own ideas about how exactly she might achieve their ends. In the midst of her performance she stepped from the makeshift stage and began to press the flesh. To the women and children she handed out sweets, and cigarettes to the men. She took hold of a baby, and with much cooing orchestrated matters so a nearby GI ended up holding the infant. By the time the show was done, there was a decidedly more fraternal atmosphere in that city square.

The troupe headed east to Blida, and from there to the capital Algiers, and everywhere they performed several shows per day.

A month after leaving Morocco, Josephine returned, her tour over. When she rendezvoused with Abtey, she struck him as looking 'exhausted and as thin as a greyhound'. As soon as she laid eyes upon him, she burst out: 'It was magnificent, Jack, magnificent! What a pity it's already over.'[14]

Old habits die hard, and she had returned from her tour with notes of all the things she had witnessed which might be of interest to Allied intelligence. The question was, just whom should she report such material to? Once again, in terms of their spymasters, they had been left in something of a limbo.

Shortly, an answer presented itself. A dinner was organised at a cosy and quiet French-style brasserie. The moving force behind the gathering was one Colonel Pierre Billotte, de Gaulle's Chief of Staff, who was most interested in their work with US and British intelligence. Billotte, a tank commander, was a standout hero of the Battle for France, and had been held prisoner by the Germans before escaping and joining the Free French. He was the kind of figure Abtey believed they could place their trust in, a man who played it with a straight bat.

It was May 1943, and de Gaulle had just moved his headquarters from London to Algiers. The intrigue and in-fighting in North Africa was at fever pitch. Even as the rift between de Gaulle and Giraud had deepened, so French Admiral François Darlan had been assassinated. Visiting Algeria when Operation Torch had been launched, Darlan had been caught by the landings and trapped. He'd gone on to cut a deal with Eisenhower, in which French forces in the region would transfer their allegiances to the Allies, in return for which he would retain a position of power and influence. But as a leading figure in the Pétain regime – he was the former de facto head of the Vichy government – Darlan had enemies.

In December 1942 he had been shot dead, in a plot that many believed had been orchestrated by the Allies.[15] Immediately after Darlan's murder, an SOE/OSS training camp in Algeria, codenamed

Brandon, had been raided, as the assassins were believed to have been trained there. Suspicion and intrigue continued to swirl and boil. In Britain, just days before he relocated to North Africa, a Wellington bomber carrying de Gaulle was sabotaged, the French leader narrowly escaping with his life. No one knew for sure who was responsible, but de Gaulle feared it was an Allied plot to have him bumped off.

One thing was for sure – the bitter enmity pitted Frenchman against Frenchman, when all needed to be united behind the cause. Certainly, Josephine had no time for such infighting. She would write of how these poisonous North African intrigues were riddled with backstabbing, tragedy, plot and counter plot, not to mention a great deal of pride and self-interest.[16]

Refreshingly, the dinner hosted by Colonel Billotte eschewed all of that. Josephine, Abtey and Zimmer were all present, and much was agreed, including that the controversy over Abtey's past service with the Free French would be sorted out, his service record being back-dated until June 1940. Colonel Billotte proposed that both Abtey and Josephine should work as agents of the Free French once more. As Abtey would later recall, this dinner was characterised by its intimacy, and was the moment when 'we finally celebrated our contact with those whom for so long we had sought in vain.'[17]

A second dinner was held, this one hosted by Colonel Paul Paillole, their long-standing Deuxième Bureau/TR boss. Paillole, who had recently been in London, was able to pass on Dunderdale's private greetings and sentiments. The SIS spymaster was hugely grateful for all the information they had provided and he apologised for erring in his treatment of Abtey, in particular. They should have spirited him to London, when Abtey had first asked, back in the winter of 1940: 'his coming would have changed everything,' Dunderdale declared.[18] Quite what that might mean wasn't entirely clear.

Confusingly, Paillole invited Abtey to join *his* intelligence apparatus, which suggested that two 'Free French' security services were somehow running side-by-side. 'In spite of my friendship and all the esteem I had for him and his high qualities, I obviously couldn't accept,' Abtey would write of Paillole's invitation.[19] As he was being courted by Colonel Billotte and de Gaulle, that was where his allegiances now had to lie. It was the same for Josephine. If she were to return to the shadow war, it would need to be for de Gaulle's Free French, which meant the BCRA.

A week later Abtey was asked formally to join the Free French. On 8 June 1943, he signed a decree, declaring that 'ABTEY Maurice, Captain . . . having taken note of the staff regulations of the FORCES FRANÇAISES LIBRES [Free French Forces], undertake to serve with Honour, Faithfulness and Discipline in the FREE FRENCH FORCES for the duration of the war . . . To be effective from . . . 25 June 1940 . . .'[20] Finally, the missing years of his service seemed to have been reclaimed.

Sadly, nothing is ever so simple, and the ghosts of Abtey's wartime secret service would continue to haunt him for decades to come.

By now the fight for Tunisia had reached maximum intensity, as British, American, French and colonial forces advanced from east and west, closing the trap. Tens of thousands of Allied troops were reported killed and wounded in that cauldron, as Rommel's Afrika Korps fought tooth and nail for every yard of territory. In the words of one American observer, the Free French forces 'fought so bravely in the front line, ill-equipped as they were, that they had lost 11,000 dead and 5,000 wounded.'[21]

Learning of the bloodshed, Josephine asked if she might fly to Tunisia, to bolster the morale of the French troops. The reply that came back from General Giraud's headquarters – he was still formally the French Civil and Military Commander-in-Chief – was a blunt no thank you: 'They do not need distractions.'[22] Churlish and self-defeating, Giraud's decision left Josephine angered and confused. All she wanted to do was to give her all for the troops, regardless of the in-fighting. But, along with Abtey, she had nailed her colours to the mast, declaring herself for de Gaulle, which meant that she could not be for Giraud.

Instead, Josephine found herself being courted by the British. Lieutenant Harry Hurford-Janes, an officer serving with

ENSA – Entertainments National Service Association – was charged with the difficult mission of finding stars to perform for the troops in North Africa.[23] Few entertainers were keen, for it generally involved a long voyage by horribly crowded troopship across U-boat infested seas. It was far preferable to entertain the mass of Allied soldiers gathering in Britain. As Josephine realised, London's top stars weren't so keen to travel far from home, to perform on the frontline of battle.

In short order, Hurford-Janes secured Josephine's services for a month-long tour. In late-June 1943 she boarded an RAF bomber for a flight east to Libya, again with Zimmer and Fred Rey as her escorts (Abtey was still trying to square away his Free French status and activities).[24] In Libya she would perform beside the towering form of the 'Arc de Triomphe', on an airbase scorched by a merciless sun. (As a monument to his North African conquests, Mussolini had erected a huge white marble arch in the deserts of Libya, formally called the *Arco dei Fileni*, but commonly known to the Allies as the 'Marble Arch', after the London landmark, or the 'Arc de Triomphe', after the one in Paris.)

Her tour would take her from there onwards to Egypt and Syria, performing for British troops and soldiers from Greece, Belgium, Czechoslovakia, Australia, New Zealand, South Africa, Canada and across the British Commonwealth. At each stop she was deeply touched by her encounters. 'They did not know that the Sicilian landing was to come so soon,' she would write, of those who were poised to embark on Operation Husky, the thrust into southern Italy. 'And to see them so full of enthusiasm, when so many were already marked by the sign of death . . .'[25] She found this hugely moving, as she did her tours of the Cairo hospitals, which were full of the wounded from the battles at El Alamein, Mersa Matruh, Bir Hakeim and other iconic battlegrounds.[26]

Josephine's efforts won her enormous affection and admiration, especially among the rank and file. Hurford-Janes shepherded her everywhere and the two would become lifelong friends. He would write to her of the impromptu shows she gave at the hospitals: 'One of my most treasured memories is the night when we dragged the little piano into the ward of the Canadian hospital and you sang "I'll Be Seeing You" until you nearly dropped. How even the nurses stood with tears in their eyes and [of] those poor helpless men – many of whom would never recover – lying on their backs unable to move, only their eyes showing the relief and comfort you gave them.'[27]

She danced for the troops, performing everything from ballet to samba. She sang all kinds of tunes – lullabies, love songs, hilarious ditties, sentimental numbers that spoke of home. The First World War refrains – those she had recorded in 1940, and performed along the Maginot Line – proved favourites: 'Tipperary', and 'If You Were The Only Girl In The World'. She sang 'My Yiddishe Momme' and 'Darling, Je Vous Aime Beaucoup', plus a piece of riotous friskiness called 'Dirty Gertie From Bizerte', which was fast becoming the number one favourite among Allied troops. And at every turn she sang 'J'ai Deux Amours'.[28]

Being the star of an ENSA tour, Josephine found herself rubbing shoulders with those famous British entertainers who had the guts and gusto to make it to North Africa. They included the likes of Laurence Olivier, Vivien Leigh and Noël Coward, who was himself a former/ sometime agent with the SIS. Having served in a top secret role – and earning himself a place in Hitler's Black Book; the Nazi's 'most-wanted list' of those to be seized once Britain was invaded – Coward had been urged by Churchill to abandon his secret assignments, so as to entertain the troops. 'Go and sing for them when the guns are firing,' Britain's wartime leader urged, and Coward had paid heed.[29]

Kindred spirits – fearless superstars and veterans of the shadow wars – Josephine and Noël Coward hit it off. When she met him in a simple tent in the midst of a military camp in the desert, she could appreciate exactly why he was so beloved of the British troops. The heartfelt warmth and generosity of the man shone through. His smile was a blessing that he gifted to you.[30] Coward reciprocated such sentiments, echoing Josephine's enthusiasm and amity. 'She is doing a wonderful job with the troops,' he would write of Josephine's tour, 'and refuses to appear anywhere where admission is charged . . .'[31]

At several junctures on her tour a Colonel Eric Dunstan – another of her ENSA minders – declared to the crowd: 'We couldn't find a better ambassador for the morale of the troops than Miss Josephine Baker.'

Josephine countered, self-effacingly: 'I don't think so. I know someone who thrills the soldiers: Noël Coward.'[32]

Josephine's signature toughness and her fire was back. In Cairo she faced down King Farouk, the royal head of Egypt. She had gone to a nightclub with an English officer who was acting as her escort for the evening. The club's owner came and sought her out, with a message from the King: he would like her to sing. She declined, after which a second message arrived at their table: 'It is an order. You do not refuse a king.'[33] When the music began playing again, Josephine got to her feet, but not to sing. Instead, she took to the dance floor on the English officer's arm.

King Farouk was not pleased. He ordered the orchestra to stop playing. As panic spread, the conductor called for a policeman, who begged Josephine to leave. 'I will not,' she countered, 'because I feel like dancing.'[34] Beneath her seemingly wilful defiance lay a set of very real and solid reasons. As she knew full well, King Farouk had yet to declare himself for the Allies. Josephine sought to lure him into a public show of where his proper loyalties should lie.

The matter was settled when the King booked the Royal Theatre Cairo for Josephine to perform. She had agreed to do so, but only if the event were held under the banner of Franco-Egyptian friendship. Egypt had yet to recognise the French Committee of National Liberation, the political wing of the Free French movement. For months, General de Gaulle's man in Egypt had failed to get an audience with King Farouk, who was suspected by some of having pro-Nazi sympathies. Josephine's performance at the Royal Theatre Cairo would go a long way to addressing such failings.

Old habits die hard. During her month-long ENSA tour, Josephine was struck repeatedly by what she heard – on the streets, from Arab chiefs, from royalty, from those in places of high authority. The people of North Africa knew the Atlantic Charter off by heart, and had taken its promised freedoms as their driving inspiration.[35] A region-wide uprising threatened, as nations reached boiling point, their populations hungering to throw off the yoke of colonial rule. Josephine felt gripped by an anxiety that was hard for her to articulate. While she supported their calls for freedom, her message, as always, was – *not just yet. Once we have defeated the overarching evil of Nazism, but not before . . .*

In fact, the British and American secret services had deliberately stoked those fires. In the run-up to the Torch landings, the SOE and OSS had offered backing to Arab leaders seeking independence, including weaponry, if they in turn would support the Allied cause. But what had then seemed like a sound policy threatened to backfire now. Fuelled by the sentiments underpinned by the Atlantic Charter, the Berber (Rif) and Arab tribes looked set to take the path of war. 'The subsequent control of such a rising might well prove impossible,' warned a SOE report, which 'would be a considerable embarrassment to the Allies . . .'[36] From what Josephine was hearing, far more than an 'embarrassment' threatened.

By mid-July 1943 she was back in Morocco, where she shared her fears with her friends. Abtey fed the intelligence to Colonel Billotte, who passed it on to those on high. He came back with an urgent request. Would Josephine consider doing a tour under de Gaulle's personal patronage, in support of the Free French troops? It would have a two-fold agenda. In addition to boosting morale, she was also being asked to raise money for those Resistance groups active across France sabotaging and ambushing German forces. They were in desperate need of funds, and as Josephine was unpaid, always and everywhere a volunteer, they hoped she could help. Josephine said she could.

That agreed, Colonel Billotte explained there would also be a third, hidden role, if she were willing. He wished Josephine, together with Abtey – for he was very much back in business now – to return to their roots; to gather intelligence, but this time specifically concerning the unrest that threatened to engulf North Africa. 'As you are used to working with Captain Abtey, he will accompany you,' Billotte promised, adding that General de Gaulle was 'very interested' in what they might discover.[37]

'Josephine Baker . . . was going to be called upon to carry out her activities for the Intelligence Services until the Allied landings on the French coast,' was how Abtey would describe her forthcoming role. 'I was to be entrusted once again with guiding her steps, directing her efforts and pursuing joint actions with her.'[38] This time, they would be doing so under de Gaulle's direct patronage. For now at least Abtey's chequered past – his spying for the British and Americans – would be ignored.

The old-faithfuls of Josephine's entourage were reassembled: Ferdinand Zimmer and Fred Rey, plus the band of assorted musicians. Bearing in mind their new clandestine role, a fresh recruit was brought in. Si Mohamed Menebhi – the son of the former Grand Vizier of Morocco – was to join them, for his presence would open many doors. A 4,500-kilometre journey lay ahead of them, just to reach Cairo, so they also recruited several drivers, including a young French naval officer who hailed from Brittany (his name seems lost to time).

Using their high-level contacts across Morocco and the wider region, Josephine and Abtey, aided by Si Mohamed Menebhi, were to seek out the unvarnished truth, and if possible to suggest 'conclusions and offer solutions'.[39] They were to do so fearlessly, and reporting freely whatever they found. They would not always get it spot on. Sometimes they called it wrong, but more often than not their reports proved accurate and incisive, even if the message they embodied was not always welcome.

'Sometimes we were appreciated, often we were hated because our weapon was our nerve to say what had to be said,' Abtey would write of their new-found mission. All too often, their reports would be met with 'indifference and disbelief, or even hostility'.[40] Unwittingly, their work would lead them into the darkest kind of trouble, for theirs was a message that many did not want to hear.

Yet again, it would take them to the very brink of death.

CHAPTER TWENTY-FOUR

Liberation Day

Come Bastille Day – the French National Day, 14 July 1943 – in Algiers, the new capital of Free France, there was much to celebrate. Five days earlier Allied forces had landed in Sicily, signifying that the long-awaited liberation of Europe was finally under way. After reviewing the Bastille Day parade, General de Gaulle spoke to the crowds: 'France is a tortured prisoner who is under the lash in her prison and who measures once and for all the cause of her unhappiness and the infamy of her tyranny . . .'[1]

He rounded off his speech with a strident call to arms, pointing out that while the Nazi tyranny was not yet over, the long darkness was lifting and that French unity would be crucial to securing victory. Cometh the hour, cometh the man. In North Africa in the summer of 1943 de Gaulle appeared to have found his calling, managing to capture the hearts and minds of the Free French as no other leader seemed able. He was never going to do so with the hard-line Vichyites, but few of them were ever going to come onside, and in any case the tide was turning against them.

To celebrate the dawning of the light across occupied Europe, a gala ball was planned at the city's grand theatre, the L'Opéra d'Alger. In a 'thunderous coup', de Gaulle's people secured Josephine to headline the show.[2] In spite of her growing penury, it was to be another benefit for the Red Cross. As with previous such shows, the Red Cross trumpeted how it was being staged with 'the gracious assistance of Mademoiselle Josephine BAKER accompanied by her American Army orchestra'.[3]

Both de Gaulle and Giraud were expected to attend. In recent days they had agreed to form an administration of national unity, the French Committee of National Liberation, but residual tensions simmered, and the night promised friction and celebration in equal measure. The hall was packed, as the great and the good of Algiers gathered. As the evening progressed, a list of French showbusiness types was read out, those who were considered to be collaborators, Maurice Chevalier's name among them.[4] The auditorium dripped anger and resentment – bordering on hatred – but when Josephine stepped onto the stage the atmosphere was transformed.

Time and again during the war she somehow managed to achieve this, bringing peace and unity solely by her presence and her example. People rose to their feet with tears in their eyes when she began to sing. At first, she stumbled upon her lyrics, being overcome by the momentous nature of the occasion. De Gaulle was the almost-mythical figure whose words in the summer of 1940 had first roused her to action, showing her the path of resistance. She had sung to royalty, celebrities of all types and to senior political leaders, but in this one instance she felt almost overawed.[5]

In the hours prior to the gala's opening, she had conceived of a dramatic grand finale: a giant Tricolour (the French flag), overlain with a Cross of Lorraine (the symbol of Free French resistance) would drop from the ceiling, filling the entire stage. In a frenetic whirl she had managed to find the material with which to make it, and even to persuade the mother superior of a local convent to put her nuns to work, sewing together the enormous flag. But before it could close out her act, there was the intermission, during which she was invited to meet with de Gaulle.

He rose from his seat to greet the iconic superstar, offering her his place next to Madame de Gaulle. As a token of his appreciation he pressed into Josephine's hands a tiny gold Cross of Lorraine, exquisite in its Cartier design. Afterwards, Josephine appeared so incredibly moved that when she took to the stage again it was to give one of the greatest performances of her life. To close out the show she started to sing 'La Marseillaise' – she would always ensure that the national anthem of those to whom she sang was the last to be played – and when the massive flag, all of eighteen feet in depth, dropped from its hiding place, the audience went wild.

That, of course, was her special gift for de Gaulle.

She would write of de Gaulle that without his courageous stand and his stirring words, France would have been thrust into 'the blackest night'.[6] All her life she had been showered with fabulous gifts by her admirers, but that small gold cross from de Gaulle would prove the one she would treasure most. Even so, in the months to come she would auction it off to raise money for the Resistance, so driven was she by the cause (it would raise 350,000 francs from a member of her audience; no small sum).

She didn't regret auctioning it for the cause. She didn't even feel as if she had lost it. She would remark, sagely, that the things 'we truly love stay with us always, locked in our hearts'.[7]

Just over a month after that historic gala ball, the Allies would recognise de Gaulle as the Chief of the Resistance. By force of personality and clever manoeuvring he had outsmarted Giraud, who, by November 1943, was being increasingly sidelined.[8] Long before that, Josephine and her tour entourage had departed, commencing what would prove to be a truly epic North African odyssey.

The drama began as they pressed east out of Algiers, their small convoy consisting of a lone jeep trailed by a Hotchkiss saloon car – a luxury French model from the time – which was piled high with Josephine's trunks. It was a warm July evening as they left the city behind, nosing into the rugged and isolated Kabylia Mountains, a name which means 'Land of the Tribes'. Aiming to make Tunis in one go, they pressed on through the gathering night, the way ahead stretching across 800 kilometres of remote desert and coastline.

The trouble came about due to a forgotten map and a wrong turn, leading onto a narrow, winding road. The route proved increasingly precipitous, carving a tortuous path through the mountains. For several hours the convoy crawled through a ravine seemingly without bottom, or at least none that was visible in the thick night. 'Sometimes black and threatening, sometimes pale like spectres, peaks rose every moment from the darkness,' Abtey would write.[9] It was obvious that they were lost, yet there seemed no option but to press on.

Come first light, they found themselves in rolling desert country, the road hugging the meanders of a wadi. To left and right the landscape bore the ravages of recent fighting, the terrain riven with jagged-edged craters, the blasted ruins of villages and the skeletal forms of bombed-out bridges. It was at this moment that the Hotchkiss decided to give up the ghost. They were forced to abandon the motorcar, loading aboard as many of Josephine's trunks as the jeep could carry, and struggling on hopelessly overloaded. Then the engine of the jeep blew up, leaving them utterly stranded.

It was only thanks to a good Samaritan – a rare vehicle happened to be passing – that they were able to secure a tow the final fifty kilometres to Tunis, the recently liberated capital of Tunisia. In a brutal and bloody campaign, which had cost tens of thousands of Allied lives, Tunisia – the last bastion of German resistance in North Africa – had fallen in May 1943, with 230,000 Axis soldiers taken prisoner. The city seemed to have suffered remarkably little damage, apart from the port area. The day after their arrival Josephine gave her first concert, as they launched into the punishing schedule that Zimmer had prepared.

It was here that a new figure joined their tour group, Captain Paul-Hémir Mezan of the Free French forces. Tall, blond, blue-eyed, Mezan had the dash of an athlete and the poise of a born warrior. He had been tasked by de Gaulle's people to oversee the Tunis side of Josephine's tour, and he would do so with remarkable aplomb. One of the earliest volunteers for de Gaulle's Free French, he had fought a long and bloody war and seemed utterly unperturbed by past defeats. Armies were made to win and to lose battles, he argued. It was only the ultimate victory that mattered.[10]

In war, Captain Mezan had proven true to his word. In June 1940, even as France had fallen to the enemy, so Mezan – then stationed in Morocco – had joined a group of Polish airmen seeking to embark clandestinely from the coast at Casablanca, to reach Britain and to join the Allies. The boat that had collected them – the *Djebel Dersa* – was one of the Gibraltar fishing/smuggling fleet, and Mezan would reach Britain – via a short stopover at the Rock – in late July 1940. There, he signed up for service with de Gaulle's Free French, volunteering to be sent 'anywhere, as long as we fight'.[11]

Sent back to North Africa, Mezan served with various Free French forces, including a long stint with a camel platoon, before being assigned as liaison officer to the British 8th Army. He was to play a key role in guiding their forces across the Mareth Line, a system of defences in Tunisia originally built by the French. For his actions he would be awarded a Military Cross by the British, and he would also win a Croix de Guerre and be appointed as a Knight of the Légion d'Honneur by the French.[12]

Josephine's first few performances in Tunis went down a treat, after which she suggested they mount two further shows with a deliberate Anglo-French friendship theme. All was duly arranged, when, on the opening of the first night, they were shocked to see how the theatre had been set up. A cordon of British Royal Military Police (RMP) had been thrown around it, and only British troops were being allowed in. Rather than cause a scene, they decided to let matters lie, but the following evening it all came to a head. Zimmer flew into one of his signature rages, ensuring that the French/British segregation came to an end, all be it with 'a certain liveliness'.[13]

By way of response, the British officer who was overseeing matters chose to insult Zimmer's honour. On hearing of this, Captain Mezan sought out the guilty party with vengeance in mind. With gun and blade in hand, Mezan challenged him to a duel. 'I give you the choice between the sabre and the machinegun,' he announced, to the British officer's astonishment. Alternatively, he could apologise for the insult and they would call it quits. Sensibly, he plumped for the latter option, and the incident ended with a soldier's handshake 'devoid of rancour'.[14]

After two years or more of soldiering across North Africa, Mezan had a decidedly piratical appearance – dirty and oil-stained shorts, a sand-encrusted faded blue peaked kepi, plus the sabre, of course – but it seemed somehow to suit his martial attitude. 'If I come to be killed in battle,' he would write, 'I ask of my comrades, and this is my last wish, to pull on white gloves, to lay my sabre at my side, and to place on my forehead the Cross of Lorraine.'[15] Sadly, a year later in Italy, he would be killed by a mortar shell, when preparing his men for an attack on German positions.

But for now, Mezan was about to lead a mission of an altogether different nature. In order to serve as one of Josephine's troupe, Si Mohamed Menebhi had been appointed as a lieutenant-interpreter in the Free French forces. But as his clearance to travel on American or British warplanes had failed to come through, they could not continue the tour by air, and their wheeled means of transport were, of course, kaput. No problem, Mezan declared. Give him a few hours and he would have the answer to all their worries.

Shortly, he took Abtey to check out two brand-new-looking American jeeps, painted in smart desert khaki. They were carefully tucked away in the garage of a Tunis villa. When Abtey tried to slide into the driver's seat, Mezan warned him, with a roguish smile: 'Don't touch them. The paint isn't yet dry.'[16] It turned out that Mezan had 'borrowed' the jeeps from the American military, repainting them in Free French colours, complete with a Cross of Lorraine on the bonnets. Apparently, the American military police knew they had gone missing, so they would need to depart Tunis in such a way as to avoid discovery.

In the depths of the night they loaded up their two pilfered transports, a third legitimate jeep rounding off the convoy. In the lead vehicle rode Mezan, who had selected a route out of the city designed to avoid any watchful eyes. Abtey followed, with Josephine and Si Mohamed riding with him. In the rear vehicle went Fred Rey plus a Free French volunteer, Sergeant Modica, and the youthful sailor from Brittany.

Josephine would describe a flight from Tunis shrouded in subter-fuge. It was well past midnight as their convoy of jeeps tore through the city streets, using speed, plus the cloak of darkness to evade the RMPs. The route ahead to Cairo stretched across thousands of kilo-metres of desert, so those purloined jeeps were about to be tested to the full. Before them lay achingly sad and haunting terrain. Between the occasional oasis – a splash of verdant green amidst the sun-bleached ochres and browns – lay graveyard after graveyard, where the countless victims of this war lay largely unidentified, bereft of headstones or flowers. They paused to pay their respects, and come nightfall the starlit heavens seemed as if they were awash with tears.[17]

Sometime after dawn on the first day of their journey, they reached the Mareth Line, and Mezan called a halt. He wished to show his comrades the place where his British commanding officer had been killed by a mine, when Mezan was serving with the 8th Army. His body lay in a military cemetery near by. They drove on through the heat of the day, the windscreens of the jeeps folded down to take advantage of any cooling breezes. 'The white road stretched out to infinity in a desert landscape, constantly sunken, cratered with deep holes,' towns to either side 'destroyed by the bombardments'.[18]

Just prior to sunset, the convoy came to a fork in the road. This was the parting of the ways. Captain Mezan was turning in one direction, to join a combat unit of the Free French forces. Josephine's tour group was taking the other road, which led to Tripoli, the capital of Libya, a hundred kilometres away.

'The time has come for us to separate,' Mezan announced. 'See you soon, in Paris, Josephine!' Sadly, he would not live to see that day.[19]

Beyond the Libyan capital, the going became horrendous, the road 'torn up by the tracks of the tanks, turned over by shelling . . . it put the jeeps to a hard test.'[20] Abtey called a halt before sunset. It made little sense to press onwards in the dark. Sleeping bags were laid out on the stony ground. Exhausted from the long day's drive, they drifted into sleep, cradled beneath a wide starlit sky.

By day, the desert had seemed wildly beautiful, but at night it appeared to be haunted, sinister, as shadows came to life on all sides and seemed to creep up on their encampment. Some of the spectral figures were very real – prowlers seeking valuables to loot, scavenging within the broken, twisted debris of tanks, or abandoned trucks or the burned-out wrecks of warplanes.[21] There were four-legged scavengers too – fast-moving shadows that flitted across the desert like spectres, letting out spine-chilling howls and screams. Jackals and hyenas were on the prowl, sniffing out corpses and digging for their next meal.[22] Their fearful cries echoed through the night. Fetching weapons from the jeep, Abtey set a sentry rotation, to make sure they weren't surprised in the darkness and robbed or killed.

Early the following morning they were back on the road, crawling across punishing terrain under a burning sun. The Sirte desert stretched like a shimmering mirage – an impossible sea – in all directions, the wreckage of aircraft and military vehicles scattered far and wide, as if afloat on the ethereal waters. It all seemed utterly deserted, until a pair of British military policemen (MPs) emerged from out of the late afternoon heat, signalling the convoy to a halt to check over their papers. That done, they wished the tour group good luck and waved them on their way.

Some sixty kilometres further on the two MPs reappeared, speeding past in their car, which they drew to a halt blocking the way. The route was heavily mined, they explained, and if anyone strayed off the road they were likely to get blown up. With nightfall approaching, they'd prefer it if Josephine and her entourage might deign to spend the night as guests 'in our shack'. That roadside 'shack' proved spartan in the extreme. Despite this, the MPs were faultless in their dress. With their white gloves, 'carefully brushed uniforms . . . boots impeccably polished, they controlled the traffic in this hell of heat and dust as they would have done in the middle of Piccadilly.'[23]

As the British soldiers dug out their finest rations in honour of their guests, the tour group reciprocated, rustling up 'a meal to remember'. Afterwards, 'Josephine sang for them as she would have done for her audience at the Casino de Paris.'[24] They departed at dawn, motoring

346

on through Benghazi, Derna, Tobruk, Bardia, Sollum, but finding so many of those places lying in ruins. For five days they slogged on, eyes shielded in motorcycle glasses with tinted lenses, a thick layer of sand and dust caking every inch of skin and clothing, and making them look like a ghostly, demonic host.

The heat, the relentless pace and the punishing conditions began to take their toll. Nerves became frayed. At one point they halted among a particularly perilous stretch of terrain. Abtey made a remark to Josephine that seemed to enrage her. By way of response she slid behind the wheel of the vehicle in which they had been riding, and sped off along the twisting track, leaving Abtey for dust. Knowing she had never driven a jeep before – 'a delicate instrument for angry people' – Abtey sped after her in the other vehicle. Eventually he caught up and managed to coax her away from the wheel.[25]

Still angry with him, for a while she chose to travel in the second jeep along with Fred Rey, and with Sergeant Modica at the wheel, plus the young sailor from Brittany riding shotgun. Finally, Abtey and Si Mohamed managed to entice her back into her usual spot, sitting with the two of them in the lead vehicle. By doing so they would very likely save her life, or at least save her from serious injury.

A while later they reached a fork in the road. One route led towards the jumbled, cratered ruins of the village of El Alamein. Pausing to wait for jeep number two to catch up, there seemed to be no sign of it. Thinking it must have broken down, they turned back. Shortly, they encountered a truck coming in the opposite direction, the driver of which gave them the shocking news: the other jeep had overturned a little further along.

'With a terrible feeling in my heart, I accelerated,' Abtey would write of this moment.[26] They reached the crash site, only to discover the jeep had veered off the road, rolling several times, before coming to a halt. A group of passing British soldiers had stopped to help, and they were inspecting the damage. Besides them stood Fred Rey, looking ghostly pale but apparently unharmed. Sergeant Modica was covered in blood and cradling his head in his hands.

Nearby lay the figure of the young sailor from Brittany, face up and stone-cold dead. As best he could Modica told them what had happened. The road had been straight, running flat through the desert, and he was unable to explain how they had come to crash. It was a mystery. Maybe he had fallen asleep at the wheel? He just didn't know.

Even as Sergeant Modica spoke, Abtey was gripped by a dark sense of unease. A while before, they had paused at an isolated British encampment to enjoy a cup of tea. Abtey had got out his cigarettes, offering them to the others. He'd stuck a match, lit his own, then another and then a third – that being the cigarette of the young man who was now dead. The words of Major Bacon, his SIS handler in Lisbon, came back to haunt him: *Never three . . . or the youngest will die.* Abtey had given that young sailor the fateful third light, and if he hadn't persuaded Josephine to return to her place in their vehicle, she too would have been caught in the accident, with unimaginable consequences.

It was a dark day. The body was fetched by some British MPs and taken to the morgue in nearby Alexandria, while the injured Modica was rushed to the local hospital. Finally, late at night the reduced tour party limped into Alexandria, Josephine's face lit by the moon and seeming 'hollowed out with grief'.[27] If anything, Abtey felt even worse. Shortly, they buried the unfortunate victim in Alexandria's military cemetery.

This epic odyssey brought Josephine closer to the death and horror of war than ever, with profound consequences. 'The powdered, pampered Josephine' of the pre-war years was a stranger to her now, she would declare. With death a constant companion, life had attained a far deeper significance, this closeness to suffering forcing her to dig deep to find compassion and 'tenderness'.[28] She did so for all of her performances, but especially at the hospitals, which were overflowing with Allied wounded.

From Alexandria to Cairo and onwards through Jerusalem, Damascus and finally to Beirut, the capital of the Lebanon, the tour continued. At all points Josephine danced and she sang. But equally, as she was feted by high society, diplomats, royalty and Arab chiefs alike, she talked, and most importantly, she listened. So too did her partner in espionage, Abtey. Across the entire region the momentum for liberation was building. It seemed unstoppable. The report they compiled made all of this clear, as it did the pressing need for the Allies to keep a lid on the unrest, at least until the war against the enemy could be won. The transition to independence needed to be smooth and untroubled, and managed properly so as not to erupt in a paroxysm of violence.

By early November 1943 they were back in Cairo, having raised over 3 million French Francs – a staggering amount in today's money – for the French Resistance. Equally, they had garnered a thick file of intelligence, and were keen to spirit it into Colonel Billotte's hands, and from there to de Gaulle. It proved impossible to do so, and mostly due to the obduracy of some of those serving at de Gaulle's intelligence HQ, in Algiers. There, a mysterious figure trashed the reports they sent by coded radio messages, consigning them to the dustbin. This was happening, even as angry crowds stoned the windows of the Egyptian minister's house in which they were being entertained, and mobs hit the streets demanding all they had been promised under the Atlantic Charter, and chiefly freedom from colonial rule.[29]

Faced with animosity and antagonism from Algiers, and blocked from getting their reports to Billotte, Josephine and Jacques decided they would have to deliver them in person. On 15 November 1943 the much-reduced party – most of the troupe, including Fred Rey, would follow later – departed Cairo, to retrace their steps across North Africa using the one battered jeep that remained. Upon reaching Alexandria they paused to place flowers on the grave of the young naval officer who had died in the jeep accident, and to pay their respects.

They also managed to track down the jeep that had run off the road, realising that it should be possible to get it just about roadworthy. Sergeant Modica was due to be released from hospital, and he volunteered to get back behind the wheel. The jeep still looked a wreck, with its windscreen gone, no spare wheel and only one head-lamp which was distinctly boss-eyed. Even so, two vehicles were far better than one for such a journey.

With winter now upon them the desert had turned bitterly cold, and especially when moving in open-topped vehicles, with the result that the jeeps' occupants looked even less presentable than their wheeled transport. Josephine shivered under a thick woollen cap with 'donkey ears', and with the giant Tricolour hugged closely around her. Si Mohammed Menebhi was wrapped in a khaki Berber djellaba – a thick woollen robe – with the hood pulled up over the top of a fez, a traditional felt hat. Abtey wore one coat over another, and had long yellow gloves pulled up to his elbows, while Sergeant Modica looked positively bursting at the seams – 'like a real Michelin Man' – with a thick wax camouflage raincoat thrown over all.[30]

They pressed ahead, but just before they reached Tobruk the jeep driven by Abtey collapsed onto its side, with one of its suspension springs cracked in two. There was almost no water left in the radiator or fuel in the tank. Just then, like an impossible apparition, Josephine spied a seeming mirage. A vehicle melted out of the haze. It turned out that a unit of Austrian Jews – die-hard anti-Nazis fighting in the Allied cause – was stationed in the desert near by. They agreed to repair the stricken jeep, on one condition: 'Miss Baker comes to sing at our camp . . .'[31] The deal was struck, Josephine did as promised, and the next day they got back on the road.

Perhaps unsurprisingly, due to his recent injuries Sergeant Modica was plagued by exhaustion. Abtey was forced to take over driving his jeep, as Josephine took the wheel of the other. Passing Benghazi, they pushed into the Sirte desert once more, but shortly Abtey's vehicle blew out two of its tyres. Josephine set out in her vehicle, seeking help. She returned with a 'curious figure, nonchalantly lying on the hood of the jeep'[32] Dressed in torn and patched trousers and battered shirt, he had a faded cap on his head topped off by a large pom-pom. He slid off the vehicle and with some glue and spare rubber got to work repairing the burst tyres.

'A great guy,' Josephine explained. 'He's an English soldier, a de-miner, who lives with a comrade in a hut, along with a dog and a black rooster called Achilles, who he's trying to keep alive until Christmas.'[33] The hut was so bare and plain, its only luxury was a tiny radio which they'd scavenged from an abandoned tank. Every morning, they'd set out with their kit to clear the desert of mines. 'Three months ago, they were four. The other two were blown up: one, the day after his arrival, the other two weeks ago. That doesn't stop them from whistling all the time . . .'

Once the soldier was done fixing the tyres, he called over to the superstar: 'Josephine! You have to pay for the repairs!'

'Of course! Of course!'

'Well! Would you agree to sing on the BBC, on Christmas Eve, "I'm Dreaming of a White Christmas"?'

'Sure!'

'Don't forget. We'll be listening . . .'[34]

That Christmas Josephine would keep to her side of the bargain. But shortly after making that BBC broadcast, she would learn that the soldier who had so gallantly repaired her tyres had been blown up by a mine on Christmas Eve . . .

On the approach to Misrata, still 1,500 kilometres short of their destination, the engine of Abtey's jeep began to knock alarmingly. A British Army truck towed it to their base, which by luck was near by. That night Josephine and her entourage slept in the back of that truck, as they waited for the jeep to be repaired.

At dawn, a British officer poked his head through the canvas: 'Miss Josephine Baker?' he demanded, in mock dismay. 'What are you doing in this miserable tumbril? Come down at once, your breakfast awaits you. When you are such a person, how is it possible to hang out like a gipsy!'[35] (A tumbril is an open-backed wooden cart, often used to convey the condemned to the guillotine.)

That day, Abtey's jeep was fitted with a new engine and Josephine's vehicle was completely overhauled. By the evening, the workshop had been transformed into a makeshift theatre, and Josephine proceeded to dance and to sing. The following morning, they discovered that the British soldiers had painted in bright lettering across the front of Josephine's spruced up vehicle: 'JOSE'S JEEP'. It was a fine and a beautiful way to part company with those who had made them so very welcome.

They set off for Algiers, but what awaited them there was a very different kind of reception. Upon arrival, they delivered their intelligence dossier, just as intended and damn the consequences, but there were many who wanted to bury the message that it embodied. To some – those intent on France retaining her colonies and the supposed 'glory' that came with them – it contained a series of deeply inconvenient truths. They were determined to 'shoot the messengers', at least metaphorically.

Yet via Colonel Billotte's good offices, the two intrepid special agents finally managed to get their warnings into de Gaulle's hands – that French North Africa was a powder keg primed to blow.

Even so, a cold wind was blowing through the world of French intelligence, and Josephine's days of spying were numbered.

CHAPTER TWENTY-FIVE

A Song For Buchenwald

Six months after completing her epic North African tour, Josephine prepared to board a French Air Force Caudron C.440 Goéland – 'seagull' – light aircraft, for a flight north across the Mediterranean, to set foot on French soil once more. She had been away for three-and-a-half years. It was the eve of the June 1944 Normandy landings, and at the behest of one of Eisenhower's deputies she had been asked to fly to Corsica, the island lying just off the coast of southern France and the first French department to have been liberated by the Allies. The US military had established seventeen airbases across the island, which had earned the nickname the 'USS Corsica'.

Her mission was to perform to the troops stationed there, as they prepared for a massive series of air-operations in support of Operation Dragoon – the Allied landings on the shores of southern France, designed to open up a new front against the forces of the enemy. Josephine's very presence on French soil would serve as a powerful symbol for the coming liberation of Europe, acting as a spur to those Allied troops charged to drive out the forces of the enemy. But the flight across the Mediterranean was not without its risks.

With rancour and resentment still swirling around de Gaulle, and with the rump of Vichyite hardliners fighting for their reputations, their liberty and very possibly their lives, Josephine had been warned that de Gaulle faced on-going assassination plots. In recent months there had been that aircraft that had taken off from British soil carrying de Gaulle, only to suffer a cataclysmic malfunction and an emergency landing. It was only due to the pilot's incredible skill that all aboard weren't killed. An investigation concluded that the aircraft had been sabotaged. Unidentified 'German agents' got the blame, but de Gaulle wasn't convinced. He feared those trying to kill him were far closer to home. Accordingly, Josephine had been warned that she should avoid travelling on any of de Gaulle's personal aircraft, for fear of sabotage.[1]

For her Corsica tour – for her highly-symbolic return to France – she had reassembled her A Team: Jacques Abtey and Ferdinand Zimmer had both been released from their duties. The morning of their departure, they gathered at the airport, only to hear the long-awaited news that the Normandy landings had begun. It was 6 June 1944 and a force of 150,000 Allied troops were even then fighting their way ashore on the northern French coastline. Josephine and her crew were overjoyed at hearing the news, but they were somewhat less enamoured by the means of air transport that awaited them. The Caudron C.440 Goéland was a twin-engine aircraft of underwhelming performance, especially compared to the sleek American-built Glenn Martin plane parked near by.

In typical style, Zimmer demanded that they take the Glenn-Martin. He was told in no uncertain terms that the Goéland was a perfectly fine aircraft, and that the pilot and co-pilot were among the best. They waited for Josephine's trunks to be loaded into the cramped interior, then clambered aboard. As the plane went to take off, it seemed to struggle even to get airborne. All aboard had their hearts in their mouths as it lumbered 'like a drunken bumblebee' towards the trees at the end of the runway . . . clearing them, but only just.[2]

As the heavily laden aircraft clawed into the skies, the weather was radiant, the views breathtaking. A swathe of mountains, desert and emerald coastline rolled out before them, much of which the three travellers had experienced up close and personal, as they had nursed their jeeps across punishing terrain during Josephine's series of tours. Since their last, which had ended in Algiers the previous November, Josephine and Abtey had mostly turned their backs on the world of intelligence and espionage, as they were drawn into the ranks of the Free French armed services.

Josephine had been appointed as a Second Lieutenant in the Women's Air Force Corps, with the role of Propaganda Officer, under commander Alla Dumesnil-Gillet, who'd won a Croix de Guerre in 1940, and who was to become one of Josephine's foremost champions.[3] Having volunteered for special forces, Abtey would end up serving in the regular French military as the liberation of Europe got under way. But the long and punishing desert tours had taken a heavy toll, especially on Josephine, and that winter she had been struck down by yet another debilitating sickness. There were rumours that she may even have been poisoned, and she certainly had her enemies.[4]

In many ways, these troubling winter months of 1943–44 were the closest that Josephine had ever come to death. So dire was her condition that Colonel Billotte had ordered Abtey to abandon all other duties and to remain by her sickbed, doing all in his power to save her. Eventually, after yet more surgery, she had won through, though it had proven a Herculean trial. She would joke that the doctors may as well have inserted a zipper in her abdomen, so many operations had she undergone. By her own estimation she had teetered on the very brink – her life had been hanging by the faintest of threads.[5]

Across occupied Europe the war was entering its final desperate stages, wherein the excesses of the Nazis would become ever more execrable. Many of those who had played a part in Josephine Baker's war would be mired in the darkness. Hans Müssig – their chisel-faced Lisbon fixer extraordinaire – would be captured by the Gestapo, though somehow, miraculously he would turn the table on his captors and weather the worst of their predations. Sadly, Father Victor Dillard, the Jesuit priest and war hero who had dispatched young Le Besnerais to Château des Milandes with his precious suitcase stuffed with intelligence, would not.

In the autumn of 1943, the venerable father had volunteered to go to Germany, posing as a worker in the STO (Service du Travail

Obligatoire) programme – the deportation of hundreds of thousands of French men and women to Germany, as forced labour. Once there, he had practised openly as a priest – indeed, that had been his sole purpose in volunteering – and in spite of the aggressive programme of de-Christianisation and Nazification that permeated the STO. Arrested by the Gestapo's specialist anti-ecclesiastical section, in April 1944 Father Dillard was condemned as a 'spy' and deported to Dachau concentration camp. He would die there, resisting to the last.[6]

Now, in early June 1944, as the Goéland droned northwards and the sleek form of a Spitfire swooped in to serve as escort, it seemed as if all was set for the triumphant return to France of Josephine and her crew, having braved the long years of struggle. That was until the Goéland's first engine spluttered, coughed and then died. As the propellers came to an ominous standstill, the plane seemed to chug ever onwards, a little slower and a little more ponderously perhaps, but still somehow clinging to the skies.

Abtey went forward to investigate. 'The left engine is dead,' the pilot told him. 'But one is enough. I promised the General to drop you off in Ajaccio and I will do so.'[7]

The rugged Corsican coastline was visible up ahead, with Ajaccio, its capital, lying on the western flank of the island. Steadily losing altitude, the Goéland pitched towards a narrow gap in the Corsican mountains, swerving between two massive cliffs, a 'granite wall whose top was at our height' looming first on one side and then the other.

'Never will we pass,' Zimmer remarked, as, with extraordinary calm, he pulled out a comb from his pocket and began to tidy up his hair.[8]

The gap loomed closer, 'a damned wall coming at us at an incredible speed', as Abtey would describe it. Josephine and her crew squeezed shut their eyes and prepared for the worst.

At the very last moment the pilot coaxed an extra gasp from the one surviving engine, and the Goéland appeared to buck up for an instant, clearing the rock walls by a whisker. Below them stretched the Corsican sea, and with each passing second it seemed to be drifting closer. The cover of the one surviving Renault engine started to blacken, blister and smoke, as the heat thrown off by the over-stressed mechanics became too much.

'Hold on!' the pilot cried.

They drifted still lower. Again, with his signature calm Zimmer went forward and started to build a barricade out of Josephine's tour cases, sheeted over with the giant Tricolour, as a rampart to prevent her from being thrown forward. That done, he stood with his back braced against the aircraft's bulkhead, facing Josephine, so as to shield her with his body. Abtey poked his head into the cockpit, eyeing the onrushing sea. He intended to yell out a warning when they were about to ditch, so all could brace themselves.

Seconds later he did just that, as the Goéland was lit from end to end in a blinding flash of white, a massive plume of water being thrown up as the aircraft's belly ploughed into the waves. As they came to a shuddering, hissing halt, so one of the aircrew smashed the windows out with an axe, and one by one the survivors clambered onto the Goéland's wing. By an odd quirk of fate the airframe was almost entirely of wooden construction, so it should stay afloat for a while at least.

The stricken aircraft was surrounded by a mass of flotsam and jetsam – mostly Josephine's tour trunks. Fortunately help was at hand. A squadron of Senegalese Tirailleurs – colonial French infantry, recruited from the West African nation of Senegal – happened to be bathing in a nearby cove. As one they dived in, swam out to the slowly sinking aircraft, seized individuals and tour luggage and brought all to land. Thus it was that Josephine was saved, and set foot once more on French soil held aloft by a phalanx of African warriors.[9]

Apart from cuts and bruises, the main damage done was to Josephine's tour luggage. Soaked in seawater though it all was, the show had to go on, especially as two of the anti-aircraft batteries that defended the Corsican airbases had been christened *Josephine* and *J'ai Deux Amours* in her honour. While *Josephine* had claimed two enemy warplanes shot down, *J'ai Deux Amours* had accounted for double that number. With the Goéland being a write-off, they used a trusty Glenn Martin for all further transport, the tour group flitting from airbase to airbase, where Josephine performed to crowds of 30,000 at a time.

Her final show was at a vast military base 'floodlit' with truck lights, where ranks of warplanes were lined up, heavy with their bomb loads, and poised to fly into mainland France. Josephine sang with an emotion and intensity rarely witnessed, as she tried to tear away 'the great black veil thrown over the country' – over France – so that every single one of those bombers could make it through to their targets.[10] After she was finished she threw herself down on a camp-bed, fully clothed and exhausted, even as the first of the bomber formations roared thunderously into the skies.

Four months later, in October 1944, Josephine sailed for France aboard a Liberty Ship – mass-produced cargo-vessels built in their thousands for the Allied war effort – which would dock at recently liberated Marseilles. Her espionage role was pretty much finished by now, but much else remained to be done. Josephine's morale-boosting duties would last until the final guns had fallen silent, as she performed throughout the winter of 1944–45 to front-line troops across Europe and even as far away as Great Britain.

One of her biggest regrets was leaving behind her menagerie – her tour animals – in North Africa. During the long years of sickness they had gradually been lost to her, including even Bonzo, her Great Dane. In any case she was formally a soldier now, and there was little scope for carrying such wayward cargoes aboard Allied warships. There was one consolation. She'd acquired a small dog, which she had managed to sneak aboard hidden under her coat. She'd given him the martial-sounding name of Mitraillette – little machinegun – not because he was particularly fierce, but because he peed like that, in little rat-tat-tat bursts.

Mitraillette was smuggled aboard secreted beneath her Air Force blue uniform coat, complete with the gold epaulettes of a lieutenant.

Over the decades, Josephine had had the world's top designers competing with each other to fashion clothes especially for her, and she had worn some of the world's most famous – and famously-revealing – examples of haute couture on stage. But it was of this outfit, her French military uniform, that she would remain most proud for the rest of her days.

That same month, October 1944, Josephine arrived back in Paris. The war would continue for another seven months, but to many the liberation of this city felt like victory. Across Paris a witch-hunt was under way for collaborators. Passions were running high, and the most egregious offenders more often than not met with unfortunate ends. By contrast, Josephine was viewed as an outstanding heroine . . . but not by all. 'She came back to France more French than Louis XIV,' musician Alain Romains, who had worked on some of her movie scores, remarked. 'I said to her, "It was very nice of you to save France for us, Josephine."'[11]

Yet such criticism was rare.

Shortly after arriving back in Paris, Josephine was invited to sing there once more – now that the enemy had been evicted – in a gala show in aid of the French Air Force. It was in three sections, the final of which was entirely hers. Discarding her lieutenant's uniform, she chose to wear a sweeping, elegant, high-waisted dress, with ruched – pleated, puffy – shoulders, based upon a classic 1900s design. Many of the songs she sung were the old favourites composed for her by Vincent Scotto, whose classic – 'J'ai Deux Amours' – rounded off her repertoire, to which she received a standing ovation.

Columbia Records invited her into their studio, to record some tunes to celebrate victory. They were released in early 1945, together with the caption: 'Thank you, charming officer, for having been heroic and for singing once again for us.'[12]

But of course, the liberation of Paris didn't mean the war was at an end. As General de Lattre de Tassigny's French 1st Army advanced towards Germany – the general had escaped from prison to command the French ground war – Josephine was asked to restart her morale-boosting work. As a lieutenant in the French Air Force, her orders were to carry out 'theatrical tours for the units engaged', and 'galas organised for the benefit of the troops or of prisoners and deportees'.[13]

Over the winter of 1944–45, Josephine returned to her front-line duties with a vengeance. From Belfort, Mulhouse, Colmar, Strasbourg and Nancy she followed the foremost units as they punched across the Rhine and into Germany itself, to Karlsruhe, Stuttgart, Hamburg . . . She sang in the biting chills and cold, in the thick and clinging mud, and even as the enemy counter-attacked, shells bursting violently in the snow. Everywhere she went – sometimes on foot, sometimes by jeep, singing to groups of soldiers in barns lit by oil-lanterns, or in the open in the freezing conditions – she eschewed special treatment, declaring, defiantly: 'I'm a soldier too . . .'[14]

With Allied forces driving ever deeper into Germany, the war in Europe would be declared won on VE Day, 8 May 1945 (VJ Day – Victory in Japan – being declared on 2 September 1945). Nine days earlier, on 29 April, Josephine had visited London, at Churchill's personal behest, headlining a victory show in aid of Allied forces and performing at the Adelphi Theatre.[15] From there she would travel north, to RAF Elvington, in Yorkshire, to perform to the 25,000 mostly French Air Force personnel who were based there. In his diary, airman Pierre-Célestin Delrieu noted his surprise and wonder that a figure of her stature had somehow found the time and wherewithal to visit.

'Josephine Baker, yes, Josephine Baker, came to surprise us one day, in all her charm,' he wrote. 'Proudly wearing the cap and uniform of the French Air Force, with two gold stripes, we saw Lt. Baker climb onto an improvised stage inside the largest of the hangars . . . It was a spectacular triumph. The climactic point was when she sang "Two Loves: My Country and Paris" [J'ai Deux Amours]. There were cheers, encores and tears on people's faces.'[16]

Josephine returned to Paris, appearing at the Théâtre des Champs-Élysées, where she had performed two decades earlier in an altogether different kind of a show – *La Revue Nègre*. General de Gaulle was in the audience, and in the programme was reprinted one of his wartime letters in which he commended 'the few', those who had listened to their hearts and joined the Resistance. 'It is the heart that was right,' de Gaulle concluded.[17] This time, all was elegance for Josephine's show, in which she changed costumes fully nine times. She was also invited to be the guest of honour at a dinner held for the Resistance – those involved in some of the most bitter and bloody fighting, and who were celebrating not only victory but sheer survival.

Shortly, Josephine's duties would take her into recently liberated Berlin, where she would perform at a gala dinner for senior Allied generals hosted at the world-famous *Justizpalast* – the Palace of Justice – on Littenstrasse. The *Justizpalast* was the city's second largest building and a stunning architectural triumph, but it had been reduced to a rat-infested semi-ruin by the predations of the war. Four artistic troupes were on the programme, hailing from Great Britain, the USSR, the USA and France. Josephine had the honour of representing France, along with Colette Mars, the young singer and actress with whom she would strike up a close friendship.

The *Justizpalast* was illuminated by searchlights, reminiscent of so many of Josephine's North African shows, but thankfully there was little danger of coming under attack. Still, the impression cast on the harshly lit and bomb-damaged building was as if it were burning – fire-racked and war-ravaged. Josephine was last to take the stage, enjoying rapturous applause from an audience dripping with glittering medals and braid. She told herself the clapping was not for her. It was for a country that had adopted her two decades earlier, embracing her hunger to flourish and to shine. A nation that had risen phoenix-like from the horrors of the Occupation, to be present at the triumph of good over evil.[18]

That *Justizpalast* gala was fine for the top brass and the dignitaries, but it did little for the common soldier. Josephine and her troupe sought out a small cinema in Berlin's French quarter. There, they began a daily routine, non-stop from ten in the morning until just short of midnight. Troops were ushered in two hundred at a time, the theatre crammed to bursting. To show their appreciation, the soldiers handed Josephine bundles of 'good conduct' certificates, which had been doled out by the Nazis, and which they'd salvaged from the cellars beneath the Reichstag building. Via those, they joked, with biting irony, Josephine was guaranteed a fine Aryan heritage for the rest of her days.[19]

Josephine would be made the principal guest at any number of Allied victory ceremonies, most notably at the magnificent hilltop fortress of the Hohenzollern Castle, the historic seat of the German royal family, the imperial House of Hohenzollern. There, she would take the seat of honour in the grandiose throne room, her very presence representing a powerful symbol of the triumph over Nazi-era prejudices and evils.[20]

If Josephine had ever had cause to doubt the justness of her struggle and of the Allied cause, all such misgivings were about to be swept away. Her visit to Germany would end with her performing for the sick and the dying of the Buchenwald concentration camp, on the outskirts of Weimar in east-central Germany. The terrible things she bore witness to at Buchenwald would underscore the righteousness of all that she had been fighting for, proving a powerful embodiment both of the horrors of Nazism and of the need for good to prevail.

The Allied high command had asked for someone – any entertainer –who might be willing to enter the Buchenwald death camp, which was riven with typhus, a highly-infectious and potentially deadly disease. Despite her long history of sickness, Josephine stepped forward. Upon arrival at Buchenwald she became aware of hordes of ghostly, skeletal figures – inmates from across the nations of the world who had crawled towards the camp's cruel perimeter, interlocking their fingers with the barbed wire; who had perished like that, collapsing, their hands ripped to shreds, their dead eyes staring empty and wide. She went wherever she was asked in the camp, regardless of the risk, seeking to comfort and to give solace, and to embue a spirit of hope which might save any who could be saved. But many in the typhus wards were already too far gone.[21]

Regardless, she sang for them, her voice low and lilting, suffused with raw emotion. All around her, faces lit up with smiles. Even on the verge of death the prisoners of Buchenwald were still trying to live. To hold onto life. So brave. Josephine had to reciprocate – and so she sang. She sang a song called "In My Village" – one she hoped would speak to every person who was there. But even as she sang, the words were choked with emotion. The song portrays a simple village, the paths winding through it, and of the church and the ringing of the bells. But for Josephine, it evoked dark memories.

A few weeks back she had witnessed how, in their death throes, the forces of Nazi Germany had stolen bells from churches across occupied Europe, to melt down so they could be transformed into weapons of war. In fact, over 175,000 had been looted, as the Nazis plundered the very soul and the beliefs of the nations they had invaded.[22] Now, as she sang, she saw the steeples of those dessecrated churches reflected in the gaze of the Buchenwald imates, those who were on the verge of death. She heard the sound of the bells pealing in the gasping and the hollow rasp of their breathing. Somehow, it gave her strength. Somehow, she found again her voice. As she poured out her heart, her compassion, her pain at their pain, she began to notice that all around her faces were streaked with tears. And then she realised that she too was crying. But as the tears poured down, she understood how it was no longer with grief or with despair. Instead, these were tears of joy and tears of love.[23]

For her wartime service, Josephine Baker would duly be awarded the Medal of the Resistance with Rosette, the Croix de Guerre, and she would be appointed a Chevalier of the Légion d'Honneur. Approaching five decades after her death in 1975, she would be interred in the crypt of the Panthéon, a foremost monument in Paris reserved as a resting place for those considered as the nation's foremost National Heroes. Less than one hundred individuals – and only five women – have been awarded such a high distinction. The ceremony at the Panthéon concentrated on Josephine Baker's legacy as a Resistance figure and as an anti-Nazi, and a figurehead for the civil rights movement – a 'life dedicated to the twin quests for liberty and justice', according to the French president's office.

As one of Josephine's senior commanders would declare of her North African work, in particular: 'Her actions in Morocco during the troubled period at the end of '43 and beginning of '44 were officially recognised as having powerfully underpinned a very precarious situation . . . For a year General Billotte . . . charged "Josephine" with particularly delicate missions, which she always fulfilled with an intelligence and devotion . . .'[24] It was a view that General Billotte had himself fully endorsed. Colonel Paul Paillole, the 12 Apostles, Commander Wilfred Dunderdale and countless others would echo such sentiments, declaring that Josephine – and Jacques Abtey's – work on behalf of the French, British and American intelligence services had been of crucial importance.

The war years had proved transformational for Josephine. They were her awakening; truly her coming of age. From global superstar and darling of stage, screen and song, she had become a heroine of the Resistance and a secret hero of the shadow wars of espionage on behalf of the Allies. She had also become, and would increasingly serve as a powerful advocate for freedom and justice in all its forms. It was the dawn of a new mission for Josephine, which would go on to distinguish her post-war life and work. In that, she would remain unwavering and unbreakable until her dying day.

Epilogue

In the spring of 1946, Josephine Baker would return to Château des Milandes, with the help of Don Wyatt, the United Services Overseas representative who had first proposed that she should tour Allied troops, in North Africa. Wyatt drove a Red Cross truck laden with her possessions, and he helped her retrieve many of her valuables, which had been hidden with friends in the surrounding community during the war years. Jacques Abtey joined them, but he would confide in a private moment to Wyatt that he was not intending to marry Josephine – if that were indeed on the cards – because he could not countenance being 'Monsieur Baker'; in other words, living in her shadow.[1]

Whatever the truth of the matter, Josephine didn't seem to take great umbrage. Indeed, she vowed to keep a house for Abtey in the château grounds, for whenever he wanted to visit. The partnership forged between them during the war years would prove powerful and enduring, as would Josephine's connection to North Africa. Shortly, she would throw a party at her Le Vésinet, Paris, home. It had been seized by the enemy during the Occupation and so had required some tender loving care and renovation. The guest of honour was El Glaoui, the Governor of Marrakesh and Lord of the Atlas. El Glaoui was the Moroccan chief with closest ties to the French Government at that time, but he had paid a high price for victory. He had lost a son in the battle for Monte Cassino in spring 1944.

Amid the victory celebrations and the reclaiming of her two

homes, perhaps unsurprisingly the heavy toll of the war years began to catch up with Josephine. Testament to the risks she had run, another American woman, Mildred Harnack, had been beheaded in February 1943, on Hitler's personal orders, due to the resistance and espionage work she had carried out in Germany.[2] In June 1946, a few months after her fortieth birthday, Josephine was rushed into hospital, facing her fifth operation in as many years. Four months later, she was still in hospital, when, on 6 October 1946, she was awarded her first decoration for her war service, the Medaille de la Résistance Avec Rosette. In an emotionally-charged ceremony, it was presented to her by General de Gaulle's daughter, Madame de Boisseau, along with senior figures from the French military, plus a representative of the League Against Racism and Anti-Semitism, Jean-Pierre Bloch.

General de Gaulle had penned a letter to accompany the medal. It read:

Dear Mademoiselle Josephine Baker,

In full awareness of the present circumstances I wish to address to you my wholehearted congratulations on your receipt of the Distinction of the Résistance Française Award. I was in recent years able to see and fully appreciate the great services you rendered at some of the most critical moments. I was subsequently all the more moved to learn of the enthusiasm and generosity you deployed to put your immense talent at the disposal of our cause and those who served it. My wife and I wish you a speedy recovery . . .

Charles de Gaulle[3]

There were headlines in the newspapers, proclaiming how this showbiz star was actually a secret agent of France, and how she had been decorated in recognition of her war service. Very few Frenchwomen would be granted such an honour, though there had been many who had served in the Resistance.

That same month Jacques Abtey would get married to Jacqueline

Cellier. Josephine, recently released from hospital, would offer them her Paris home for the wedding. Around a hundred guests attended. Josephine, still weak from her recent hospitalisation, descended the staircase supported by Abtey on the one side, and his bride-to-be on the other. But the wedding party soon exhausted her, and she asked to be helped back to her bedroom. She had paid a heavy price for the war years.

A campaign was already under way to get her awarded the Légion d'Honneur, France's highest gallantry medal, along with the Croix de Guerre. In the citations for the former, the ex-head of the French counter-espionage service confirmed Josephine's pre-war recruitment to the 'French Special Services', and much of her wartime work in Spain, Portugal and elsewhere.[4] French Air Force General René Bouscat underlined all of this, outlining her role 'in the fight against espionage . . . her collaboration with the forces of the Resistance; missions abroad and liaison with the Allied intelligence services.' He also stressed her missions to Portugal, Spain, Morocco and across North Africa, 'with her chief, Captain ABTEY (Hébert)', plus the fact that she had raised over 10 million francs for the French military.[5]

Despite such backing, the proposal for the Légion d'Honneur was refused. At this point, Josephine's former chief in the French Air Force, the war hero Commander Alla Dumesnil-Gillet, stepped into the fray, as did Major-General Billotte. Billotte stressed the enormous benefits Josephine had delivered for the Allied war effort. He wrote of how, at the cost of her good health, she had 'put her great talent into the service of French propaganda and French works'.[6] If anything, Dumesnil-Gillet – who was the daughter-in-law of French Admiral Charles-Henri Dumesnil – went further, questioning whether Josephine's colour or her gender may have influenced the rejection, and stressing how she was 'an admirable and a great patriot . . . we owe her the almost irremediable compromise of her health.' Dumesnil-Gillet begged 'to have this error of prejudice rectified', as the 'honest and just action to take'.[7]

On 14 February 1947, the recommendation for Josephine Baker's

Légion d'Honneur was again rejected. Undaunted, her supporters immediately put her forward for the decoration once more, but on 8 March 1949 it was rejected for a third time. There would then ensue what can only be described as a galactic tug-of-war between Josephine Baker's supporters and her apparent detractors, which would only be drawn to a close almost a decade later. On 9 December 1957, Josephine was finally made a Chevalier (Knight) of the Légion d'Honneur. (She was also granted the Croix de Guerre Avec Palme.)[8]

Her Légion d'Honneur citation reflected her wartime heroics, and the high price she had paid:

> Sick, exhausted with fatigue, stays for nineteen months in a clinic in CASABLANCA, where her room serves as a meeting place for the Allies' agents . . . Despite a state shaken by illness and fatigue, never ceases to set a fine example of patriotism and a spirit of sacrifice. Has carried the prestige of France very high, setting an example of the most wonderful national virtues and the most ardent patriotism. Renouncing her fans [her star status] to fight the enemy, gave precious service to the cause of the Resistance, representing one of the most remarkable elements of a . . . French woman who gave up and sacrificed everything to serve her country . . .[9]

Much had happened in Josephine Baker's life in the interim. In 1947 she had herself got married to the French composer and conductor, Jo Bouillon. Bouillon had accompanied Josephine during much of her winter 1944–45 tour, as the conductor for her touring orchestra. Together they set up home at Château des Milandes, and as Josephine had been told she could not conceive, they decided they would adopt children and so raise a family that way. They would do just that throughout the 1950s, adopting young children from around the world. They would raise twelve in all, which was their way to prove that people of a variety of races could live in harmony.[10]

In 1949, Josephine felt well enough to return to the Paris stage, performing at the Folies-Bergère, and she soon re-established herself as one of the city's most popular entertainers. Typically, she had not forgotten her pledges to the black GIs to whom she had performed in North Africa – *let's win the war on racial segregation, but let's win the war against the Nazis first.* In 1951 she was invited to the USA to perform at a Miami nightclub, but she insisted on winning a public battle first – that her audiences would not be segregated. She followed up her sold-out Miami shows with a national tour, and was greeted everywhere with rave reviews. Her future looked golden, with six months of bookings lying ahead of her across America, and with promises of more to follow.

But upon reaching New York, she and her husband, Jo Bouillon, were refused a room repeatedly, dozens of the city's hotels rejecting them. Their reason was squeamishness about the supposedly 'unseemly' nature of a black woman and a white man sharing the same room, and what impact that would have on the rest of their guests. Josephine was appalled, saddened and incensed. She began writing news articles about her experiences, and she boycotted selected venues, arguing that if African Americans were banned from attending her shows, she would refuse to perform to segregated audiences (as she had done in North Africa during the war). By way of response, she received abusive and threatening phone-calls from the Ku Klux Klan, among others. Typically, she declared publicly that she was not afraid.

At one stage she even made a citizen's arrest of a man in a hotel, who had levelled the N-word at her. Matters finally came to a head at the Stork Club in Manhattan, where she had been refused service. Storming out of the venue, along with the actress Grace Kelly, and others – she and Kelly would become lifelong friends – they vowed never to return. Publicly they criticised the Stork Club's unwritten policy of ostracising black patrons. As the controversy raged, Josephine got into a spat with the famous American newspaper columnist Walter Winchell, who hit back that she supposedly had 'Communist sympathies', which was viewed as being a serious accusation at that point in history.

In an era of McCarthyism, the 'communist' label was a serious slur – at least in the United States. The outcry resulted in Josephine's work visa being terminated – she was a French citizen, so did require a visa – which in turn forced her to leave the US. The allegations would prompt the FBI to open a file on Josephine, and it would be years before she was allowed back into the nation of her birth.[11] Even so, her feisty stance and her campaigning against segregation had hit home. As a result, the NAACP (National Association for the Advancement of Coloured Peoples) – the foremost US civil rights organisation of the day – declared that 20 May 1951 would be known as 'Josephine Baker Day'.

In memory of the war years, she would tour Germany, Norway, Italy, Spain, Algeria and Morocco, finally reaching Japan in April 1954. There she visited both Hiroshima and Nagasaki, where the dropping of the atomic bombs by US warplanes had finally forced an end to the Second World War. She would also perform for free for the American troops who were heading off to war again, this time in Vietnam.

Josephine would remain grateful to France – and wider Europe – for the sense of freedom from prejudice that she encountered there, and certainly compared to what she had experienced in the USA. On May 12, 1957, she gave a speech at the closing banquet of the XIX National Congress of the Ligue Internationale Contre l'Antisémitisme (International League Against Antisemitism – LICA), at the Hotel Lutétia, Paris, in which she summed up her feelings most eloquently: 'When I arrived in Paris ... I was happy to feel all the same, in the street, that I could ask for a taxi without having the fear that he would refuse to take me. I was happy to think that if I were hungry I could stop at any restaurant. When I was sick, I was so happy to think that a white doctor and also a white nurse were not ashamed to treat me ... Here I knew that ... I could live for a cause, and this cause is human brotherhood ...' She would be an energetic supporter and spokesperson for LICA over the years.[12]

By the early 1960s, Josephine Baker was back in the US, this time her message of equality seeming to be more universally accepted.

She spoke at the 1963 March on Washington, alongside Rev. Dr Martin Luther King Jr, the eloquent and inspirational figurehead of the American civil rights movement. Resplendent in her French Air Force uniform, and with her decorations – including her 1957 Légion d'Honneur – proudly on display, she was the only official female speaker at the historic civil rights rally.

There were some critics who believed her long sojourn in France had disconnected her from the struggle for equality in the USA. Josephine's powerful speech silenced most. 'I have walked into the palaces of kings and queens and into the houses of presidents,' she declared. 'And much more. But I could not walk into a hotel in America and get a cup of coffee, and that made me mad. And when I get mad, you know that I open my big mouth. And then look out, 'cause when Josephine opens her mouth, they hear it all over the world.'[13]

Josephine's words, delivered on the steps of Washington's Lincoln Memorial, came shortly before Dr King's historic 'I have a dream' speech, in which he called for an end to racial segregation across the USA. Five years later, on 4 April 1968, Martin Luther King Jr would be assassinated. In the immediate aftermath of his death, Josephine Baker was offered the leadership of the US Civil Rights Movement, by Coretta Scott King, his widow. She reluctantly declined. She was concerned that to do the movement justice she would be forced to spend precious little time with her adopted children, and so she made the tough decision that family came first.

Josephine continued to tour widely, from Cuba to Yugoslavia, and always returning to perform in Paris. In the early-to-mid-1960s, by her own account, she exchanged telegrams with Sir Winston Churchill. Churchill, then in the twilight years of his career and his life, would continue to serve as an MP until shortly before his death in January 1965. Not long before that, Josephine wished him one hundred further happy birthdays, to which he had replied with suitable vim and vigour, and typically feisty humour.[14]

Josephine would forever cherish the Anglo-French relationship, or rather the core of those who had stood firm at the darkest hours of the war. In 1969 she would tell a BBC radio presenter, speaking of the war years: 'I was in England many times, as we were all together, as we still are. They'll certainly never be able to separate us, will they? I don't care what people say or what happens, there is something amongst people who have suffered together that unites us for ever, don't you think.'[15]

In her later years Josephine would face financial woes. In 1967 she lost Château des Milandes, which had been forced into bankruptcy and was sold to the highest bidder.[16] It was Princess Grace of Monaco – the actress Grace Kelly – who stepped in to help, offering Josephine the use of a modest home in Monaco for her and her family. Despite such setbacks, she continued to enthral and captivate audiences world-wide. In 1973 she won a standing ovation at New York's Carnegie Hall, as well as at the Royal Variety Performance at the London Palladium, and at Paris' Gala du Cirque the following year.

But the passing years and the punishment she had put her body through began to weigh heavy. In April 1975, aged sixty-eight, Josephine starred in a revue at the Bobino Theatre in Paris, entitled *Josephine à Bobino*, to celebrate fifty years in showbusiness. A 'comeback' tour, the show was scheduled to go to London and New York, and further afield. It opened to rave reviews, many claiming that a mature Josephine Baker sounded the best that she had ever done. The show made maximum play on her wartime role. French President Valéry Giscard d'Estaing had sent a telegram to Josephine, which she read live for the opening night, and in which d'Estaing pledged that France would never forget what she had done for the nation and for the Allied war effort. In a press interview, when asked what was the highlight of her fifty-year career, Josephine answered simply: 'The war years.' On stage she would repeat the lines that she had uttered to Jacques Abtey, almost word for word, when he went to recruit her as an Honourable Correspondent: 'I gave my heart to Paris, as Paris gave me hers . . . I am ready to give my country my life.'[17]

Josephine had always vowed to stay young, bold and free and maybe even to die dancing . . . Four days into the Bobino's run, she was found lying peacefully in her bed, surrounded by newspapers full of glowing reports of her performances. She had suffered a cerebral haemorrhage and had fallen into a coma. She was taken to Paris' Pitié-Salpêtrière Hospital, where she would die on 12 April 1975.

Josephine Baker would receive a Roman Catholic funeral at L'Église de la Madeleine, in the 8th arrondissement, becoming the only women of American birth to receive full French military honours. Her death was the occasion of a vast procession in the city, as 20,000 people turned out to pay their final respects. Her remains were interred at Monaco's Cimetière de Monaco. Shortly before her death, she had told a TV interviewer, 'I don't like the word hatred . . . We weren't put on earth for that, more to understand and to love each other.'[18] It was a fitting epitaph.

Approaching five decades after her death Josephine Baker was granted a final honour, and the greatest accolade of all - entry into France's Panthéon, where she would rest among foremost French figures, including the writers Victor Hugo and Voltaire, and the cele-brated physicist Marie Curie. While her family asked that her remains should stay in the Monaco cemetery, on Tuesday 20 November 2021, in an elaborate ceremony presided over by President Emmanuel Macron, members of the French Air Force carried a symbolic coffin containing handfuls of soil from the four main places that she had made her home: St Louis, Paris, Château des Milandes, and Monaco, her final resting place. The coffin was placed within a tomb reserved for her in the crypt of the Panthéon in Paris, a grand church and mausoleum built in the 1700s in the 5th arrondissement.

Josephine Baker was just the sixth woman and the fourth person of colour to be honoured in this way, one of only eighty-one individuals interred in the Panthéon at that time. That high honour seems entirely justified, in that she was not only a groundbreaking and glittering superstar and a foremost champion for civil liberties and democratic freedoms, but she was also a 'world-class spy', as others have recently concluded of her role during the war years.[19]

*

In December 1944, Captain Jacques Abtey had returned to Paris and sought out his wartime partner in espionage. He discovered her in the depths of a bitter Paris winter, intent on a personal mission of mercy, doling out essentials – coal, meat and other foodstuffs – to the city's war-destitute. Though she claimed that all of this was a Red Cross-funded initiative, in truth it was a solo mission of mercy, one that Josephine had financed through the sale of some of her few remaining precious gems and jewellery. Typically, she persuaded Abtey to lend her a hand.

Since their North African adventures, Abtey had fallen out of favour with some in power within the French military-intelligence-political hierarchy. Seemingly, his wartime record, allegiances and liaisons still counted against him. Not one to turn his back on former friends and comrades, Abtey had learned that Hans Müssig – his and Josephine's Lisbon fixer – was then in custody in Paris, and facing possible charges of war crimes. Going to his aid, Abtey discovered that Müssig had handed himself in to French forces once Paris was liberated, and freely confessed what he had been up to in the final stages of the war in France.

Arrested by the Gestapo in late 1943, he had been tortured and beaten up for two days solid, but had refused to divulge the names and identities of those within French intelligence and the Resistance with whom he had had dealings. Instead, he'd turned the tables on his captors, convincing them that as the war was all but lost, they needed to concentrate on lining their own pockets before there came a reckoning. There was no one better placed to help them, he argued. So it was that Müssig had become a sometime agent of the Gestapo and SS, deploying his unique skills to fleece the Paris underworld and to feather the nests of his captors.

Thus were the grim imperatives of survival in the winter of 1943–44. Müssig was accused of serving with the Rote Kapelle – the Red Orchestra – a Soviet intellience network, and also with Sonderkommando Pannwitz, a Gestapo unit which specialised in combatting the French Resistance and the Rote Kapelle. Whatever the truth of the matter, with Müssig facing such serious charges, Abtey managed to pull strings and argue successfully for his release, springing him from incarceration. During Müssig's interrogation by his French accusers, he had revealed that 'Captain ABTEY had procured a visa for PORTUGAL for MUSSIG Hans,' as a note records in the French Government files. Of course, Abtey had done just that, for at that stage Müssig was his and Josephine Baker's fixer at the Lisbon end of operations.[20]

Müssig's release without charge had one condition attached to it, that he serve with the DGSS/SDECE, the then French foreign intelligence service – which had subsumed its forerunners, including the BCRA and the Deuxième Bureau – until the end of the war. He was to help track down Nazi war criminals; arguably, who better was there to do so? Müssig would do just that, serving until September 1945 under the cover name 'Captain René Clairmont'.

Sometime after the war Müssig would emigrate to the United States, where he would find gainful employment, very possibly spending some of his time on assignment with the US security services or the FBI. Some years after the war's end, Müssig would learn that there was an arrest warrant for him in France, and that he was very possibly facing a death sentence for being a member of the SS and allegedly operating against the French special services. He had visited the country several times in the interim, but had never faced arrest or any kind of censure.[21]

In 1960, Johannes Mario Simmel, an Austrian writer, published a book in German, entitled *Es muss nicht immer Kaviar sein* – It Can't Always Be Caviar. The promotional blurb for the book reads: 'Europe 1939–1945 was a bad time for a good living. Not, however, for Thomas Lieven, ex-London banker: perhaps the most reluctant of spies, his taste as a gourmet and his skill as a seducer are indispensable in his adventures. Equally at home working for M.I.5, the Deuxième Bureau, the Abwehr and the F.B.I., Lieven knows who can best forge a passport, how to dine well in a Portuguese gaol and how, when it all becomes too much, to supervise his own assassination.'[22]

As Simmel noted on the opening pages of the book, 'This novel is based on first-hand information.'[23] In fact, the book is a thinly disguised treatment of Hans Müssig's wartime adventures, carried out by Simmel's protagonist Thomas Lieven. It includes sections detailing Lieven's relations with 'Major Maurice Debras . . . of the Deuxième Bureau' – Captain Jacques Abtey – and with Josephine Baker, whose real name is used by Simmel. Lieven first meets her at Château des Milandes and later in Marseilles, when Josephine saves his life in the most dramatic fashion. At Lieven's first meeting with Josephine he cooks her a meal in the château's kitchen – he was a celebrated gourmet – and apologises when serving it, as so many ingredients are lacking in wartime. She tells him, teasingly, not to worry, for: 'It can't always be caviar.'[24] It is Josephine's phrase that makes the title of Simmel's book.

The book includes an account of how Lieven is recruited by the Deuxième Bureau, to operate a fabulously clever currency manipulation scheme, running suitcases of cash to Belgium, Switzerland and other countries, so raising millions of dollars for the cash-strapped French security services – their slush fund. It includes an account of Lieven's winter 1940 Lisbon mission with 'Major Debras' – Abtey – wherein Lieven is imprisoned due to a passport faking scam, in which his partners were the consul of a South American country living in Lisbon, plus Lisbon's top passport forger. It relates the shocking tale of Lieven's later arrest by the Gestapo, his interrogation, and how he strikes a deal with them to ensure his survival by engineering black market stings to enrichen his new taskmasters.

By his own account, Simmel met Müssig prior to writing the book and interviewed him over several days.[25] Indeed, Simmel claims that the tale told in *It Can't Always Be Caviar* is wholly true, and that only certain names and other key details have been changed. It is also of note that Colonel Rémy – real name Gilbert Renault – the legendary French Resistance hero and prolific author, wrote a book about Jacques Abtey and Josephine Baker's war years, entitled *J.A. Épisodes de la vie d'un agent du S.R. et du contre-espionnage français.*

In it there is a lengthy telling of Hans Müssig's story, which again closely mirrors that told in Simmel's book. It is equally of note that Colonel Rémy and Josephine remained friends and mutual admirers for life, bound together by their shared history during the war years.[26]

Even when taken with a pinch of salt, Simmel's book makes for a fascinating read. Unfortunately, it is long out of print, and the 1965 English language version – translated from the German by James Cleugh – is only rarely available from second-hand book sellers, and even then at a price that reflects its rarity. By his end-of-war actions, Jacques Abtey rescued Hans Müssig from a seemingly gruesome fate, without which Simmel's account of Müssig's – Lieven's – exploits would never have been written. In 2019, Thomas Bürkle, a German economist and author who had become fascinated by Lieven/Müssig's tale, carried out a detailed investigation into its veracities. He concluded that the story as related by Simmel is almost entirely true, that Mussig first met Josephine in 1940, when she was 'in the service of the Deuxième Bureau [sic],' and that Lieven/Müssig 'remained to the end what he was throughout his life – uncatchable.'[27]

Jacques Abtey, Müssig's saviour, had the one son, Jean-Louis, by his first wife, Emma Kuntz, and would have a second, Bertrand-Hugues, with his second wife, Jacqueline Cellier. She gave birth in Casablanca in 1948. Working for a few months in Paris with the SDECE in 1945, Abtey had returned to North Africa and would remain there for eight years, upon what appears to have been some kind of attachment to the French intelligence services. In 1946 he appears to have been in charge of overseeing 'US arrivals' in Morocco. But by late 1947 the SDECE would deny that Abtey was serving as one of their agents, concluding that his 'current activities in Morocco are considered very suspicious'.[28]

SDECE in Morocco would go on to suggest that Abtey had somehow gone rogue, serving as some kind of freelance agent working with his old friends Si Mohamed Menebhi, the son of the former Grand Vizier, and Moulay Larbi, cousin of the Sultan of Morocco. He was labelled as an adventurer who was liable to immediate arrest. By 1949, SDECE had disowned Abtey: 'Mr Abtey does not belong to the D.E.C. [short-hand for SDECE] and can in no way be covered by the Service.' In several of the reports on Abtey's supposedly wayward activities at this time, he was accused of using high-level political contacts to oil the wheels in North Africa, and his name is at times misspelt as 'Astey'.[29]

Whatever aspersions may have been cast, Abtey seems to have come through largely unscathed. In 1953 he would return to France, and thanks largely to the support of his former chiefs in the Deuxième Bureau, including the then General Louis Rivet, he would be re-instated to the French security services. Seconded to the Direction des Études et Fabrications d'Armement (DEFA), he took control of security of a top-secret facility, the Laboratoire de Recherches de Saint-Louis (L-RSL). There, one hundred-odd German scientists, mostly high-level physicists, were working for DEFA, continuing to develop the kind of ground-breaking rocketry and related armaments that they had done at their previous posting, at the Nazi-era Hermann Goering Ballistic Academy.

When General de Lattre de Tassigny's French forces had advanced into Germany, they had overrun the German facility, securing those high-level physicists for the post-war French armaments industry. The scientists lived in Weil am Rhein, a town lying on the German side of the River Rhine, but in what was then the French zone of occu-pation of Germany. Abtey would take up residence himself in that town. Each morning the scientists would be bussed to work across the Rhine, to the L-RSL laboratory. In 1956, Germany became a sov-ereign nation again, and the French and German governments signed a treaty whereby the L-RSL laboratory became a Franco-German joint venture. It is known to this day as the French-German Research Institute of Saint-Louis. In helping broker this partnership, Abtey was assisted greatly by his old comrade from North African days, General Billotte.[30]

Still troubled by what Abtey believed were powerful enemies within the French political establishment – they nursed grudges dating back to his Second World War service – he found himself posted to a sinecure, and not for the first time since his wartime service had ended. Unable to endure life in such a banal position, in 1959 Abtey secured a posting to the Military Centre for European Studies, in Paris, serving as a lecturer and examiner in the Superior War School, German language section. But after two decades' service in the French security services, Abtey felt underwhelmed and as if he had been abandoned and betrayed. He sought retirement in March 1961 at fifty-two years of age.

In April 1958, Abtey had received a letter informing him that he was to be granted the Légion d'Honneur, and also that he would be promoted to the rank of Lieutenant-Colonel. By Abtey's own account neither of those decisions appears to have been ratified, and among other slights this underpinned his decision to retire. The official French service files held on Abtey seem to contradict this, several stating that he was made a Chevalier of the Légion d'Honneur on 7 August 1959. Abtey states he rejected the decoration, in large part because there was no citation making mention of any of his war service, which he found both unacceptable and deeply insulting.[31]

What is abundantly clear from a close reading of Abtey's post-war government files is that significant and on-going efforts were made to disavow his wartime service, particularly that prior to the date when it was 'regularised', in Morocco, in the spring of 1943. It is also clear that some of Abtey's superiors had concluded of him that he was only fit for 'special services' type work, and that there was little scope to use such skills in peacetime, when France was no longer embroiled in a world war.[32]

Sometime after his retirement, Abtey would explain away his 'missing years' – those from 1946–1953, in North Africa – by stating officially that he had been on a personal assignment at the behest of the then French president, Vincent Auriol. The president, who knew of Abtey due to his wartime service with the Deuxième Bureau, had given him a special mission in North Africa, which had been overseen by none other than the president's own head of security.

As such, Abtey had served in North Africa in some kind of grey role – in 'clean air, on a civilian mission', as he would describe it – during which time he had on occasion reported directly to the French president. That would explain why the SDECE and French military security had no record of him working to their orders or as one of their agents, and why they had concluded that he had somehow 'gone rogue'. It would also explain why and how his return to France in 1953 saw him quietly taken back into the French security services, and in spite of the apparent missing years.

Still, Abtey believed – and the files suggest with ample justification – that he had enemies in the French political establishment. Their enmity led directly back to Abtey's war work, but the cause and effect of this lie beyond the scope of this book. Abtey chronicled this in his French government files (some of which were only released to the public in 2020). To be forced into early retirement after all he had done for France, for the Allies and for freedom, left Abtey feeling 'disgusted, and doubly so: I was one of the very first F.F.L. [volunteers for Free France] – the only active officer of the Deuxième Bureau to have joined the F.F.L. as early as 1940 . . .' Certainly, his wartime service alone meant he deserved far better.[33]

In 1949 Abtey had penned a memoir of his wartime service, or rather an account of both his and his famous fellow agent's wartime adventures, entitled *La Guerre Secrète de Josèphine Baker* – The Secret War of Josephine Baker. (In this and his subsequent book Abtey relates chapter and verse concerning the Hans Müssig story.) There is a well-understood rule in the French secret service that no agent, nor Honourable Correspondent for that matter, should write about or otherwise publicise his or her secret work until at least three decades have passed, and preferably not at all. Although the book is somewhat elliptical and often couched in coded, veiled language, it doubtless ruffled feathers.

Having retired from the French secret service in 1961, Abtey must have felt he was free to say more. That same year he published a new account of his and Josephine Baker's war years, written with/by Colonel Rémy (Gilbert Renault). Colonel Rémy's book – *J.A.: Épisodes de la vie d'un agent du S.R. et du contre-espionnage français* – is published only in French and alas is long out of print. While Rémy's account is more forthright and revealing than Abtey's 1948 telling, it still falls short of full disclosure, and no doubt both men were aware of the expectations of secrecy by which Abtey at least was still bound.

In 1967 Abtey (co-)authored a third account of his wartime exploits with the French security services, entitled *2ème Bureau Contre Abwehr* – Deuxième Bureau Against the Abwehr. A fascinating and detailed account concerning his service with the Deuxième Bureau, which ended in the summer of 1940, many of the missions covered are pre-war, so the thirty-year secrecy rule would have been largely over. The book is co-written by the former Abwehr agent Dr Fritz Unterberg Gibhardt, the same individual who, during the run-up to the war had orchestrated French Navy officer Aubert's treachery, including the betrayal of the French naval codes. Incidentally, this book also includes a detailed rendering of Hans Müssig's early wartime adventures.

In 1951 Josephine Baker had asked Abtey to travel to the USA, to support her in her fight against segregation and to clear her name of the accusations of communist leanings. He would do just that, testifying to her long fight for freedom in the Second World War on behalf of the Allies, and her unbending commitment to struggle for justice no matter what the cost might be. This was but one of many instances in which the two wartime colleagues and lovers would work closely together, supporting each other in their lives, their careers and their adventures and misadventures.[34]

Shortly after his retirement, Abtey seems to have taken Josephine up on her 1949 offer, that she would always keep a house for him at Château des Milandes. In 1962 he went to live there, and took up a part-time profession as an artist, painting any number of pictures of the château itself (among other subjects). At least one of those paintings he signed 'J. Brad' – short for James Bradford, as a nod to the wartime cover name that the British Secret Intelligence Service had given him in the autumn of 1941. After the war Josephine had written of how, of all her partners, Abtey was the one that she truly loved and with whom she should have settled down.[35]

Josephine and Jacques Abtey were truly inseparable, that was until she sang and danced her last shows at the Bobino, going out as she had fully intended, in a blaze of euphoria, showbiz success and light. Indeed, in 1957 and again in 1958 Josephine had written to her French Government contacts on Abtey's behalf, in support of his on-going attempts to get all of his wartime service regularised and his war-time role properly recognised. Her intervention seems to have had some effect. By 1959 the then French prime minister, Michel Jean-Pierre Debré, who served under President de Gaulle from 1959 to 1962, interceded on Abtey's behalf, investigating the apparent 'career prejudices that he may have suffered . . . without any well-founded grievances . . .'[36]

In March 1999 Jacques Abtey passed away, just a few months short of his ninetieth birthday. He was at that time living in Sarlat-la-Canéda, a beautiful and historic medieval town in the Dordogne, founded around a Benedictine Abbey, Sarlat Cathedral. Sarlat lies a short drive away from Château des Milandes, although of course for the last thirty years of Abtey's life it was no longer owned or lived in by Josephine Baker. He was survived by his wife, Jacqueline, and Bertrand-Hugues, their son.

Needless to say, alongside Josephine Baker, Jacques Abtey is one of the standout heroes and individuals of courage and grit who dared all in freedom's cause, as related in these pages.

Wilfred 'Biffy' Dunderdale CMG MBE would forge a long and distinguished career post-war with the Secret Intelligence Service. Typically, he refused to take an office in SIS's Whitehall headquarters, as the atmosphere and outlook was intolerable as he saw it. Instead, he was able to establish a small private office near by, which he furnished with rich oriental rugs, a portrait of the British King and the Russian Tsar, plus a beautifully crafted model of a Russian destroyer of First World War vintage. Among many other intelligence coups, following

General de Gaulle's resignation in 1946 – which was due to a political row within the post-war French Government – there was a shake-up of the French intelligence services, and Dunderdale provided the bridge between the old guard and the new recruits, as far as the SIS was concerned.[37]

In recognition of his wartime efforts on behalf of the Allies, Dunderdale was awarded the French Légion d'Honneur, the Croix de Guerre Avec Palme and the American Legion of Merit, a military award granted by the US Armed Forces. He would separate from June Ament-Morse in 1947, and in 1952 would marry Dorothy Mabel Brayshaw Hyde, the daughter of James Murray Crofts DSC. They lived near London until her death, in 1978. Theirs had been a happy marriage, and upon her death Dunderdale decided to start afresh. He moved to New York where he had a group of old friends. In 1980 he married Deborah McLeod (née Jackson), of Boston, Massachusetts. There were no children from any of the marriages. Dunderdale would die in 1990, in New York, of natural causes, aged ninety-one. His wife Deborah would pass away three years later.

Much of Dunderdale's post-war intelligence work remains untold, due to the intense secrecy that enshrouds SIS activities. However, the role he performed to win the intelligence war in France, North Africa and the wider region – not to mention his Enigma coups – was so masterful that in 1965 Admiral John Henry Godfrey CB, the Director of Britain's Naval Intelligence from 1939–42, wrote to Dunderdale, in praise of his long years of service. 'Starting in a humble capacity you have chosen to become an elder statesman, continuing to work almost full time after official retirement . . . In this respect the country has been fortunate in being able to retain your services, and make use of your unique gifts, specialised knowledge and wisdom over nearly half a century, an achievement which you share with very few . . .'[38]

Citing their 'four years of close collaboration during World War Two,' Godfrey praised Dunderdale's ability to survive the 'vicissitudes' of so many decades of outstanding service, after which he was 'still actively employed on the retired list, enjoying your work and the esteem and confidence of your Chief and colleagues. They have acquired the habit, after years of experience, of leaning heavily on your shoulder – and, of course, a shoulder cannot be leant on unless it is offered.' Admiral Godfrey was also Ian Fleming's boss during much of the war, and is reputed to be the basis of the character known as 'M', James Bond's boss in the early novels.[39]

As late as 1991 the then chief of the Secret Intelligence Service, Sir Colin Hugh Verel McColl KCMC, would write, in memoriam – it was a year after Dunderdale's death – praising 'the outstanding contribution made by one of its best-loved and respected officers . . . I like to think that generations of our staff will . . . hear the story of Biffy's historic contribution to this Service's work and so be set an example which they shall be proud to follow.'[40] High praise indeed.

Stephen R. Hill, the biographer of Boodle's – the London club that Dunderdale shared with Ian Fleming, and which is portrayed as 'Blades' in the Bond books – would say of Dunderdale: 'He was undoubtedly another hero incorporated into the myth of James Bond, embracing espionage, underwater activities and sheer style, with his mission duly accomplished with whatever it took.' On that last note, there is an ornate silver bowl that commemorates Dunderdale's service, which has pride of place in the mess at Fort Monckton, SIS's training base located near Gosport, on the south coast of England, which is known simply as the No. 1 Military Training Establishment.

As the Fort is the 'spiritual home' of the SIS and the dining room in the Main Mess is the 'heart of the Fort', the fact that the bowl forms the centrepiece of the 'splendid dining table' seems entirely fitting, as Sir Colin McColl would write to Dunderdale's widow. He would add: 'I can think of no more appropriate way for the Service to remember the outstanding contributions made by one of its best-loved and respected officers.' The inscription on the bowl reads: 'In memory of Commander Biffy Dunderdale CMG MBE (MIL) R.N.V.R. (RET'D) 1899–1990.'[41]

There is also a plaque to Dunderdale, located in Bletchingley, a village to the south of London, which reads: 'COMMANDER WILFRED

'ALBERT DUNDERDALE CMG MBE RNVR 1899–1990 Distinguished Diplomat and Naval Officer 1918–1959 Decorated by five countries for his outstanding contributions in peace and wars. Biffy lived in Bletchingley for 31 years.'

By the summer of 1944, Commander Paul Paillole was back in Paris and busy establishing a new base there, at 2 Boulevard Suchet, which had been the headquarters of the Luftwaffe in France during the Occupation. Serving now as part of the DGSS (soon to be the SDECE), his priority was to transfer all the surviving Deuxième Bureau files to the new HQ. While the Abwehr had been eviscerated in recent months, a particularly virulent branch of the SS had filled the vacuum so caused, organising 'stay-behinds' across France, who were to be the eyes and ears of the German high command. Paillole's priority was to hunt them down, along with the foremost Nazi collaborators who were still active.

To that end, Paillole founded a tripartite Inter-Allied Counter-Espionage Bureau (the BICE), which pooled the resources and intelligence of the three foremost Allied powers – France, the USA and Great Britain. BICE's remit was to follow the advance of the Allied troops as they pushed into Germany, but sadly Paillole's role within it would be short-lived. By November 1944, the cumulative stress and strain of the war years had caught up with him – just as it would with Josephine Baker – and he would resign from the French intelligence services. He also felt that he was being frozen out of the heart of things, having been tainted with the accusations of being a Vichy intelligence agent for much of the war.

Paillole went into business after the war, but he would remain committed to defending the reputation of his wartime intelligence apparatus for the remainder of his days. In 1953 he founded a secret service veterans association, the Amicale des Anciens des Services Spéciaux de la Défense Nationale, which published a regular bulletin. He also donated his personal wartime archives to the French military's national archive service, the Service Historique de l'Armée de

Terre (SHAT). In 1975 he published his wartime memoirs, *Services Spéciaux 1935–1945*, also published in English as *Fighting the Nazis*.

The publication prompted protests from some quarters, as those who believed they had fallen foul of Paillole's TR network, and who had been involved in legitimate Resistance activities, questioned his wartime record as he related it. That debate lies outside of the scope of this book. Moreover, it bears little relevance to Josephine Baker's or Jacques Abtey's wartime stories, and certainly in their depictions of Colonel Paillole he is only ever portrayed as operating in the very best interests of the Allies.

Paillole retired to the region of La Queue-les-Yvelines, to the north of Paris, and would serve as the mayor for that region from 1965 to 1983. He died in 2002 aged ninety-seven.

On 18 June 2020, French President Emmanuel Macron joined Prince Charles in London, to inspect a guard of honour of Grenadier Guards, at Clarence House – a British Royal residence – as part of a series of events to commemorate the eightieth anniversary of General de Gaulle's historic June 1940 call to arms, issued from London over the BBC. Praising London as a 'city of wartime hope', Macron conveyed upon London France's highest distinction, the Légion d'Honneur.

Today, Josephine Baker's former home, Château des Milandes – her French wartime Resistance headquarters – is maintained as a shrine and memorial to her life and works. The château is run as a public monument and deserves a visit of several hours, for there is a great deal to see and experience, including the Resistance Room, which is a living memorial to Josephine's wartime activities. Angélique de Saint-Exupéry is both the chatelaine and the guiding light of the château-as-museum, which 'pays tribute to Josephine Baker and devotes all of its interiors to this great artist, Resistance member, activist and mother . . .' For Mme. de Saint-Exupéry, the period of the war remains the most exciting of Josephine Baker's life, during which she demonstrated the most incredible 'courage, intuition and intelligence . . .'[42]

In the booklet *Château et Jardins des Milandes*, Angélique de Saint-Exupéry writes of the French Resistance room, and Josephine's wartime work: 'Her commitment to France during the Second World War was one of her greatest achievements and one she was incredibly proud of.' The displays in the château's French Resistance room tell that story. 'Josephine was awarded the highest honours in recognition of her dedicated work for France during World War Two.' Two statues in the Resistance Room 'serve as a testament to Josephine Baker receiving her Légion d'Honneur medal.'[43]

The Château des Milandes receives 120,000 visitors per year, testament to the long-lived and enduring appeal of Josephine Baker's timeless story. 'I felt driven by fate,' Angélique de Saint-Exupéry explains, of her dedication to maintaining this living memorial. 'I didn't want anyone to forget Josephine. By her commitment to the Resistance and her fight against racism, she deserved it.' Of the château itself she remarks that 'I always have the impression that Josephine is there . . . She is very cheerful but it is also here that she lived her last so painful moments at Milandes . . .'[44]

Acknowledgements

First and foremost, I must say thank you to my esteemed readers. You go out and buy my books, in the hope that each will deliver an enjoyable, rewarding, illuminating read; another work that brings a story to life in vivid detail. I am most grateful to you and I hope I have managed to deliver that kind of reading experience in this book. Without you, there could be no author such as myself. You enable individuals like me to make a living from writing. You deserve the very first mention.

I also wish to say thank you to all those individuals who helped me to tell this story, in all the innumerable and kind ways that you have. This is certainly not limited to those mentioned below, and I extend my apologies to anyone that I may have inadvertently forgotten.

Primarily, thank you to the Abtey family, chiefly Bertrand-Hugues Abtey and Benoît Abtey, without whose kind assistance I would not have been able to tell their father and grandfather's incredible and courageous wartime story. I am especially grateful for their permission to quote from Jacques Abtey's accounts of his wartime tale, which has proven invaluable, and also for discussing with me Jacques Abtey and Josephine Baker's wartime story.

Enormous thanks also are due to the family of Colonel Rémy – Gilbert Renault – for your kind assistance in so many ways, and especially for looking into the Rémy family archive on my behalf, and for providing the documents you were able to and also for allowing me to quote from Colonel Rémy's book, which tells the story of

Captain Jacques Abtey and Josephine Baker's wartime exploits. My sincere gratitude is extended to Ian and Marie-Françoise Renault (last son of the Colonel), Brigitte Renault (wife of Mic-Mic Michel Renault), Marie-Anne Renault de Castilho (first, and representative, of Catherine Renault's eight daughters), Frédéric and Isabelle Genty (child of Cécile Renault) and Franck and Emmanuelle Genty (children of Cécile Renault).

Thank you to Jean-Pierre Reggiori, one of Josephine Baker's dance partners, for the time you generously dedicated to interviews and cor-respondece and for sharing your special reminiscences over Josephine, plus the photos and documents you were able to provide, and for your perceptive comments on an early manuscript of this book. I am most grateful.

My warmest gratitude is also extended to Anne-Marie and Catherine Paillole, daughters of Colonel Paul Paillole, for pointing me in the direction of her late father's Association, which was cre-ated to honour the memory of her father and all those who served in similar roles during the Second World War – L'Amicale des Anciens des Services Spéciaux de la Défense Nationale (AASSDN). This has proved a rich resource for my research. Thank you also for giving me the kind permission to quote from your father's books that tell of his wartime story, for which I am most grateful.

I extend my sincere thanks to Angélique de Saint-Exupéry, the chatelaine and leading light behind the living memorial to Josephine Baker which is today's Château des Milandes. Thank you for your generous time in corresponding with me as you have, and your sup-port for this book from the moment I first reached out to you. I am most grateful.

Thank you to the family of Kenneth Pendar, for allowing me to use select quotations from his book, *Adventures in Diplomacy*. Thank you to Emmanuel de Crits for permitting me to quote material from Alain Gilles-Minella's book, *L'Homme des Services Secrets,* the full reference to which is included in the bibliography. Thank you to Père (Father) Philippe Verrier, in France, author of the seminal book on Père Victor

Dillard, for corresponding with me and sharing your insight into this immensely brave and principled figure from the Second World War, who gave the ultimate sacrifice in the fight against the scourge of Nazism.

A very special mention must go to my researcher, producer and sometime translator into English, Julie Davies. Far more than that, you were someone who shared with me the passion, insight, intuition and vision regarding this story from the earliest stages to the very last. You buoyed me up when I flagged, shored me up when I was in danger of losing my enthusiasm and my way, and provided crucial insights when they were most needed. I could not have persevered in the writing of this book without you. Thank you.

Thank you to my good friend and sensei Sally Allcard, for your work as a French-to-English translator and also for taking the time to read an early draft of the manuscript. It would have been so difficult for you to have assisted me in those translations, correspondence and discussions without knowing the full story, and I remain very grateful.

Thank you to Ros Schwartz, for generously putting me on the right track translation-wise. Thank you to Joanna Coryndon, for your trenchant advice on all things translation-related, without which I would have been all at sea. Thank you to Nicholas Rose, of Perfect Pitch Translations, for your invaluable assistance with my work and interviews in France. Hugely appreciated.

Thank you to Nina Staehle for your research in Germany concerning this story and for your translations from German to English. With remarkable tenacity you unearthed some true gems and for that I am very grateful.

Enormous thanks as always to Simon Fowler, my researcher in the UK – your hard work and insight was invaluable, as ever, and your perseverance during the trials and tribulations of the Covid lockdown was admirable.

Enormous thanks once again to Sim Smiley, in the US, brilliant historical and archival researcher and translator from the French. Your early work on and your belief in this book from the very outset proved inspirational. Thank you. I am only sorry that Covid restricted some of our travel/research plans, but I am pleased to say we endured anyhow.

Massive thanks to Laurence Abensur-Hazan, in France, genealogist and very talented archival researcher – your tenacity in winkling out the relevant archival files in France, often at the height of the Covid lockdown, was remarkable and invaluable. Thank you.

I extend gratitude to M. Richard Ravalet, Chef de la division défense, Département des fonds d'archives, Centre historique des archives, Service historique de la défense, Château de Vincennes, for assistance with the French archival research, which of course proved so vital to the telling of this story. I also wish to thank Thibault Fanton, Responsable des relations et opérations médias, secrétariat général pour l'administration, Ministère des Armées, for your kind assistance in locating relevant Second World War archive material and granting permission to use them in this book.

Thank you to fellow author and Second World War historian Paul McCue, for enabling contact with Colin Cohen, the son of the Secret Intelligence Service officer of the same surname who served in that era. Enormous thanks for the correspondence I was able to exchange with Colin Cohen, whose father, Kenneth Cohen, features in this book, and who was a wartime colleague of Wilfred Dunderdale, among others.

Thank you to Richard Neave, of the Royal British Legion Paris Branch, for your assistance with the French side of the research for this book – this was much appreciated. Thanks to Paul Woodage, for corresponding with me over the French archives and other resources, and insight into the same, and for your invaluable help and advice on all things French in the Second World War.

Thank you to Elodie Massaro and Rhoda Cohen of the American Society of the French Legion of Honor, in New York, for corresponding with me over Josephine Baker's story, for your considerate responses to the plethora of questions that I kept firing your way. Much appreciated and keep up the good work.

Thank you to the UK-based Josephine Baker Trust for informing me about the genesis and objects of their charitable organisation and its work, and corresponding with me on the matter. It came as a revelation, needless to say.

Thank you to Natalia Sciarini and colleagues at the Yale Beinecke Rare Book & Manuscript Library, Access Services, for enabling me to access archival research documents remotely, during a time of Covid, when visits in person were not allowed. I am enormously grateful.

Huge thanks (once again) to Dr Phil Judkins, for your expert advice and guidance on all aspects of the Third Reich's labyrinthine security and foreign intelligence apparatus, which proved invaluable, as did your tip about the 'Q Ship' HMS *Fidelity*, and her incredible story.

Thank you to Ian Piper FCPFA, Senior Research Fellow at the University of Portsmouth's Faculty of Business and Law, for sharing with me your excellent, unpublished academic paper on the financial warfare of the SOE, and for the communications we shared concerning the same. Utterly fascinating.

Huge thanks to Paul Biddle MBE, international security specialist, who gave freely of his time to help me research the extraordinary history of Commander Wilfred 'Biffy' Dunderdale. Your generosity in sharing with me the documents, photographs and other wartime memorabilia from the Dunderdale family archive was invaluable in helping me to tell a small part of his wonderful story. This was very appreciated, and especially as you took the trouble to answer my repeated queries and to read early drafts.

Thanks also to Colonel Tim Spicer, for providing me with your insights into the life and times of Commander Wilfred 'Biffy' Dunderdale CMG, MBE, and his wartime exploits with those portrayed in this book, and for sharing with me sections of your forthcoming biography of Dunderdale, and for the photos and document you were able to provide as part of that process.

Enormous thanks as ever to my superlative 'early readers', who went through first drafts of this manuscript with a fine tooth comb, winkling out errors of fact and of diction, advising, inspiring and enthusing me in equal measure. My dear friends Paul and Anne Sherratt, your painstaking input was extraordinarily helpful, pertinent and encouraging, and as always you were the first to deliver. Bravo!

I especially valued my mother, Christine Major's, refreshing thoughts, enthusiasm and input. Thank you for those. New to the 'early reader' club, my neighbours, Sandy and Erica Moriarty, truly excelled themselves: your detailed handwritten notes in pencil were invaluable. Thank you – good neighbours are a special thing and to be especially cherished.

Thanks also to Paul Hazzard, long-standing reader and friend, for perusing an early draft and for your deeply perceptive comments. Thanks to John R. McKay, a fellow author and Second World War historian of great talent, for reading an early iteration of this book and for all your invaluable comments. It was great to have that support, as ever, my friend. Thank you also to Richard Domoney-Saunders for reading an early copy of the manuscript and for your comments and suggestions. Thank you to Paul Hughes for your perceptive comments on an early draft, which proved especially useful.

A very special thanks to my dear friend Dr Mukesh Kapila CBE, fellow author – we have collaborated on books together in the past – for your excellent and heartfelt comments on an early draft of the manuscript. Coming from your good self, these were especially appreciated.

Thanks to budding author and former intelligence/special operations supremo Michael Chavarria, for reading an early draft of this book and for offering your comments from an American and an intelligence/ security services perspective. Again, the specialist knowledge and the decades of experience you brought to bear were invaluable.

Enormous thanks to my dear friend and fellow author Dr Halima Bashir – we have worked together in the past on books, and your input into this one proved priceless. Thank you, and I look forward to working with you in the future on other important tales to be told. So much to be done!

Enormous and heartfelt thanks to the amazing Second World War special forces veteran Jack Mann, whom I count as a dear, dear friend. That you took the effort to read this book from cover to cover at your advanced age, giving your line by line comments, and bringing to bear all the experience that you have, means a great deal to me. Thank you as ever, Jack. Bravest of the brave.

Thank you to the Churchill Fellowship, for two things. Firstly, for backing me with a Fellowship many years ago, which ignited the spark in a young man to be curious about all things Winston Churchill, and especially the legacy of this extraordinary wartime leader. Thank you also for the *Churchill Fellowship News & Views,* Issue 58, 2021, the quote on the rear cover of which inspired me to such a degree that it graces the opening page of this book.

I have also benefited in the research for this book from the resources that the French, British, American, German and other governments have invested into preserving for posterity the archives from the Second World War era. The preservation and cataloguing of a mountain of papers – official reports, personal correspondence, telegrams, etc. – plus photographic, film and sound archives is vital to authors such as myself, without which books of this nature could not be written. Devoting resources to the preservation of this historical record, and to making it accessible to the public, is something for which these governments deserve praise.

All at my publishers' deserve the highest praise for their committed, enthusiastic and visionary support of this project from the get-go. In the UK, Richard Milner, my long-standing editor and good friend, provided likeminded guidance and feedback, as always, and in the USA Clive Priddle proved a dynamic editor especially from the North American perspective. Thank you to the both of you. The Quercus team in the UK also deserve the highest praise, and especially Charlotte Fry, Hannah Robinson, Bethan Ferguson, Ben Brock, Dave Murphy, and Jon Butler.

My gratitude as always to my literary agent, at Curtis Brown, Gordon Wise. I do believe we felt a special affinity and connection with this story and I remain enormously grateful for your sage advice, your steering hand and your encouragement. Enormous thanks to George Lucas, at Inkwell Management Literary Agency, my literary agent in the USA, for your enthusiasm and dynamism in ensuring this book found the right home with a US publisher.

Thank you also to Sophie Ransom, of Ransom PR, for your huge enthusiasm for this story from the very outset, and for working your special magic, as always.

Finally, of course, I need to extend my deep thanks and gratitude to my family – Eva, David, Damien Jr and Sianna – who once again had to put up with 'Pappa' spending far too long locked in his study trying to do justice to this story. That I have – if I have – I owe to you all; to your forbearance, your love and support and kindness, and for putting up with me through it all.

This, of course, is a very special story for the Lewis family, for many reasons – not least of all that you were there with me when it all began, during our visit to Château des Milandes. It is also a special story because my wife has played a very hands-on and indispensable role in the research, the writing and the revisions of this book. You stayed the course over the long years that it has taken to come to fruition, for which I am hugely grateful.

A Note On Sources

I am hugely indebted to the following authors and key texts, without which this book could not have been written, or at least not in its present form. As detailed in the Author's Note, I extend my deep gratitude to those who granted me kind permission to quote from their material:

Jacques Abtey, whose books – published in French, and alas long out of print – provide the key accounts of his and Josephine Baker's war. These are *La Guerre Secrète de Joséphine Baker* and *2ème Bureau Contre Abwehr* (for full details, see bibliography: all rights reserved).

Colonel Rémy, whose book – published in French, and alas long out of print – provides the other key account of Jacques Abtey and Josephine Baker's war (it is based upon a series of interviews with Abtey). Its title is *J.A.: Épisodes de la vie d'un agent du S.R. et du contre-espionnage français* (for full details, see bibliography: all rights reserved). For details of the Foundation set-up by Colonel Rémy's family and its excellent work, see the entry that follows.

Colonel Paul Paillole, whose books – published first in French, and also sadly out of print – provide detailed accounts of the shadow war fought by the French intelligence services, including his work with Jacques Abtey and Josephine Baker. These are *Services Spéciaux 1935–1945* (entitled *Fighting the Nazis* in the English edition) and *L'Homme des Services Secrets,* written with Alain-Gilles Minella (for full details, see bibliography: all rights reserved).

I am also grateful to the following publishers, authors and estates for granting me the permission to quote from their works:

Keith Jeffrey and A. M. Heath, *MI6*, 2010 – all rights reserved.

Tim Newark and Greenhill Books, *The Mafia at War*, 2007 – all rights reserved.

Charles Onana and Éditions Duboiris, *Joséphine Baker Contre Hitler*, 2006 – all rights reserved.

The family and estate of Kenneth Pendar, *Adventure In Diplomacy*, 1945 – all rights reserved.

Ean Wood and Omnibus Press, *The Josephine Baker Story*, 2000 – all rights reserved.

Hal Vaughan and Rowman & Littlefield, *FDR's 12 Apostles*, 2006 – all rights reserved.

Emmanuel de Crits and Éditions Julliard/Robert Laffont, *L'Homme des Services Secrets: Entretiens avec Alain-Gilles Minella*, 1995 – all rights reserved.

Selected Bibliography

Jacques Abtey, *La Guerre Secrète de Joséphine Baker*, Siboney, 1948

——, *2ème Bureau Contre Abwehr*, La Table Ronde, 1967

Patrick Atkinson, *An Army at Dawn*, Henry Holt & Company, 2002

Josephine Baker and Marcel Sauvage, *Les Mémoires de Joséphine Baker*, Editions Correa, 1949

Josephine Baker and Jo Bouillon, *Josephine*, WH Allen, 1978

Jean-Claude Baker and Chris Chase, *Josephine: The Hungry Heart*, Random House, 1993

James Barr, *Lords of the Desert*, Simon & Schuster, 2019

Leon Borden Blair, *Western Window in the Arab World*, University of Texas Press, 1970

Martin Blumenson, *The Patton Papers: 1940–1945*, Houghton Mifflin, 1974

René Bouscat, *De Gaulle–Giraud: Dossier d'une mission*, Flammarion, 1992

Rodney Campbell, *The Luciano Project*, McGraw-Hill, 1977

Peggy Caravantes, *The Many Faces of Josephine Baker*, Chicago Review Press, 2015

Winston Churchill, *The Hinge of Fate: The Second World War*, Volume 4, Bantam, 1965

Ian Dear, *Sabotage and Subversion: the SOE and OSS at War*, Arms and Armour Press, 1996

Rebecca Donner, *All The Frequent Troubles Of Our Days*, Canongate, 2021

Charlie Erswell & John R. McKay, *Surviving the Arctic Convoys*, Pen & Sword, 2021

Hugh Mallory Falconer, *The Gestapo's Most Improbable Hostage*, Pen & Sword, 2018

M. R. D. Foot, *SOE 1940–1946*, The Bodley Head, 2014

Robert Forczyk, *We March Against England: Operation Sea Lion 1940–41*, Osprey Publishing, 2016

Brian Hammond and Patrick O'Connor, *Josephine Baker*, Jonathan Cape, 1988

Lynn Haney, *Naked at the Feast*, Robson Books, 1981

Linda Hervieux, *Forgotten: The Untold Story of D-Day's Black Heroes*, Amberley, 2016

Stephen R. Hill, *Boodle's Apocrypha*, Duckworth, 2009

Meredith Hindley, *Destination Casablanca*, PublicAffairs, 2017

Alistair Horne, *To Lose A Battle: France 1940*, Macmillan, 1969

George F. Howe, *Northwest Africa: Seizing the Initiative in the West*, University Press of the Pacific, 2005

Mark Hull and Vera Moyes, *Masquerade: Treason, the Holocaust, and an Irish Impostor*, University of Oklahoma Press, 2017

Robert Hutton, *Agent Jack: The True Story of MI5's Secret Nazi Hunter*, Weidenfeld & Nicolson, 2018

Keith Jeffery, *MI6*, Bloomsbury, 2010

Marcel Jullian, *H.M.S. Fidelity*, Souvenir Press, 1957

Bennetta Jules-Rosette, *Josephine Baker in Art and Life*, University of Illinois Press, 2007

David Kahn, *Hitler's Spies: German Military Intelligence in WWII*, Macmillan, 1978

Simon Kitson, *The Hunt for Nazi Spies*, University of Chicago Press, 2008

Neill Lochery, *Lisbon*, PublicAffairs, 2011

Robert Lyman, *The Rise of the Third Reich*, Amberly, 2018

William Manchester and Paul Reid, *The Last Lion: Winston Spencer Churchill: Defender of the Realm, 1940–1965*, Bello, 2015

Gavin Maxwell, *Lords of the Atlas*, Eland London, 1966

Andy Merriman, *Greasepaint & Cordite*, Aurum Press, 2013

Christopher Moore, *Fighting for America: Black Soldiers – The Unsung Heroes of WWII*, One World, 2005

Brendan M. Murphy, *Turncoat*, Harcourt Brace Jovanovich, 1987

Robert Murphy, *Diplomat Among Warriors*, Collins, 1964

Tim Newark, *Mafia at War*, Greenhill Books, 2007

Jean-Yves Le Naour, *La Honte Noire*, Hachette, 2003

Alan Ogden, *Tigers Burning Bright: SOE Heroes in the Far East*, Bene Factum Publishing, 2013

Sybil Oldfield, *The Black Book: The Britons on the Nazi Hitlist*, Profile Books, 2020

Charles Onana, *Joséphine Baker Contre Hitler*, Editions Duboiris, 2006

Paul Paillole, *L'Homme des Services Secrets*, Éditions Julliard, 1995

——, *Fighting the Nazis*, Enigma Books, 2003

——, *The Spy in Hitler's Inner Circle*, Casemate, 2016

Kenneth Pendar, *Adventure in Diplomacy*, Cassell, 1945

Nicholas Rankin, *Defending the Rock*, Faber & Faber, 2017

Anthony Read and David Fisher, *Colonel Z: The Secret Life of a Master of Spies*, Hodder & Stoughton, 1984

Colonel Rémy (Gilbert Renault), *J.A.: Épisodes de la vie d'un agent du S.R. et du contre-espionnage français*, Éditions Galic, 1961

Francis Brooks Richards, *Secret Flotillas, Volume 1: Clandestine Operations to Brittany 1940–44*, Frank Cass Publishers, 2004

——, *Secret Flotillas, Volume 2: Clandestine Operations in the Western Mediterranean, North African and the Adriatic 1940–44*, Frank Cass Publishers, 2004

Alan Schroeder, *Josephine Baker: Entertainer*, Chelsea House Publishers, 1991

Hugh Sebag-Montefiore, *Enigma: The Battle for the Code*, Weidenfeld & Nicolson, 2000

Margot Lee Shetterly, *Hidden Figures*, William Morrow, 2016

Major General Rygor Słowikowski, *In the Secret Service*, The Windrush Press, 1988

Tim Spicer, *A Dangerous Enterprise*, Barbreck, 2021

David Stafford, *Britain and European Resistance 1940–1945*, David Stafford Publishing, 2013

Philip John Stead, *Second Bureau*, Evans Brothers, 1959

Dermot Turing, *X, Y & Z*, History Press, 2018

Hal Vaughan, *FDR's 12 Apostles*, The Lyons Press, 2006

Philippe Verrier, *Victor Dillard, SJ*, trans. Theodore P. Fraser, Marquette University Press, 2017

Edward Wake-Walker, *A House for Spies: SIS Operations into Occupied France*, Robert Hale, 2011

Nigel West, *MI6*, Panther Books, 1985

——, *The Guy Liddell Diaries, 1939–1942: MI5's Director of Counter-Espionage in WWII*, Routledge, 2005

Charles Wighton and Gunter Peis, *They Spied on England*, Odhams, 1958

Ean Wood, *The Josephine Baker Story*, Sanctuary Publishing, 2000

Sources

UNPUBLISHED/ARCHIVAL

Material quoted from the UK archive files listed below, and referenced in the endnotes, is courtesy of the British National Archives, with enormous thanks. Note: this book contains public-sector information licensed under the Open Government Licence v3.0.

British National Archives, Kew

CAB 80-24-86 France and French colonies. Review of situation IN.

CAB 85-22-1 Committee on French Resistance/Committee on Foreign (Allied) Resistance.

CAB 67-7-5 The Economic Consequences of a Complete or Partial Collapse of French Resistance.

CAB 85-23-1 Committee on French Resistance/Committee on Foreign (Allied) Resistance.

CAB 85-27-1 Committee on French Resistance: Table of Contents.

CAB 85-30 Foreign (Allied) Resistance Sub-Committee on Welfare Security.

CAB 85-28-1 Committee on French Resistance: Table of Contents.

CAB 85-30-1 War Cabinet Anglo-French Committee; Foreign (Allied) Resistance Sub-committee.

CAB 85-30-40 Memoranda Papers: CFR (WS) (40) 1–41.

CAB 85-30-3 Minutes of Meetings: CFR (WS) (40) 14th–23rd.

CAB 85-30-2 Minutes of Meetings: CFR (WS) (40) 1st–13th.

CAB 80-14-55 French Hostility. Implications of: Note by JPC submitting draft Report for the C.O.S.

CAB 65-7-33 Record Type: Conclusion Former Reference: WM (4) 138 Attendees.

CAB 65-7-39 Record Type: Conclusion Former Reference: WM (4) 144 Attendees.

CAB 65-7-46 Record Type: Conclusion Former Reference: WM (4) 151 Attendees.

HW 48 Government Code and Cypher School: Hut 3: Intelligence Reports on German Plans for the Sea-borne Invasion of Britain (Operation Smith/Sea Lion).

ADM 199-2477 Director of Naval Intelligence: reports of invasion exercises and craft, anti-invasion.

WO 193-141 Threatened German invasion of United Kingdom: notes on possible developments.

AIR 75-7 German Invasion May 1940.

CAB 80-13-50 Eire: German Invasion: Plans to Meet: Aide-memoire.

CAB 84-22-34 German invasion of Eire by Air. Note by Secretary.

CAB 84-19-43 German Invasion of Eire.

HS 6-308 HMG's relations with French governing authorities.

T 160-1102-1 Committees. England: Vansittart Committee on French Resistance; Campbell Sub-committee.

KV 6-30 Paul Laurent Louis Burdet: French. Burdet was a Free French Resistance member whose case . . .

HS 13 SOE France Index

HS 9-877-5 An unusual file containing detailed reports written by Lake of the subject's mission to train the French Resistance in the Dordogne area . . .

FO 1055 Foreign Office, French Welfare Section and War Cabinet, Welfare and Security Sub-committee: Papers

FO 1055-3 Notes concerning meetings of the Committee on Foreign (Allied) Resistance, including attitude of the French colony in the UK.

FO 892-8 Recruitment minutes.

FO 892- Lord Bessborough's Sub-Committee – Minutes.

WO 193/1007 SOE Anglo-American Collaboration.

FO 892-6 General Catroux file

FO 892-5 Morton Committee – Minutes

CAB 85-94 Civil resistance.

ADM 199-1100 Free French Movement: minutes of committee on Foreign (Allied) Resistance.

ADM 199-1098 Free French Movement: minutes of committee on Foreign (Allied) Resistance.

KV 6-125 Serge Lucien COLLIN. In July 1940 COLLIN was appointed second in command of the Free French Deuxième Bureau in London . . . He fabricated evidence against the head of the Free French Navy, Admiral Musilier . . .

HS 13 Special Operations Executive: Registry: France Nominal Index.

KV 2-848 Dusko POPOV, codenamed TRICYCLE.

KV 2-863 Dusko POPOV, codenamed TRICYCLE.

KV 2-845 Dusko POPOV, codenamed TRICYCLE.

KV 2-849 Dusko POPOV, codenamed TRICYCLE.

KV 2-449 Selected Historical Papers from the SNOW case.

KV 2-448 Selected Historical Papers from the SNOW case.

KV 2-2630 Kurt Frederick LUDWIG: American. In 1941 LUDWIG was arrested in the USA on charges of espionage . . .

KV 2-2631 Kurt Frederick LUDWIG: American. In 1941 LUDWIG was arrested in the USA on charges of espionage . . .

KV 2-2632 Kurt Frederick LUDWIG: American. In 1941 LUDWIG was arrested in the USA on charges of espionage . . .

KV 2-3431 Max AZANCOT: Portuguese. In 1938 AZANCOT was reported to be working for the Germans . . .

T 160-1080-3 FINANCE. Currency: Countries – Morocco / T421/10 Recommendations for the King's Medal for Courage in the Cause of Freedom: Morocco.

CAB 80-83 Memoranda (0) Nos. 391–471.

CAB 21-1464: Free French Forces: operations by General de Gaulle.

CAB 21-1451: General de Gaulle's organisation.

FO 660-47 Negotiations for French Union (Free French Unity).

WO 106-5193 Strategical aims of the Free French.

FO 892-129 Communications Aircraft for Free French Africa.

FO 660-68 Free French.

PREM 3-442-11 Proposed Free French mission to North Africa.

WO 193-859 Free French in Africa.

PREM 3-317-3 Various.

PREM 3-416 Operation Susan in French Morocco (PM's Office, July 1940).

PREM 3-431 Operation THREAT in French Morocco (PM's Office, Sept 1940).

PREM 3-317-3 VARIOUS (PM's Office, Morocco, Oct 1940 – Feb 1944).

HS 3-203 Top Level planning activities: OSS/SOE coordination in Morocco.

HS 3-204 Politics: use of political groups for SOE activities.

FO 371-32221-9 Correspondence from the London Chamber of Commerce to the Foreign Office dated 6 October 1942 . . . Louis Dreyfus Company.

BT 103-532 Trading with the enemy Act 1939; Louis Dreyfus and Co.; instructions to Counsel . . .

KV 6-80 Helmut Clissmann / Elizabeth Clissmann: German. A student and leading Nazi Party member in Dublin, working for both Abwehr and Jahnke Bureaux . . .

KV 2-769 Dr. K HALLER, alias VOGE: German HALLER was from September 1939 to December 1942 head of a small group of Abwehr Abteiling II (sabotage) dealing with Ireland.

CAB 103-457 Publication of enemy document section appreciations: Operation SEALION.

GFM 33-399-694 Under State Secretary: France: Armistice Commission, July 1941–Sept 1942.

GFM 33-1847-4382 Commercial Policy Department; Clodius Papers: Armistice Commission (Turkey neutrality and trade negotiations/policy).

GFM 33-2062-4635 German Embassy Paris: Armistice Commission (Wako) Nov 1940–Dec 1942.

GFM 33-877-2358 Under State Secretary: Oct–Dec 1941.

GFM 33-1575-3839 German Embassy Paris: German Armistice Commission Wiesbaden, Nov 1942–May 1944.

GFM 33-499-1067 Etzdorf Papers: Armistice Commission, June 1940–June 1942.

GFM 33-1529-3697 German Embassy Paris: Armistice Commission June 1940–Dec 1942.

FO 371-31921 Activities of the German Armistice Commission in France, Code 17 file 28 (papers 5259-6804), 1942.

WO 219-3763 The German Armistice Commission, Wiesbaden, for the military government of occupied France, 1943.

KV 2-468 Selected Historical Papers from the GW case. GW was a Welsh retired Police Inspector, recruited by SIS as a Welsh Nationalist plant in the Abwehr.

FO 954-8B-512 France: Algiers telegram No. 1126. Giraud has left for US.

WO 204-9945 French Expeditionary Force reports, April–July 1944.

PREM 3-271-10 Operation Dragoon (Anvil) – Allied landings in Southern France, Aug–Sept 1944.

CAB 106-1032 Operation Dragoon: Address by General L. Devers on the invasion of Southern France, Aug 15 1944. (General Devers, US military commander of Op Dragoon).

CAB 119-5 Operation Dragoon: operations in the Mediterranean against the South of France.

PREM 3-227-4 Plans and Directive.

FO 371-36173 Relations between General de Gaulle and General Giraud. Code 69 file 30 (papers 2867-3978), 1943.

FO 954-16B-282 North Africa: Resident Minister, Algiers telegram No. 37, Giraud and Godefroy.

FO 954-16B-303 Resident Minister, Algiers telegram to Foreign Office, No. 161 Eisenhower–Giraud.

FO 954-8B-494 France: Algiers telegram No. 1047. Visit of Giraud to US, 24 June 1943.

FO 954-8B-350 France: Foreign Office dispatch to Mr. Peake, No. 39, Conversation with General Catroux (Giraud–de Gaulle relations) 12 Jan 1943.

FO 954-8B-436 France: Private Secretary No. 10 to Private Secretary Foreign Office Letter from Giraud to the Prime Minister 27 May 1943.

FO 954-8A-227 FRANCE: Secretary of State Minute to Prime Minister Movement of General Giraud 29 April 1942.

FO 954-9A-67 FRANCE: Algiers (Ambassador) telegram No. 425 (for the Prime Minister). Giraud will not resign.

FO 954-9A-69 FRANCE: Algiers (Ambassador) telegram No. 428 (for the Prime Minister). Clash between Giraud and de Gaulle, 9 April 1944.

FO 954-8B-561 France: Algiers telegram No. 1441. Message from Prime Minister given to de Gaulle, Giraud and others . . . 11 Aug 1943.

CAB 80-39 Memoranda Nos. 1–100 Jan 1943–March 1943.

PREM 3-442-19 Negotiations between Gen. Giraud and Gen. de Gaulle May–June 1943.

FO 954-8B-577 France: Algiers telegram No. 1915. Giraud retains his co-Presidency, 1 Oct 1943.

PREM 3-181-1 Gen. Giraud's visit to USA, June–July 1943.

PREM 3-442-16 Meeting between Gen. Giraud and Gen. de Gaulle, Jan 1943.

FO 660-76 Desertions Giraud to de Gaulle Feb–Jul 1943.

PREM 3-182-1 Position of General Giraud, Mar–May 1944.

KV 2-2296 Lothar WITZKE: German. WITZKE worked for the JAHNKE Bureau in the 1920s, later becoming an Abwehr officer.

HS 3/52 ZODIAC two agents landing Tunisian coast.

HS 6/973 Gun-running and Toys to North Africa.

HS 3/203 Top-level planning SOE/OSS Morocco.

HS 3/59 Liaison SIS/ISLDF C and MI6.

HS 3/56 SOE/OSS Coordination.

HS 3/41 French Special Services.

· WO 373/153 Recommendation for Award for Gérar-Dubot, Paul.

French National Archives (Vincennes, etc.)

Material quoted from the French archive files listed below, and referenced in the endnotes, is courtesy of and © Service Historique de la Défense, with enormous thanks.

GR 28 P9 14280, MAURICE, LEONARD (JACQUES) ABTEY

GR 28 P9 390, JOSEPHINE BAKER

GR Z 2000 1618 7959, MAURICE, LEONARD (JACQUES) ABTEY

AI P 6679 (1), JOSEPHINE BAKER

FOLDER 1 FOLDER 2 FOLDER 3 FOLDER 4 PAUL BAPTISTE SABIN PAILLOLE, Paillole Archive Folder 4 Final (29.4.21)

GR 16 P 116346, GEORGE, JEAN, EMILE, RENE CHADEBAC DE LAVALADE

GR 16P 127284, MAURICE CHEVALIER

GR 16P 275626, ALBERT, JEAN MARIE GUERVILLE

GR 16P 373520, VICTOR DILLARD

GR 16P 373520, JEAN LION (20.1.2021)

GR 16P 28445, JOSEPHINE BAKER

GR 16P 2170, MAURICE, LEONARD (JACQUES) ABTEY

Federal Bureau of Investigation Archives on Josephine Baker, FBI Vault

BUFILE: 62-95834 Josephine Baker, Part 1 & 2.

OTHER (UNPUBLISHED) RESEARCH RESOURCES

Foreign Relations of the United States, Diplomatic papers, 1940, General and Europe Volume 2. Credit US Department of State. https://history.state.gov/historicaldocuments/frus1940v02/d490

""Double Jeu": The foreign relations of Vichy France with Germany and Great Britain June 1940 to February 1941', David Jan Austin, University of Montana, 1971 – https://scholarworks.umt.edu/etd/5196/

"'Of Historical Interest Only": The Origins and Vicissitudes of the SOE Archive', Duncan Stuart, *Intelligence and National Security*, 24 May 2006 – https://www.tandfonline.com/doi/abs/10.1080/0268 4520500059338?tab=permissions&scroll=top

AASSDN, the L'Amicale des Anciens des Services Spéciaux de la Défense Nationale – https://aassdn.org/amicale/

International Churchill Society – https://winstonchurchill.org/

Association for the Defence and the Memory of Colonel Rémy – https://www.association-memoire-colonel-remy.com

Henry Hurford Janes-Josephine Baker Collection, Call Number JWJ MSS 2, Archives at Yale – https://archives.yale.edu/repositories/11/resources/967

Notes

ABBREVIATIONS

NARA – National Archives and Records Administration (US)
SHD – Service Historique de la Défense, French national defence archives.
TNA – The National Archives (UK)
USHMM – US Holocaust Memorial Museum
* Notes marked with an asterisk denote texts read partially in translation – pagination may differ from original.

AUTHOR'S NOTE

1   Josephine Baker and Jo Bouillon, *Josephine*, WH Allen, 1978, p. 144.
2   Paul Paillole, *Fighting the Nazis*, Enigma Books, 2003, p. xxv.
3   Colonel Rémy, *J.A.*, Éditions Galic, 1961, p. 178.*
4   Ibid., p. 2.*
5   SHD GR 28 P9 14280, Abtey, p. 1.

PREFACE

1   Paul Paillole, *L'Homme des Services Secrets: Entretiens avec Alain-Gilles Minella*, Éditions Julliard, 1995, p. 78.*

CHAPTER ONE

1   Duncan Gardham, 'Real James Bond snuck into Russia wearing school uniform', *The Telegraph*, 27/9/2010; Stephen R. Hill, *Boodle's Apocrypha*, Duckworth, 2009, p. 118; Keith Jeffery, *MI6*, Bloomsbury, 2010, p. 199.

2   Brian Cathcart, 'The Name's Dunderdale, Biffy Dunderdale', *The Independent*, 23/06/1996.

3   Hill, *Boodle's Apocrypha*, p. 118; Jeffery, *MI6*, p. 200; Documents and photographs held in private Dunderdale family archive, courtesy of Paul Biddle MBE.

4   Gardham, 'Real James Bond'; 'Commander Wilfred Dunderdale', Obituaries, *The Times*, 16/11/1990; Documents and photographs held in private Dunderdale family archive, courtesy of Paul Biddle MBE.

5   Paul Paillole, *Fighting the Nazis*, Enigma Books, 2003, p. 83; Documents and photographs held in private Dunderdale family archive, courtesy of Paul Biddle MBE.

6   Tim Spicer, *A Dangerous Enterprise, Secret War At Sea*, Barbreck, 2021, p. 32.

7   Paul Paillole, *L'Homme des Services Secrets: Entretiens avec Alain-Gilles Minella*, Éditions Julliard, 1995, pp. 3, 41–2.*

8   Colonel Rémy, *J.A.*, Éditions Galic, 1961, p. 2.*

9   SHD GRZ 2000 1618, J Abtey, p. 1; Colonel Rémy, *J.A.*, Éditions Galic, 1961, p. 2.*

10 SHD GRZ 2000 1618, J Abtey, p. 24.

11 Colonel Rémy, *J.A.*, p. 4.*

12 Jacques Abtey and Dr Fritz Unterberg Gibhardt, *2ème Bureau Contre Abwehr*, La Table Ronde, 1967, p. 57.*

13 Ibid.

14 Paillole, *Services Speciaux, 1935–1945*, Robert Laffont – Opera Mundi, 1975, p. 118.

15 Britannica.com, Electric Boat Company – https://www.britannica.com/topic/Electric-Boat-Company ; Wikipedia, General Dynamics Electric Boat, pp. 1–3: https://en.wikipedia.org/wiki/General_Dynamics_Electric_Boat

16 'Commander Wilfred Dunderdale', Obituaries, *The Times*, 16/11/1990; Documents and photographs held in private Dunderdale family archive, courtesy of Paul Biddle MBE.

17 Hill, *Boodle's Apocrypha*, p. 117.

18 Gardham, 'Real James Bond'; MBE letter of 27 June 1921, private Dunderdale family archive, courtesy of Paul Biddle MBE.

19 Dunderdale, Wilfred Albert, 23/9/2004, *Oxford Dictionary of National Biography* – https://www.oxforddnb.com/view/10.1093/ref:odnb/9780198614128.001.0001/odnb-9780198614128-e-40173; Documents held in private Dunderdale family archive, courtesy of Paul Biddle MBE.

20 Abtey and Unterberg Gibhardt, *2ème Bureau Contre Abwehr*, p. 5.*
21 Ibid., p. 14.*
22 Paillole, *L'Homme des Services Secrets*, p. 69.*
23 Ibid., p. 30.*
24 Paillole, *Fighting the Nazis*, p. 83–4.
25 Abtey and Unterberg Gibhardt, *2ème Bureau Contre Abwehr*, p. 58.*
26 Jean-Claude Baker and Chris Chase, *Josephine: The Hungry Heart*, Random House, 1993, p. 144.
27 Ean Wood, *The Josephine Baker Story*, Sanctuary Publishing, 2000, p. 127.
28 Review in *Le Soir*, quoted in Baker and Chase, *Josephine: The Hungry Heart*, p. 143.
29 Wood, *The Josephine Baker Story*, p. 129.
30 Ibid.
31 Abtey and Unterberg Gibhardt, *2ème Bureau Contre Abwehr*, p. 59.*
32 Ibid., p. 58.*
33 Paillole, *Fighting the Nazis*, pp. 84–5.
34 Paillole, *Services Speciaux 1935–1945*, p. 122.
35 Abtey and Unterberg Gibhardt, *2ème Bureau Contre Abwehr*, p. 57.*
36 Paillole, *Services Speciaux, 1935–1945*, p. 123.
37 Abtey and Unterberg Gibhardt, *2ème Bureau Contre Abwehr*, pp. 66–7.*
38 Ibid.
39 Paillole, *Fighting the Nazis*, p. 273; Abtey and Unterberg Gibhardt, *2ème Bureau Contre Abwehr*, pp. 66–7.*
40 Abtey and Unterberg Gibhardt, *2ème Bureau Contre Abwehr*, pp. 66–7.*
41 Ibid., p. 57.*
42 Paillole, *Services Speciaux, 1935–1945*, p. 123.
43 Paillole, *L'Homme des Services Secrets*, p. 43.*
44 Abtey and Unterberg Gibhardt, *2ème Bureau Contre Abwehr*, p. 62.*
45 Paillole, *L'Homme des Services Secrets*, pp. 55–7.*
46 Paillole, *Fighting the Nazis*, pp. 3, 42–3.
47 Paillole, *Services Speciaux, 1935–1945*, p. 67
48 Wood, *The Josephine Baker Story*, pp. 202–4.
49 'The Spanish Civil War', United States Holocaust Memorial Museum – https://encyclopedia.ushmm.org/content/en/article/spanish-civil-war
50 Wood, *The Josephine Baker Story*, pp. 205–6.
51 Paillole, *Services Speciaux, 1935–1945*, p. 89.
52 Ibid., p. 53; Paillole, *L'Homme des Services Secrets*, p. 56.*
53 Paillole, *Fighting the Nazis*, p. 89.
54 Philip John Stead, *Second Bureau*, Evans Brothers, 1959, p. 22.

55 Jeffery, *MI6*, p. 157.

56 Ibid., pp. 289–90, 291; Documents and photographs held in private Dunderdale family archive, courtesy of Paul Biddle MBE.

57 Ibid., p. 293.

58 Paillole, *Fighting the Nazis*, p. 13; Abtey and Unterberg Gibhardt, *2ème Bureau Contre Abwehr*, pp. 106–7.*

59 Hugh Mallory Falconer, *The Gestapo's Most Improbable Hostage*, Pen & Sword, 2018, p. 71.

CHAPTER TWO

1   Jacques Abtey and Dr Fritz Unterberg Gibhardt, *2ème Bureau Contre Abwehr*, La Table Ronde, 1967, pp. 4–14.*

2   Ean Wood, *The Josephine Baker Story*, Sanctuary Publishing, 2000, p. 213; Colonel Rémy, *J.A.*, Éditions Galic, 1961, p. 8.*

3   Jacques Abtey, *La Guerre Secrète de Joséphine Baker*, Siboney, 1948, p. 5.*

4   Abtey and Unterberg Gibhardt, *2ème Bureau Contre Abwehr*, pp. 107–8.*

5   Abtey and Unterberg Gibhardt, *2ème Bureau Contre Abwehr*, pp. 20–1*; Wood, *The Josephine Baker Story*, pp. 108–9.

6   Abtey and Unterberg Gibhardt, *2ème Bureau Contre Abwehr*, p. 19.*

7   Wood, *The Josephine Baker Story*, pp. 119, 121.

8   Ibid., p. 16; Jean-Claude Baker and Chris Chase, *Josephine: The Hungry Heart*, Random House, 1993, pp. 13–14.

9   Wood, *The Josephine Baker Story*, p. 13; Baker and Chase, *Josephine: The Hungry Heart*, pp. 13–14. Note: in some version of Josephine Baker's story, the tribe is given as Cherokee.

10 Abtey, *La Guerre Secrète*, p. 4.*; Wood, *The Josephine Baker Story*, p. 213.

11 Baker and Chase, *Josephine: The Hungry Heart*, p. 226.

12 Wood, *The Josephine Baker Story*, p. 175.

13 Colonel Rémy, *J.A.*, p. 8.*

14 Ibid.

15 Ibid.

16 Ibid.

17 Ibid.

18 Wood, *The Josephine Baker Story*, p. 214.

19 Abtey, *La Guerre Secrète*, p. 4.*

20 Josephine Baker and Jo Bouillon, *Josephine*, WH Allen, 1978, p. 118.

21 Jean-Pierre. Reggiori, interview with author, 2021; Wayne Bernath, 'French dancer tells Josephine Baker story', Cable Update, March 1991.

22 Colonel Rémy, *J.A.*, pp. 8–9.*

23 Ibid.

24 Ibid.

25 Abtey, *La Guerre Secrète*, p. 6.*

26 Colonel Rémy, *J.A.*, pp. 8–9.*

27 Ibid.

28 Ibid.; Baker and Chase, *Josephine: The Hungry Heart*, pp. 190, 227.

29 Wood, *The Josephine Baker Story*, pp. 176–7, 186–7.

30 Lynn Haney, *Naked at the Feast*, Robson Books, 1981, pp. 186, 196.

31 Paul Paillole, *Fighting the Nazis*, Enigma Books, 2003, pp. 36, 54, 72.

32 Wood, *The Josephine Baker Story*, p. 165.

33 Colonel Rémy, *J.A.*, p. 9.*

34 Abtey, *La Guerre Secrète*, p. 6.*

35 Josephine Baker and Marcel Sauvage, *Les Mémoires de Joséphine Baker*, Éditions Corrêa, 1949, p. 71.

36 Wood, *The Josephine Baker Story*, pp. 94–5.

37 Baker and Sauvage, *Les Mémoires*, pp. 12–13.

38 Wood, *The Josephine Baker Story*, p. 95.

39 Ibid., pp. 119, 121.

40 Ibid., pp. 94–5; Baker and Chase, *Josephine: The Hungry Heart*, p. 155.

41 Wood, *The Josephine Baker Story*, p. 96.

42 Wood, *The Josephine Baker Story*, pp. 141–51.

43 Ibid.

44 Ibid.

45 Baker and Chase, *Josephine: The Hungry Heart*, p. 159–61.

46 Baker and Sauvage, *Les Mémoires*, p. 25.

47 Bryan Hammond and Patrick O'Connor, *Josephine Baker*, Jonathan Cape, 1988, pp. 81–2.

48 Haney, *Naked at the Feast*, p. 215; Wood, *The Josephine Baker Story*, p. 213.

49 Wood, *The Josephine Baker Story*, p. 146.

50 Baker and Bouillon, *Josephine*, p. 117.

51 Ibid., p. 146.

52 Géraud Létang, *Joséphine Baker, figure emblématique des Armées*, Service Historique de la Défense (SHD) – https://european-security.com/josephine-baker-in-the-pantheon/

53 Baker and Bouillon, *Josephine*, p. 117.

54 Colonel Rémy, *J.A.*, pp. 10–13.*

55 Ibid.

56 Abtey, *La Guerre Secrète*, p. 11.*
57 Colonel Rémy, *J.A.*, pp. 10–12.*
58 Baker and Sauvage, *Les Mémoires*, p. 20.
59 Baker and Chase, *Josephine: The Hungry Heart*, p. 146.
60 Baker and Sauvage, *Les Mémoires*, p. 87.
61 Colonel Rémy, *J.A.*, p. 13.*
62 Ibid; Abtey, *La Guerre Secrète*, p. 11.*
63 Abtey, *La Guerre Secrète*, p.11.*.
64 Ibid.
65 Colonel Rémy, *J.A.*, p. 13.*
66 TNA CAB 66/7/14, pp. 1–9 – 21/4/1940, War Cabinet report on Italian Action in the Mediterranean.
67 TNA CAB 65/7/33, War Cabinet, pp. 1, 6 – 25/5/40, War Cabinet meeting.
68 Baker and Sauvage, *Les Mémoires*, p. 37.

CHAPTER THREE

1   Paul Paillole, *Fighting the Nazis*, Enigma Books, 2003, pp. 113–14.
2   Paillole, *Services Speciaux, 1935–1945*, Robert Laffont – Opera Mundi, 1975, p. 155.
3   Paul Paillole, *L'Homme des Services Secrets: Entretiens avec Alain-Gilles Minella*, Éditions Julliard, 1995, pp. 39–40.*
4   Pesonal correspondence and interviews with Colonel Tim Spicer, 2021–2022, author of the forthcoming biography of Wilfred 'Biffy' Dunderdale, provisionally entitled *A Suspicion Of Spies*; Documents and photographs held in private Dunderdale family archive, courtesy of Paul Biddle MBE.
5   Paillole, *L'Homme des Services Secrets*, p. 57.*
6   Keith Jeffery, *MI6*, Bloomsbury, 2010, p. 371.
7   TNA CAB 65/1/19, p. 5 – 18/9/39 – Shipping arms to Poland.
8   Paillole, *Fighting the Nazis*, pp. 116–17.
9   TNA CAB 65/1/19, p. 8 – 18/9/39 – Japan jockeying for power and shadowy allegiances.
10 Jacques Abtey, *La Guerre Secrète de Joséphine Baker*, Siboney, 1948, pp. 13–14.*
11 Ibid.
12 Jean-Claude Baker and Chris Chase, *Josephine: The Hungry Heart*, Random House, 1993, p. 185.
13 Ibid., p. 175.
14 Baker and Chase, *Josephine: The Hungry Heart*, p. 227.

15 Paillole, *Fighting the Nazis*, p. 55; Jacques Abtey and Dr Fritz Unterberg Gibhardt, *2ème Bureau Contre Abwehr*, La Table Ronde, 1967, p.12.*

16 TNA ADM 199/2477, Op Sealion, p. 30 – Dec 1940, invasion fleet in French ports.

17 TNA CAB 65/2/15, p. 5 – November 1939, War Cabinet meeting.

18 TNA CAB 65/2/35, pp. 6–7 – 2/12/39, War Cabinet minutes.

19 Ibid.

20 Julie Davies perscom/timeline, p. 11 – J Baker via Portuguese embassy learns of German U-boat base plans.

21 Abtey, *La Guerre Secrète*, p. 3*; Paillole, *Fighting the Nazis*, p. 76.

22 SHD GR 16P 28445, Baker Josephine, p. 3.

23 SHD AI 1P 66791, p. 40.

24 SHD GRZ 2000 1618, J Abtey, p. 53; SHD GRZ 2000 1618 7959 J Abtey, p. 4.

25 Colonel Rémy, *J.A.*, Éditions Galic, 1961, p. 10.*

26 Angélique de Labarre, *Château et Jardins des Milandes*, Joseph'in Les Milandes, 2019, p. 28. Note: Angélique de Labarre became Angélique de Labarre de Saint Exupéry upon her marriage. I have used both names according to publication date and authorship.

27 Ean Wood, *The Josephine Baker Story*, Sanctuary Publishing, 2000, p. 97.

28 Wood, *The Josephine Baker Story*, pp. 24–5; Baker and Sauvage, *Les Mémoires*, pp. 11–12.

29 Wood, *The Josephine Baker Story*, pp. 24–5.

30 Ibid., pp. 24–5; Baker and Sauvage, *Les Mémoires*, pp. 11–12.

31 Baker and Sauvage, *Les Mémoires*, pp. 11–12.

32 Josephine Baker and Jo Bouillon, *Josephine*, WH Allen, 1978, p. 118.

33 Baker and Chase, *Josephine: The Hungry Heart*, p. 257.

34 Abtey and Unterberg Gibhardt, *2ème Bureau Contre Abwehr*, p.13.*

CHAPTER FOUR

1 Ean Wood, *The Josephine Baker Story*, Sanctuary Publishing, 2000, pp. 13–15.

2 Melanie Zeck, 'Josephine Baker, the most sensational woman anybody ever saw', 3 June 2014, Oxford University Press, OUPblog – https://blog.oup.com/2014/06/josephine-baker-sensational-woman/

3 Jean-Claude Baker and Chris Chase, *Josephine: The Hungry Heart*, Random House, 1993, p. 216.

4 Wood, *The Josephine Baker Story*, 2000, pp. 164–6.

5   Ibid.

6   Ibid.

7   Ibid., p. 168.

8   Alan Schroeder, *Josephine Baker: Entertainer*, Chelsea House Publishers, 1991, pp. 65, 69.

9   Jacques Abtey, *La Guerre Secrète de Joséphine Baker*, Siboney, 1948, p. 12.

10 Wood, *The Josephine Baker Story*, p. 167.

11 Ibid., pp. 215–16.

12 Ibid.

13 Ibid.

14 Josephine Baker and Jo Bouillon, *Josephine*, WH Allen, 1978, pp. 117–18.

15 Ibid.

16 Ibid.

17 Wood, *The Josephine Baker Story*, pp. 216–17.

18 Ibid.

CHAPTER FIVE

1   Hal Vaughan, *FDR's 12 Apostles*, The Lyons Press, 2006, p. 3.

2   Paul Paillole, *Fighting the Nazis*, Enigma Books, 2003, pp. 140–3.

3   Ibid.

4   TNA CAB 65/7/46, War Cabinet, pp. 12–14 – 1/6/40, Shattering effect of Blitzkrieg.

5   Meredith Hindley, *Destination Casablanca*, PublicAffairs, 2017, p. 17.

6   TNA CAB 65/7/39, War Cabinet, p. 5 – 28/5/40, War Cabinet meeting.

7   'Blood, Toil, Tears and Sweat', 13 May 1940, International Churchill Society – https://winstonchurchill.org/resources/speeches/1940-the-finest-hour/blood-toil-tears-sweat/

8   Vaughan, *FDR's 12 Apostles*, pp. 4–8.

9   Ibid.

10 Jean-Claude Baker and Chris Chase, *Josephine: The Hungry Heart*, Random House, 1993, p. 220 – in theory Josephine Baker was still married to Willie Baker and was still a US citizen.

11 Paul Paillole, *L'Homme des Services Secrets: Entretiens avec Alain-Gilles Minella*, Éditions Julliard, 1995, pp. 74–5.*

12 Baker and Chase, *Josephine: The Hungry Heart*, pp. 229–30

13 Ean Wood, *The Josephine Baker Story*, Sanctuary Publishing, 2000, p. 218

14 Paillole, *Fighting the Nazis*, pp. xvii–xviii.

15 Paillole, *L'Homme des Services Secrets*, pp. 74–5.*

16 Paillole, *Services Speciaux, 1935–1945,* Robert Laffont – Opera Mundi, 1975, p. 199.

17 Ibid., p. 156.

18 Quoted in Jean-Yves Le Naour, *La Honte Noir*, Hachette, Paris, 2003, p. 240.

19 Louis Snyder, *The War: A Concise History 1939–1945*, Julian Messner, 1960, p. 99.

20 Baker and Chase, *Josephine: The Hungry Heart*, pp. 229–30.

21 Ibid., p. 240.

22 Josephine Baker and Jo Bouillon, *Josephine,* WH Allen, 1978, p. 119.

23 Ibid.

24 Colonel Rémy, *J.A.*, Éditions Galic, 1961, p. 15.*

25 Angélique de Saint-Exupéry, Josephine Baker Honourable Correspondent, Charles de Gaulle Foundation, 12/2/21, p. 5.

26 Baker and Chase, *Josephine: The Hungry Heart*, pp. 229–30.

27 Ibid., p. 240.

28 Vaughan, *FDR's 12 Apostles*, pp. 5–7.

29 Paillole, *Fighting the Nazis*, p. 168.

30 Paillole, *L'Homme des Services Secrets*, p. 75.*

31 Ibid.

32 Paillole, *Services Speciaux, 1935–1945*, p. 206.

33 Paillole, *Fighting the Nazis*, pp. 157–8.

34 Jacques Abtey, *La Guerre Secrète de Joséphine Baker,* Siboney, 1948, pp. 14–15.*

35 Paillole, *Services Speciaux 1935–1945*, p. 207.

36 Paillole, *L'Homme des Services Secrets*, pp. 75–9.*

37 Ibid.; Paillole, *Fighting the Nazis*, pp. 6–7.

38 Paillole, *Fighting the Nazis*, , p. 49.

39 Ibid., p. 159.

40 Hindley, *Destination Casablanca*, pp. 17–19.

41 Ibid.

42 Paillole, *Fighting the Nazis*, pp. 160, 164.

43 Paillole, *Services Speciaux 1935–1945*, p. 212.

44 Paillole, *L'Homme des Services Secrets*, p. 136.*

45 Ibid., pp. 81, 84.*

46 Ibid.

47 Angélique de Labarre, *Chateau et Jardins des Milandes*, Joseph'in Les Milandes, 2019, p. 5.

48 Ibid.

49 Agrippa d'Aubigne, *Les Tragiques*, Book V, vv. 1149–60; *Museum of Medieval Warfare*, Castelnaud Castle.

50 Josephine Baker and Marcel Sauvage, *Les Mémoires de Joséphine Baker*, Éditions Corrêa, 1949, p. 86.

51 Baker and Bouillon, *Josephine*, p. 6.

52 Colonel Rémy, *J.A.*, p. 15*; Abtey, *La Guerre Secrète*, p. 18*; Paillole, *Fighting the Nazis*, p. 49.

CHAPTER SIX

1 Dunderdale, Wilfred Albert, 23/9/2004, *Oxford Dictionary of National Biography*, pp. 10–11 – https://www.oxforddnb.com/view/10.1093/ref:odnb/9780198614128.001.0001/odnb-9780198614128-e-40173

2 Stephen R. Hill, *Boodle's Apocrypha*, Duckworth, 2009, p. 118.

3 Clive Priddle private collection of Dunderdale papers, 30 May 1919 CAVA 'Carte D'Identité' for Wilfred Dunderdale.

4 'Commander Wilfred Dunderdale', Obituary, *The Times*, 16 November 1990 ; Documents and photographs held in private Dunderdale family archive, courtesy of Paul Biddle MBE.

5 Keith Jeffery, *MI6*, Bloomsbury, 2010, p. 200.

6 Paul Paillole, *Fighting the Nazis*, Enigma Books, 2003, pp. 123–4.

7 Paillole, *Services Speciaux, 1935–1945*, Robert Laffont – Opera Mundi, 1975, p. 167.

8 Hill, *Boodle's Apocrypha*, pp. 131–3.

9 Ibid.

10 Jeffery, *MI6*, pp. 293–4; Hill, *Boodle's Apocrypha*, pp. 131–3.

11 Jeffery, *MI6*, p. 390; Pesonal correspondence and interviews with Colonel Tim Spicer, 2021–2022, author of the forthcoming biography of Wilfred 'Biffy' Dunderdale, provisionally entitled *A Suspicion Of Spies*.

12 Meredith Hindley, *Destination Casablanca*, PublicAffairs, 2017, p. 25.

13 Kenneth Pendar, *Adventure in Diplomacy*, Cassell, 1966, p. 245.

14 Neill Lochery, *Lisbon*, PublicAffairs, 2011, pp. 21, 41.

15 TNA CAB 65/2/39, pp. 7–8 – 6/12/39, War Cabinet discussions for Franco-British financial union . . .

16 Dominic Tierney, 'When Britain and France almost merged into one country', *The Atlantic*, 8 August 2017, pp. 1–3.

17 Ibid.

18 Ibid.

19 Ibid.

20 Pendar, *Adventure in Diplomacy*, p. 338.

21 Hindley, *Destination Casablanca*, p. 25.

22 Jacques Abtey, *La Guerre Secrête de Joséphine Baker*, Siboney, 1948, pp. 18–19.*

23 Josephine Baker and Jo Bouillon, *Josephine*, WH Allen, 1978, p. 119.

24 Quoted in Jules-Rosette Bennetta, *Josephine Baker in Art and Life*, University of Illinois Press, 2007, p. 47.

25 Josephine Baker and Marcel Sauvage, *Les Mémoires de Joséphine Baker*, Éditions Corrêa, 1949, p. 86.

26 Jean-Claude Baker and Chris Chase, *Josephine: The Hungry Heart*, Random House, 1993, p. 232.

27 Johannes Mario Simmel, *It Can't Always Be Caviar*, Anthony Blond, 1965; Jacques Abtey and Dr Fritz Unterberg Gibhardt, *2ème Bureau Contre Abwehr*, La Table Ronde, 1967, pp. 89, 91–3.*

28 Ulrich Stoldt, 'Der Legendare Agent Thomas Lieven', Stuttgarter Zeitung, 12/11/2019; Simmel, *It Can't Always Be Caviar*.

29 Abtey, *La Guerre Secrête de Joséphine Baker*, pp. 37–41.*

30 Abtey and Unterberg Gibhardt, *2ème Bureau Contre Abwehr*, p. 92–3.*

31 Ibid; Ulrich Stoldt, Der Legendare Agent Thomas Lieven, Stuttgarter Zeitung, 12/11/2019.

32 Abtey, *La Guerre Secrête de Joséphine Baker*, pp. 37–41.*

33 Abtey and Unterberg Gibhardt, *2ème Bureau Contre Abwehr*, pp. 92–3.*

34 French TNA GR 28 P9 14280, Abtey, p. 80; Abtey, *La Guerre Secrête de Joséphine Baker*, pp. 37–41.*

35 Abtey and Unterberg Gibhardt, *2ème Bureau Contre Abwehr*, p. 94.*

36 Ibid.

37 Ibid.

38 Colonel Rémy, *J.A.*, Éditions Galic, 1961, pp. 28–30.*

39 Ibid., p. 15.*

40 Abtey, *La Guerre Secrête de Joséphine Baker*, pp. 16–17*; Colonel Rémy, *J.A.*, p. 15.*

41 Baker and Bouillon, *Josephine*, p. 119.

42 Colonel Rémy, *J.A.*, p. 15.*

43 Abtey and Unterberg Gibhardt, *2ème Bureau Contre Abwehr*, p. 50.*

44 Colonel Rémy, *J.A.*, p. 16.*

45 Ibid.

46 Philip John Stead, *Second Bureau*, Evans Brothers, 1959, p. 49.

47 Paul Paillole, *L'Homme des Services Secrets: Entretiens avec Alain-Gilles Minella*, Éditions Julliard, 1995, p. 82.*

48 Baker and Bouillon, *Josephine*, p. 120.

49 Paillole, *L'Homme des Services Secrets*, p. 88.*

50 TNA ADM 223/484, German Invasion of UK, p.3 – Germans awaiting air superiority prior to invasion; TNA ADM 223/484 German Invasion of UK, pp. 11–13 – German AF briefs Hitler.

51 'Their Finest Hour', 18 June 1940, International Churchill Society https://winstonchurchill.org/resources/speeches/1940-the-finest-hour/their-finest-hour/

52 Jeffery, *MI6*, pp. 371, 389, 392.

53 Ibid., pp. 346–7.

54 Ibid., p. 390; Documents and photographs held in private Dunderdale family archive, courtesy of Paul Biddle MBE.

55 Paillole, *Services Speciaux 1935–1945*, p. 223.

56 Paillole, *Fighting the Nazis*, p. 180.

57 Paillole, *Services Speciaux 1935–1945*, p. 223.

58 Ibid., pp. 245-6.

59 Ibid., pp. 246.

60 Stead, *Second Bureau*, p. 53.

61 Mémoires de Résistances de la Dordogne, Camouflage du matériel (CDM), http://memoires-resistance.dordogne.fr/dossiers

62 Paillole, *Fighting the Nazis*, pp. 185–6.

63 Quoted in Baker and Bouillon, *Josephine*, p. 121.

64 Hindley, *Destination Casablanca*, p. 91.

65 Ean Wood, *The Josephine Baker Story*, Sanctuary Publishing, 2000, pp. 220–1.

66 Baker and Sauvage, *Les Mémoires*, pp. 128–9.

67 Paillole, *Services Speciaux 1935–1945*, p. 250.

CHAPTER SEVEN

1 French TNA GRZ 2000 1618, J Abtey, p. 1.

2 Paul Paillole, *Fighting the Nazis*, Enigma Books, 2003, p. 188.

3 *Studies in Intelligence*, Vol. 62, No. 1 (Extracts, March 2018), p. 53.

4 Colonel Rémy, *J.A.*, Éditions Galic, 1961, pp. 18–19.*

5 Josephine Baker and Marcel Sauvage, *Les Mémoires de Joséphine Baker*, Éditions Corrêa, 1949, p. 87.

6 Colonel Rémy, *J.A.*, pp. 18–19.*

7 Ibid.

8 Ibid.

9   Ibid.; for wider insight into the veracities, origins and controversies over the 'scalp dance' see https://www.ferris.edu/HTMLS/news/jimcrow/native/homepage.htm

10   Ibid.

11   Ibid.

12   Ean Wood, *The Josephine Baker Story*, Sanctuary Publishing, 2000, p. 222.

13   French Archives File GR 16P 28445, Baker Josephine, pp. 3, 11; French TNA AI 1P 66791, p. 54.

14   Baker and Sauvage, *Les Mémoires*, p. 87.

15   Josephine Baker and Jo Bouillon, *Josephine*, WH Allen, 1978, pp. 120–1.

16   TNA ADM 223/484, German Invasion of UK, pp. 14–16, 17.

17   Jean-Claude Baker and Chris Chase, *Josephine: The Hungry Heart*, Random House, 1993, p. 232.

18   Colonel Rémy, *J.A.*, pp. 16–17.*

19   Ibid.

20   Jacques Abtey, *La Guerre Secrète de Joséphine Baker*, Siboney, 1948, p. 20.*

21   Colonel Rémy, *J.A.*, pp. 16–17.*

22   Ibid.; Abtey, *La Guerre Secrète*, p. 20.*

23   Colonel Rémy, *J.A.*, pp. 16–17.*

24   Abtey, *La Guerre Secrète*, p. 20.*

25   Colonel Rémy, *J.A.*, pp. 16–17.*

26   Abtey, *La Guerre Secrète*, p. 20.*

27   Colonel Rémy, *J.A.*, pp. 16–17.*

28   Ibid.

29   Ibid., p. 10; French TNA GRZ 2000 1618 7959 J Abtey, pp. 4, 41.

30   Colonel Rémy, *J.A.*, pp. 16–17.*

31   Philippe Verrier, *Victor Dillard, SJ*, Marquette University Press, 2017, pp. 38–9, 45.

32   Ibid., pp. 11, 63–70, 72, 73–80, 81.

CHAPTER EIGHT

1   Colonel Rémy, *J.A.*, Éditions Galic, 1961, pp. 16–20.*

2   Ibid.

3   Ibid.

4   Note: Le Besnerais is recorded as 'La Besnerais' in contemporary sources. This has to be a typographical error, for the Director of the SNCF at the time was R. H. Le Besnerais.

5   Robert Lyman, *The Rise of the Third Reich*, Amberley, 2018, p. 235;
    French Archives GR 16P 275626, Albert Guerville File pp. 31–2.

6   Ibid., pp. 17–18.

7   Ibid., pp. 1–7, 14, 15.

8   Colonel Rémy, *J.A.*, pp. 19–20.*

9   Jacques Abtey, *La Guerre Secrète de Joséphine Baker*, Siboney, 1948,
    pp. 24–5.*

10 Ibid.

11 Colonel Rémy, *J.A.*, p. 21.*

12 J. Davies perscom/timeline, p. 15 – J Abtey and J Baker receive Paillole
    telegram.

13 Philippe Verrier, *Victor Dillard, SJ*, Marquette University Press, 2017,
    pp. 83, 170.

14 Ibid., pp. 85, 91, 92–3; Ean Wood, *The Josephine Baker Story*, Sanctuary
    Publishing, 2000, p. 222.

15 Colonel Rémy, *J.A.*, p. 21.*

16 Verrier, *Victor Dillard, SJ*, p. 170.

17 French Govt. Archives File GR 16P 185679, Dillard French Archive,
    pp. 2, 7.

18 Jean-Claude Baker and Chris Chase, *Josephine: The Hungry Heart*,
    Random House, 1993, p. 235.

19 Ibid.

20 Josephine Baker and Jo Bouillon, *Josephine*, WH Allen, 1978, p. 120.

21 Colonel Rémy, *J.A.*, p. 24.*

22 Baker and Bouillon, *Josephine*, pp. 120–1.

23 Paul Paillole, *Fighting the Nazis*, Enigma Books, 2003, p. 196.

24 Abtey, *La Guerre Secrète*, pp. 29–30.*

25 Ibid.

26 Ibid.

27 Paul Paillole, *L'Homme de Services Secrets: Entretiens avec Alain-Gilles
    Minella*, Éditions Julliard, 1995, pp. 7, 14.*

28 Ibid., pp. 16–17, 22, 23.*

29 Ibid.

30 Abtey, *La Guerre Secrète*, p. 20.*

31 Colonel Rémy, *J.A.*, pp. 23, 197.*

32 Ibid.

33 Baker and Bouillon, *Josephine*, p. 120.

34 Meredith Hindley, *Destination Casablanca*, PublicAffairs, 2017, p. 92.

35 Colonel Rémy, *J.A.*, pp. 23, 197.*

36   Baker and Bouillon, *Josephine*, WH Allen, 1978, p. 120.

37   Ibid.

CHAPTER NINE

1   Colonel Rémy, *J.A.*, Éditions Galic, 1961, p. 25.*

2   Meredith Hindley, *Destination Casablanca*, PublicAffairs, 2017, p. 81.

3   Ibid.

4   The Churchill Society, '*Dieu Protége La France*', 21/11/1940, London – http://www.churchill-society-london.org.uk/LaFrance.html

5   Stephen R. Hill, *Boodle's Apocrypha*, Duckworth, 2009, p. 110.

6   Ibid.

7   Mavis Batey, *From Bletchley with Love*, Bletchley Park Trust, 2008

8   Ibid.

9   Ibid.

10   Colonel Rémy, *J.A.*, pp. 24–5.*

11   Jacques Abtey, *La Guerre Secrète de Joséphine Baker*, Siboney, 1948, p. 32.*

12   Ibid.

13   Colonel Rémy, *J.A.*, pp. 24–5.*

14   French Archives File GR 16 P 2170, Abtey Maurice Leonard, p. 28.

15   Colonel Rémy, *J.A.*, p. 24.*

16   Ibid.

17   Abtey, *La Guerre Secrète*, pp. 31–2.*

18   Renée Mussot-Goulard, *Histoire de la Gascogne*, PUF, 1996 – the legend of the Cadets of Gascony.

19   Alan Schroeder, *Josephine Baker Entertainer*, Chelsea House Publishers, 1991, p. 59.

20   Colonel Rémy, *J.A.*, pp. 21–4.*

21   Abtey, *La Guerre Secrète*, pp. 27–8.*

22   Colonel Rémy, *J.A.*, pp. 21–2.*

23   Abtey, *La Guerre Secrète*, p. 27–8.*

24   Colonel Rémy, *J.A.*, pp. 21–2.*

25   Josephine Baker and Marcel Sauvage, *Les Mémoires de Joséphine Baker*, Éditions Corrêa, 1949, pp. 60–1.

26   Ibid.

27   Paul Paillole, *Fighting the Nazis*, Enigma Books, 2003, p. 302.

28   Keith Jeffery, *MI6*, Bloomsbury, 2010, pp. 66–7.

29   Abtey, *La Guerre Secrète*, p. 30*; TNA ADM 223/484, German Invasion of UK, pp. 4–5 – Invasion fleet mustering at French ports.

30 Nicholas Rankin, *Defending the Rock*, Faber & Faber, 2017, p. 1.

31 Paillole, *Services Speciaux, 1935–1945*, Robert Laffont – Opera Mundi, 1975, p. 247.

32 Rankin, *Defending the Rock*, p. 1.

33 TNA CAB 65/1/19, p. 6 –18/9/39 – Fears of HMG that Ireland is ripe for German take-over.

34 TNA KV2-769 Irish Invasion Files/Haller Dr. Kurt, p. 46–8.

35 Ibid., pp. 32, 137.

36 Ibid., p. 108.

37 TNA KV2-769-1, Irish Invasion Files, pp. 6–7; TNA KV2-769, Irish Invasion Files/Haller Dr. Kurt, pp. 56–7.

38 TNA KV2-769, Irish Invasion Files/Haller Dr. Kurt, pp. 107, 114.

39 TNA KV2-769, Irish Invasion Files, pp. 1–2.

40 TNA KV2-769-1, Irish Invasion Files, pp. 6–7.

41 Paillole, *Services Speciaux 1935–1945*, pp. 251–2.

42 TNA KV2-769, Irish Invasion Files/Haller Dr. Kurt, p. 35.

43 Ibid., p. 15.

44 TNA ADM 199/2477, Op Sealion, p. 12.

45 TNA KV2-769, Irish Invasion Files/Haller Dr. Kurt, p. 35.

46 Ibid., p. 14.

47 Ibid., p. 114.

48 Paillole, *Services Speciaux 1935–1945*, pp. 252; TNA KV 2-486, Abwehr and Welsh Nationalists, p. 11.

49 Ibid., p. 3.

50 TNA KV2-769, Irish Invasion Files/Haller Dr. Kurt, p. 55.

51 TNA KV 2/2296, Jahnke Bureau, pp. 13–15.

52 Ibid.

53 TNA KV 2/755, Kurt Jahnke.

54 Hindley, *Destination Casablanca*, p. 92.

55 Ibid.

56 Abtey, *La Guerre Secrète*, p. 33.*

57 Rankin, *Defending the Rock*, pp. 1–5.

58 Ibid.; David A Messenger, 'Against the Grain: Special Operations Executive in Spain, 1941–45', Intelligence & National Security 20:1 (2005), pp. 173–77.

59 Colonel Rémy, *J.A.*, p. 25.*

60 Abtey, *La Guerre Secrète*, p. 33.*

61 Ibid.

CHAPTER TEN

1   Josephine Baker and Marcel Sauvage, *Les Mémoires de Joséphine Baker*, Éditions Corrêa, 1949, p. 88.
2   Neill Lochery, *Lisbon*, PublicAffairs, 2011, pp. 9, 10–11.
3   Ibid., p. 1.
4   Colonel Rémy, *J.A.*, Éditions Galic, 1961, p. 26.*
5   Ibid.
6   Baker and Sauvage, *Les Mémoires*, p. 88.
7   Jacques Abtey, *La Guerre Secrète de Joséphine Baker*, Siboney, 1948, pp. 40–2.*
8   Lochery, *Lisbon*, p. 67.
9   Ibid.
10 Ibid., pp. 179, 201, 203, 211; David A Messenger, 'Against the Grain: Special Operations Executive in Spain, 1941–45', Intelligence & National Security 20:1 (2005), p. 182.
11 Ibid.
12 Ibid.
13 Colonel Rémy, *J.A.*, pp. 28–30.*
14 Abtey, *La Guerre Secrète*, pp. 40–2.*
15 Ibid.
16 Ulrich Stoldt, 'Der Legendare Agent Thomas Lieven', *Stuttgarter Zeitung*, 12/11/2019; Johannes Mario Simmel, *It Can't Always Be Caviar*, Anthony Blond, 1965, London, pp. 76–9.
17 Colonel Rémy, *J.A.*, pp. 28–30*; Jacques Abtey and Dr Fritz Unterberg Gibhardt, *2ème Bureau Contre Abwehr*, La Table Ronde, 1967, pp. 96–7.*
18 Colonel Rémy, *J.A.*, pp. 28–30.*
19 Abtey and Unterberg Gibhardt, *2ème Bureau Contre Abwehr*, pp. 96–7.*
20 'Hotel Palácio Estoril', On The Tracks of 007, – https://www.onthetracksof007.com/palacio
21 Abtey and Unterberg Gibhardt, *2ème Bureau Contre Abwehr*, pp. 96–7.*
22 TNA KV2-769, Irish Invasion Files/Haller Dr. Kurt, p. 134.
23 Lochery, *Lisbon*, p. 148.
24 SHD GR 28 P9 14280, Abtey, pp. 104–5.
25 Ibid., p. 98.
26 Ibid.
27 Lochery, *Lisbon*, p. 158.
28 SHD GR 16P 28445, Baker Josephine, p. 3.
29 SHD AI 1P 66791, p. 54.

30 SHD GR 16 P 2170, Abtey Maurice Leonard, p. 28.

31 Abtey, *La Guerre Secrète*, pp. 35–7.*

32 SHD GR 16 P 2170, Abtey Maurice Leonard, pp. 28, 31.

33 Colonel Rémy, *J.A.*, p. 27.*

34 SHD GR 16 P 2170, Abtey Maurice Leonard, p. 28.

35 Colonel Rémy, *J.A.*, p. 27.*

36 private Dunderdale family archive, various wartime documents and photographs, courtesy of Paul Biddle MBE.

37 Keith Jeffery, *MI6*, Bloomsbury, 2010, pp. 393–4.

38 Philip John Stead, *Second Bureau*, Evans Brothers, 1959, p. 55.

39 Ibid.

40 Sébastien Albertelli, 'The Officers of the BCRA, London, 1940–1944', Prosoprographical study essay, Ministère des Armées, DGSE.

41 Jeffery, *MI6*, pp. 397–8; Rygor Słowikowski, *In the Secret Service*, The Windrush Press, 1988, p. 233; Documents and photographs held in private Dunderdale family archive, courtesy of Paul Biddle MBE.

42 SHD GR 28 P9 14280, Abtey, p. 98.

43 Ibid.

44 Abtey, *La Guerre Secrète*, p. 34.*

45 Colonel Rémy, *J.A.*, p. 31.*

46 Abtey, *La Guerre Secrète*, p. 35.*

47 Abtey and Unterberg Gibhardt, *2ème Bureau Contre Abwehr*, pp. 96–7.*

48 Abtey, *La Guerre Secrète*, p. 47.*

49 Ibid.

50 Ibid., p. 36.*

51 Pedro Cravinho, 'The "Black Angel"', in *Lisbon, EU-topias*, 2019, vol. 18, pp. 121–31.

52 Colonel Rémy, *J.A.*, p. 27.*

CHAPTER ELEVEN

1 Paul Paillole, *L'Homme des Services Secrets: Entretiens avec Alain-Gilles Minella*, Éditions Julliard, 1995, p. 98.*

2 Ibid., p. 87.*

3 Colonel Rémy, *J.A.*, Éditions Galic, 1961, pp. 23, 197.*

4 Jacques Abtey, *La Guerre Secrète de Joséphine Baker*, Siboney, 1948, p. 44.*

5 Josephine Baker and Marcel Sauvage, *Les Mémoires de Joséphine Baker*, Éditions Corrêa, 1949, p. 20.

6   Rygor Słowikowski, *In the Secret Service*, The Windrush Press, 1988, p. 24.

7   'Gay Men Under The Nazi Regime', 2021, United States Holocaust Memorial Museum – https://encyclopedia.ushmm.org/content/en/article/gay-men-under-the-nazi-regime

8   Jean-Claude Baker and Chris Chase, *Josephine: The Hungry Heart*, Random House, 1993, p. 63.

9   Ean Wood, *The Josephine Baker Story*, Sanctuary Publishing, 2000, p. 112.

10 Josephine Baker and Jo Bouillon, *Josephine*, WH Allen, 1978, p. 121.

11 Ibid.

12 Ibid.

13 Baker and Sauvage, *Les Mémoires*, pp. 2–4.

14 Wood, *The Josephine Baker Story*, pp. 184–5.

15 Baker and Chase, *Josephine: The Hungry Heart*, p. 184.

16 Baker and Sauvage, *Les Mémoires*, p. 83.

17 Ibid.

18 Colonel Rémy, *J.A.*, p. 35.*

19 Jacques Abtey and Dr Fritz Unterberg Gibhardt, *2ème Bureau Contre Abwehr*, La Table Ronde, 1967, p. 98.*

20 Colonel Rémy, *J.A.*, p. 34.*

21 'Grand Hôtel Noailles-Métropole, Lieux et Histoires Remarquable', Tourisme-Marseille – https://tourisme-marseille.com/fiche/grand-hotel-noailles-metropole-marseille/

22 Colonel Rémy, *J.A.*, pp. 30–1, 33.*

23 Abtey, *La Guerre Secrète*, p. 52.*

24 Colonel Rémy, *J.A.*, pp. 30–1, 33.*

25 Ibid.

26 TNA FO 371/32221/9, Louis Dreyfus Company, pp. 1–3.

27 SHD GR 16 P 2170, Abtey Maurice Leonard, pp. 28, 32.

28 Abtey, *La Guerre Secrète*, pp. 47–8.*

29 SHD GR 16 P 2170, Abtey Maurice Leonard, p. 32.

30 Ibid.

31 Ibid., pp. 28, 32.

32 Abtey, *La Guerre Secrète*, pp. 47–8.*

33 Colonel Rémy, *J.A.*, pp. 33–4.*

34 SHD GRZ 2000 1618, J Abtey, p. 41.

35 Colonel Rémy, *J.A.*, p. 34.*

36 Hanna Diamond, 'The Starlet-Spy', Medium.com – https://medium.com/truly-adventurous/she-was-a-global-superstar-she-was-a-world-class-spy-df5263d51adc

37 Abtey, *La Guerre Secrète*, p. 52.*

38 Paillole, *L'Homme des Services Secrets*, p. 119.*

39 TNA PREM 3/416, Op Susan, pp. 3–4 – 1/7/1940, War Cabinet briefing on Op Susan.

40 Ibid., pp. 3–10.

41 Ibid.

42 Charles Onana, *Joséphine Baker Contre Hitler*, Éditions Duboiris, 2006, p. 26.

43 Baker and Chase, *Josephine: The Hungry Heart*, p. 267.

44 TNA CAB 12106, 4 July 1940, WSC on need to take Casbalanca.

45 Paillole, *Services Speciaux, 1935–1945*, Robert Laffont – Opera Mundi, 1975, pp. 248–9.

46 Ibid., p. 249.

47 Paul Paillole, *Fighting the Nazis*, Enigma Books, 2003, pp. 198–9, 201.

48 Paillole, *Services Speciaux 1935–1945*, p. 254.

49 Colonel Rémy, *J.A.*, p. 35.*

50 Wood, *The Josephine Baker Story*, p. 227.

51 Ibid.

CHAPTER TWELVE

1 Colonel Rémy, *J.A.*, Éditions Galic, 1961, p. 35.*

2 Jacques Abtey, *La Guerre Secrète de Josephine Baker*, Siboney, 1948, p. 53.*

3 Ibid.

4 Ibid.

5 Ibid.

6 Josephine Baker and Marcel Sauvage, *Les Mémoires de Joséphine Baker*, Éditions Corrêa, 1949, p. 89.

7 Josephine Baker and Jo Bouillon, *Josephine*, WH Allen, 1978, p. 122.

8 Baker and Sauvage, *Les Mémoires*, pp. 12, 50.

9 Ibid., pp. 22–3.

10 Ibid.

11 Ibid., pp. 89–90.

12 Lloyd's Register of Shipping: Steamers and Motorships 1941–42, p. 2 – details of *Gouverneur-Général Gueydon*.

13 SHD GR 28 P9 14280, Abtey, p. 108.

14 Ean Wood, *The Josephine Baker Story*, Sanctuary Publishing, 2000, p. 229.

15 Abtey, *La Guerre Secrète*, p. 56.*

16 Baker and Sauvage, *Les Mémoires*, pp. 15–16.

17 Ibid.

18 Hal Vaughan, *FDR's 12 Apostles*, The Lyons Press, 2006, p. 73.

19 Ibid., pp. 26–7.

20 Ibid., pp. 30–1.

21 Ibid.

22 Ibid., pp. 36–7.

23 Kenneth Pendar, *Adventure in Diplomacy*, Cassell, 1966, pp. 4–5.

24 Marc Wortman, '12 Amateur Spies Paved the Way to War Against the Nazis', *Daily Beast*, 4 September 2018.

25 Robert Murphy, *Diplomat Amongst Warriors*, Collins, 1964, pp. 78–9.

26 Ibid.

27 Letter from President Roosevelt to Ambassador Leahy, 20 December 1940, in *Foreign Relations of the United States: Diplomatic papers, 1940, General and Europe*, Volume 2. Document 490, Credit: US Department of State – https://history.state.gov/historicaldocuments/frus1940v02/d490

28 Ibid.

29 Baker and Bouillon, *Josephine*, p. 123.

30 Baker and Sauvage, *Les Mémoires*, p. 90.

31 Ibid., pp. 78–9.

32 SHD GR 16P 28445, Baker Josephine, p. 11.

33 SHD File GR 16 P 2170, Abtey Maurice Leonard, p. 32.

34 Baker and Bouillon, *Josephine*, p. 124.

35 Colonel Rémy, *J.A.*, p. 38.*

36 Ibid., p. 38.*

37 SHD GR 28 P9 14280, Abtey, p. 107.

38 SHD File GR 16 P 2170, Abtey Maurice Leonard, p. 28.

39 Colonel Rémy, *J.A.*, p. 38.*

40 SHD GR 28 P9 14280, Abtey, p. 107.

41 Abtey, *La Guerre Secrète*, p. 59.*

42 Colonel Rémy, *J.A.*, p. 38.*

43 Abtey, *La Guerre Secrète*, p. 59.*

44 Kevin Labiausse, 'Josephine Baker at the service of the Free French' – http://www.fndirp.asso.fr/josephine%20baker.htm

45 Abtey, *La Guerre Secrète*, p. 59.*
46 Ibid.
47 SHD GR 28 P9 14280, Abtey, p. 107.
48 Meredith Hindley, *Destination Casablanca*, PublicAffairs, 2017, p. 94.
49 Baker and Bouillon, *Josephine*, p. 123.
50 SHD GR 16 P 2170, Abtey Maurice Leonard, p. 28.

CHAPTER THIRTEEN

1   Colonel Rémy, *J.A.*, Éditions Galic, 1961, p. 38.*
2   SHD GR 16 P 2170, Abtey Maurice Leonard, pp. 29, 33.
3   Meredith Hindley, *Destination Casablanca*, PublicAffairs, 2017, pp. xi–xviii.
4   Hal Vaughan, *FDR's 12 Apostles*, The Lyons Press, 2006, p. 45.
5   Ibid., p. 70.
6   Paillole, *Services Speciaux, 1935–1945*, Robert Laffont – Opera Mundi, 1975, p. 285.
7   Paul Paillole, *Fighting the Nazis*, Enigma Books, 2003, p. 272.
8   TNA KV2-769, Haller Dr. Kurt, p. 83.
9   Kenneth Pendar, *Adventure in Diplomacy*, Cassell, 1966, p. 34.
10 Paillole, *Services Speciaux 1935–1945*, p. 343.
11 Ibid., p. 342.
12 Josephine Baker and Marcel Sauvage, *Les Mémoires de Joséphine Baker*, Éditions Corrêa, 1949, p. 91.
13 Keith Jeffery, *MI6*, Bloomsbury, 2010, pp. 320–3.
14 Ibid., pp. 320–3, 414.
15 Ibid.
16 Ibid., p. 415.
17 Colin Cohen, perscom, August 2021 – suggests the rivalry of SIS and SOE is overblown.
18 Jeffery, *MI6*, p. 342.
19 Ibid.; David A Messenger, 'Against the Grain: Special Operations Executive in Spain, 1941–45', Intelligence & National Security 20:1 (2005), p. 175.
20 Jacques Abtey, *La Guerre Secrète de Joséphine Baker*, Siboney, 1948, p. 62.*
21 Jean-Claude Baker and Chris Chase, *Josephine: The Hungry Heart*, Random House, 1993, p. 240.

22 Hindley, *Destination Casablanca*, pp. xi–xviii.

23 Abtey, *La Guerre Secrète*, p. 65.*

24 Baker and Sauvage, *Les Mémoires*, p. 91.

25 Ean Wood, *The Josephine Baker Story*, Sanctuary Publishing, 2000, p. 230.

26 Colonel Rémy, *J.A.*, p. 39.*

27 Abtey, *La Guerre Secrète*, p. 61.*

28 SHD GR 28 P9 14280, Abtey, p. 107.

29 Colonel Rémy, *J.A.*, p. 39.*

30 Hanna Diamond, 'The Starlet-Spy', Medium.com – https://medium.com/truly-adventurous/she-was-a-global-superstar-she-was-a-world-class-spy-df5263d51adc

31 Jeffery, *MI6*, p. 743.

32 Hindley, *Destination Casablanca*, p. 94.

33 Baker and Chase, *Josephine: The Hungry Heart*, Random House, 1993, p. 227.

34 Baker and Sauvage, *Les Mémoires*, p. 91.

35 Abtey, *La Guerre Secrète*, p. 62.*

36 Ibid.

37 Damien Lewis, *SAS Ghost Patrol*, Quercus, 2017, p. 19.

38 Baker and Chase, *Josephine: The Hungry Heart*, p. 240.

39 Abtey, *La Guerre Secrète*, p. 62.

40 Ibid.

41 Jeffery, *MI6*, p. 408.

42 SHD GR 28 P9 14280, Abtey, p. 108.

43 Abtey, *La Guerre Secrète*, p. 129.*

44 Paul Paillole, *Fighting The Nazis*, Enigma Books, 2003, p. 197; Stephen R. Hill, *Boodle's Apocrypha*, Duckworth, 2009, p. 134.

45 Dermot Turing, *X, Y & Z*, The History Press, 2018, pp. 175–6, 185.

46 Neill Lochery, *Lisbon*, PublicAffairs, 2011, p. 151.

47 TNA F0 950/965, 7 OCTOBER 1941 H TO D/FIN & F0 950/965, 9 JANUARY 1941: A/DW TO CD – paranoia in Lisbon that Portugal will be invaded.

48 Lochery, *Lisbon*, p. 151.

CHAPTER FOURTEEN

1 Jacques Abtey, *La Guerre Secrète de Joséphine Baker*, Siboney, 1948, pp. 62–3.*

2 Ibid.

3   'Churchill's World – Hotel La Mamounia', The International Churchill Society – https://winstonchurchill.org/publications/finest-hour/finest-hour-108/churchill-s-world-hotel-la-mamounia-marrakech-morocco/

4   Con Coughlin, 'Marrakesh: where Churchill and Roosevelt played hookey', The Telegraph, 10 April 2013.

5   Gavin Maxwell, Lords of the Atlas, Eland Publishing, 2004, p. 198.

6   Kenneth Pendar, Adventure in Diplomacy, Cassell, 1966, pp. 57–9.

7   Ean Wood, The Josephine Baker Story, Sanctuary Publishing, 2000, p. 231.

8   Jean-Claude Baker and Chris Chase, Josephine: The Hungry Heart, Random House, 1993, p. 241.

9   Colonel Rémy, J.A., Éditions Galic, 1961, pp. 40–1.*

10 Abtey, La Guerre Secrète, p. 65.*

11 Ibid.

12 Colonel Rémy, J.A., Éditions Galic, 1961, pp. 40–1.*

13 Bennetta Jules-Rosette, Josephine Baker in Art and Life, University of Illinois Press, 2007, p. 117.

14 Colonel Rémy, J.A., pp. 40–1.*

15 Josephine Baker and Jo Bouillon, Josephine, WH Allen, 1978, p. 136.

16 Jean-Claude Baker and Chris Chase, Josephine: The Hungry Heart, Random House, 1993, p. 250.

17 Ibid.

18 Ibid.

19 Ibid.

20 Ibid.

21 Colonel Rémy, J.A., pp. 40–1.*

22 Baker and Bouillon, Josephine, p. 125.

23 Abtey, La Guerre Secrète, p. 67.*

24 Paul Paillole, Fighting the Nazis, Enigma Books, 2003, p. 273.

25 TNA HS 3/203, SOE/OSS Morocco, p. 72; TNA HS9/1221/3, Hugh Quennell; TNA HS9/1332/5, Charles Hilary Scott.

26 TNA HS 9/1332/6, Charles Hilary Scott.

27 TNA HS 3/203, SOE/OSS Morocco, p. 72.

28 Neill Lochery, Lisbon, PublicAffairs, 2011, pp. 61–3.

29 Colonel Rémy, J.A., p. 41.

30 Ibid.

31 Abtey, La Guerre Secrète, p. 66–7.*

32 Ibid.

33 Ibid.

34 Paul Paillole, *L'Homme des Services Secrets: Entretiens avec Alain-Gilles Minella*, Éditions Julliard, 1995, p. 47.*

35 Baker and Sauvage, *Les Mémoires*, pp. 43–7.

36 Ibid.

37 Ibid.

38 Colonel Rémy, *J.A.*, p. 41.*

39 Ean Wood, *The Josephine Baker Story*, Sanctuary Publishing, 2000, p. 230.

40 Ibid.

CHAPTER FIFTEEN

1   Hal Vaughan, *FDR's 12 Apostles*, The Lyons Press, 2006, p. xiv; Marc Wortman, '12 Amateur Spies Paved the Way to War Against the Nazis', *Daily Beast*, 4 September 2018, p. 6.

2   Meredith Hindley, *Destination Casablanca*, PublicAffairs, 2017, p. 109.

3   Robert Murphy, *Diplomat Among Warriors*, Doubleday, 1964, p. 91.

4   Vaughan, *FDR's 12 Apostles*, pp. 46–7.

5   Murphy, *Diplomat Amongst Warriors*, p. 91.

6   Kenneth Pendar, *Adventure in Diplomacy*, Cassell, 1966, pp. 24–5.

7   Vaughan, *FDR's 12 Apostles*, p. 61.

8   Ibid.

9   Ibid., p. 72.

10 Ibid., p. xiv.

11 'Kenneth Pendar, Ex-Vice Consul', obituary, *New York Times*, 8 December 1972.

12 Pendar, *Adventure in Diplomacy*, pp. 22–3.

13 Ibid.

14 Ibid.

15 Ibid., p. 38.

16 Vaughan, *FDR's 12 Apostles*, p. 66.

17 Pendar, *Adventure in Diplomacy*, p. 23.

18 Jacques Abtey, *La Guerre Secrète de Joséphine Baker*, Siboney, 1948, p. 68.*

19 'The Aesthete Looks at Hotels and Restaurants in Marrakech', *The Aesthete*, 31 July 2021 – https://www.architecturaldigest.com/story/the-aesthete-marrakech-morocco-architecture (NB: The Villa Taylor is also known by its local name, La Saadia.)

20 Vaughan, *FDR's 12 Apostles*, pp. 67–9.

21　Ibid.

22　Pendar, *Adventure in Diplomacy*, p. 63.

23　Vaughan, *FDR's 12 Apostles*, p. 67–9.

24　Pendar, *Adventure in Diplomacy*, p. 12.

25　TNA HS 3/203, SOE/OSS Morocco, pp. 11–12.

26　Abtey, *La Guerre Secrète*, pp. 68–9.*

27　Hindley, *Destination Casablanca*, pp. 142–3.

28　Vaughan, *FDR's 12 Apostles*, pp. 131–2.

29　TNA HS 3/203, SOE/OSS Morocco, pp. 62, 63, 64.

30　private Dunderdale family archive, various wartime documents and photographs, courtesy of Paul Biddle MBE; SHD GR 16 P 2170, Abtey Maurice Leonard, p. 32.

31　SHD GR 16 P 2170 Abtey Maurice Leonard, p. 29.

CHAPTER SIXTEEN

1　Josephine Baker and Jo Bouillon, *Josephine*, WH Allen, 1978, pp. 125–6.

2　SHD AI 1P 66791, p. 54.

3　Baker and Bouillon, *Josephine*, p. 126.

4　Kenneth Pendar, *Adventure in Diplomacy*, Cassell, 1966, p. 73.

5　Ibid.

6　Jacques Abtey, *La Guerre Secrète de Joséphine Baker*, Siboney, 1948, p. 68.*

7　Colonel Rémy, *J.A.*, Éditions Galic, 1961, p. 42.*

8　Josephine Baker and Marcel Sauvage, *Les Mémoires de Joséphine Baker*, Éditions Corrêa, 1949, p. 93.

9　Ean Wood, *The Josephine Baker Story*, Sanctuary Publishing, 2000, p. 175.

10　Baker and Bouillon, *Josephine*, pp. 126–7.

11　Colonel Rémy, *J.A.*, p. 42.*

12　Baker and Bouillon, *Josephine*, pp. 126–7; Meredith Hindley, *Destination Casablanca*, PublicAffairs, 2017, pp. 183–4. Some sources argue J. Baker's illness may had been due to other causes – a miscarriage, or even poisoning. See this entry. But most sources – Abtey and Baker included – cite the botched X-ray as the cause.

13　Colonel Rémy, *J.A.*, p. 43.*

14　Ibid.

15　Abtey, *La Guerre Secrète*, pp. 71–2.*

16　Lynn Haney, *Naked at the Feast*, Robson Books, 1981, pp. 225–6. There are conflicting reports as to what exactly made J. Baker ill at this time; these include that she had been poisoned, or that she had been pregnant and that the child was stillborn. For an alternative account see this reference.

17 Abtey, *La Guerre Secrète*, pp. 71–2.*
18 Baker and Bouillon, *Josephine*, pp. 126–7.
19 Abtey, *La Guerre Secrète*, pp. 71–2.*
20 Wood, *The Josephine Baker Story*, p. 134.
21 Ibid.
22 Abtey, *La Guerre Secrète*, pp. 71–2.*
23 Ibid.
24 Ibid.
25 Ibid.
26 Ibid.
27 Ibid., pp. 73–6.*
28 Jean-Claude Baker and Chris Chase, *Josephine: The Hungry Heart*, Random House, 1993, p. 244.
29 Abtey, *La Guerre Secrète*, pp. 73–8.*
30 Ibid.
31 Baker and Sauvage, *Les Mémoires*, p. 94.
32 Abtey, *La Guerre Secrète*, pp. 73–8.*
33 Ibid.
34 Baker and Sauvage, *Les Mémoires*, p. 94.
35 Pendar, *Adventure in Diplomacy*, p. 39.
36 Baker and Bouillon, *Josephine*, pp. 126–7.
37 SHD GR 16P 28445, Baker Josephine, p. 9.
38 Ibid., p. 11.
39 Abtey, *La Guerre Secrète*, pp. 73–8.*
40 Baker and Sauvage, *Les Mémoires*, p. 6.
41 WO 373/153 Recommendation for Award for Gérar-Dubot, Paul.
42 Paul Paillole, *Fighting the Nazis*, Enigma Books, 2003, p. 281.
43 Colonel Rémy, *J.A.*, p. 43.*
44 Kevin Labiausse, 'Josephine Baker at the Service of the Free French', www.fndirp/fr, p. 3.
45 Charles Onana, *Joséphine Baker Contre Hitler*, Éditions Duboiris, 2006, p. 36.

CHAPTER SEVENTEEN

1 TNA HS 6/345 SOE France, "SAVANNA" & "JOSEPHINE B", pp. 3–39.
2 Ibid.

3   Francis Brooks Richards, *Secret Flotillas*, Vol. 1, Pen & Sword, 2012, pp. 88–9.

4   TNA HS 6/345 SOE France, "SAVANNA" & "JOSEPHINE B", pp. 3–39.

5   Paul Paillole, *L'Homme des Services Secrets: Entretiens avec Alain-Gilles Minella*, Éditions Julliard, 1995, p. 4*; Paul Paillole, *Fighting the Nazis*, Enigma Books, 2003, p. 269.

6   'Einsatzgruppen, An Overview', United States Holocaust Memorial Museum – https://encyclopedia.ushmm.org/content/en/article/einsatzgruppen

7   TNA ADM 199/2477, Op Sealion, pp. 44–6.

8   Kenneth Pendar, *Adventure in Diplomacy*, Cassell, 1966, p. 66.

9   Colonel Rémy, *J.A.*, Éditions Galic, 1961, p. 44–6.*

10 Ibid.

11 Ibid.

12 Ibid., p. 50.

13 Ibid.

14 Ibid.

15 Ibid.

16 Ibid.

17 Ibid., pp. 52–3.

18 Ibid.

19 Tim Newark, *The Mafia at War*, Frontline Books, 2007, pp. 70–3.

20 Keith Jeffery, *MI6*, Bloomsbury, 2010, p. 439.

21 Newark, *The Mafia at War*, pp. 90–8.

22 Ibid., p. 135.

23 Colonel Rémy, *J.A.*, p. 54.*

24 'H for History, Pearl Harbor' – https://www.history.com/topics/world-war-ii/pearl-harbor

25 Jacques Abtey, *La Guerre Secrète de Joséphine Baker*, Siboney, 1948, pp. 79–80.*

26 Ibid.

27 Ean Wood, *The Josephine Baker Story*, Sanctuary Publishing, 2000, p. 234.

28 Pendar, *Adventure in Diplomacy*, p. 69.

29 Ibid., p. 74.

30 Pearl Harbor! 80th Anniversary of the Attack that brought the United States into the Second World War, International Churchill Society, 28 November 2021

31 Josephine Baker and Marcel Sauvage, *Les Mémoires de Joséphine Baker*, Éditions Corrêa, 1949, p. 94.

32 Jean-Claude Baker and Chris Chase, *Josephine: The Hungry Heart*, Random House, 1993, p. 145.

33 Abtey, *La Guerre Secrète*, p. 80.*

34 Colonel Rémy, *J.A.*, pp. 54–5.*

35 Ibid.

36 Ibid.

37 Newark, *The Mafia at War*, pp. 129–30.

38 SHD GRZ 2000 1618, J Abtey, p. 29.

CHAPTER EIGHTEEN

1 TNA HS 6-971, Musson's Smuggling Fleet, p. 1.

2 'Secret Fishing Fleet Carried Spies to France', *The Times*, 5 February 1996, p. 1.

3 Quoted in Nicholas Rankin, *Defending the Rock*, Faber & Faber, 2017, pp. 13–15.

4 TNA HS 9/1080/5, Musson, pp. 25–6.

5 Ibid., p. 6.

6 Ibid., pp. 18, 21, 23, 24.

7 TNA HS 6-971, Musson's Smuggling Fleet, p. 129; TNA HS 3/203, SOE/OSS Morocco, pp. 3, 14.

8 Ian Piper FCPFA, 'John Venner FCA: A virtuous man and Baker Street Irregular: The accountant at the centre of the Special Operations Executive's web of financial warfare 1940-45,'(2022 unpublished academic paper, under peer review); Personal communications with Ian Piper FCPFA, PhD Student at University of Portsmouth.

9 TNA HS 6-971, Musson's Smuggling Fleet, pp. 126–7.

10 Francis Brooks Richards, *Secret Flotillas*, Frank Cass Publishers, Volume 2, 2004, pp. 23–4. NB: Kadulski adopted the *nom de guerre* of Krajewski; TNA HS 6-971, Musson's Smuggling Fleet, pp. 10–16.

11 Ibid., p. 86.

12 Ibid., p. 122.

13 Ibid., p. 25.

14 Ibid., p. 58.

15 Ibid., p. 60.

16 TNA HS 3/203, SOE/OSS Morocco, pp. 16, 19.

17 Ibid., p. 62.

18 Brooks Richards, *Secret Flotillas*, Volume 2, p. 92.

19 Colonel Rémy, *J.A.*, Éditions Galic, 1961, pp. 55–67.*

20 Marcel Jullian, *H.M.S Fidelity*, Souvenir Press, 1957, pp. 128–60.

21 Colonel Rémy, *J.A.*, p. 55–6.

22 Ibid.

23 Tim Newark, *The Mafia at War*, Frontline Books, 2007, p. 194.

24 Colonel Rémy, *J.A.*, pp. 55–6.*

25 Ibid.

26 Rygor Słowikowski, *In the Secret Service*, The Windrush Press, 1988, pp. 21–2.

27 Ibid., p. 83.

28 Ibid, p. xvii.

29 American Society of the Legion of Honour, 'Josephine Baker, Chevalier (1906–1975)', *ASFLH Newsletter*, Summer 2020, Vol. 27, No. 2, p. 3.

30 Charles Onana, *Joséphine Baker Contre Hitler*, Éditions Duboiris, 2006, p. 36.

31 Jean-Claude Baker and Chris Chase, *Josephine: The Hungry Heart*, Random House, 1993, p. 245.

32 Lynn Haney, *Naked at the Feast*, Robson Books, 1981, p. 226.

33 Quoted in Onana, *Joséphine Baker Contre Hitler*, pp. 35–6.

34 Ibid.

35 Josephine Baker and Marcel Sauvage, *Les Mémoires de Joséphine Baker*, Éditions Corrêa, 1949, p. 94.

CHAPTER NINETEEN

1 Colonel Rémy, *J.A.*, Éditions Galic, 1961, pp. 59–60.*

2 Ibid.

3 Ibid.

4 'Night & Fog Decree', United States Holocaust Memorial Museum, https://encyclopedia.ushmm.org/content/en/article/night-and-fog-de-cree

5 Colonel Rémy, *J.A.*, p. 62–5.*

6 Ibid.

7 Ibid.

8 Ibid.

9 Hal Vaughan, *FDR's 12 Apostles*, The Lyons Press, 2006, pp. 76–7.

10 Colonel Rémy, *J.A.*, p. 68.*

11 Ibid.

12 Ibid.

13 Ibid., pp. 69–71.*

14   Ibid., pp. 78–9.*

15   Ibid., p. 90.*

16   Jacques Abtey, *La Guerre Secrète de Joséphine Baker*, Siboney, 1948, p. 81.*

17   Paul Paillole, *L'Homme des Services Secrets: Entretiens avec Alain-Gilles Minella*, Éditions Julliard, 1995, pp. 118–19.*

18   Vaughan, *FDR's 12 Apostles*, p. 127.

19   SHD GR 16 P 2170, Abtey Maurice Leonard, p. 32.

20   Colonel Rémy, *J.A.*, pp. 92–3.*

21   Ibid., p. 104.*

22   Abtey, *La Guerre Secrète*, p. 82.*

23   Tim Newark, *The Mafia at War*, Frontline Books, 2007, p. 99.

24   Josephine Baker and Jo Bouillon, *Josephine*, WH Allen, 1978, p. 128.

25   Ibid.

26   Abtey, *La Guerre Secrète*, p. 82.*

27   Ibid.

28   Colonel Rémy, *J.A.*, p. 117.*

29   Abtey, *La Guerre Secrète*, pp. 85-6.*

30   Ibid.

31   Ibid.

CHAPTER TWENTY

1   Ean Wood, *The Josephine Baker Story*, Sanctuary Publishing, 2000, p. 42.

2   Josephine Baker and Marcel Sauvage, *Les Mémoires de Joséphine Baker*, Éditions Corrêa, 1949, p. 74.

3   Jacques Abtey, *La Guerre Secrète de Joséphine Baker*, Siboney, 1948, pp. 90–1.*

4   Ibid.

5   Ibid., p. 85.*

6   Ibid., p. 91.*

7   Ibid.

8   Baker and Sauvage, *Les Mémoires*, p. 94.

9   Abtey, *La Guerre Secrète*, p. 85.*

10   Baker and Sauvage, *Les Mémoires*, p. 94.

11   Ibid.

12   Kenneth Pendar, *Adventure in Diplomacy*, Cassell, 1966, pp. 328–30.

13   Ibid.

14   Meredith Hindley, *Destination Casablanca*, PublicAffairs, 2017, pp. 155–164.

15 Winston Churchill, *The Hinge of Fate: The Second World War*, Vol. 4, New York, Bantam, 1965, p. 335.

16 Ibid., p. 404.

17 Ibid., p. 405.

18 Hal Vaughan, *FDR's 12 Apostles*, The Lyons Press, 2006, pp. 72, 143–4, 158.

19 Lynn Haney, *Naked at the Feast*, Robson Books, 1981, p. 219.

20 'France, Key Facts', United States Holocaust Memorial Museum – https://encyclopedia.ushmm.org/content/en/article/france

21 Abtey, *La Guerre Secrète*, pp. 119–20.*

22 Haney, *Naked at the Feast*, p. 228.

23 Ibid.

24 Josephine Baker and Jo Bouillon, *Josephine*, WH Allen, 1978, p. 128.

25 Abtey, *La Guerre Secrète*, p. 119.*

26 Langston Hughes, 'Josephine Baker Obituary', *Chicago Defender*, quoted in Christopher Klein, 'Josephine Baker's Daring Double Life as a WWII Spy', 15 March 2021 – https://www.history.com/news/josephine-baker-world-war-ii-spy

27 Jean-Claude Baker and Chris Chase, *Josephine: The Hungry Heart*, Random House, 1993, p. 248.

28 Wood, *The Josephine Baker Story*, p. 15.

29 Daisy Fancourt, 'Maurice Chevalier, Music and the Holocaust', ORT – https://holocaustmusic.ort.org/resistance-and-exile/french-resistance/maurice-chevalier/

30 TNA HO 382/10, M Chevalier, pp. 1–37.

31 Ibid.

32 Ibid.

33 Baker and Bouillon, *Josephine*, p. 129.

34 Vaughan, *FDR's 12 Apostles*, p. 153.

35 Abtey, *La Guerre Secrète*, pp. 93–4.*

36 Ibid.

37 Hindley, *Destination Casablanca*, p. 181.

38 Colonel Rémy, *J.A.*, Éditions Galic, 1961, p. 125.*

39 Abtey, *La Guerre Secrète*, p. 95.*

40 Vaughan, *FDR's 12 Apostles*, pp. 112, 127.

41 Baker and Sauvage, *Les Mémoires*, p. 7.

42 Keith Jeffery, *MI6*, Bloomsbury, 2010, pp. 529, 531.

43 Hindley, *Destination Casablanca*, pp. 180, 214–16.

44 Martin Blumenston, *The Patton Papers: 1940–1945*, Houghton Mifflin, 1974, p. 68.

45 'Operation Torch', *Encyclopaedia Britannica* – https://www.britannica.com/event/North-Africa-campaigns/Operation-Torch

46 Abtey, *La Guerre Secrète*, p. 95–6.*

47 Ibid.

48 Colonel Rémy, *J.A.*, pp. 123–5.*

49 'Correct Attributions or Red Herrings?', International Churchill Society, 23 May 2013 – https://winstonchurchill.org/publications/finest-hour/finest-hour-130/correct-attributions-or-red-herrings/

50 Vaughan, *FDR's 12 Apostles*, pp. 175–6.

51 Paillole, *Services Speciaux, 1935–1945,* Robert Laffont – Opera Mundi, 1975, p. 409.

52 Rick Atkinson, *An Army at Dawn*, Henry Holt & Company, 2002, p. 3.

53 Vaughan, *FDR's 12 Apostles*, pp. 184–5.

54 Ibid., p. 199.

CHAPTER TWENTY-ONE

1 Meredith Hindley, *Destination Casablanca*, PublicAffairs, 2017, p. 253.

2 Quoted in George F. Howe, *Northwest Africa*, University Press of the Pacific, 2005, p. 125.

3 Colonel Rémy, *J.A.*, Éditions Galic, 1961, p. 126.*

4 Josephine Baker and Jo Bouillon, *Josephine*, WH Allen, 1978, p. 129.

5 Colonel Rémy, *J.A.*, p. 126.*

6 Jacques Abtey, *La Guerre Secrète de Joséphine Baker*, Siboney, 1948, p. 103.*

7 Hindley, *Destination Casablanca*, pp. 259–63.

8 Hal Vaughan, *FDR's 12 Apostles*, The Lyons Press, 2006, p. 219.

9 Hindley, *Destination Casablanca*, pp. 300–5.

10 Ibid.

11 Abtey, *La Guerre Secrète*, p. 99.*

12 Baker and Bouillon, *Josephine*, p. 129.

13 Colonel Rémy, *J.A.*, p. 114–15.*

14 Abtey, *La Guerre Secrète*, pp. 99–100.*

15 Ibid.

16 Colonel Rémy, *J.A.*, p. 127.*

17 Abtey, *La Guerre Secrète*, p. 101.*

18 Ibid., p. 98.*

19 SHD GR 16 P 2170, Abtey Maurice Leonard, p. 32.

20 Abtey, *La Guerre Secrète*, p. 101.*

21 Josephine Baker and Marcel Sauvage, *Les Mémoires de Joséphine Baker*, Éditions Corrêa, 1949, p. 95.

22 Ibid.

23 Marc Wortman, '12 Amateur Spies Paved the Way to War Against the Nazis', *Daily Beast*, 4 September 2018, p. 14.

24 Rygor Słowikowski, *In The Secret Service*, The Windrush Press, 1988, p. 248.

25 'The End of the Beginning', The Churchill Society, London – http://www.churchill-society-london.org.uk/EndoBegn.html

26 Hindley, *Destination Casablanca*, pp. 320–7.

27 Martin Blumenston, *The Patton Papers: 1940–1945*, Houghton Mifflin, 1974, pp. 94–6.

28 Paul Paillole, *Fighting the Nazis*, Enigma Books, 2003, p. 330.

29 Paillole, *Services Speciaux, 1935–1945*, Robert Laffont – Opéra Mundi, 1975, p. 407.

30 Ibid., p. 428.

31 Baker and Sauvage, *Les Mémoires*, p. 91.

32 Colonel Rémy, *J.A.*, pp. 128–9.*

33 Ibid.

34 Ibid.

35 Ean Wood, *The Josephine Baker Story*, Sanctuary Publishing, 2000, pp. 237, 235.

36 'Josephine Baker Is Safe', *New York Times*, 6 December 1942.

37 Christopher Klein, 'Josephine Baker's Daring Double Life as a WWII Spy', 15 March 2021 – https://www.history.com/news/josephine-baker-world-war-ii-spy

CHAPTER TWENTY-TWO

1 Meredith Hindley, *Destination Casablanca*, PublicAffairs, 2017, p. 385.

2 William Whitworth, 'African-American Red Cross Social Clubs', Northeastern University, 24 April 2020, p. 2 – https://dcrn.northeastern.edu/african-american-red-cross-social-clubs/

3 Colonel Rémy, *J.A.*, Éditions Galic, 1961, p. 131.*

4 Ean Wood, *The Josephine Baker Story*, Sanctuary Publishing, 2000, pp. 29–31.

5 Jacques Abtey, *La Guerre Secrète de Joséphine Baker*, Siboney, 1948, p. 107.*

6 Josephine Baker and Jo Bouillon, *Josephine*, WH Allen, 1978, p. 130.

7   Ibid., p. 137.

8   Hindley, *Destination Casablanca*, p. 385; Baker and Bouillon, *Josephine*, p. 130.

9   Josephine Baker and Marcel Sauvage, *Les Mémoires de Joséphine Baker*, Éditions Corrêa, 1949, p. 96.

10 Ibid., pp. 80–1.

11 Colonel Rémy, *J.A.*, p. 131.*; Letter from Josephine Baker to Colonel Remy (sic), 22 January 1962, courtesy of the Association for the Defence and the Memory of Colonel Rémy.

12 Ken Crawford, *Report on North Africa*, Farrar & Rinehart, 1943, p. 43.

13 Baker and Bouillon, *Josephine*, p. 131.

14 Abtey, *La Guerre Secrète*, p. 108.*

15 Lynn Haney, *Naked at the Feast*, Robson Books, 1981, pp. 231–2.

16 Colonel Rémy, *J.A.*, p. 131.*

17 Abtey, *La Guerre Secrète*, p. 108.*

18 Colonel Rémy, *J.A.*, pp. 131–2.*

19 Ibid.

20 Jean-Claude Baker and Chris Chase, *Josephine: The Hungry Heart*, Random House, 1993, pp. 251–2.

21 Ibid.

22 'The Theatre: New Plays in Manhattan', *Time*, 10 February 1936 – http://content.time.com/time/subscriber/article/0,33009,755816,00.html

23 Baker and Chase, *Josephine: The Hungry Heart*, pp. 251–2.

24 'The Theatre: New Plays in Manhattan', *Time*.

25 Abtey, *La Guerre Secrète*, p. 109.*

26 Ibid., p. 214. *

27 Abtey, *La Guerre Secrète*, p. 110.*

28 Baker and Bouillon, *Josephine*, pp. 131–2.

29 Abtey, *La Guerre Secrète*, p. 112.*

30 Baker and Bouillon, *Josephine*, pp. 131–2.

31 Abtey, *La Guerre Secrète*, p. 108.

32 Kenneth Pendar, *Adventure in Diplomacy*, Cassell, 1966, p. 131.

33 Abtey, *La Guerre Secrète*, p. 108.* NB: Some accounts record Archie Roosevelt, FDR's fifth son, as also being present at this party, but he was not in North Africa at this time; Hindley, *Destination Casablanca*, p. 355.

34 Colonel Rémy, *J.A.*, p. 133–4.*

35 Ibid.

36 Ibid.

37 Ibid.

38 Hindley, *Destination Casablanca*, p. 407.

39 SHD GR28 P9 390, J Baker, p. 16.

40 Ibid.

41 Ibid.

42 Abtey, *La Guerre Secrète*, p. 111.*

43 Hindley, *Destination Casablanca*, pp. 380–1.

44 Press Conference, 24 January 1943, The Conference at Washington, 1941–1942, and Casablanca, 1943, *FRUS*, p. 727.

45 Meeting of Combined Chiefs of Staff, Roosevelt, and Churchill, 18 January 1943, *FRUS*, 1943, p. 635.

46 Paul Paillole, *Fighting the Nazis*, Enigma Books, 2003, p. 379.

47 Abtey, *La Guerre Secrète*, pp. 133–5.*

48 SHD GR 28 P9 14280, Abtey, p. 102.

49 Ibid., p. 98.

50 Ibid., p. 95.

51 1943.-D.-No. 465, In The High Court of Justice. King's Bench Division. Folio 23. Writ issued the 6th day of August, 1943, Thomas Cooper & Co., London, pp. 1–5 – Dufour's case as brought in High Court.

52 Ibid.

53 Ibid.

54 Ibid.

55 TNA CAB 66/50/36, War Cabinet, The Dufour Case, p. 23.

56 'The Dirty War on our Doorstep', *The Times*, 1 April 2021, pp. 14–15 (Dufour case).

57 Ibid., pp. 18–19.

58 Ibid., pp. 14–15.

59 Ibid.

60 Ibid.

61 Abtey, *La Guerre Secrète*, p. 123.*

CHAPTER TWENTY-THREE

1 Josephine Baker and Marcel Sauvage, *Les Mémoires de Joséphine Baker*, Éditions Corrêa, 1949, pp. 98–9.

2 Josephine Baker and Jo Bouillon, *Josephine*, WH Allen, 1978, p. 132.

3 Jean-Claude Baker and Chris Chase, *Josephine: The Hungry Heart*, Random House, 1993, pp. 253.

4 Baker and Bouillon, *Josephine*, WH Allen, 1978, p. 133.

5   Baker and Sauvage, *Les Mémoires*, pp. 97–8.
6   Baker and Chase, *Josephine: The Hungry Heart*, pp. 252–4.
7   Ibid.
8   Baker and Sauvage, *Les Mémoires*, pp. 97–8.
9   Baker and Bouillon, *Josephine*, WH Allen, 1978, p. 133.
10 Jacques Abtey, *La Guerre Secrète de Joséphine Baker*, Siboney, 1948, p. 126.*
11 Jean-Pierre. Reggiori, interview with author, 2021, p. 2.
12 Alan Schroeder, *Josephine Baker: Entertainer*, Chelsea House Publishers, 1991, p. 75.
13 Abtey, *La Guerre Secrète*, pp. 126–7.*
14 Ibid.
15 Francis Brooks Richards, *Secret Flotillas*, Vol. 2, Frank Cass Publishers, 2004, pp. 212–13.
16 Baker and Sauvage, *Les Mémoires*, p. 98.
17 Abtey, *La Guerre Secrète*, pp. 130–1.*
18 Ibid.
19 Ibid.
20 SHD GR 16 P 2170, Abtey Maurice Leonard, pp. 29, 38, 50.
21 Abtey, *La Guerre Secrète*, p. 132.*
22 Ibid.
23 Henry Hurford Janes – Josephine Baker Collection, Collection Call Number JWJ MSS 2, Beinecke Rare Book and Manuscript Library, Archives at Yale
24 SHD GR28 P9 390, J Baker, pp. 9–10.
25 Abtey, *La Guerre Secrète*, pp. 133.*
26 Bryan Hammond and Patrick O'Connor, *Josephine Baker*, Jonathan Cape, 1988, p. 178.
27 Ean Wood, *The Josephine Baker Story*, Sanctuary Publishing, 2000, pp. 238–9.
28 Ibid.
29 Sheridan Morley, *A Talent to Amuse*, Heinemann, 1969.
30 Baker and Sauvage, *Les Mémoires*, p. 133.
31 Baker and Chase, *Josephine: The Hungry Heart*, pp. 252–3.
32 Abtey, *La Guerre Secrète*, p. 139*; E.N.S.A. (Inquiry), HC Deb 29 November 1945 vol. 416 cc1725-34m, *Hansard*, p. 1. NB: 'Colonel Dunstan' appears to be the correct spelling of this individual's name, though it is also rendered 'Dunston' and 'Dunstean' in other sources.
33 Abtey, *La Guerre Secrète*, p. 137.*

34　Ibid.

35　Colonel Rémy, *J.A.*, Éditions Galic, 1961, pp. 166-7.*

36　TNA HS 3/203, SOE/OSS Morocco, p. 3–7.

37　Abtey, *La Guerre Secrète*, pp. 140–1.*

38　Ibid., pp. 134–5.*

39　Ibid.

40　Ibid.

CHAPTER TWENTY-FOUR

1　'De Gaulle Calls For 4th Republic', *New York Times*, 15 July 1943.

2　Jean-Claude Baker and Chris Chase, *Josephine: The Hungry Heart*, Random House, 1993, p. 256.

3　SHD GR28 P9 390, J Baker, p. 6.

4　Baker and Chase, *Josephine: The Hungry Heart*, p. 256.

5　Meredith Hindley, *Destination Casablanca*, PublicAffairs, 2017, p. 415.

6　Josephine Baker and Jo Bouillon, *Josephine*, WH Allen, 1978, p. 130.

7　Ibid., p. 135.

8　Hindley, *Destination Casablanca*, p. 416.

9　Colonel Rémy, *J.A.*, Éditions Galic, 1961, p. 148.*

10　Ibid.

11　'Paul-Hémir Mezan', Musée de l'Ordre de la Libération, pp. 1–2 – https://www.ordredelaliberation.fr/fr/compagnons/paul-hemir-mezan

12　Ibid.

13　Jacques Abtey, *La Guerre Secrète de Joséphine Baker*, Siboney, 1948, p. 150.*

14　Colonel Rémy, *J.A.*, pp. 148–9.*

15　Ibid.

16　Ibid.

17　Josephine Baker and Marcel Sauvage, *Les Mémoires de Joséphine Baker*, Éditions Corrêa, 1949, p. 99.

18　Colonel Rémy, *J.A.*, p. 150.*

19　Ibid.

20　Ibid.

21　Baker and Sauvage, *Les Mémoires*, p. 100.

22　Abtey, *La Guerre Secrète*, p. 158.*.

23　Colonel Rémy, *J.A.*, pp. 150–2.*

24　Ibid.

25　Ibid.

26 Ibid.

27 Ibid.

28 Baker and Bouillon, *Josephine*, p. 136.

29 Abtey, *La Guerre Secrète*, p. 175.*

30 Colonel Rémy, *J.A.*, pp. 160–3.*

31 Ibid.

32 Ibid.

33 Ibid.

34 Ibid.

35 Ibid.

CHAPTER TWENTY-FIVE

1 Jacques Abtey, *La Guerre Secrète de Josephine Baker*, Siboney, 1948, p. 202.*

2 Ibid.

3 SHD AI 1P 66791, p. 35.

4 Alan Schroeder, *Josephine Baker: Entertainer*, Chelsea House Publishers, 1991, pp. 73. NB: J. Baker will claim the Nazis/enemy poisoned her, hence the source of her illness. See also Hanna Diamond, 'The Starlet-Spy', Medium.com – https://medium.com/truly-adventurous/she-was-a-global-superstar-she-was-a-world-class-spy-df5263d51adc

5 Josephine Baker and Marcel Sauvage, *Les Mémoires de Joséphine Baker*, Éditions Corrêa, 1949, p. 101.

6 Philippe Verrier, *Victor Dillard, SJ*, Marquette University Press, 2017, pp. 14, 140, 144–5, 146, 161.

7 Abtey, *La Guerre Secrète*, p. 202.*

8 Ibid.

9 Marion Soutet, 'Joséphine Baker, figure emblématique des Armées, Conservatrice du patrimoin', Service Historique de la Défense (SHD), 16 November 2021 – https://european-security.com/josephine-baker-in-the-pantheon/

10 Abtey, *La Guerre Secrète*, p. 211.*

11 Ean Wood, *The Josephine Baker Story*, Sanctuary Publishing, 2000, pp. 242–3.

12 Ibid.

13 SHD AI 1P 66791, pp. 17, 21.

14 Jean-Claude Baker and Chris Chase, *Josephine: The Hungry Heart*, Random House, 1993, pp. 262–3.

15 Ibid.

16 'The day a French part of Yorkshire welcomed a star', Yorkshire Air Museum, 15 May 2020 – https://yorkshireairmuseum.org/remembrance/josephine-baker-1945-elvington-york-visit/

17 Baker and Chase, *Josephine: The Hungry Heart*, p. 267.

18 Baker and Sauvage, *Les Mémoires*, p. 109.

19 Ibid.

20 Abtey, *La Guerre Secrète*, pp. 219–20.*

21 Baker and Sauvage, *Les Mémoires*, pp. 82, 83–4; Baker and Chase, *Josephine: The Hungry Heart*, p. 266.

22 'When Nazis Took All The Bells', National Bell Festival – https://www.bells.org/blog/when-nazis-took-all-bells

23 Baker and Sauvage, *Les Mémoires*, pp. 82, 83–4; Josephine Baker and Jo Bouillon, *Josephine*, WH Allen, 1978, p. 142.

24 SHD AI 1P 66791, p. 36.

EPILOGUE

1 Jean-Claude Baker and Chris Chase, *Josephine: The Hungry Heart*, Random House, 1993, p. 268.

2 Rebecca Donner, *All the Frequent Troubles of Our Days*, Canongate, 2021, pp. 375–445

3 SHD AI 1P 66791, p. 44; Alain Juillet and Marie Gatard, 'Josephine Baker in the Panthéon', AASSDN, 19 September 2021 – https://aassdn.org/amicale/josephine-baker-in-the-pantheon/

4 SHD AI 1P 66791, p. 17.

5 Ibid., p. 29.

6 Ibid.

7 Ibid.

8 Ibid., pp. 51, 54.

9 SHD GR 16P 28445, Baker Josephine, p. 11.

10 'Josephine Baker, Chevalier (1906–1975)', *American Society of the French Legion of Honour*, Vol. 27, No. 2, Summer 2020, pp. 3–4.

11 Federal Bureau of Investigation, Josephine Baker, PART 1 of 2, BUFILE: 62-95834

12 Personal communications with Jean-Pierre Reggiori, 2022; Courtesy of Jean-Pierre Reggiori private collection: Emmanuel Debono, 'De quel antiracisme Joséphine Baker est-elle le nom?', 29 November 2021, LEDDV Le Droit De Vivre.

13 Jessica Goldstein, 'March on Washington had one female speaker: Josephine Baker', 23 August 2011, *Washington Post* – https://www.washingtonpost.com/lifestyle/style/march-on-washington-had-one-female-speaker-josephine-baker/2011/08/08/gIQAHqhBaJ_story.html

14 Baker and Chase, *Josephine: The Hungry Heart*, p. 267.

15 'Josephine Baker', *Woman's Hour*, BBC Radio 4, 30 November 2021.

16 Henry Hurford Janes – Josephine Baker Collection, Collection Call Number JWJ MSS 2, Beinecke Rare Book and Manuscript Library, Archives at Yale

17 Author interview with Jean-Pierre Reggiori, pp. 2, 9.

18 Angelique Chrisafis, 'Josephine Baker, music hall star and civil rights activist, enters Panthéon', 30 November 2021, *The Guardian* – https://www.theguardian.com/world/2021/nov/30/black-french-american-rights-activist-josephine-baker-enters-pantheon

19 Hanna Diamond, 'The Starlet-Spy', Medium.com – https://medium.com/truly-adventurous/she-was-a-global-superstar-she-was-a-world-class-spy-df5263d51adc

20 US CIA/Paul L. Kesaris (editor), *The Rote Kapelle: The CIA's History of Soviet Intelligence and Espionage Networks in Western Europe, 1936–1945*, University Publications of America Inc., 1979, in Classified Studies in Twentieth-Century Diplomatic And Military History, pp. 120, 121, 317, 347; SHD GR 28 P9 14280, Abtey, p. 80.

21 Jacques Abtey and Dr Fritz Unterberg Gibhardt, *2ème Bureau Contre Abwehr*, La Table Ronde, 1967, pp. 99–105.*

22 Johannes Mario Simmel, *It Can't Always Be Caviar*, Anthony Blond, 1965, prelim pages.

23 Ibid., p. 3.

24 Ibid., p. 77.

25 Ibid., pp. 440–7.

26 Personal correspondence between the author and Gilbert Renault's relatives, 2021; Letter from Josephine Baker to Colonel Remy (sic), 22 January 1962, courtesy of the Association for the Defence and the Memory of Colonel Rémy; Colonel Rémy, *J.A.*, Éditions Galic, 1961, pp. 28–30.*

27 Ulrich Stolte, 'Der Legendare Agent Thomas Lieven', *Stuttgarter Zeitung*, 12/11/2019; Note: strictly speaking, Josephie Baker wasn't serving as a Deuxième Bureau agent by this time.

28 SHD GR 28 P9 14280, Abtey, p. 74.

29 Ibid., pp. 38, 81, 87.

30 SHD GRZ 2000 1618, J Abtey, pp. 5–6, 7, 31, 34, 35.

31 SHD GR 16 P 2170, Abtey Maurice Leonard, pp. 4, 15, 22, 26, 27.

32 SHD GRZ 2000 1618, J Abtey, p. 34.

33 Ibid., pp. 5–6, 7, 31, 34, 35.

34 Ader-Nordmann Auction Notes, p. 13.

35 Baker and Chase, *Josephine: The Hungry Heart*, p. 275.

36 SHD GRZ 2000 1618. J Abtey, p. 49.

37 'Dunderdale, Wilfred Albert', 23 September 2004, *Oxford Dictionary of National Biography*, – https://www.oxforddnb.com/view/10.1093/ref:odnb/9780198614128.001.0001/odnb-9780198614128-e-40173

38 private Dunderdale family archive, various wartime documents and photographs, courtesy of Paul Biddle MBE.

39 Ibid.

40 private Dunderdale family archive, letter of 5 December 1991, to Mrs Dunderdale from Sir Colin McColl KCMG, courtesy Paul Biddle MBE.

41 Ibid.

42 Angélique de Saint-Exupéry, 'Josephine Baker, honourable correspondent', Fondation Charles de Gaulle, 12 February 2021 – https://www.charles-de-gaulle.org/blog/2021/02/12/josephine-baker-honorable-correspondante-par-angelique-de-saint-exupery/

43 Angélique de Saint-Exupéry, *Château et Jardins des Milandes*, 2019.

44 'Angélique de Saint-Exupéry, dynamic guardian of the Milandes, the former castle of Joséphine Baker', Archyde, 29 November 2021.

Index

Association for the Defence and the Memory of Colonel Rémy

The Association supports the work of Colonel Rémy, so that it does not disappear, and ensuring that it is preserved for posterity.

The Association pays homage to so much incredible work and heroism, so many small defeats and great victories, so many joys, sorrows, sacrifices and the suffering of all those who were members of the Brotherhood Networks (*Confrérie Notre-Dame*), which did so much for the cause of the Resistance in World War Two. Also known as the 'Dame-Castille' and 'Centurie' networks, it included those who made up the 'Sussex' teams, and this Franco-British unit served with great courage and honour in the war.

Colonel Rémy was their leader, General de Gaulle their inspiration, France their supreme goal and raison d'être.

The Association is a non-profit organisation, which falls under the Law of 1 July 1901 and the Decree of 16 August 1901. Its purpose, to the exclusion of any political or campaigning ends, is to:

- Defend the memory and work of Colonel Rémy, whose real name is Gilbert Renault.
- Carry out educational and civic action aimed at the younger generations by organising exhibitions on the work of Colonel Rémy.

It was created on 29 September 2020, at the Sous-Préfecture de Guingamp, under the number W222005617 by members of the family, direct descendants of Gilbert Renault.

Membership is open to everyone, the Association being inclusive. Becoming a member obliges one to 'commit oneself to respecting the statutes and the ethical charter, to pay, if necessary, an annual subscription'.

To join the association please visit the website:

https://www.association-memoire-colonel-remy.com/

Or contact:

Email: Asso.mdcr@gmail.com
Phone: +33 (0) 650 610 599
Address: Chez Franck Genty, Pont Léan 22170 Lanrodec, France

About the Author

© Andrew Millard

Damien Lewis is an award-winning writer who spent twenty years reporting from war, disaster, and conflict zones for the BBC and other global news organizations. He is the bestselling author of more than twenty books, many of which are being adapted into films or television series, including military history, thrillers, and several acclaimed memoirs about military working dogs. Lewis lives in Dorchester, England.

PublicAffairs is a publishing house founded in 1997. It is a tribute to the standards, values, and flair of three persons who have served as mentors to countless reporters, writers, editors, and book people of all kinds, including me.

I. F. STONE, proprietor of *I. F. Stone's Weekly*, combined a commitment to the First Amendment with entrepreneurial zeal and reporting skill and became one of the great independent journalists in American history. At the age of eighty, Izzy published *The Trial of Socrates*, which was a national bestseller. He wrote the book after he taught himself ancient Greek.

BENJAMIN C. BRADLEE was for nearly thirty years the charismatic editorial leader of *The Washington Post*. It was Ben who gave the *Post* the range and courage to pursue such historic issues as Watergate. He supported his reporters with a tenacity that made them fearless and it is no accident that so many became authors of influential, best-selling books.

ROBERT L. BERNSTEIN, the chief executive of Random House for more than a quarter century, guided one of the nation's premier publishing houses. Bob was personally responsible for many books of political dissent and argument that challenged tyranny around the globe. He is also the founder and longtime chair of Human Rights Watch, one of the most respected human rights organizations in the world.

. . .

For fifty years, the banner of Public Affairs Press was carried by its owner Morris B. Schnapper, who published Gandhi, Nasser, Toynbee, Truman, and about 1,500 other authors. In 1983, Schnapper was described by *The Washington Post* as "a redoubtable gadfly." His legacy will endure in the books to come.

Peter Osnos, *Founder*